P9-EMH-288

Guns, Gun Control, and Elections

DISCARD

Guns, Gun Control, and Elections

The Politics and Policy of Firearms

Harry L. Wilson

ROWMAN & LITTLEFIELD PUBLISHERS, INC.
Lanham • Boulder • New York • Toronto • Oxford

ROWMAN & LITTLEFIELD PUBLISHERS, INC.

Published in the United States of America
by Rowman & Littlefield Publishers, Inc.
A wholly owned subsidiary of The Rowman & Littlefield Publishing Group, Inc.
4501 Forbes Boulevard, Suite 200, Lanham, Maryland 20706
www.rowmanlittlefield.com

PO Box 317
Oxford
OX2 9RU, UK

Copyright © 2007 by Rowman & Littlefield Publishers, Inc.

All rights reserved. No part of this publication may be reproduced,
stored in a retrieval system, or transmitted in any form or by any
means, electronic, mechanical, photocopying, recording, or otherwise,
without the prior permission of the publisher.

British Library Cataloguing in Publication Information Available

Library of Congress Cataloging-in-Publication Data

Wilson, Harry L., 1957–
    Guns, gun control, and elections : the politics and policy of firearms / Harry L.
Wilson.
        p. cm.
    Includes index.
    ISBN-13: 978-0-7425-5347-7 (cloth : alk. paper)
    ISBN-10: 0-7425-5347-7 (cloth : alk. paper)
    ISBN-13: 978-0-7425-5348-4 (pbk. : alk. paper)
    ISBN-10: 0-7425-5348-5 (pbk. : alk. paper)
    1. Gun control—United States. 2. Gun control—Political aspects—United States.
3. Gun control—United States—Public opinion. 4. Firearms ownership—United
States. 5. Firearms—Government policy—United States. I. Title.
HV7436.W55 2006
363.330973—dc22   2006003835

Printed in the United States of America

♾ ™ The paper used in this publication meets the minimum requirements of American
National Standard for Information Sciences—Permanence of Paper for Printed Library
Materials, ANSI/NISO Z39.48-1992.

ACC Library Services
Austin, Texas

To my mother, Catherine Wilson,
who is still loved as much as ever
and missed terribly.

Contents

Acknowledgments

This book could not have been written without the generous support of Roanoke College. A sabbatical leave and several research grants provided the time and resources necessary to think, research, and write. The resources of the Center for Community Research at Roanoke College were essential in conducting several public opinion polls. Directing the center is a great job.

I thank two colleagues, Roger Hartley and Todd Peppers, for their encouragement and insights, which helped me to keep plugging away and improve the work. Three anonymous reviewers forced me to focus more clearly on the topic while providing much-needed context for several of the chapters. The suggestions of each made this book better.

Judi Pinckney proofread several versions of this book, formatted all of it, and remained very pleasant throughout the process. For those largely thankless tasks, I say a big thank you. Rebecca Heller, the research librarian at Roanoke College, helped track down several important sources and uncovered some on her own. Renee Legatt, the editor at Rowman & Littlefield, was consistently pleasant, very helpful, and understanding.

Many undergraduate students helped in researching and organizing parts of the manuscript. The assistance of Bridget Tainer, Aaron Cook, Michael Kessler, and Jonathon Preedom was particularly helpful. Literally dozens of students worked on the surveys. Some of them were captives in research methods courses, but others were volunteers for special polling courses. Judith Daniel is a capable and enthusiastic survey supervisor.

Several political actors in Virginia generously gave me their time and insights in interviews. These include elected officials on both sides of the aisle as well as lobbyists and political operatives. Their views give the book a real-world feel, and their contributions are greatly appreciated.

Finding the time to work on a project of this size is never easy. My wife, Donna, never complained when I said I had to work or when I took time off to watch Penn State football. More important, her love and support allow me to concentrate on work when I am on a self-imposed deadline. I could not ask for a better partner or a better friend.

Kathy Wilson helped teach me what it means to be a professional. I regret that she is not here to read this. I also thank Abby, Lady, and Mindy, my children who happen to have four legs and bark, for their unconditional love.

Preface

Why are you writing a book on gun control? What's your position? Those are the two questions commonly asked when I tell someone about my research. The answer to the first question is because it is a subject I believe is important and one that I find extremely interesting. When I was a child, my grandmother had guns around her farmhouse to shoot snakes or varmints and defend herself in case any convicts from a nearby prison escaped. I was fascinated from an early age, but I was told not to touch them because they were very dangerous, and I was an obedient child. Only in my midteens was I allowed to shoot.

The second question is more difficult to answer. To say you are for or against gun control obscures a great deal of gray area and many nuances. A more important question, but one equally difficult to answer, concerns the value of regulations on firearms. Like most Americans, I favor "reasonable" regulations, but my definition of reasonable may differ considerably from yours.

This book focuses on the political aspects of gun control. My training as a political scientist lends a perspective to the issue that differs from those of many other scholars who have written on the subject. My interests go beyond the actual policies to investigate how those policies are made. Policy making includes many actors, and most of them are covered in some respect in this book.

This book builds on the foundation laid by many others who have written in the field. Much of what is contained here has been discussed in other works, but I hope I have added some thoughts not found elsewhere. Original research on media coverage and public opinion as well as discussion of gun control in Virginia help differentiate this book. I also spend more time discussing the role of gun control in elections than most other authors.

For reasons I do not fully understand, researchers in the field of gun control feel compelled to state their affiliations and whether they own any firearms. People who study political parties do not reveal their partisanship, nor do those who write about elections reveal their voting decisions. In the interest of full disclosure, I own several guns, and I am an avid, if not very successful, hunter. To go a step beyond the norm, I have never used any of my guns illegally or in the commission of a crime. I have never used a firearm defensively, and I have never shot at any other person. I joined the National Rifle Association when I began my research in order to get full access to their publications and communications, but I will most likely renew my membership.

I personally knew two people who used firearms to kill themselves. I know another who lost a leg in a shooting accident, and the sister of a good friend was murdered in a random shooting.

Regardless of my personal experiences, I would be remiss as a researcher if I allowed any of them to directly influence my work. I have done my best not to allow that to happen. You can judge the degree to which I was successful.

Tables

Introduction

Mr. Dixon was upstairs, in bed, when he heard a noise in the hallway. Half asleep, he opened his eyes and saw a man at the top of the stairs heading toward the bedroom of Mr. Dixon's 2-year-old son, Kyle. . . . He grabbed a 9-millimeter pistol that he kept in a closet, walked toward the man and asked what he was doing there. The man, Mr. Dixon said, ran at him, screaming. That's when he pulled the trigger. He shot the intruder twice. . . . Mr. Dixon is your basic straight arrow, a Navy veteran. . . . The man accused of being the intruder . . . is a career low-life with a blocklong record of burglaries and other crimes. . . . Mr. Dixon's gun was illegal. He had no New York license for it. . . . Mr. Hynes [borough district attorney] wants Mr. Dixon to do jail time. . . . "Nobody is going to get a bye" on a gun charge.[1]

A 14-year-old student shot and killed his principal today in a crowded junior high cafeteria and then killed himself, the authorities said. . . . Everyone ran out of the cafeteria yelling. "He has a gun!" said an eighth grader, Danny Dulin. The principal, Eugene Segro, 51, was shot once in the chest with a .44-caliber handgun and was pronounced dead at the hospital. The student, James Sheets, 14, died at the scene of a shot to the head from a .22-caliber gun, the coroner, Barry Bloss, said. The youth apparently carried three guns in his backpack, Mr. Bloss said. . . . The guns belonged to the boy's stepfather, Arthur Blake, the police said. The boy used a key to remove the weapons from a safe at his house, they said. The teenager was not known for being a disciplinary problem, and the police and the Red Lion Area school superintendent, Larry Macaluso, said they did not know of any disputes he might have had with Mr. Segro. Mr. Segro had been at the school more than a decade, a school official said. "He tried to find the most lenient way to punish the kids," said Nicole Wisor, 16, a 10th grader who had attended the school. "It wasn't just a job for him. He truly loved the kids."[2]

Gun control is a hotly contested issue in the United States. As the temperature of the debate rises, which it does frequently, it generates both smoke and fire.

1

While the light from the fire helps illuminate the details of the issue, the smoke obscures the facts. The facts are often either lost or ignored in the exchanges between the supporters of stronger gun control laws and those who argue for the rights of gun owners. Some of the facts are disputed.

As these newspaper article excerpts demonstrate, there are ample anecdotes to indicate that gun control in the United States is necessary and needs to be strengthened, or that gun laws seem to punish the law-abiding as much as, if not more than, the criminals. They suggest that firearms can be used for self-protection or to protect one's family. Guns can also be used to injure or to kill innocent people. Where is the truth? Most would agree that it is somewhere in the middle, but many would argue that one of the above stories is much closer than the other to reality. Which story you think is more reflective of the truth largely depends upon preconceived notions regarding guns and gun control, many of which may not be accurate.

Those ideas may have developed through socialization in the family, the schools, the media, or your friends and acquaintances. Your thoughts about firearms may depend upon where you live or where you were raised. Guns in major cities such as New York, Atlanta, or Chicago are viewed very differently than they are in more rural areas of New York, Georgia, or Illinois. Your view of guns is probably influenced by their presence or absence in the household when you were growing up, whether you are familiar with guns or even own one yourself. Do you see a gun as something to be avoided and feared or as an instrument that can be used for protection or pleasure that should be respected?

GUNS IN AMERICA

There is no doubt that crime and gun violence are important issues in contemporary America. The crime rate, which fell throughout much of the 1990s, has begun to level off, with 2003 rates virtually unchanged from the previous year.[3] This estimate included some 5.4 million violent crimes. The 16,200 murders and nonnegligent manslaughters reported by the FBI in 2002 represented a slight increase from 16,040 in 2001.[4] In a typical year, nearly two out of every three murders is committed with a firearm.

Violent crime does not affect all demographic groups in the population equally. Those with lower income levels, those who live in an urban area, and single African-American males between sixteen and twenty years old are more likely to be victims of violent crime.[5] Members of those same demographic groups are also more likely to be perpetrators. To look at this another way, 3 percent of the nation's households had a member age twelve or older who experienced one or more violent crimes in 2003.[6]

Sometimes the crime story is told in statistical terms, but very often it is told in the recounting of real-life stories. Countless times we have watched the news on television report a shooting—in a school, a mall, the workplace, a home—and seen the tragic results. Countless times we have read the newspaper account of yet another gun murder in our city or maybe even a killing in our small town. Many of us know all too well the cost of losing a loved one to an armed assailant. Even more of us know someone who has been the victim of a violent crime, perhaps being targeted by a criminal carrying a firearm. Some of us know someone who has used a gun to defend himself from a would-be criminal and thus prevented himself from becoming another crime statistic.

Many of us live in households where firearms are present and some of us own guns, but more of us do not. Fewer households today have guns than in the past.[7] The number of firearms in the United States is estimated at between 200 and 230 million, and it continues to increase each year.[8] Many of us are relatively familiar with guns. We may be target shooters, hunters, or gun collectors. Some of us have little or no experience with firearms. We may never have fired a gun; some have never even seen a gun.

Many Americans who are relatively unfamiliar with guns confuse pistols and revolvers. Many more are unaware of the differences between a semiautomatic and fully automatic firearm. Few of us can identify or define an assault weapon or describe how it is similar to or different from weapons commonly used for hunting.

Still, most of us have an opinion regarding the gun "problem" and gun control. We think that we need more gun control laws or tougher enforcement of existing laws. Some of us think we should ban all guns because they are objects designed to destroy other objects—or living creatures. As some say, "No one *needs* to own a gun."

Others see guns as objects that can be used recreationally in target shooting or hunting, to help provide a sense of accomplishment, and as a means of connecting with their heritage. For some, guns are seen as a necessary part of life, needed to defend themselves, their property, or their livelihood. Others simply like to collect firearms, just as many Americans collect other items. A few would even argue that most citizens should be armed in order to promote a more polite and civil society. To quote the ubiquitous bumper sticker, "Guns don't kill people. People kill people."

To see guns as the cause of crime and violence or to see stricter gun control laws as the answer to those problems is too simplistic. Unfortunately, listening to the spokespersons for the various sides in the debate often provides

only one side of the story. Sometimes the version of reality reflected in statements of the Brady Campaign to Prevent Gun Violence or the National Rifle
Association (NRA) is fairly accurate. All too often, though, these interest
groups serve up more misinformation than fact. Usually they tell only one
side of the story. Depending upon the source of the information, you can be
led to believe that gun registration will either (a) enable the police to catch
most criminals, or (b) help law enforcement officials catch no one, but enable
the government to compile a list of citizens who have guns so they can be
confiscated in the future. Similarly, "ballistic fingerprinting" is either a
costly technology that can be easily circumvented by criminals or an effective
high-tech tool in the fight against crime. Requiring background checks at gun
shows will either prevent criminals and terrorists from easily obtaining weapons to use against average citizens or they will prevent average citizens from
buying and selling guns they collect, use for self-defense, or use to hunt. With
all the hyperbole, it is difficult to separate fact from fiction, truth from half-
truth.

Many elected officials follow the lead of the interest groups and use scare
tactics rather than reason when they discuss gun control. A piece of gun control legislation may be described as a panacea for reducing criminal violence
or as an unwarranted intrusion into the personal affairs of law-abiding citizens. In recent debates over the now-expired assault weapons ban and limiting liability for gun manufacturers and dealers, the U.S. Senate, which is
often regarded as more measured and cerebral than the U.S. House of Representatives, engaged in debate that was not at all senatorial. Both sides alleged
that a vote cast against their position would support terrorism by either allowing terrorists to legally purchase weapons in the United States or preventing
private citizens from defending themselves and bankrupting the weapons
manufacturers who supply our troops with firearms. It is difficult to imagine
that senators on either side actually believed their own rhetoric.

Academics have also been caught up in this debate. Unlike most areas of
study, many of the scholars in the field of gun control have become strong
advocates of one position or the other, and they have engaged in some rancor-
ous squabbling. Perhaps the best example of this is the debate over how often
guns are used defensively to thwart a potential crime. The estimates of the
frequency of these events vary by up to a factor of five, depending upon the
researcher and the method used to obtain the estimate.[9]

The media play an important role in shaping our view of guns and gun
control just as they impact our opinions regarding other issues. The ways in
which the news media describe the debate over gun control can influence the
type of policies adopted in Congress and in state legislatures. Those policies
affect all of us, although the impact is not always obvious to us.

We know there is a large number of firearms in circulation in the United States—over 200 million. We also know that guns are associated with almost thirty thousand deaths annually.[10] While the number of homicides in the United States is high, it is not clear that they result from the number of guns available. First, the number of guns in circulation increased greatly throughout the 1990s, while crime and murder rates fell. Second, the vast majority of gun owners do not commit crimes with their weapons. In fact, many crimes are committed by individuals who cannot legally purchase guns. Firearms are often cited as a cause of the high murder rate, but other factors are mentioned, too, including a violent culture, a decline of individual responsibility, violent entertainment media, video games, and, at the extreme, eating too much sugary junk food.

Reducing the number of gun-related murders, decreasing gun violence in general, and keeping firearms out of the hands of criminals are goals that are shared by those on both sides of the gun control debate. The means that are best suited to achieve those ends, however, are hotly contested. Would society be better served by strengthening gun regulations, more harshly punishing offenders who use firearms, allowing more law-abiding citizens to carry guns to protect themselves, or trying to change our culture of violence that seems to be prevalent in some areas? The answer to that question will vary considerably depending upon whom you ask.

More gun deaths result from suicides than homicides, but we can not be certain that stricter laws will reduce those numbers. Relatively few people purchase a firearm for the purpose of killing themselves, and those who do are very difficult to identify. It is likely that many of those who use a gun to end their lives would substitute another means if a firearm were not readily available. Devising a scheme that would prevent those with suicidal thoughts from obtaining a gun but would permit access to other law-abiding citizens is not an easy task. Legitimate concerns about protecting the privacy of those who seek counseling or treatment for mental illness make it even more difficult to limit their access to firearms.

Laws that are designed to disarm criminals may only serve to disarm potential victims, leaving the criminals with free rein. Beyond that, how do we prevent a criminal from obtaining a firearm on the black market or from a friend who is willing to make a legal purchase and give the gun to the criminal?

The number of accidental shooting deaths is smaller than many of us would guess. Gun accidents claim fewer than one thousand lives annually, and relatively few of those killed are children. In comparison, automobile accidents account for more than forty thousand deaths each year.[11] The number of fatal car accidents could be significantly reduced by reducing speed limits, but the cost to society in lost time would be great. Restricting those who could obtain a driver's license by raising the age at which one can legally drive and imposing tougher testing on senior citizens could also save lives. Among children, drowning and poison are more common causes of accidental death than accidental shootings. Should we pass legislation to ban swimming pools and liquid drain cleaners? This does not imply that accidental shootings are not tragic or that we should not try to reduce their number. It does, however, suggest that school shootings and other gun accidents in which children die are not an epidemic. Why, then, do we see it that way?

Perhaps firearms are qualitatively different from other objects.

> The primary and unique purpose of firearms is to provide an efficient means of destruction of people, animals, and objects. While some may admire firearms for aesthetic, artistic, sporting, or other qualities, no one can dispute this central purpose of firearms. . . . Other objects in society cause great destruction, of course, from knives to automobiles, but these objects exist or were created to serve other purposes.[12]

Guns are indeed different than knives or cars insofar as they are designed to be destructive, but we must examine how an object is used as well as its intended use. Like the vast majority of knives and automobiles, most guns are not used to injure or kill humans or to commit crimes.

THE NATURE OF THE
GUN CONTROL DEBATE

Gun control is both an emotional and a factual issue. The emotion is strongly felt by both sides. Those who favor gun control look at the injuries and deaths related to firearm use, and they feel that many of these lives could have been saved and the injuries prevented. When the victim is a child, emotions run even higher. For many, a gun can be seen only as a dangerous weapon that, for most people, is not a necessity. Guns are little more than death waiting to happen. Many supporters of strong gun control laws can not comprehend why someone would want to own a gun. For them, reducing the number of guns produced and restricting who can legally possess them can only be beneficial for society.

> These actions [gun violence] disrupt American lives, inflame public sentiment, and interrupt the societal concept of ordered liberty. While the absence of guns would not end violence and mayhem in America, the presence and easy availability of guns magnify the violent strain in the American character, multiplying its deadly consequences.[13]

Those who favor gun rights view firearms as protection against a criminal element that society has been unable to effectively control. Their guns are their last line of defense against a potential murderer or rapist. Others own guns as collectible items they may never even use; some are antiques or family heirlooms. Sport shooting and hunting are other reasons to own guns and protect the rights of gun owners. Firearms provide some owners with a link to the past, not just the days of the Wild West, but also the days when self-reliance, independence, and fortitude were both more valued and more necessary in society. This is part of what is commonly referred to as a gun culture. Finally, the Second Amendment is as important to many gun owners, and some nonowners, as the First Amendment is to religious leaders and journalists. For both supporters of gun control and supporters of gun rights, their views seem to be self-evident. Bridging the gap between the two sides is no easy task.

The concept of a gun culture is one that warrants a closer look. Political scientist Robert J. Spitzer argues that it arises from the presence and proliferation of firearms throughout the country's history, the link between gun ownership and the struggle for independence and westward expansion, and a mythology that has been perpetuated in popular culture.[14] He differentiates the hunting/sporting ethos from the militia/frontier ethos as two separate traditions that feed into the current gun culture.

The gun culture may be a result of American history or the product of popular culture. For better or worse, guns were important in the settling of the nation. Firearms have also been a staple in American entertainment from the old Westerns portrayed in early film and television to the gangsta rap music of today. While the patrons of those genres are certainly different, the gun is central to both forms of entertainment. There is little question that Americans see firearms differently than do most citizens in most nations, but the gun culture can be viewed from different perspectives. For some, the image is that of a trigger-happy yahoo who can hardly wait to find something to shoot. Others might have a vision of a father and son sharing time together as they shoot targets or enjoying quiet time in the woods while hunting. Neither of these depictions captures the most common perpetrators of gun crimes today—the urban male youth.

GUN CONTROL AND PUBLIC POLICY

There are also different ways of looking at gun control from a public policy perspective. Many researchers classify gun control as a social regulatory policy, in the same category as abortion, women's rights, school prayer, pornography, gay rights, and affirmative action.[15] Social regulatory policy generally deals with the state's authority to regulate values, norms, and relationships. In terms of governmental involvement, the states retain significant powers, while Congress is active at the national level with less judicial and little executive involvement. Among the public, these issues tend to be quite controversial, yet rousing the masses to action can be difficult.

Others argue that gun control better fits into the concept of morality politics introduced by political scientist Kenneth J. Meier.[16] Gun control has been lumped together with religion and abortion in the phrase "God, gays, and guns," but the connection between it and the other issues is not obvious. Religion and gay rights clearly and easily fit in the moral politics mold, primarily because they are matters of personal conviction and belief and involve questions of right and wrong. Guns do not fit as neatly into that category, and although gun control is at least in part a social issue, it is not usually discussed in moral terms. No one uses biblical references to justify their position on guns, and religious leaders rarely, if ever, inject themselves into the debate over guns. The so-called three Gs are important because they represent issues that are crucial to the same set of voters.

A recent article in the *Christian Century* suggests that compromise on the issue is difficult from both a political and moral perspective. At the same time, both sides tend to shy away from a moral debate. Those who support stronger gun control can point to the immorality of senseless violence, while gun rights advocates can raise the morality of self-defense or protection of family.[17] Most of the debate, however, focuses on legal, constitutional, and utilitarian concerns. Other research has found that the media portray the issue in ethical terms about 30 percent of the time. The ethical discussion usually centers on constitutional interpretation rather than morality.[18]

While there is little doubt that the gun control issue exhibits some of the characteristics of a moral debate and fits some criteria of social regulatory policy, to see the issue only in these terms is too limiting. For some participants, it is a political debate or a battle over culture, morals, and values. For many others it is a fight over saving lives, whether they believe those lives would be saved by preventing people from owning firearms or by allowing more people to own and carry guns. Members of both groups believe that lives are literally at stake in this debate. Unlike, for example, abortion, where there are questions regarding the definition of life and what constitutes a person, all of the victims of gun violence are considered by everyone to be persons. Much of the debate over gun control centers on the question of how best to save lives. To be sure, discussions of the Second Amendment are not as concrete, but questions regarding the impact of the assault weapons ban or limiting liability for gun manufacturers are more material.

Criminal justice scholar William J. Vizzard describes several different paradigms or perspectives from which one can examine gun control.[19] The crime control paradigm is self-explanatory and one that is at times adopted by both sides of the debate. Everyone is interested in reducing gun crime. The cultural paradigm views gun control as a largely symbolic conflict between two identifiable groups—the "cosmopolitans," well-educated urban dwellers who usually hold liberal Democratic positions on most social issues, and the "traditionalists," people who are more small-town or rural in origin and less tolerant in their outlook. The individualistic and libertarian strain in the American political culture, which is more prevalent in rural America, has fed the support for gun rights. This has been reinforced by the suspicion of authority that was present from the American Revolution to today, the individualism so important in the frontier experience, and the tradition of Protestantism that emphasizes the individual's relationship with God. To some extent, the debate is over whether the individual or the community is more highly valued.

One can also view gun control from a sovereignty and social-order perspective, which is strongly related to values. Underlying this paradigm is the question of who legitimately holds the power in society. This perspective directly addresses the "individual versus society" question. For Vizzard, this is the core of the gun control debate, and it is central to interpreting the Second Amendment. The public health paradigm emerged in the past few decades and seeks to place gun control in a completely different context. Gun violence should be seen as a public health issue and shootings as an epidemic. Viewed from this perspective, strict gun control is a logical choice as a treatment for the disease. Finally, one can view gun control as political symbolism, the dance between groups that compete for power as much for the sake of power itself as for the issue of gun control.

Each of these paradigms is relevant for different aspects of the gun control debate. At times, gun control is a debate over values. Sometimes it is a discussion of policy outcomes or the proper limits of state power over individuals. It can be and is used for partisan or political advantage. For the true believers on both sides, it is a question of values, history, and culture. Most citizens do not see gun control as a public health issue, but there is considerable concern over the number of deaths and injuries associated with firearms. Regardless of how the issue is classified, gun control is very controversial in contemporary politics, and the debate is not likely to be settled in the foreseeable future.

Gun control defies easy classification in policy terms because it involves so many actors and all levels of government. It is a local, state, and national issue simultaneously. The legislative, executive, and judicial branches of government are all influential in the politics of gun control. At the same time, the issue demonstrates the importance of political parties and interest groups in policy making. The mass media help citizens frame the questions regarding firearms, and public opinion is important, both in terms of shaping the policy debates among elected officials and in the elections in which we choose who will represent our interests. Gun control is an excellent example of the multiple influences in the formation and implementation of American public policy.

The purpose of this book is to show how gun control policy is made and to examine the influence of the many actors who are involved in the policy-making process. In addition, the reader will become informed regarding the important debates that surround the issue. The intent is to get you to think about the issue, not to lead you to a specific position, although, of course, this work does reach some conclusions.

REGULATING FIREARMS

Conventional wisdom holds that gun control pits gun owners against those who do not own guns. We might qualify the conventional wisdom and modify the groups slightly to those who are and those who are not familiar with firearms. Many people who want to regulate guns are not gun owners and are not familiar with guns. Moreover, even among those who advocate stricter gun laws, many feel they will not be effective against crime, accidents, or suicides.[20] If new laws will not achieve their goal, then how can we justify the "cost" that will be borne by others? On the other hand, many gun owners are willing to accept some restrictions or regulations regarding their ability to purchase or possess certain types of firearms. Overall, self-interest is thought to be very influential in determining policy preferences with regard to gun control.[21]

As previously discussed, the debate over gun control focuses partly on the question of whether the government has the authority to regulate firearms. The reality, however, is that we have already passed that hurdle in that we do regulate guns. We regulate what types of firearms can be sold and who can purchase or possess them. We have prohibited certain types of ammunition. Some weapons must be registered in specific jurisdictions. The wisdom and effectiveness of the laws can be debated, but we have, in fact, enacted gun control laws at all levels of government throughout the United States.

One of the few areas of agreement between supporters of gun control and supporters of gun rights is that the overall impact of these laws has been minimal. Gun control supporters suggest that the laws have had some impact, but it has been limited because the regulations are not sufficiently extensive. They argue, for example, that background checks should be required for all firearms purchases. All guns should be registered with the state. Safe storage laws and gun safety requirements should be universal. Some supporters of gun control think that certain types of firearms, like the inexpensive handguns referred to as Saturday night specials, should be prohibited. Others suggest that it should be illegal to possess broad categories of guns, such as handguns.

Supporters of gun rights argue that control policies are doomed to failure because most criminals do not obtain guns through legal means. While we can make it more difficult for criminals to legally purchase guns, we can not prevent them from buying guns on the black market, stealing them, or having someone else purchase them, a so-called straw purchase. Prohibition did not eliminate alcohol sales or consumption. Illegal drug traffic has increased and decreased slightly over several decades, but these small changes have been largely due to a shift in consumer preferences, not an overall reduction in addiction. Can we reasonably expect greater restrictions on firearms to reduce crime? Gun rights advocates suggest that stricter gun laws might actually increase crime by emboldening criminals who know they are less likely to face an armed victim.

This is not to say that guns should be totally unregulated. The background checks mandated by the Brady Bill are viewed by most citizens, including gun owners, as reasonable restrictions.[22] Those checks prevent some criminals from purchasing guns at gun shops, although at least some of them get their guns through other channels.[23] Age requirements to purchase or own firearms, similar to those imposed on tobacco and alcohol, are almost universally recognized as reasonable regulations.

Gun control advocates argue that policies that would greatly restrict the number of firearms available would reduce the number of guns that could be used to kill or injure. Those effects may not be felt immediately, but they might be greater over time as the guns currently in circulation begin to leave the market. Of course, this would also mean that many law-abiding citizens would be denied access to firearms.

For example, creating a national gun registration and requiring all transfers to go through a federally licensed firearms dealer may be effective in reducing crime. In order to work, however, those laws would have to include all existing guns as well as those manufactured in the future. They would have to be backed up by stiff penalties for anyone who violated those laws, and would have to require that all stolen guns be reported to the police within a very short period of time.

Politically, those laws can not be passed in the United States because of the opposition of gun rights interest groups and citizens. In addition, mandatory registration of existing guns would be nearly impossible to enforce. Finally, this would not preclude the emergence of a black market that would still supply guns to the most dangerous criminals. Gun control, like other public policies, has both positive and negative consequences.

Any gun control legislation must also pass the hurdles created by the Second Amendment. While the specific meaning of that amendment remains unsettled after more than two hundred years, many gun rights advocates argue that it prohibits many, if not all, restrictions on the purchase of firearms by law-abiding citizens. Conversely, gun control advocates suggest that it is a collective right that pertains only to the national militia and protects the nation's right to self-defense.[24] A more moderate interpretation recognizes an individual right that is balanced against other rights and the government's responsibility to protect the lives of all its citizens.

This book helps the interested reader navigate through the muddy waters of research regarding guns and gun control. While the emphasis is on the evidence provided by sound empirical research, at times we will employ what might be referred to as a "common sense" test. For example, the actual number of defensive gun uses each year is most likely far less than that claimed by gun rights academics, although it is probably greater than the number asserted by pro-control researchers. The Second Amendment may well protect an individual's right to own a gun, but it does not prevent regulation of that right, as is true of all other constitutional rights. It is not an absolute right any more than the First Amendment is an absolute right to speech or religion, although it may prohibit Congress from banning firearm possession by law-abiding citizens in the United States.

Gun regulations may prevent some murders and gun-related violent crimes, reduce accidental shootings, and prevent some suicides, but we have to balance that gain against the cost of those regulations to sportsmen and those who wish to assert their right to self-defense. In short, gun control is a complex, multifaceted issue that defies the simple solutions that are frequently offered to the problem of violence in America.

For many citizens, gun control does not assume the salience of other social and political issues such as the war on terror, health care, or abortion. Changes in gun control policy do not result in major shifts of wealth or power within the country. It has virtually no impact on the national debt or budget deficit. So why is it important?

First, firearms are related to more than thirty thousand deaths and tens of thousands of injuries annually. At the same time, guns are used to prevent hundreds of thousands of crimes, some of which would result in injury or death.

As discussed above, gun control is also an emotional issue that is related to several other important concepts such as trust in government, individual versus collective rights, and a clash of cultures. It is a political battle that to some extent pits Democrats against Republicans and conservatives against liberals. It also reflects a conflict between those who live in large cities and those who live in more rural areas. To some extent it is also a geographical division, more complex than just red and blue states. The South and the West are most supportive of gun rights, while the Northeast is generally more supportive of gun control, although many residents of Vermont and New Hampshire would dispute that stereotype. Gun control is a clash of values and worldviews as much as it is a debate over statistics.

From a purely political perspective, gun control is important because it can influence voters. Although we can rarely attribute an electoral victory to a single issue, we will identify individual contests and some states in presidential elections that probably turned on the issue of gun control. The issue consumes considerable time in legislative sessions, both state and national, including several days of debate in 2004 and 2005 in the U.S. Senate.

OUTLINE OF THIS BOOK

This book provides a balanced discussion of the gun control issue. Each chapter presents arguments on both sides of the debate and explains the importance of that aspect of the issue for policy making. While the conclusions lean more toward the gun rights perspective, those conclusions are based on evidence, not conjecture. This book does not answer all of the questions surrounding gun control. It does, however, provide you with the information you need to intelligently and rationally discuss the issue and to reach your own conclusions.

We begin by examining the Second Amendment and the important court decisions dealing with gun rights. While the Supreme Court has been largely silent on this topic, lower federal courts have begun to address the issue. There is also a robust debate within academia regarding the meaning of the Second Amendment. The fundamental question is whether the right conferred in the Second Amendment is an individual or a collective right. Is the right enjoyed by individual citizens or does the reference to militia mean that it applies only to defense of the nation?

We then focus on the magnitude of the "gun problem" in America by analyzing statistics related to firearms—the number of guns in circulation, the number of firearm deaths, the types of guns used to commit crimes, and the number of times guns are used to prevent a crime. In each of these cases, the numbers are put into perspective by examining trends and comparing them with other data. Too often these numbers are simply "thrown out there" to make the gun situation appear more or less serious to support a particular position. Context for the statistics will be provided as often as possible. In that way, we can form tentative conclusions regarding the extent of the problem of gun violence.

The book then examines the ways in which guns and gun owners can be regulated. Regulations may focus on preventing certain types of people from purchasing or owning guns, the types of firearms that can be sold, or safety devices that may be required to be installed on firearms prior to their sale. Some of these regulations have been enacted by legislatures within the states or by Congress, while others are still policy recommendations only. This discussion is followed by a brief summary of current policies at the state level. Each of the major pieces of national gun legislation is then examined in more detail.

We also discuss the relatively recent spate of private and public lawsuits filed against gun dealers and firearms manufacturers. Congress passed legislation that limits liability for gun manufacturers and dealers in 2005.[25] This prevented many lawsuits from being filed and preempted those already in the courts.

The next topic addressed is public opinion. Most surveys simply ask which gun control policies are favored by the public. Relying on original data sets from both the national and state levels, we focus on the perceived utility of potential gun regulations and the respondents' background characteristics to analyze public opinion from a different perspective. Familiarity with firearms is at least as important as the more commonly considered demographic characteristics such as sex, political ideology, and political party (which remain important explanatory variables). The data also indicate that a majority of respondents support many specific gun regulations, but not all those who support more restrictive laws think that policies will be effective at reducing violent crime, accidents, or suicides.

Next, we turn our attention to the interest groups that are actively involved in influencing firearms policy. We trace the history and mission of several of the most important groups on both sides of the issue. Topics covered include lobbying strategies, short-term and long-term goals of the groups, and measuring success. We examine the groups' involvement in drafting legislation, influencing legislators, and enacting retribution on recalcitrant legislators. The focus in this chapter is on both lobbying and electoral activity.

Interest group participation in political campaigns and the importance of the gun control issue in elections are also examined in this chapter. Campaign contributions, while important, are not the only important measure for the major players in the gun control arena. For the National Rifle Association, it is the group's membership, both in terms of numbers and in terms of commitment, that is critical to its success. For the Brady Campaign and Million Mom March, it is the emotion of the gun control issue and the images of innocent gunshot victims and their families. Federal Election Commission data detailing campaign contributions and other electoral activities are summarized and discussed in the context of recent national elections.

A major point of focus is the 2000 and 2004 presidential elections. The importance of George W. Bush's carrying West Virginia, Tennessee, and Arkansas in 2000 has been overshadowed by the disputed outcome in Florida. Without those three states, Bush would not have won the election, even with Florida's electoral votes. Without the support of large numbers of pro-gun voters, it is likely that he would have lost those states, particularly West Virginia. Gun control was also important in the 2004 campaign, although it was clearly overshadowed by the war in Iraq.

Media coverage of guns and gun control is the topic of the next chapter, which includes a content analysis of both the *New York Times* and the *CBS Evening News*. While it is simplistic to say that the media are biased toward the pro-control position, the evidence does indicate that the gun rights position is treated less favorably by at least some reporters. And, while the National Rifle Association does not lack for attention in the news media, the coverage it receives is often negative. The definition of "news" tends to move media coverage to pay more attention to unusual events, major tragedies, and incidents that are more emotional, so coverage of gun use is generally the result of guns used in killings. Sporting use of guns does not fit the definition of "news" and receives scant attention from the news media, as does defensive use of guns.

Virginia provides the backdrop for an analysis of an individual state. While generally thought of as being pro-gun, Virginia adopted and implemented several gun control measures in the early 1990s. Virginia is interesting because in 2001 it elected a Democratic governor, Mark Warner, who openly courted gun owners in the commonwealth and managed to persuade the NRA to remain neutral throughout most of the campaign. Warner's campaign is now considered by some to be a model for other Democrats to emulate, and he is mentioned as a possible presidential candidate in 2008. This chapter also discusses the consideration of gun-related legislation in the commonwealth's General Assembly.

The concluding chapter ties together the previous discussions and offers suggestions regarding what policies are both politically possible and likely to reduce gun violence.

NOTES

1. Clyde Haberman, "Protecting a Gun Law, or a Family," *New York Times*, February 15, 2003.

2. Associated Press, "Middle School Boy Shoots His Principal, Then Kills Himself," *New York Times*, April 25, 2003.

3. Shannan M. Catalano, "Criminal Victimization, 2003," Bureau of Justice Statistics, September 2004, at www.ojp.usdoj.gov/bjs/pub/pdf/cv03.pdf.

4. Catalano, "Criminal Victimization," 2.

5. Catalano, "Criminal Victimization," 4.

6. Patsy A. Klaus, "Crime and the Nation's Households, 2003," Bureau of Justice Statistics, October 2004, at www.ojp.usdoj.gov/bjs/pub/pdf/cnh03.pdf.

7. Tom W. Smith, "1999 National Gun Policy Survey of the National Opinion Research Center: Research Findings" (paper presented at the annual meeting of the American Association for Public Opinion Research, Portland, OR, May 2000), 54. Part of this decline may be due to the increase in the number of households headed by single females, a demographic group very unlikely to own a gun.

8. Philip J. Cook and Jens Ludwig, *Guns in America: Results of a Comprehensive National Survey on Firearms Ownership and Use* (Washington, D.C.: Police Foundation, 1996); Gary Kleck, *Targeting Guns: Firearms and Their Control* (New York: Aldine de Gruyter, 1997), 63–70; and William J. Vizzard, *Shots in the Dark: The Policy, Politics, and Symbolism of Gun Control* (Lanham, MD: Rowman & Littlefield, 2000), 21.

9. See David Hemenway, "Survey Research and Self-Defense Gun Use: An Explanation of Extreme Overestimates," *Journal of Criminal Law and Criminology* 87, no. 4 (1997): 1430–45; Gary Kleck and Marc Gertz, "The Illegitimacy of One-Sided Speculation: Getting the Defensive Gun-Use Estimate Down," *Journal of Criminal Law and Criminology* 87, no. 4 (1997): 1446–62; and Tom W. Smith, "A Call for a Truce in the DGU War," *Journal of Criminal Law and Criminology* 87, no. 4 (1997): 1462–69.

10. National Center for Injury Prevention and Control, Centers for Disease Control and Prevention, "Leading Causes of Death by Homicide in Various Age Groups, by Race, 2001," at webapp.cdc.gov/sasweb/ncipc/leadcaus.html.

11. See National Center for Injury Prevention and Control, "Leading Causes of Death."

12. Robert J. Spitzer, *The Politics of Gun Control*, 3d ed. (Washington, D.C.: CQ Press, 2004), 5–6.

13. Spitzer, *Politics of Gun Control*, 7.

14. Spitzer, *Politics of Gun Control*, 9–10.

15. Spitzer, *Politics of Gun Control*, 4–5; John M. Bruce and Clyde Wilcox, eds., *The Changing Politics of Gun Control* (Lanham, MD: Rowman & Littlefield, 1998), 7–13.

16. Kenneth J. Meier, *The Politics of Sin: Drugs, Alcohol, and Public Policy* (Pacific Grove, CA: Brooks/Cole, 1994).

17. "Middle Ground Elusive on Gun-Control Issue," *Christian Century* 122, no. 9 (May 3, 2005): 17.

18. Dhavan Vinod Shah, "Value Judgments: News Framing and Individual Processing of Political Issues" (PhD diss., University of Minnesota, 1999).

19. Vizzard, *Shots in the Dark*, 4–11.

20. Harry L. Wilson, "Public Opinion and Gun Control Utility: Not as Simple or Coherent as We Thought?" (paper presented at the Joint Meetings of the Canadian Law and Society Association and the Law and Society Association, Vancouver, B.C., May 30–June 1, 2002).

21. Robin M. Wolpert and James G. Gimpel, "Self-Interest, Symbolic Politics, and Public Attitudes toward Gun Control," *Political Behavior* 20, no. 3 (1998): 241–62.

22. Smith, "Gun Policy Survey."

23. Philip J. Cook and Jens Ludwig, "Pragmatic Gun Policy," in *Evaluating Gun Policy*, ed. Jens Ludwig and Philip J. Cook (Washington, D.C.: Brookings Institution, 2003), 20–22.

24. For opposing views of the meaning of the Second Amendment, see Saul Cornell, "Commonplace or Anachronism: The Standard Model, the Second Amendment, and the Problem of History in Contemporary Constitutional Theory," *Constitutional Commentary* 16 (1999): 221–46; and Michael C. Dorf, "Symposium on the Second Amendment: Fresh Looks: What Does the Second Amendment Mean Today?" *Chicago-Kent Law Review* 76 (2000): 291–347.

25. S. 397 passed in the Senate on July 29, 2005 on a 65–31 vote. The House of Representatives approved the bill by a 283–144 margin on October 20, 2005.

Chapter One

Guns and the Constitution

A well regulated Militia, being necessary to the security of a free State, the right of the people to keep and bear Arms, shall not be infringed.

—Second Amendment, U.S. Constitution

Any consideration of guns and gun control in the United States must begin with the Second Amendment. This chapter describes the two major competing theories of interpretation of the Second Amendment.[1]

We begin by examining the theoretical and philosophical history of the right to bear arms. We then focus on the specific right in the American context, again considering the history and the philosophical underpinnings of the Second Amendment. This leads us to a search for the actual meaning(s) of the Second Amendment. It is here that we see the diversity of opinion between those who believe the amendment guarantees an individual right and those who believe that the right conferred is collective in nature.

The Supreme Court's rulings on the Second Amendment have been few and somewhat vague. None of them are very recent. In addition, the Court has not yet made the right applicable to the states through the process known as incorporation. Rulings in the lower courts have generally favored the collective-right approach, although there have been exceptions. In 2004 the Justice Department registered its support of the individual right interpretation.

For most of our history the Second Amendment received little attention from scholars or citizens. One prominent scholar has described the progression from the "relative obscurity" of the amendment for the first two hundred years of its existence to its emergence as a "virtual cottage industry among law professors."[2] The description that follows is a brief introduction to the subject of Second Amendment scholarship. A full treatment of the subject is beyond the scope of this book. Nonetheless, the Second Amendment is the elephant in the room during any discussion of gun control policy.

PHILOSOPHICAL BACKGROUND
OF THE RIGHT

The primary arguments in favor of an individual right to bear arms include the right of self-defense, the need to be able to overthrow a tyrannical government, and to defend the nation against foreign invasion. There are counterarguments for the first two of these. The last argument, defense of country, is the basis of the collective right interpretation as well.

The right to self-defense is described in the ancient writings of the Roman orator Cicero. "[T]here exists a law . . . inborn in our hearts; a law which comes to us . . . from nature itself . . . if our lives are endangered by . . . violence or armed robbers or enemies, each and every method of protecting ourselves is morally right."[3] John Locke argued to the contrary that an ordered society requires that this right rest with the society and not the individual. Even today there are differences of opinion regarding the existence of the right to self-defense and its extent.

Arguments regarding the right to self-defense are both practical and moral. Practically, there is the question of being prepared to injure or perhaps kill another person to protect yourself or others. Some of us would be able to do that; others would not. If one is not prepared to fight, then the weapon may be taken by the attacker. Many professionals advise some crime victims not to resist in order to reduce the risk of injury or death. Others argue that resisting an attack is less likely to lead to injury or death.

Morally, the question is whether we ever have the right to injure or kill another person. While not the norm, such moral objections to violence have been recognized by the government. For example, members of some religions who disdain all forms of violence qualified for conscientious objector status under the military draft. They would be assigned to noncombat roles rather than being placed in combat duty.

A reference to the potential crime-reducing benefit of an armed citizenry was supplied by Cesare Beccaria, who suggested, "[T]he laws which forbid men to bear arms are of this sort [a false idea of utility]. They only disarm those who are neither inclined nor determined to commit crimes."[4]

While Aristotle seemed to believe that an armed citizen is a good citizen, Niccolo Machiavelli argued that only the state can exercise the war power.[5] Some philosophers have warned that despots and their regimes have a tendency to disarm the citizenry, while others have disagreed. Thomas Paine suggested that citizens should be reluctant to surrender their arms to the government.[6]

James Madison, in Federalist No. 46, stated, "To these (the regular army) would be opposed a militia . . . with arms in their hands . . . the advantage of being armed, which the Americans possess over the people of almost every other nation."[7] On the other hand, Alexander Hamilton, Madison's *Federalist Papers* coauthor, argued that, "If a well-regulated militia be the most natural defense of a free country, it certainly ought to be under the regulation and at the disposal of that body which is constituted the guardian of the national security."[8] In Federalist No. 28, Hamilton wrote, "[I]f the representatives of the people betray their constituents, there is then no recourse left but in the exertion of that original right to self-defense which is paramount to all positive forms of government," and in Federalist No. 29, he said, "[L]ittle more can be reasonably aimed at, with respect to the people at large than to have them properly armed and equipped."[9]

During the discussions prior to ratification of the Constitution, supporters of ratification "promised all individuals that the right to keep and bear arms would be more than a paper right."[10] Anthony Gallia argues that the individual right to keep and bear arms was generally accepted throughout the ratification debates.[11]

Perhaps the strongest argument in favor of the historical antecedent of an individual right to bear arms is offered by Robert E. Shalhope.[12] He argues that the belief system that emerged in colonial America reflected classical philosophy and a tradition of republicanism that joined the themes of personal right and communal responsibility. In this way, the collective right to bear arms does not preclude the individual right to own firearms, but rather it is a derivative of the individual right.

Each of these arguments may also be found in current writings and the justifications offered by those who favor an individual right to bear arms and those who oppose it. On an even more practical level, the two major interest groups involved in the modern debate, the National Rifle Association and the Brady Campaign to Prevent Gun Violence base much of their rhetoric on these arguments. These philosophical issues are not easy to resolve, and the answers depend upon one's own moral and religious beliefs in addition to one's political beliefs.

THE SECOND AMENDMENT

Background

The history of the Second Amendment is inextricably linked with several of the important debates that faced the Founding Fathers. The relationship between the government and its citizens, as well as the relationship between the federal and state governments, are closely tied to the right to bear arms.

Did a citizen's right to rebel against a government end when the Revolutionary War was concluded? How were states to defend their sovereignty against possible incursions from the federal government? When, if ever, does the nation's need for a citizen militia disappear?

The ideal of a citizen militia has deep roots in the American political culture and colonial history. Part-time citizen soldiers were largely responsible for the local defense. There was a strong distrust of standing armies, given the experience with European armies that often served more to tyrannize than to free citizens. Therefore, both citizens and local authorities often relied on the militia.[13]

Despite the somewhat spotty record of the militia in the Revolutionary War, many Americans continued to hold the militia in high esteem. Seven of the former colonies adopted state constitutions that included a formal declaration on rights of the militia. Each prohibited a standing peacetime army and asserted civilian control of the military. Three explicitly protected the right to bear arms.[14]

The Pennsylvania Anti-Federalists suggested an amendment in their Dissent of the Minority of the Pennsylvania Convention that explicitly recognized an individual's right to bear arms, a right to self-defense, and a right to hunt. The amendment was not adopted, and it applied only to the federal government. To the contrary, Pennsylvania enacted a law that disarmed up to 40 percent of the state's adult white male population.[15] Pennsylvania's Test Acts imposed penalties on those citizens who refused to take a state loyalty oath. Those who refused to take the oath were disarmed.[16] And while the Pennsylvania Constitution did recognize a right to hunt, restrictions on that right indicate that it was not viewed with the same importance as fundamental rights such as speech.[17] The Virginia ratifying convention offered an amendment similar to that of Pennsylvania, but excluded the hunting references.[18]

The early years of the Republic saw several important constitutional issues raised, but few of them dealt with the Bill of Rights. States passed a variety of laws that infringed on rights guaranteed in the Bill of Rights, and few of those were challenged in court. Still, there is ample evidence that the intent of many of the framers was to create an individual right to possess firearms, although it is also clear that this freedom was not without limits.[19] Still, other scholars place the emphasis on the role of the militia in society and suggest that the constitutional right is limited to that context.[20]

The Meaning of the Second Amendment

While the original intent of the framers is hotly debated, the discussion regarding the contemporary meaning of the right to bear arms is no more settled. The Second Amendment has emerged as an important topic of discussion within the academic community in the past several decades.

In what is perhaps the most frequently cited discussion of the history of the Second Amendment, Shalhope examines several historical principles related to the formation of the right to bear arms. These include the individual right to bear arms, the fear of standing armies, the concomitant reliance upon citizen-formed militias, and civilian control of the military.[21]

A few years later, the article that reinvigorated the debate, "The Embarrassing Second Amendment," spawned a new school of thought referred to as the Standard Model.[22] In that article, Sanford Levinson suggests that the Second Amendment protects an individual's right to bear arms:

> I cannot help but suspect that the best explanation for the absence of the Second Amendment from the legal consciousness of the elite bar, including that component found in the legal academy, is derived from a mixture of sheer opposition to the idea of private ownership of guns and the perhaps subconscious fear that altogether plausible, perhaps even "winning," interpretations of the Second Amendment would present real hurdles to those of us supporting prohibitory regulation.[23]

While not insisting that an individual right is the only reasonable way to interpret the Second Amendment, Levinson suggests that to dismiss it out of hand, as many constitutional scholars have done, is equally incorrect. He argues that the right conferred is indeed an individual right, but it is not absolute.[24]

Levinson's article generated a great deal of scholarship on both sides of the debate, and it helped push the Standard Model into the mainstream of academic writing.[25] While those who subscribe to the Standard Model differ in the degree to which they would hold various—or any—gun control statutes to be unconstitutional, they all agree that there is an individual right conferred on the people by the Second Amendment.

In further explaining this line of thought, Eugene Volokh suggests that the Second Amendment has been viewed differently by some scholars because it contains both an operative clause, which protects the right to bear arms, and a justification clause, which explains why this right is important.[26] While no other amendment in the Bill of Rights contains such language, Volokh points out that many state constitutions use similar language, and it does not limit the rights only to that instance or situation. Echoing a point raised by Levinson, he notes that the First, Fourth, and Ninth Amendments also refer to "the right of the people," and they have been consistently interpreted to confer an individual right.[27]

David C. Williams argues that this right refers not to individuals, but to the "Body of the People."[28] If the people two hundred years ago were somewhat homogeneous, those similarities have dissipated over time to the extent that today's society is much more diverse and that this "Body of the People" no longer exists. As such, the Second Amendment's meaning has changed, and to look to the framers for guidance in interpretation is to look in the wrong place. The Second Amendment must be interpreted in light of the situation that exists today. That would include changes in both the way we provide for national defense and the nature of crime and criminals. Citizen militias are obsolete, and violent crime has become both more common and more lethal. We might also consider the technological changes that have made firearms much more dangerous in modern times. Taking all of that into consideration clearly suggests that the Second Amendment's interpretation should evolve to fit the reality of twenty-first-century America.

While Williams's response might be described as challenging the basis for the Standard Model, historian Saul Cornell's might be called an attack: "Indeed, recent writing on the Second Amendment [Standard Model] more closely resembles the intellectual equivalent of a check kiting scheme than it does solidly researched history."[29] Cornell argues that the Standard Model misinterprets history, misreads the text of the Constitution, and recycles the ideas of its adherents until they become accepted as legitimate. Cornell suggests there is little, if any, evidence that even the states were unwilling to disarm the citizenry at the time the Constitution was written. In addition, the term "the people" was applied in a much more restrictive fashion two hundred years ago.

Michael C. Dorf argues that the Second Amendment is best interpreted to mean only that the federal government may not abolish state militias.[30] Because this prohibition is largely meaningless in America today, the amendment itself is largely meaningless in the contemporary context.[31] Thus, any regulation regarding firearms would be constitutionally permissible.

The individual-right interpretation can be rejected through the application of commonly used criteria applied to other constitutional provisions— doctrine, text, original understanding, structural inference, and history after adoption. Dorf admits, however, that the Second Amendment has always been "somewhat puzzling" and that "deciding which interpretation best hangs together admittedly requires a somewhat subjective judgment, and that those who favor gun control as a policy matter are likely to be more sympathetic to the interpretation I offer than are those who oppose it."[32]

For those who are unsatisfied with declaring a part of the Bill of Rights to be meaningless, Dorf suggests that we might entertain three possible alternative interpretations.[33] The first would be to recognize a limited right to armed self-defense, although he defines that right more as a right to police protection.

A second possibility would recognize a right of law-abiding citizens who complete a gun safety course to own or possess a small number of long guns. This would cover guns that were deemed useful to the militia at the time of the founding. Pragmatically, this would also protect hunting to some extent while reducing the number of homicides, which are most often committed with handguns. Depending upon how this right is interpreted, it could also permit some self-defense by the individual.

A third possibility is to view the Second Amendment as ensuring a right to serve in the military, a right that would protect the ideal of the citizen-soldier so prevalent in the early writings in American history.

While one can agree or disagree with Dorf's suggestion, echoed by many others, that the Second Amendment is meaningless in today's society, critiquing his suggestions for those who feel that a part of the Constitution must mean something is akin to shooting fish in a barrel (pun intended).

It is not clear how the right he refers to as a "limited right of armed self-defense" can be operationalized as a right-to-police protection. He seems to suggest that police reforms to increase patrols in minority neighborhoods might meet the requirements of this right. While this might be a wise policy to pursue, Dorf fails to explain how all citizens would be a part of this expanded police force or how the police would actually be present at all times to defend against criminal attack.

The second suggestion is slightly more clever in that it attempts to address the wishes of those who want to look to the original intent of the Second Amendment. If the intent dealt with the militia, then we should preserve the right to possess those firearms that were useful at that time. As we shall see in the next section, this interpretation also pays homage to the legacy of the major Supreme Court decision in the field. The protection of the rights of hunters, the majority of whom use long guns, is a practical consideration. However, if the intent were to protect guns that were useful two-hundred-plus years ago, then no modern firearms would be protected. At best, hunters would be able to use primitive flintlock rifles only. Most of today's muzzle-loaders, the most "primitive" firearms commonly used, would not meet those criteria.

Finally, the idea that the Second Amendment protects our right to serve in the military may have some merit, although it is difficult to think why that right would ever be denied to large numbers of citizens without good reason—such as not meeting minimum physical, intellectual, psychological, and behavioral criteria for acceptance into the military. Even so, this right today would be defined more as a right to join the national military, not the state militia.

In recent scholarship it appears that the Standard Model has been gaining prominence. Constitutional scholar Don Kates asserts that forty-two of forty-eight law review articles in the 1990s endorsed the Standard Model.[34] Even some of the more liberal scholars and standard constitutional law textbooks, most notably the one authored by Laurence Tribe, have agreed that the collective-right interpretation has fallen into disfavor.[35] Still, many texts simply ignore the Second Amendment altogether, perhaps because of the dearth of cases, the debate over interpretation, or for ideological reasons.

Yet even if one adopts the Standard Model, it does imply an unfettered right to own, possess, carry, or use firearms. There is no absolute right guaranteed by the Constitution. All rights must be balanced against others. This is evident from even a cursory examination of the history of Supreme Court decisions with regard to any of the other amendments in the Bill of Rights as well as that of the Fourteenth Amendment. Neither freedom of speech, nor freedom of the press, freedom of religion, or any of our guarantees of due process or equal protection is absolute. There are times we may constitutionally be constrained from speaking or practicing our faith, and the government can infringe on other fundamental rights as well when it has a compelling reason to do so.

To argue that the Second Amendment would not be subject to these same potential restrictions would imply that it is *the primary* right and the only one that enjoys absolute protection. Few, if any, mainstream scholars would make this argument. Kates, one of the strongest proponents of the individual-rights theory, clearly states, "[T]he amendment does not forbid gun *control*, as opposed to wholesale prohibition. Registration, licensing and other regulations are permissible if, but only if, they do not unreasonably hinder the freedom of law-abiding adults to choose to acquire firearms."[36] A one-day waiting period to conduct a background check would likely pass constitutional muster, while an eight-month waiting period would not.

Shalhope has revisited his earlier article, particularly in light of the firestorm that followed. In summarizing and lamenting the modern debate over both the Second Amendment and the history and political thought of early America, he noted:

> Most [scholars] displayed little if any interest in the political culture that spawned the Second Amendment; those that did displayed an appalling ignorance of this intellectual climate. The result was . . . [q]uotations taken entirely out of context were strung together as if the language conveyed the same meaning at all times and in all circumstances. . . . The end result has been the "Standard Model" of interpreting the Second Amendment and an equally strained and intemperate opposition.[37]

It is reasonable to conclude that the Second Amendment does indeed confer an individual right as well as one that protects state militias. It is, however, clearly not an absolute right. Not every citizen will enjoy the right. Various types of regulations, wise or unwise, effective or ineffective, are permissible even if they impact law-abiding citizens to some degree. Citizens may be prevented from acquiring certain types of weapons. How far these regulations can go before they infringe too far on the Second Amendment right is an issue for the courts to decide.[38]

The Constitution does not protect us against unwise or ineffective regulations in any policy area or at any level of government. There is no section of the Constitution that declares that only wise or effective policies can legally be enacted. Even if such a clause existed, we would be unlikely to reach a consensus regarding which policies were wise or effective. That is the purview of politics, the political process, and policy analysis.

The Department of Justice and the Second Amendment

Different presidential administrations adopt different positions on a variety of issues, including the interpretation of the Second Amendment. While it is not binding on any court, the position influences the cases that will be pursued by the Justice Department. The Bush administration represented a clear break with the past in general, and especially with the Clinton administration.

In a 2001 memo Attorney General John Ashcroft adopted the individual-right interpretation of the amendment. This was followed in 2004 by a lengthy memorandum opinion produced by the Justice Department that supported the Ashcroft memo. The DOJ opinion reads in part:

> [W]e conclude that the Second Amendment secures a personal right of individuals, not a collective right that may only be invoked by a State or a quasi-collective right restricted to those persons who serve in organized militia units. Our conclusion is based on the Amendment's text, as commonly understood at the time of its adoption and interpreted in light of other provisions of the Constitution and the Amendment's historical antecedents. . . . We do not consider the substance of that right, including its contours or the nature or type of governmental interests that would justify restrictions on its exercise, and nothing in this memorandum is intended to address or call into question the constitutionality, under the Second Amendment, of any particular limitations on owning, carrying, or using firearms.[39]

Although one may disagree with the conclusions of the memorandum, it provides an excellent summary of the current state of the issue. The memo is important primarily because it guides decisions of the Bush administration regarding cases that may be brought before the federal courts. While that in no way guarantees a victory for the individual-right interpretation, it would presumably be beneficial to have the attorney general or solicitor general support an argument in front of the Supreme Court.

THE SUPREME COURT AND THE
SECOND AMENDMENT

One of the reasons for the ongoing discussion related to interpreting the Second Amendment is that the U.S. Supreme Court has been largely silent regarding its meaning. A definitive Supreme Court pronouncement would not end the debate, but it would clarify what restrictions on firearms and gun owners are permissible. This would take time and several decisions, but we have not as yet started down that path.

Early Supreme Court Cases

Two nineteenth-century cases deal at least indirectly with the right to bear arms. In *United States v. Cruikshank*, Chief Justice Morrison R. Waite wrote:

> The right there specified is that of "bearing arms for a lawful purpose." This is not a right granted by the Constitution. Neither is it in any manner dependent upon that instrument for its existence. The second amendment declares that it shall not be infringed; but this, as has been seen, means no more than that it shall not be infringed by Congress.[40]

The Second Amendment claim in this case was one of many, and this is all the attention it received in the Court's opinion. This passage seems to indicate that the states were free to infringe upon the right although the national government could not. This is not surprising, given that the Supreme Court did not begin to incorporate the Bill of Rights, that is, make them applicable to the state governments, until 1897, nearly thirty years after the decision in *Cruikshank* was handed down.

In *Presser v. Illinois*, Justice William B. Woods reasserted the statement from *Cruikshank* that the Second Amendment did not apply to the states. Woods clearly stated that the defendant did not have a right to band together with other citizens to form their own militia, but he offered some support for an individual-right interpretation and addressed the right to bear arms as follows:

> It is undoubtedly true that all citizens capable of bearing arms constitute the reserved military force or reserve militia of the United States as well as of the states, and . . . the states cannot, even laying the constitutional provision in question out of view, prohibit the people from keeping and bearing arms.[41]

The opinion in *Presser* concluded that the Illinois law that prohibited Presser from parading, drilling, and forming a citizen militia without state authorization did not violate the Second Amendment. It is not clear from the opinion if the law was constitutional because the right is not an individual right or because it was the state and not the national government that was infringing upon the right. The opinion does state, however, that the government, both national and state, has the power to regulate and control military organizations and that citizens do not enjoy the right of association as a military company or organization.

While these cases provide some support for both a collective right and an individual right to bear arms, respectively, neither directly confronts the meaning of the Second Amendment. Both cases are cited as evidence that the Court subscribes to a collective-right interpretation, although this is not entirely obvious from the opinions. Both opinions suggest that the national government may not infringe the right to bear arms but state governments may regulate firearms. It is clear that the Second Amendment was not and has not been incorporated by the Supreme Court.[42]

United States v. Miller, 307 U.S. 174 (1939)

"Both sides of the gun control debate draw support from this ambiguous decision,"[43] and they like to claim the decision in *Miller* as their own: "[T]he Court stated that citizens could possess a constitutional right to bear arms only in connection with service in a government-organized and -regulated militia."[44] An alternative interpretation suggests that the Supreme Court held that the Second Amendment "protects possession of only military type and quality weapons. If so, then the amendment covers high-quality handguns and other firearms, but not poor-quality or gangster-type weapons."[45] A closer examination may help shed some light on this confusing case.

The facts of the case are fairly straightforward. Jack Miller and Frank Layton were charged with violating the National Firearms Act by transporting a sawed-off shotgun across state lines. The act required that the men needed a certified order stating that a $200 tax had been paid. The defendants claimed that the National Firearms Act was an attempt to usurp the police power reserved for the states and not a revenue measure, and was therefore unconstitutional. They also argued that it violated the Second Amendment. The district court that first heard the case held that the act did indeed violate the Second Amendment.

Justice James Clark McReynolds's opinion for the unanimous Supreme Court in its review of the district court's decision stated, in part:

> In the absence of any evidence tending to show that possession or use of a "shotgun having a barrel of less than eighteen inches in length" at this time has some reasonable relationship to the preservation or efficiency of a well regulated militia, we can-

not say that the Second Amendment guarantees the right to keep and bear such an instrument. Certainly it is not within judicial notice that this weapon is any part of the ordinary military equipment or that its use could contribute to the common defense."[46]

The Court continued to discuss the role and the history of the militia in America at great length while saying little about the Second Amendment itself. The opinion stated that the amendment was adopted "to assure the continuation and render possible the effectiveness of such forces [the militia] and "it must be interpreted and applied with that end in view."[47]

While this provides comfort to the collective-right argument, the logic of these passages and the rest of the opinion indicate that firearms that can be effectively used in a military context may be protected under the Second Amendment. "Ironically, *Miller* can be read to support some of the most extreme anti-gun control arguments, that the individual citizen has a right to keep and bear bazookas, rocket launchers, and other armaments . . . including, of course, assault weapons."[48]

Some scholars have even argued that the fact that neither the government nor the Court raised a challenge regarding standing[49] implies that Miller and Layton could, as citizens, assert a Second Amendment defense.[50] If citizens do not enjoy a right to bear arms, then they would not have standing, that is, meet the standards of the Supreme Court to bring the case before the Court. The Court could have overruled the district court's decision on the basis that the defendants were not a state or members of a militia and therefore did not have standing to claim protection under the Second Amendment.

Yet a third alternative exists. Perhaps *Miller* means . . . nothing.

It was the opinion of the Court that these regulations did not have a "reasonable relationship between such weapons and a well-regulated militia." That was it. What bearing does the Court's decision in *Miller* have on an individual's right to keep and bear arms? Sawed-off shotguns don't have a reasonable relationship with a well-regulated militia?[51]

Miller is the Supreme Court's most recent case that directly confronts the Second Amendment, and, contrary to the protestations of both sides of the gun control debate, this case did not clarify the meaning of the right to bear arms. Unfortunately, the Supreme Court has not heard a case in which it has had to directly interpret the Second Amendment in more than sixty years. As a result, the apparent contradictions in *Miller* have never been resolved, and the Court has yet to unambiguously interpret the Second Amendment.[52]

Incorporation of the Second Amendment and Other Supreme Court Cases

"Incorporation" is the term used to describe the method employed by the Supreme Court to make the Bill of Rights applicable to the states. This process uses the Fourteenth Amendment to require that states adhere to the restrictions placed on the federal government in the Bill of Rights. It has been applied on a selective basis, although most of the Bill of Rights has now been incorporated.[53] Those rights that are deemed to be fundamental to the due process of law have been incorporated.

While everyone agrees that the Second Amendment has not been incorporated, not surprisingly, there is disagreement over whether it should be. Those who argue that the amendment is irrelevant today would obviously argue that incorporation would be unwise and ridiculous because there is nothing to incorporate. On the other hand, some academics have gone to great lengths to argue why incorporation would be good policy and sound constitutional reasoning. For example, Janice Baker has suggested that the Second Amendment meets the modern test for incorporation.[54] She goes beyond that to argue that once incorporated, Second Amendment cases should be reviewed using a midlevel of scrutiny: that is to say that the right is fundamental, but it is qualified and subject to some restrictions.[55]

In several cases since *Miller*, individual justices have expressed their personal views regarding the Second Amendment. In *Adams v. Williams*,[56] a man was convicted in a Connecticut state court for illegal possession of a handgun found during a police "stop and frisk" operation. The Supreme Court upheld the conviction, reversing a lower court decision that had found a Fourth Amendment violation. Justice William O. Douglas's dissenting opinion discusses the Second Amendment, but it is not explicit except his note that "I would prefer to water down the Second than the Fourth Amendment" implies that he saw the Fourth Amendment as more important.[57]

In *Lewis v. United States*, a defendant challenged his conviction under a federal law that prohibited convicted felons from purchasing firearms.[58] The Court held that the law did not violate the Sixth Amendment. Justice Harry Blackmun wrote, "These legislative restrictions on the use of firearms are neither based upon constitutionally suspect criteria, nor do they trench upon any constitutionally protected liberties," citing the Court's decision in *Miller*. Both of these decisions are cited by supporters of a collective-right interpretation.[59]

United States v. Verdugo-Urquidez dealt with the Fourth Amendment and noncitizens, but in explaining the nature of the rights afforded by the Fourth

Amendment, Chief Justice William Rehnquist, writing for the 7–2 majority, stated:

> That text [the Fourth Amendment], by contrast with the Fifth and Sixth Amendments, extends its reach only to "the people." . . . "the people" seems to have been a term of art employed in select parts of the Constitution. The Preamble declares that the Constitution is ordained and established by "the people of the United States." The Second Amendment protects "the right of the people to keep and bear Arms," and the Ninth and Tenth Amendments provide that certain rights and powers are retained by and reserved to "the people." . . . While this textual exegesis is by no means conclusive, it suggests that "the people" protected by the Fourth Amendment, and by the First and Second Amendments, and to whom rights and powers are reserved in the Ninth and Tenth Amendments, refers to a class of persons who are part of a national community.[60]

Finally, Justice Clarence Thomas, appointed to the Court after *United States v. Verdugo-Urquidez* was decided, provided the strongest statement of support for an individual-right interpretation in *Printz v. United States.* Despite the fact that this case dealt with the Brady Bill, it did not focus on the Second Amendment. The issue raised was a potential federalism violation in the provision that required local law enforcement personnel to conduct the background checks of prospective firearms purchasers. In a concurring opinion, Thomas wrote at length about the Second Amendment:

> The Constitution . . . places whole areas outside the reach of Congress' regulatory authority. The First Amendment, for example, is fittingly celebrated for preventing Congress from "prohibiting the free exercise" of religion or "abridging the freedom of speech." The Second Amendment similarly appears to contain an express limitation on the government's authority. . . . This Court has not had recent occasion to consider the nature of the substantive right safeguarded by the Second Amendment. If, however, the Second Amendment is read to confer a personal right to "keep and bear arms," a colorable argument exists that the Federal Government's regulatory scheme, at least as it pertains to the purely intrastate sale or possession of firearms, runs afoul of that Amendment's protections. As the parties did not raise this argument, however, we need not consider it here. Perhaps, at some future date, this Court will have the opportunity to determine whether Justice Story was correct when he wrote that the right to bear arms "has justly been considered, as the palladium of the liberties of a republic." [Footnotes deleted][61]

Thomas' footnotes argue that in *Miller*, "[t]he Court did not, however, attempt to define, or otherwise construe, the substantive right protected by the Second Amendment."

It is interesting that several different analyses of this case also fail to discuss the Second Amendment.[62] For example, the perceived irrelevance of the Second Amendment in relation to gun control legislation is obvious in

Melissa Ann Jones's analysis of the *Printz* decision.[63] Jones suggests that Congress enact future gun control legislation under the spending clause "to get around *Printz* and obtain state participation."[64] At no point in this argument does Jones even suggest that the Second Amendment might be an impediment to enacting gun control legislation.

Recent Lower Court Decisions

While the Supreme Court has been vague in terms of its interpretation of the Second Amendment, most lower federal courts have adopted a collective-right approach.[65] The approach used by most of these courts has been a two-tiered test—the first part for the weapon and the second for the person possessing the weapon.[66] This test implies that the right guaranteed by the Second Amendment applies to those who need such arms to serve in the militia—an organized, government-sanctioned militia.

There are several cases that fit these criteria and reached the conclusion outlined above.[67] In *Hickman v. Block*, the Ninth Circuit Court of Appeals went so far as to rule that a man who was denied a permit to carry a concealed weapon did not have standing to challenge the ruling under the Second Amendment.[68]

The single exception to this line of cases was handed down in 1999. One group of scholars describe the decision in *United States v. Emerson*[69] as follows: "Considering all the aforementioned cases that have held how the Second Amendment grants a collective right, it is hard to imagine that any responsible court, even a trial court, could hold differently."[70] Not surprisingly, the *Emerson* decision is hailed by gun rights supporters and dismissed as simple "dicta" and not binding on any other court by gun control advocates.[71]

The facts of the case follow: Timothy Emerson was indicted for possessing a firearm while he was subject to a restraining order, a violation of federal law. His wife had gotten a temporary restraining order alleging that he had threatened her and their children. Emerson argued that the indictment should be dismissed because the law violated the Second Amendment. The district court agreed. In his opinion, Judge Sam Cummings wrote, "*Miller* did not answer the crucial question of whether the Second Amendment embodies an individual or collective right to bear arms . . . and left for another day further questions of Second Amendment construction."

The district court also ruled that the Second Amendment guarantees an individual right to bear arms for self-defense.[72] Arguing that the Supreme Court had provided little, if any, guidance for lower courts allowed the district court in *Emerson* to adopt the individual-right approach to the Second Amendment.

The government appealed the decision, and the appeals court found that there was sufficient evidence that Emerson presented a threat to his wife and children, so he could be barred from possessing a firearm. At the same time, though, the appeals court also rejected the collective-right approach to the Second Amendment:

> We hold, consistent with *Miller* that it [the Second Amendment] protects the right of individuals, including those not then actually a member of any militia or engaged in active military service or training, to privately possess and bear their own fire-arms.[73]

The appeals court suggested that other courts that had adopted the collective-right interpretation erroneously believed that the Supreme Court had adopted that approach in *Miller* or they did not sufficiently examine the history or the text of the amendment. Sometimes overlooked in this decision is the appeals court's assertion that, although

> [t]he Second Amendment does protect individual rights, that does not mean that those rights may never be made subject to any limited, narrowly tailored specific exceptions or restrictions for particular cases that are reasonable and not inconsistent with the right of Americans generally to keep and bear their private arms as historically understood in this country.

In a concurring opinion, Judge Parker argued that the court's recognition of an individual right to bear arms was not relevant, and he questioned the importance of the entire debate: "In the final analysis, whether the right to keep and bear arms is collective or individual is of no legal consequence. It is . . . a right subject to reasonable regulation . . . simply another example of a reasonable restriction on whatever right is contained in the Second Amendment."

Emerson is important for several reasons. First, it is the first in a long line of cases to recognize an individual right to bear arms. Whether this case is simply an aberration or the beginning of a new jurisprudence is impossible for anyone to say. Second, the opinions in the case provide an excellent summary of the disparate views of the Second Amendment and its interpretation. Finally, the opinions place the constitutional discussion in the context of the world in which we live.

A more recent decision came from the Ninth Circuit Court of Appeals (generally thought to be a more liberal circuit than the Fifth) that reasserts the federal courts' recognition of the collective right approach. In *Silveira v.*

Lockyer, California's ban on assault weapons was challenged under the Second Amendment. The district court held that it was constitutional and an appeal was made to the Ninth Circuit. The opinion by Judge Stephen Reinhardt clearly addresses the court's choice of interpretation schemes as well as the decision in *Emerson*:

> There are three principal schools of thought that form the basis for the debate. The first, which we will refer to as the "traditional individual rights" model, holds that the Second Amendment guarantees to individual private citizens a fundamental right to possess and use firearms for any purpose at all, subject only to limited government regulation. This view, urged by the NRA and other firearms enthusiasts, as well as by a prolific cadre of fervent supporters in the legal academy, had never been adopted by any court until the recent Fifth Circuit decision in *United States v. Emerson*. The second view, a variant of the first, we will refer to as the "limited individual rights" model. Under that view, individuals maintain a constitutional right to possess firearms insofar as such possession bears a reasonable relationship to militia service. The third, a wholly contrary view, commonly called the "collective rights" model, asserts that the Second Amendment right to "bear arms" guarantees the right of the people to maintain effective state militias, but does not provide any type of individual right to own or possess weapons. Under this theory of the amendment, the federal and state governments have the full authority to enact prohibitions and restrictions on the use and possession of firearms, subject only to generally applicable constitutional constraints, such as due process, equal protection, and the like. Long the dominant view of the Second Amendment, and widely accepted by the federal courts, the collective rights model has recently come under strong criticism from individual rights advocates. After conducting a full analysis of the amendment, its history, and its purpose, we reaffirm our conclusion in *Hickman v. Block* that it is this collective rights model which provides the best interpretation of the Second Amendment.
>
> Despite the increased attention by commentators and political interest groups to the question of what exactly the Second Amendment protects, with the sole exception of the Fifth Circuit's *Emerson* decision there exists no thorough judicial examination of the amendment's meaning. The Supreme Court's most extensive treatment of the amendment is a somewhat cryptic discussion in *United States v. Miller*. [Citations deleted][74]

As was the case in *Emerson*, the *Silveira* opinion is instructive for those interested in gun control. It summarizes the different views of Second Amendment interpretation, and it directly addresses and rejects the decision in *Emerson*. In that sense, *Silveira* may represent a "return to normalcy" in Second Amendment jurisprudence. At the same time, it recognizes the limitations of the Supreme Court's decision in *Miller* in terms of offering a clear meaning of the right to bear arms.

Why Is the Supreme Court Silent?

The Supreme Court has denied *certiorari* in at least nine circuit court rulings dealing with the Second Amendment.[75] There are several possible explanations for this. First, the Supreme Court traditionally has avoided issues that are not "ripe" for adjudication, that is, cases that are too "political." While one can point to the abortion decisions and several related to freedom of religion as very politically charged issues, we can also see the difficulties the Court has created for itself by wading into these topics. Recently, the Supreme Court declined to become involved in the Terri Schiavo "right to die" case. Perhaps the justices prefer not to inject themselves into the political fray until opinion is more settled on the issue of gun control—if that ever happens.

Second, it is possible that the Court is not ready to start down what might be a long, winding path of several decisions over several years to flesh out the meaning of the Second Amendment. Again, if we use abortion as an example, more than thirty years after the decision in *Roe v. Wade*, the Court has yet to fully define and limit rights with regard to abortion, to say nothing of the larger right to privacy. Of course, a decision ruling that the Second Amendment right is a collective right would essentially terminate the flow of cases immediately because any infringement of an individual right to possess firearms would then be constitutional.

Third, regardless of how the Supreme Court would rule, one side would be very unhappy, and it could put the Court's prestige in jeopardy. However, we can point to cases such as *Bush v. Gore*, the decision regarding the Florida recount in the 2000 presidential election, and the challenge to segregated schools in *Brown v. Board of Education* as examples of controversial cases in which the Court survived challenges to its integrity. Still, the justices may see no urgent need to embark on a case or series of cases that could damage the prestige of the Court, especially when it is infrequently asked to do so. The gun control debate is playing itself out in the nation's legislatures. It can also be argued that the current debate over gun control does not rise to the level of importance of the right to privacy, equal protection for citizens of different races, or the necessity of deciding an election.

It has been suggested that the Supreme Court may be reluctant to grant *certiorari* to a Second Amendment case because several of the justices are concerned with how their colleagues will rule. It is speculated that justices are careful regarding which cases to hear because they do not want to establish a precedent that would contradict their position. In those issues and cases, they would prefer to be silent. They may not be certain how their colleagues would rule in a particular situation, and they may be wary of learning the answer to that question.

It is also possible that the Court sees no reason to enter the fray because lower courts have been applying the collective-right argument for years. There is no real issue to resolve in that situation. This, of course, assumes that a majority of the justices view the collective-right approach as correct and see no need to contradict the substantial case law that has adopted it.

A final suggestion is that both sides—or at least the pro-gun rights lobby— are afraid to bring a case to the Supreme Court because they do not want a precedent established that favors the other side.[76] Because Supreme Court precedents are both binding on lower courts and very difficult to overturn, litigants are wary of bringing a case to the Court unless they think they have a good chance of prevailing. The *Printz* case is a good example of this concept at work. The Brady Law was challenged on Tenth Amendment grounds rather than on Second Amendment considerations. Without being able to probe the minds of the justices, we have no way to determine which, if any, of the above theories is correct. Perhaps the more important question is the one raised in the opinions in the *Silveira* case. Does it really matter which interpretation is correct?

THE IMPORTANCE OF SECOND
AMENDMENT INTERPRETATION

As stated above, no constitutional right is absolute. The First Amendment is explicit in its statement that "Congress shall make no law" abridging freedom of speech, the press, or religion. Yet most of us accept the Supreme Court ruling and its logic that one is not permitted falsely to shout "Fire!" in a crowded theater. There is a consensus that certain types of materials—for example, child pornography—should be illegal. It is a widespread belief that anyone who is libeled should have a right to sue for damages. Similarly, the Supreme Court and society have long had to balance the free exercise of religion against the clause that prohibits the government from establishing a religion. Although we sometimes disagree as to where those lines should be drawn, we are virtually unanimous in our belief that lines should be drawn. Only a few Supreme Court justices have held any rights to be absolute. Why should we see the Second Amendment differently?

It is tempting to adopt the philosophy of Judge Parker in *Emerson*. Does it really matter if the right to bear arms is an individual or collective right? Maybe the answer is yes and no. If the right is an individual right, then we must balance any infringement of that right against the governmental (societal) interest that was served by the infringement. The key question then would be if the Court would require only a "rational relation" to a governmental goal or if it would hold any infringement to a higher level of scrutiny. Either way, there is no question that some infringements on the right to keep and bear arms would be permissible.

It seems unlikely, for example, that any court, the opinion in *Miller* notwithstanding, would rule that an individual has a right to own a tank, rocket launcher, a B-1 bomber, or machine gun. And there seems little doubt that prohibitions against firing weapons in crowded neighborhoods would not be lifted.

Courts could and probably would question prohibitions against possessing certain handguns or, perhaps, assault weapons. Waiting periods for purchasing firearms might also come into question. On the other hand, safety requirements, age requirements, owner licensing, and gun registration would likely pass constitutional muster.

However, if the Supreme Court adopted the collective-right approach, then virtually any gun regulation would be permissible. That is not to say that guns would immediately become illegal.[77] The Congress and the state legislatures would be free to adopt restrictions as they saw fit. This would clearly be an important development, and it would lead to major gun laws in some states, though likely not in others. Federal legislation would also be possible, but it is unlikely in the current political climate that major restrictions would be implemented.

Thus far this discussion has ignored the psychological impact of the Second Amendment. It is not surprising that the right to bear arms is rarely mentioned by supporters of gun control, but it is especially important to gun rights supporters. Virtually every fundraising letter from the NRA or mention of the issue in political campaigns involves some threat against the Second Amendment rights of gun owners.[78] Many gun rights Web sites contain numerous links to discussions of the amendment. Most often it is suggested that any governmental regulation of firearms is an infringement of the right.

The elevation of one's preferred issue position to that of a right or the loftier status of a constitutionally guaranteed right implies a higher level of legitimacy for that position. Many interest groups argue for what they refer to as rights, but few have what they believe is a clear statement in the Constitution protecting their right. Despite the disagreements over its interpretation, those who advocate for the right to bear arms have a stronger statement to which they can refer than do advocates of, say, the right to privacy. What they lack is an unambiguous endorsement of the right in a Supreme Court decision.

The belief in a constitutional right brings with it an assumption of greater importance for that right and a higher level of urgency for its protection, either by or from the government. These sentiments are clearly expressed by the panoply of interest groups and elected officials who court rank-and-file supporters of gun rights.

We would not expect any of the gun rights interest groups to present a nuanced discussion of the possible limits of the Second Amendment rights or even the nature of the rights. Rather, they are expected to assume that the right is absolute and to push for the legislative adoption of that position. Likewise, gun owners and other citizens who believe in the right to bear arms are likely to see many regulations as unnecessary infringements on their rights. In this regard, they are similar to any other group who advocates for what they define as rights—a woman's right to choose, the right to free speech, the right to practice religion, and so on. For each of these groups the right is fundamental, and the proper role of the government is to protect the right, not trample on it. While it is true that many gun owners are willing to accept some gun regulations, many also see the Second Amendment as their legal guarantee to something that is of great importance to them. As a result, for many the Second Amendment and the rights they believe it guarantees are sacred.

CONCLUSION

While it appears that the pendulum for constitutional law scholars is swinging toward the individual-right side of Second Amendment interpretation, the courts' pendulum is stationary. The U.S. Supreme Court remains silent.

Examining historical documents and writings, one can gather sufficient evidence to make a strong case that the framers intended to create an individual right to keep and bear arms. At the same time, there is ample evidence to the contrary. The question of a right to self-defense and the thorny issue of a right to insurrection will most likely never be satisfactorily resolved. The questions are difficult to answer from philosophical, moral, and legal perspectives. Discerning original intent, even if one believes that is the best way to interpret the Constitution, is a difficult task.

On the other hand, one can argue that the Second Amendment has become irrelevant because it only provides a collective right and that right's time has long since passed. Most Americans, though, would prefer that all parts of their Constitution, particularly the Bill of Rights, have some meaning. Many fear the slippery slope: If the Second Amendment is obsolete today, what rights become obsolete tomorrow?

This argument is not just academic. It matters whether the right conferred in the Second Amendment is an individual or collective right; whether it applies to all of us as individuals, those of us who are part of the state militia, or only to us as a single entity. It matters whether it provides us with a right to self-defense or permits the state to disarm us, if it would so choose.

The courts' interpretations of the Second Amendment, though ambiguous, have tended to be in the direction of a collective right. Lower federal courts have all ruled in that direction, with the exception of the 1999 *Emerson* case from the generally conservative Fifth Circuit court.

The U.S. Supreme Court has not ruled on a Second Amendment case in more than sixty years. Its 1939 ruling in *United States v. Miller* is unsatisfying due to its ambiguity regarding the interpretation of the amendment. Both sides of the gun control debate count *Miller* as a victory. Some of that, of course, is simple rhetoric, but the case has been interpreted differently by various constitutional law and Second Amendment scholars as well as the interest groups.

Thus far, the Supreme Court has chosen not to incorporate the Second Amendment, meaning that it has not been made applicable to the states. It is not obvious if that has been the Court's intent or if it is a function of the fact that the Court has not directly addressed the Second Amendment since it began the process of incorporation in earnest in the 1960s. Whether or not it should be incorporated, as most of the other rights mentioned in the Bill of Rights have been, is a matter of debate.

It is impossible to predict if or when the Supreme Court will resolve these conflicts. It is easy to say that the debate will continue at a fairly high decibel level until that happens. If and when it does, some citizens will be very disappointed, and perhaps angry. Those who firmly believe that the Second Amendment confers individual rights on them would, of course, be the most upset with a Supreme Court ruling that went against their position.

Still, it is quite possible that the Supreme Court could rule that the right to bear arms is an individual right and even incorporate the Second Amendment without setting off a jurisprudential earthquake. Even if the right was conferred on the individual, it would most likely not be an absolute right. If it was not absolute, then it must be balanced against other rights. Many legal restrictions could pass constitutional muster under this scenario. Banning broad categories of firearms, such as all handguns, might be unconstitutional under this interpretation, but many less extensive and intrusive policies would likely be constitutional.

This is the background against which the policy debates over the issue of gun control play themselves out in contemporary America. For many of those opposed to gun control, the rights they believe are guaranteed by the Second Amendment form the bedrock of their opposition to restrictions on the individual right to bear arms. Gun control advocates argue either that the right is collective or that it is anachronistic in the twenty-first century. It is to these specific policy debates that we now turn our attention.

NOTES

1. One can argue that there are three major interpretations of the Second Amendment—an individual right, a collective right, and a more limited individual right that applies to those in the militia. Practically speaking, this third option is quite similar to the second. Therefore, we refer to two major lines of thought regarding the correct interpretation of the Second Amendment.

2. Robert E. Shalhope, "To Keep and Bear Arms in the Early Republic," *Constitutional Commentary* 16 (Summer 1999): 269.

3. Cicero, "In Defense of Titus Annius Milo," in *Selected Political Speeches of Cicero*, ed. and trans. Michael Grant (New York: Penguin, 1969), 234.

4. Cesare Beccaria, "On Crimes and Punishment," in *On Crimes and Punishment and Other Essays*, ed. Richard Bellamy (New York: Cambridge University Press, 1995), 101.

5. Andrew J. McClurg, David B. Kopel, and Brannon P. Denning, eds., *Gun Control and Gun Rights* (New York: New York University Press, 2002), 122–25.

6. McClurg, Kopel, and Denning, *Gun Control*, 136. A more detailed discussion of the philosophical background of the right to bear arms may be found in Don B. Kates, "The Second Amendment: A Right to Personal Self-Protection," in *Armed: New Perspectives on Gun Control*, ed. Gary Kleck and Don B. Kates (Amherst, NY: Prometheus, 2001), 343–56.

7. James Madison, "The Federalist No. 46," in *The Federalist*, ed. Sherman F. Mittell (Washington, D.C.: National Home Library Foundation, 1938), 299–300.

8. Alexander Hamilton, "The Federalist No. 29," in *The Federalist*, ed. Sherman F. Mittell, 176.

9. Alexander Hamilton, "The Federalist No. 28," in *The Federalist*, ed. Sherman F. Mittell, 173; and "Federalist 29," 178–79.

10. Stephen P. Halbrook, *That Every Man Be Armed: The Evolution of a Constitutional Right* (Oakland, CA: Independent Institute, 1994).

11. Anthony Gallia, "'Your Weapons, You Will Not Need Them,' Comment on the Supreme Court's Sixty-Year Silence on the Right to Keep and Bear Arms," *Akron Law Review* 33 (1999): 150.

12. Robert E. Shalhope, "The Armed Citizen in the Early Republic," *Law and Contemporary Problems* 49, no. 1 (1986): 125–41.

13. For a discussion of the history of the militia in the United States, see Don Higginbotham, "The Federalized Militia Debate: A Neglected Aspect of Second Amendment Scholarship," *William and Mary Quarterly* 55, no. 1 (1998): 263–68.

14. Saul Cornell, introduction to *Whose Right to Bear Arms Did the Second Amendment Protect?* (Boston: Bedford/St. Martin's, 2000), 10. Even Robert Spitzer agrees that there was a widespread and strong bias against a standing army and in favor of an armed citizen militia in the colonial era and in the early years of the Republic; Robert J. Spitzer, *The Politics of Gun Control,* 3rd ed. (Washington, D.C.: CQ Press, 2004), 19–21.

15. Cornell, "Whose Right," 12–13.

16. Saul Cornell, "'Don't Know Much about History': The Current Crisis in Second Amendment Scholarship," *Northern Kentucky University Law Review* 29 (2002): 657–81.

17. Cornell, "Don't Know Much," 674–75.

18. Cornell, "Whose Right," 14. For more discussion on the importance and history of Pennsylvania in the gun control debate, see Saul Cornell and Nathan DeDino, "Symposium: The Second Amendment and the Future of Gun Regulation: Historical, Legal, Policy and Cultural Perspectives: Panel I: Historical Perspective: A Well Regulated Right: The Early American Origins of Gun Control," *Fordham Law Review* 73 (2005): 487–528; and James A. Henretta, "Symposium: The Second Amendment and the Future of Gun Regulation: Historical, Legal, Policy and Cultural Perspectives: Panel I: Historical Perspective: Collective Responsibilities, Private Arms, and State Regulation: Toward the Original Understanding," *Fordham Law Review* 73 (2005): 529–38.

19. Shalhope, "Armed Citizen."

20. Lawrence Delbert Cress, "An Armed Community: The Origins and Meaning of the Right to Bear Arms," *Journal of American History* 71 (June 1984): 22–42.

21. Robert E. Shalhope, "The Ideological Origins of the Second Amendment," *Journal of American History* 69 (December 1982): 599–614.

22. Sanford Levinson, "The Embarrassing Second Amendment," *Yale Law Journal* 99 (1989): 637–59. The term "Standard Model" originated in Glenn H. Reynolds, "A Critical Guide to the Second Amendment," *Tennessee Law Review* 62 (1995): 461–512.

23. Levinson, "Embarrassing Second Amendment," 642.

24. For most Supreme Court justices and legal scholars, there is no such thing as an absolute right. All rights must be balanced against other rights, and governmental restrictions are, in some circumstances, permissible.

25. Garry Wills has identified the "inner circle of Standard Modelers" as including Robert J. Cottrol, Stephen P. Halbrook, Don B. Kates, Joyce Lee Malcolm, and Robert E. Shalhope. Garry Wills, "To Keep and Bear Arms," in *Whose Right to Bear Arms Did the Second Amendment Protect?* ed. Saul Cornell (Boston: Bedford/St. Martin's, 2000), 65.

26. Eugene Volokh, "The Commonplace Second Amendment," *New York University Law Review* 73 (1998): 793–821.

27. Volokh, "Commonplace Second Amendment," 810.

28. David C. Williams, "The Unitary Second Amendment," *New York University Law Review* 73 (1998): 822–30.

29. Saul Cornell, "Commonplace or Anachronism: The Standard Model, the Second Amendment, and the Problem of History in Contemporary Constitutional Theory," *Constitutional Commentary* 16 (1999): 223.

30. Michael C. Dorf, "Symposium on the Second Amendment: Fresh Looks: What Does the Second Amendment Mean Today?" *Chicago-Kent Law Review* 76 (2000): 291–347.

31. Whether or not we retain a right to revolution is more than just an academic question to many. Jesse Ruhl, Arthur Rizer, and Mikel Wiel write, "[N]o matter how far-fetched the need to take arms against the government might seem, America was founded on the principle that professional soldiers and police should not have a monopoly on the legitimate use of force. And, at the very least, the people have the right to take back power when the government becomes abusive." Jesse Matthew Ruhl, Arthur L. Rizer, and Mikel J. Weir, "Gun Control: Targeting Rationality in a Loaded Debate," *Kansas Journal of*

Law & Public Policy 13 (Winter 2004): 448. More practically, they suggest that many modern governments have killed larger number of citizens than those of the eighteenth century. On the other hand, Robert Hardaway, Elizabeth Gormley, and Bryan Taylor point out that the Constitution itself prevents insurrection through its definition of treason, which is to make war on the United States. Also, one of the functions of the militia is to suppress insurrection, i.e., Shays' Rebellion. Robert Hardaway, Elizabeth Gormley, and Bryan Taylor, "The Inconvenient Militia Clause of the Second Amendment: Why the Supreme Court Declines to Resolve the Debate over the Right to Bear Arms," *St. John's Journal of Legal Commentary* 16 (Winter 2002): 99–102.

32. Dorf, "Symposium," 294.

33. Dorf, "Symposium," 342–44.

34. Don B. Kates, "Introduction," 24.

35. See, for example, Laurence H. Tribe, *American Constitutional Law*, vol. 1 (Westbury, NY: Foundation, 2000), pp. 901–02; and Leonard W. Levy, *Origins of the Bill of Rights* (New Haven, CT: Yale University Press, 2001), chap. 6.

36. Kates, "Introduction," 24.

37. Shalhope, "To Keep and Bear Arms," 269.

38. This interpretation fits well with the conclusions of Shalhope, who argues that the "people" did enjoy a personal right to own and possess firearms, but he recognizes a much more limited definition of the people and the power of the states to restrict the rights of citizens for the common good. Shalhope, "To Keep and Bear Arms."

39. "Whether the Second Amendment Secures an Individual Right," Memorandum Opinion for the Attorney General, August 24, 2004, at www.usdoj.gov/olc/secondamendment2.htm.

40. *United States v. Cruikshank*, 92 U.S. 542 (1876).

41. *Presser v. Illinois*, 116 U.S. 252 (1886).

42. For a discussion of several Supreme Court and lower court cases related to the Second Amendment, see McClurg, Kopel, and Denning, *Gun Control*, chap. 4.

43. McClurg, Kopel and Denning, *Gun Control*, 155.

44. Spitzer, *Politics of Gun Control*, 30.

45. Kates, "Introduction," 24.

46. *Unites States v. Miller*, 307 U.S. 174 (1939).

47. To offer two examples of interpretations of this case, an anonymous reviewer of an earlier version of this chapter suggested that this text "tries to vest the case with a meaning consistent with [Wilson's] predilections instead of offering a full or detailed account of the case." Conversely, Ian Redmond notes that "while collective rights advocates have long relied on [*Miller*] to support their contention that the Supreme Court does not believe the Second Amendment affords any individual right to possess a firearm, there is nothing explicitly stated or implicitly suggested by the Court's ruling to suggest this claim." See Ian Redmond, "Legislative Reform: The Second Amendment: Bearing Arms Today," *Journal of Legislation* 28 (2002): 343.

48. Levinson, "Embarrassing Second Amendment," 655–56.

49. In order to have standing, a litigant before the Supreme Court must have been affected personally by the action of the government and must be able to assert the right for themselves. In other words, one cannot assert rights on behalf of someone else.

50. See Ruhl, Rizer, and Weir, "Gun Control."

51. Gallia, "Your Weapons," 135.

52. For a brief but enlightening discussion of *Miller*, its interpretations, and some insights into those interpretations, see McClurg, Kopel, and Denning, *Gun Control,* 169–71.

53. For a discussion of the theory of incorporation as well as those rights that have and have not been incorporated, see David M. O'Brien, *Constitutional Law and Politics: Civil Rights and Civil Liberties*, 3rd ed. (New York: Norton,1997), 293–301; and Craig R. Ducat, *Constitutional Interpretation*, 7th ed. (Belmont, CA: West Constitutional Law, 2000), 495–500.

54. Janice Baker, "Comment: The Next Step in Second Amendment Analysis: Incorporating the Right to Bear Arms into the Fourteenth Amendment," *Dayton Law Review* 28 (Fall 2002): 35–44. See also Redmond, "Legislative Reform," 345–48; and Cornell and DeDino, "Symposium," 518–26.

55. The level of scrutiny largely determines whether an incursion into a specific right is permissible. There are three tests commonly applied by the Supreme Court. The first is the rational relation test, in which the regulation need only be rationally related to a governmental interest in order for it to be judged constitutional. Heightened scrutiny implies a higher standard, while strict scrutiny implies that the government's interest in restricting a right must be compelling.

56. *Adams v. Williams*, 407 U.S. 143 (1972).

57. The opinions of Justice Douglas tend to be absolutist in terms of the prohibition of governmental interference with the exercise of many rights, so his willingness to "water down" the Second Amendment suggests that it was lower in his hierarchy of rights than some other constitutional rights.

58. *Lewis v. United States*, 445 U.S. 55 (1980).

59. See Ruhl, Rizer, and Wier, "Gun Control," 435; and Spitzer, *Politics of Gun Control*, 31.

60. *United States v .Verdugo-Urquidez*, 494 U.S. 259 (1990).

61. *Printz v. United States*, 521 U.S. 898 (1995).

62. For example, see Dan Carney, "Brady Decision Reflects Effort to Curb Congress' Authority," *CQ Weekly Report* (June 28, 1997): 1524–25; and John A. Ducoff, "Note: Yesterday: Constitutional Interpretation, the Brady Act, and *Printz v. United States*," *Rutgers Law Journal* 30 (Fall 1998): 209–45.

63. Melissa Ann Jones, "Note: Legislating Gun Control in Light of *Printz v. United States*," *U.C. Davis Law Review* 32 (Winter 1999): 455–83.

64. Jones, "Legislating Gun Control," 482.

65. See Ruhl, Rizer, and Wiel, "Gun Control," 436–437; and McClurg, Kopel, and Denning, *Gun Control*, 180.

66. Hardaway, Gormley, and Taylor, "Inconvenient Militia Clause," 121–34.

67. For a detailed discussion, see Hardaway, Gormley, and Taylor, "Inconvenient Militia Clause," 122–30.

68. *Hickman v. Block*, 81 F. 3d 98 (9th Cir. 1996).

69. *United States v. Emerson*, 46 F. Supp. 2d 598 (N.D. Tex. 1999).

70. Hardaway, Gormley, and Taylor, "Inconvenient Militia Clause," 130.

71. Spitzer, *Politics of Gun Control,* 32, quoting from the dissenting opinion.

72. For a discussion of the court's rationale, see Hardaway, Gormley, and Taylor,

"Inconvenient Militia Clause," 130–34; McClurg, Kopel, and Denning, *Gun Control*, 184–89; and Ruhl, Rizer, and Wier," Gun Control," 37–38.

73. *United States v. Emerson*, 270 F.3d 203 (5th Cir. 2001).

74. *Silveira v. Lockyer*, 328 F.3d. 567 (9th Cir. 2003).

75. Hardaway, Gormley, and Taylor, "Inconvenient Militia Clause," 46. It is also possible that none of those cases presented the precise set of facts that the Court would like to have before issuing a ruling.

76. While Hardaway, Gormley, and Taylor, in "Inconvenient Militia Clause," 45–46, argue that this applies to the NRA and those who favor the individual-right interpretation, it can also be applied to the Brady Campaign and its colleagues. A Supreme Court ruling would be a boon to one side and a serious blow to the other, but in other ways it would aid both sides. Unless the Supreme Court adopted an unfettered individual-right interpretation, which is extremely unlikely, there would be potentially even more battles to fight in the Congress and in state legislatures. This would require that both sides in the lobbying campaign be even more active. Stirring up emotions on both sides would make all gun-related lobbying groups more powerful, and would most likely aid in fundraising. It is generally accepted that it is easier for a group to fund-raise when it is on the defensive. It is when people feel that their rights are being threatened that they become more protective of those rights and more willing to contribute money to groups that protect those rights.

77. A similar misconception surrounds the Supreme Court and the abortion debate. Overturning *Roe v. Wade* would not necessarily mean that abortion would become illegal. It would simply return that decision to the state legislatures, some of which would adopt much more stringent laws than others. Only a Supreme Court declaration that a fetus was a person would prohibit all abortions. In the same way, adoption of the collective-right interpretation of the Second Amendment by the Supreme Court would mean that both federal and state laws regarding firearms would be permissible. It would not *require* that any particular restriction be approved.

78. Following are excerpts from one such letter. "**NRA members remain strong, united and ready to do battle with any elected official who dares to try to weaken our fundamental rights in any way**. . . . They're blocking President George W. Bush's judicial nominees—judges who understand the individual right of law-abiding Americans to own firearms guaranteed by the Second Amendment—hoping that one day, they may convince a federal judge, or even the United States Supreme Court, to issue a ruling that would overturn our rights with a single stroke of the pen. . . . [W]e want action in protecting and strengthening our Second Amendment rights." [Bold and underline in original]. Chris W. Cox, letter to NRA members from the NRA Institute for Legislative Action, August 12, 2005.

Chapter Two

Statistics and Firearms

Elected officials, interest groups, and citizen activists frequently relate specific incidents or cite statistics as a way of bolstering their arguments for or against gun control. The stories or statistics typically support the individual's or group's position and are used to increase the depth or breadth of support among the public.

Sometimes this information comes in the form of an anecdote, a single event that, while true, may not reflect the overall situation or accurately depict reality. Examples of anecdotes are the implication that accidental shootings of children are common or that an average person needs to carry a concealed weapon in a restaurant to defend herself against potential criminals. These stories stir emotions, which is why they are used, but they do not offer an accurate picture of the reality of guns in America. Fortunately, very few young children are shot and restaurant shootings are rare, except on television crime dramas.

At other times, those who are interested in persuading others of their view will rely on statistics. Because they are less emotional than anecdotes, statistics are often viewed as more authoritative. Data can either help to elucidate the topic or be used to obscure the truth. It is not always easy to determine which is the case, and truth, much like beauty, can be in the eye of the beholder.[1] Both sides in the gun control debate use statistics to bolster their position, discredit the opposition, and, at times, mislead the audience.

This chapter will help you make sense of the data by placing it in different contexts. While all the numbers may seem overwhelming, it is essential to both examine the statistics and probe beneath the surface to more accurately assess the arguments in the gun control debate.

In judging the veracity of various statistics and claims, it is essential that we consider both the source of the information and how that information was gathered. While at times this may be a tedious task, it is the only way that we can separate information that may be accurate but misleading from that which is more reflective of reality.

GUN OWNERSHIP IN THE UNITED STATES

The Number of Firearms

The Bureau of Alcohol, Tobacco, and Firearms has maintained a count of the number of firearms produced and imported since 1974. Records prior to that are sketchy, although an estimate of 90 million firearms, including 24 million handguns, in 1968 is generally accepted.[2] More current estimates suggest that there are at least 200 million firearms in the United States, and the number may be closer to 230 million.[3] Because we do not know the number of guns that have been taken out of circulation through regular use, police seizure, destruction, or some other means, the exact number of guns in the United States is not known. Still, the 200 million figure is one that is generally accepted by gun control advocates and opponents alike.

The market itself has changed dramatically over the past several decades. Handguns have held an increasing share of the gun market since the mid-1960s, and they now constitute about 40 percent of the firearms sold. There are currently about 65 million handguns in circulation.[4]

In addition, the long gun market has shifted somewhat away from shotguns and traditional hunting rifles toward rifles and shotguns more commonly associated with combat use, the so-called assault weapons. While we do not know the exact number of these weapons that have been sold, it is obvious from the academic literature and a look at any gun shop, gun show, or gun magazine that these firearms have become more popular. Vizzard notes, for example, that in 1960 *Gun Digest* referenced none of these weapons, but it included more than one hundred types of combat guns by 1993.[5] Still, it is unlikely that the average gun owner would possess one.

By the mid-1990s the handgun market had shifted away from pistols and revolvers commonly used for sporting purposes and toward "medium- and large-caliber, semi-automatic pistols designed as combat weapons which can also be used for personal defense."[6] Sales of handguns and long guns have declined slightly in recent years, although there was an increase in sales following the terrorist attacks of September 11, 2001.

In short, there is a very large stockpile of firearms in the United States. No one knows exactly how many guns are in that cache or precisely who owns them. This would hinder any attempt to register those guns or collect them in the unlikely event that either of those policies was implemented. If legislation requiring gun registration was passed, even a 90 percent compliance rate—certainly an optimistic figure—would mean that at least 20 million firearms would not be accounted for.

Who Owns Guns?

The distribution of those guns is as important as the number of firearms in circulation. The percentage of households that contain firearms and the percentage of citizens who own guns are ascertainable only through public opinion surveys because most firearms are not registered with any governmental entity.

Approximately 40 percent of the households in the United States have a gun, a decline from about half the households in 1980.[7] According to General Social Survey data, the percentage of adults who personally own a gun has declined only slightly since 1980, to about 27 percent. These apparent disparate findings can be reconciled when one considers that the average household size in the United States has declined in the past twenty years, with a significant increase in the number of households headed by single females, who are not likely to own guns. In the 2000 census, single-member households constituted more than one-fourth of the households in the country.

Gun ownership is not evenly distributed throughout the country. Survey data consistently show that men are much more likely (as much as four times) than women to own a firearm. Those who live in a rural area, are white, married, middle-aged, and have an above-average income are also more likely to own a gun. These demographic groups are not those normally associated with high levels of crime, particularly violent crime. Politically speaking, self-described Republicans and conservatives are also more likely to own a gun.[8]

Even gun control advocates Philip J. Cook and Jens Ludwig concede that "gun ownership is concentrated in rural areas and small towns, and middle-aged, middle-income households . . . and it is reasonable to suppose that most guns are in the hands of people who are unlikely to misuse them."[9] Tom W. Smith argues that the pattern of gun ownership is related to the traditional gun culture of America, of which hunting is a major component.[10]

In the past several decades, those who own a gun have become more likely to own more than one, so clearly those 200 million firearms are not evenly distributed across the population. For example, most hunters own more than one gun because no single firearm is equally suited for different types of hunting. Similarly, target shooters are likely to own several guns. While the number of hunters is in decline, anecdotal evidence indicates the number of

gun collectors is increasing, as is the number of people who purchase firearms for personal protection.[11]

We know that guns are generally retained by the original owner for about
thirteen years on average. Firearms that are in the possession of criminals and
juveniles change hands more frequently,[12] and about five hundred thousand
guns are stolen each year.[13]

Between 60 and 70 percent of gun transactions are conducted through dealers who have a federal firearms license (FFL). The remainder take place
between individual buyers and sellers. Most of these transactions involve only
law-abiding citizens, while some involve transfers to, and perhaps from, a
criminal.

A survey of convicted felons found that fewer than half (43 percent) of the
guns they possessed were purchased.[14] Almost one-third (32 percent) were
stolen, and the rest were rented or borrowed (9 percent), gifts (8 percent), or
obtained through a trade (7 percent). The most common seller of those firearms that were purchased was a friend or family member (38 percent), followed closely by a retail shop (35 percent), and the black market (26 percent).
This indicates that only 15 percent of the guns possessed by these convicted
felons were purchased in gun shops prior to the implementation of the Brady
Law background check.

An important consideration, in addition to the mere presence of a gun in
the household, is how that gun is stored. A 1994 Police Foundation survey
found that 16 percent of all guns and 34 percent of handguns were kept
loaded and unlocked.[15] The storage of firearms is a critical issue in accidental
shootings, particularly among children. On the other hand, gun rights advocates argue that a gun that is locked in a gun safe with the ammunition locked
in another area cannot be easily accessed for self-protection.

FIREARMS AND DEATH

There are three ways in which a shooting can result in death—homicide, accidental shooting, or suicide. Perhaps the most authoritative source of mortality
statistics in the United States is the National Center for Injury Prevention and
Control, part of the Centers for Disease Control and Prevention. Each year
the NCIPC compiles death statistics in a variety of ways that allow us to
assess the relative impact of various diseases, homicides, suicides, accidents,
and so on. The most current statistics available at this writing are from 2001.[16]

For all ages, the most frequent causes of death were heart disease
(700,142), cancer (553,768), and stroke (163,538). Accidents were fifth on

the list of leading causes of death (101,537), suicide was eleventh (30,622), and homicide was thirteenth (20,308). In comparison, there were 16,785 homicides in 2000 and 16,889 in 1999.

Firearms deaths ranked fifteenth among causes of unintentional death, accounting for only 802, or 1 percent of accidental deaths. Motor vehicle accidents accounted for the most accidental deaths, with 42,443. Firearms were the most commonly used instrument in both suicides (16,869, or 55 percent) and homicides (11,348, or 56 percent). Overall, in 2001, firearms accounted for a total of 29,019 deaths.[17]

Firearms accounted for 28,163 deaths in 2000 and 28,251 in 1999. Most of the increase in 2001 was in homicides, although the percentage of homicides caused by firearms actually decreased that year. The overall increase in homicides in 2001 came after a decline for several years.

While you may find these statistics interesting or alarming, it is useful to examine them in more detail. The NCIPC provides breakdowns of the leading causes of death in various age groups, which can help put these numbers in perspective.

Table 2.1 begins to clarify the picture. We can see that accidents, suicides, and homicides are all major causes of death in most age subgroups. For the 15–19, 20–24, and 25–34 age groups, they are the top three leading causes of death. Obviously, as the population ages, natural causes emerge as more common causes of death.

Accidents account for a relatively large number of deaths in every age group. This is not surprising given the large number of ways in which one can die accidentally and the number of automobiles in the United States. We

Table 2.1. Leading Causes of Death in Various Age Groups, 2001

Age Group	Accident Rank/Number	Suicide Rank/Number	Homicide Rank/Number
< 1 year	7 / 976	—	14 / 332
1–4	1 / 1,714	—	4 / 415
5–9	1 / 1,283	18 / 7	4 / 137
10–14	1 / 1,553	3 / 272	5 / 189
15–19	1 / 6,649	3 / 1,611	2 / 1,899
20–24	1 / 7,765	3 / 2,360	2 / 3,398
25–34	1 / 11,839	3 / 5,070	2 / 5,204
35–44	2 / 15,945	4 / 6,635	6 / 4,268
45–54	3 / 13,344	5 / 5,942	10 / 2,467
55–64	6 / 7,658	8 / 3,317	16 / 1,018
65 +	9 / 32,964	18 / 5,393	—

Source: National Center for Injury Prevention and Control

would expect that suicide is uncommon until the middle teenage years, and the number of those who take their own life remains substantial, at least until much later in life. Much like suicide, homicides are fortunately infrequent among those under fifteen years of age, but homicides increase at that point, and they remain an important cause of death until age fifty-five or so. While these data help establish the importance of these causes of death, they still do not help us in assessing the relationship between firearms and death.

Table 2.2 details the relative frequency of various causes of accidental deaths. Two conclusions can be fairly easily drawn from these data. First, motor vehicle accidents are the leading cause of accidental deaths in the United States, accounting for 42 percent of all unintentional deaths recorded in 2001. Motor vehicle accidents are the leading cause of accidental death in every age group except for those under one year of age and those sixty-five or older.

Second, firearms account for a relatively small number of accidental deaths. Even in the age groups in which firearms are in the top ten causes of death, the numbers are dwarfed by the number of motor–vehicle-related deaths. This is not to say that firearm-related accidental deaths are not tragic or are unimportant. However, if we wish to enact public policies to save lives lost in accidents, then our attention should be focused more on motor vehicle safety than on gun safety.

A closer look at accidental deaths among the very young reveals that children are more likely to drown, suffocate, or die from poisoning or from a fall

Table 2.2. Leading Causes of Accidental Death in Various Age Groups, 2001

Age Group	Motor Vehicle Rank/ Number	Drowning Rank/ Number	Poison Rank/ Number	Fire Rank/ Number	Fall Rank/ Number	Suffocation Rank/ Number	Firearm Rank/ Number
< 1	2 / 139	3 / 68	8 / 15	4 / 50	5 / 23	1 / 614	—
1–4	1 / 558	2 / 458	8 / 31	3 / 230	7 / 32	4 / 138	13 / 15
5–9	1 / 660	2 / 168	10 / 18	3 / 164	6 / 33	5 / 44	10 / 18
10–14	1 / 884	2 / 165	9 / 32	3 / 88	8 / 33	5 / 68	6 / 39
15–19	1 / 5,106	3 / 322	2 / 406	7 / 76	6 / 88	11 / 65	5 / 110
20–24	1 / 5,407	3 / 274	2 / 956	5 / 138	4 / 168	11 / 80	9 / 96
25–34	1 / 6,759	3 / 374	2 / 2,507	6 / 250	4 / 340	10 / 156	12 / 122
35–44	1 / 6,891	4 / 462	2 / 5,036	5 / 448	3 / 647	6 / 344	14 / 146
45–54	1 / 5,422	7 / 359	2 / 3,547	5 / 434	3 / 1,024	4 / 461	16 / 103
55–64	1 / 3,328	7 / 206	3 / 798	4 / 395	2 / 1,004	6 / 381	16 / 69
65 +	2 / 7,256	9 / 391	6 / 722	5 / 1,147	1 / 11,623	4 / 3,204	16 / 82

Source: National Center for Injury Prevention and Control

than to die from an accidental gunshot wound. Even among 10-to-19-year-olds, when firearm accidents reach their highest rankings, they still account for fewer deaths than drowning. Overall in 2001 the number of accidental deaths in motor vehicles outnumbered those caused by firearms by about 53 to 1.

It is worth repeating that these statistics in no way detract from the tragedy associated with any accidental death, particularly those that could have been prevented and those that claim the lives of children. Still, it is reasonable to ask by how much we could have reduced the 182 accidental firearm deaths in 2001 among those under the age of twenty, and at what cost to whom.

In table 2.3 we see that firearms are the most frequently used method of committing suicide. This is true of every age category except the youngest, and the numbers there are relatively small. The proportion of those using a gun to commit suicide increases in the older age groups.

Sex is also an important variable in suicide. In 2001, 24,672 males and 5,950 females committed suicide. The most frequently used means for males were firearms (60 percent), suffocation (21 percent), and poison (12 percent). For females, poison was most common (37 percent), followed by firearms (36 percent), and suffocation (17 percent). Both the suicide rate and the use of firearms as a means of killing oneself is higher among males aged sixty-five and older.

These data indicate that it is worth pursuing the idea that gun control might reduce the number of suicides in the United States. Gun control as a means of preventing suicide is hotly debated, but the number of people using firearms to kill themselves suggests that we should at least consider the idea.

Table 2.4 indicates that firearms are the most commonly used weapons in

Table 2.3. Leading Causes of Death by Suicide in Various Age Groups, 2001

Age Group	Poison Rank/ Number	Fall Rank/ Number	Suffocation Rank/ Number	Cut/Pierce Rank/ Number	Firearm Rank/ Number
10–14	3 / 10	4 / 4	1 / 163	—	2 / 90
15–19	3 / 117	4 / 37	2 / 551	13 / 2	1 / 838
20–24	2 / 220	4 / 168	2 / 684	7 / 22	1 / 1,292
25–34	3 / 753	4 / 109	2 / 1,373	6 / 52	1 / 2,564
35–44	2 / 1,541	4 / 139	3 / 1,534	5 / 116	1 / 3,030
45–54	2 / 1,439	4 / 129	3 / 952	5 / 115	1 / 3,023
55–64	2 / 578	4 / 73	3 / 392	5 / 60	1 / 2,083
65 +	3 / 530	4 / 112	2 / 543	5 / 91	1 / 3,943

Source: National Center for Injury Prevention and Control

Table 2.4.   Leading Causes of Death by Homicide in Various Age Groups, 2001

Age Group	Transportation Related Rank/Number	Unspecified Rank/Number	Suffocation Rank/Number	Cut/Pierce Rank/Number	Firearm Rank/Number
1–4	10 / 5	1 / 146	6 / 18	9 / 10	3 / 55
5–9	10 / 3	2 / 19	4 / 10	5 / 8	1 / 59
10–14	8 / 4	2 / 17	6 / 6	3 / 16	1 / 121
15–19	8 / 15	3 / 65	5 / 39	2 / 165	1 / 1,529
20–24	3 / 124	4 / 99	5 / 76	2 / 316	1 / 2,675
25–34	2 / 842	4 / 204	6 / 132	3 / 472	1 / 3,308
35–44	2 / 1,061	5 / 298	7 / 145	3 / 458	1 / 1,978
45–54	2 / 644	4 / 250	6 / 88	3 / 266	1 / 934
55–64	2 / 250	3 / 117	6 / 45	4 / 112	1 / 364

Source: National Center for Injury Prevention and Control

homicides. Again, this is true in every age group except the youngest, and the numbers in that group are relatively small. Firearms are an important element in most homicides.

With more than twenty thousand homicides nationwide and more than eleven thousand of those the result of gunshot wounds, it is clear that lethal gun violence is an important issue in America. Perhaps most alarming is the number of people between the ages of fifteen and thirty who are being killed.

Sex and race are very important variables when discussing homicide. Homicide was the twelfth leading cause of death among males in 2001, claiming 15,555 victims, with 61 percent of those dying from gunshot wounds. Even more alarming is that 44 percent (6,780) of those males who were killed were African American. And 78 percent of those black murder victims were killed with guns. While firearms were the most frequently used weapon in homicides among other races, they accounted for just under half of the homicides.

Homicide was the fifth leading cause of death among black males and the fourteenth leading cause among white males. It was the leading cause of death among black males in the 15–19, 20–24, and 25–34 age groups, while it was third in those groups among whites. Overall, there were more homicides among black males between the ages of fifteen and thirty-four than among whites in the same demographic group, in spite of the fact that there are about four times as many whites in that age group.

What is obvious from these data is that African-American males are disproportionately victims of homicide, and that firearms are disproportionately used in the commission of those homicides.

WEAPONS AND VIOLENT CRIME

In order to fully assess the negative consequences of firearms, we also need to consider gun-related crime, much of which does not result in death. While firearm-related accidents often result in death, it is more common for a victim to be injured. For example, the NCIPC estimated that 58,841 persons were treated in emergency rooms for nonfatal firearm-related injuries in 2002.[18] This includes all injuries, not only those that resulted from a criminal attack.

According to the National Crime Victimization Survey, between 1993 and 2001 violent crime declined 54 percent, violence with a weapon declined 59 percent, and firearm violence went down 63 percent.[19] The drop in the crime rate throughout the 1990s was noted in many quarters and was attributed to a variety of factors, including tougher sentencing practices, a decline in the usage of crack, and economic prosperity, as well as other more specific anti-crime programs.

The rate of firearm usage while committing various crimes ranged from a high of 27 percent of the robberies to 8 percent of assaults and 3 percent of rapes. Overall, between 1993 and 2001 the annual average firearm-related crime rate was four crimes per one thousand persons twelve years old or older. Firearms were present in just under 10 percent of all nonlethal violent crimes during this time, and 87 percent of the gun-related crimes involved the use of a handgun.

Knives or other sharp objects accounted for about 6 percent of all violent crimes, while blunt objects were used in 4 percent of the crimes. African Americans had significantly higher victimization rates by an assailant with a weapon or a firearm than did whites or Hispanics. Violent victimization was especially high among eighteen- to twenty-year-old blacks. On a more positive note, the largest drops in victimization rates during this time were experienced by blacks, Hispanics, and those in the 12–14 (97 percent decrease) and 15–17 (77 percent decrease) age groups.

Victims who faced an armed assailant were about as likely to be injured as those whose attacker did not have a weapon. Attacks with blunt objects or other weapons were the most likely to result in injury (36 percent), followed by 28 percent of those with knives or sharp objects and 15 percent of the crimes committed with guns.

Overall, 61 percent of victims reported some attempt at self-defense during the crime. Fewer than 1 percent of the victims reported using a gun to threaten the offender.[20]

CAN GUN POLICY IMPACT FIREARM-RELATED DEATHS AND INJURIES?

It is axiomatic that most loss of life is to be lamented. In some cases death may be seen as a welcome relief from pain and suffering or as just desserts for an individual's transgressions, but it is far more common for us to see death and severe injury as something we should strive to prevent.

In trying to prolong life and prevent injury we generally ask two questions. First, is the consequence avoidable? That is, can we reasonably expect that measures we take will in fact prolong the life or prevent the injury? Second, what is the cost of avoiding the outcome? Costs can be measured in terms of psychology, economic impact, social costs, and the personal toll on victims or others. All of these are recognized, implicitly or explicitly, as legitimate considerations. We must be able to look at these costs and benefits in terms of the "big picture" if we are to seriously discuss issues such as drug safety, automobile laws and safety regulations, and firearms regulations.

For example, potential benefits of prescription medications must be balanced against potential side effects or misuse of the drugs. The painkiller OxyContin has provided relief for many terminally ill patients, but it has also been related to drug addictions in many who have misused the drug. Enforcement of illegal-drug laws must be balanced against civil liberties. Lower speed limits save lives, but they inconvenience all those who are stuck in slow-moving traffic. Raising the age at which teenagers can obtain a driver's license would also save lives, but there would be costs to the parents who have to drive their children around. Firearms can be lethal weapons if they are used recklessly or with that intent. In any of these cases, we must assess the effectiveness of a regulation in preventing negative outcomes and the costs associated with that law or regulation. In this section we examine the prevention side of that equation, looking specifically at suicides, accidents, and homicides.

Suicide

Whether or not gun regulations can reduce the incidence of suicide is largely dependent upon the nature of the suicide itself. How many suicides are the result of a spur-of-the-moment decision? Such a situation might involve an individual who has suicidal thoughts and has a firearm (or other means) readily available that makes the act immediately possible. If he had time to reconsider the idea, he might decide against taking his life. Conversely, how many lives are taken in a more carefully planned manner in which the individual is determined to end her life and will do so with whatever means are available or can be obtained?

If those who use a firearm to end their lives would simply substitute another method, then gun availability has no impact on the number of suicides, only on the method used. If the presence of a gun makes suicide easier or more attractive, then availability might affect the incidence of suicide. Of course, in order to reduce suicides, we would have to be able to identify those who are suicidal, prevent them from purchasing firearms, and remove existing guns from their immediate environs.

Researchers have reached different conclusions with regard to the impact of guns on suicide. We can say that the mere presence of guns does not seem to increase rates of suicide. The suicide rate in the United States is significantly lower than that in many other industrialized nations in which the rate of gun ownership is much lower.[21] Ludwig and Cook's analysis of the Brady Law found that the law did not impact the overall suicide rate, but it may have contributed to a lower rate among those aged fifty-five and older, although they also found some method of substitution.[22] Using subscriptions to *Guns & Ammo* magazine as a surrogate for gun ownership, Mark Duggan concluded that gun owners are more likely to commit suicide, but he admits that gun ownership does not explain changes in the suicide rate in the past twenty years.[23]

A substantial body of literature in the public health field has linked gun ownership and suicide. Arthur Kellerman and his colleagues, in a frequently cited study of suicides in Memphis and Seattle, found that keeping a gun in the home was associated with an almost 500 percent increase in suicide risk.[24] They compared suicide victims with a control group in each locality that was matched on sex, race, and approximate age, but the control groups may have been different with regard to their suicidal tendencies.

The instrumentality effect was advanced in the research of David A. Brent and colleagues. They found that adolescent teenage suicide completers were more than twice as likely as those who unsuccessfully attempted suicide to have a gun in their home.[25] Garen Wintemute and colleagues found that those who purchased a handgun in California in 1991 were significantly more likely to commit suicide in the week following the purchase. This effect was found up to a year after the purchase.[26] Several other studies have also suggested a link between either gun ownership or access to a firearm and suicide rates.[27]

This body of research leads Duggan to conclude that "individuals who own a gun are more likely to commit suicide than are other individuals" and that there is a "positive correlation between suicidal tendencies and gun ownership."[28] Discussing adolescent suicide, Andrew J. McClurg states the case more starkly,

> Unfettered access to millions of unlocked guns contributes to the United States having the highest adolescent suicide rate in the world. Our firearm suicide rate for children under fifteen is eleven times higher than that of any other industrialized nation. A prime explanation for this grim statistic is that we are a nation awash in readily available firearms. [Footnotes omitted][29]

On the other hand, Gary Kleck has written a lengthy and critical analysis of the studies that have purported to show a connection between gun ownership and suicide, based on a detailed discussion of the methodologies used.[30] Even Duggan admits that "available data are far from perfect."[31] Kleck cites other studies which indicate that fatality rates for suicide attempts with a gun may not be higher than those that employ hanging, poison, or gas. In addition, several studies which examined a small sample of suicide attempts found that only a small percentage of the guns used in those attempts were acquired for that purpose. Most were originally purchased for self-defense. If this pattern holds true more generally, it would be very difficult to prevent those with suicidal thoughts from gaining access to firearms. Finally, he cites data indicating that the suicide rate had fluctuated only slightly during the fifty years prior to his study, but that the number of guns in circulation per capita had more than doubled during that time. In response to Kleck, while the number of firearms has increased, the rate of gun ownership has probably not increased as much, if at all, during that time. Both the gun suicide rate and the percentage of suicides committed with a gun have increased over that time period.[32]

There are several important points raised in all the research that must be considered when discussing gun control and suicide prevention. It is assumed that a policy that reduces gun-related suicides but fails to reduce the overall suicide rate is not an effective policy. First, to what extent would people attempting suicide simply substitute the use of another method if a gun were not available? It is clear that overall suicide rates are not related to gun availability, at least insofar as international comparisons are accurate. Even domestically, the data are questionable as to whether reduced gun accessibility is related to lower overall suicide rates.[33]

Second, even if we assume that suicide fatality rates are higher with guns, does that indicate that lives could be saved with gun control, or can we infer that those who use guns are simply more serious about wanting to die? Some suicide attempts are intended to result in death, while others are a way of seeking help or attention. It is logical that those who truly wish to die would choose a more effective method, while those who do not really want to die would select a mode that may have little or no chance of success.

Finally, can we effectively identify those individuals who intend to commit suicide and prevent them from purchasing firearms (or other means to commit suicide)? Can we remove those items from their homes and environs? Even the research that supports a link between guns and suicides is inconclusive regarding the effectiveness of safe firearm storage in reducing suicides.[34]

While the research in this field is inconclusive, it does indicate that *some* lives may be saved *if* we could prevent those with suicidal thoughts from obtaining guns or having them in their homes. We might also prevent *some* suicides by removing all firearms from homes. The possibility of implementing a policy that would accomplish either of those goals is another story. We can, as we do under the Brady Law, conduct background checks and prevent some people with mental illness from purchasing a gun. However, we are not very accurate in predicting who will commit suicide, and we have no means available to take away any guns they might already own or have available. In addition, because records of suicide attempts, mental illness, or simple psychological counseling are kept confidential, they are unavailable to anyone conducting a background check.

Any policy that would try to identify suicide-prone individuals and prevent them from purchasing or accessing firearms would, by necessity, be very intrusive. There would have to be a check at purchase and some type of follow-up at periodic intervals after purchase. This would require record keeping as well as devising some follow-up mechanism. These policies might prevent or deter some suicides, but they would be unwieldy to implement and run afoul of numerous civil liberties. What types of persons would be ineligible to purchase firearms, and what records would we use to make that determination? In short, some gun control policies might result in fewer suicides, but the cost would be very high in terms of both economics and personal freedom.

Accidents

Although accidental shootings, especially those involving children, receive a great deal of attention from the news media and evoke tremendous sympathy, relatively little research has been conducted on the effects of various gun control strategies and safety measures on unintentional shootings.

Cook and Ludwig admit that "unintentional shootings form a rather small and dwindling portion of the total" number of gun-related deaths; they also note that only 7 percent of accidental shootings are fatal, and that accidental shootings account for about 15 percent of gun-related injuries.[35] Therefore, there is a cost beyond death related to accidental shootings.

Without citing any numbers, Spitzer notes similar findings, although he refers to an American Medical Association study that found that about 40 percent of gun-related injuries were unintentional, a rate that is about three times higher than that cited by Cook and Ludwig and seems logically indefensible.[36] He notes that more than half of those shot accidentally are under thirty and that one third are younger than twenty. "These statistics have put greater focus on stemming gun accidents among the young, given their preventability."[37] He refers to the Wintemute study of California accidental child shootings which found that a majority of the accidents occurred when children were playing with friends. About half the time the guns were stored in the house loaded and unlocked. Again, what is absent from Spitzer's discussion is any mention of the number of accidental shootings that actually occurred. The study analyzed the deaths of only eighty-eight children aged fourteen or younger between 1977 and 1983, a relatively small number.[38]

Deborah Azrael and colleagues present a more balanced view of unintentional shootings as part of a call for a more comprehensive national data collection and reporting system.[39] Information recorded in accidental shootings is often sketchy. For example, we do not have longitudinal data regarding how the guns used were stored or information pertaining to the shooter (age, relationship to victim, how they obtained the gun, etc.). Finally, they note that some accidental shooting deaths are miscoded as either homicides or suicides, depending upon the circumstances. For all of these reasons, the studies that have been done to assess the impact of child prevention laws are inconclusive at best.

On the other side, Kates argues that much of the health advocacy literature and gun control advocates actually "suppress" the declining number of unintentional shooting deaths that has coincided with the increasing number of guns in circulation and the replacement of long guns by handguns for personal protection.[40] He notes that health advocates rarely cite the number of accidental deaths caused by bicycles, bathtubs, swimming pools, and cigarette lighters. His use of statistics, for example, that 400 percent more children under fifteen years old die by drowning than in gun accidents is also potentially misleading because of the small number of gun-related deaths.

Kleck notes that firearms are involved in a very small percentage of accidental deaths, and he suggests that many gun-related deaths coded as accidents are really suicides or homicides.[41] While he acknowledges there are many more accidental injuries due to guns than deaths (about fourteen to one), he notes that the rate of fatal gun accidents has declined since the late 1960s.

Kleck suggests this is due, in part, to advances in medical treatment of gunshot victims, but he argues that the primary reason is that the preferred firearm kept loaded in the household for self-defense has shifted from long guns to handguns, specifically smaller caliber, cheaper, and less lethal handguns, the so-called Saturday night specials.

Perhaps Kleck's most on-target criticism of the gun accident "myth" is the perception that gun accidents primarily involve children. He cites data similar to those found in table 2.2 which indicate that there are relatively few deaths attributed to accidental shootings of children fourteen or younger (72 for 2001). The number of deaths rises to 206 for those fifteen to twenty-four years of age. The reasons the misperception of a child-shooting epidemic is so common include the tendency of control proponents to include older groups as "children" to make the problem seem more serious and the media attention that is given to accidental shootings involving children.[42]

Finally, Kleck cites studies indicating that the majority of accidental gun deaths result from reckless behavior, such as playing with a loaded gun or mixing alcohol and shooting, and that about 15 percent are hunting accidents, most of which are true accidents. Only a small number of deaths result from a malfunctioning gun.

Certain strategies and policies could reduce the number of accidental shooting deaths. Safety training may encourage some gun owners to behave more responsibly, while trigger locks and other "safe-gun technologies" may make guns safer. Safe-storage laws might also impact accidental shootings to the extent that gun owners comply with a law that could only be enforced retroactively. As with all policies, these must be evaluated in terms of their costs and expected benefits. This will be done more extensively later in this chapter when we consider the number of crimes *prevented* by firearms. For now, it is sufficient to say that the number of accidental shooting deaths that could be prevented is relatively small, so the cost of any policy would also have to be low in order for it to be efficient.

Homicides

It seems indisputable that the number of homicides would be reduced if we eliminated all firearms from the United States. While it is true that someone who really wanted to kill another person would find an alternative method, many homicides are not that carefully planned and would not occur if an easy means of killing were not available. While we do not have reliable statistics on this, anecdotal evidence indicates that many homicides are the result of heated arguments that may include the presence of alcohol or illegal substances. Even if the urge to fight were satisfied with a substitute weapon, few, if any, of them are as lethal as a firearm.

Franklin E. Zimring and Gordon Hawkins note that firearms are used in the commission of about 20 percent of the violent crimes in the United States, but 70 percent of lethal attacks are committed with a firearm.[43] This is what is referred to as the instrumentality effect, that guns make assaults more deadly.[44]

Academics on the other side of the debate counter with arguments that while firearms are indeed more lethal than other weapons, they also permit potential victims to more effectively defend themselves against crime.[45]

We know that it is not possible to get all guns out of circulation. That policy is not practical and is probably not constitutional. Short of an effective ban, the utility of various gun control laws is questionable. As previously discussed, the typical purchaser or owner of a firearm (middle-aged or older, white male) does not match the typical person who commits a homicide (younger, minority male). While restricting ownership among members of the former group would likely reduce the number of homicides they commit, it would do little to address the issue of homicides committed by (and largely against) the latter group. There may be a trickle-down effect in that if the primary market is squeezed, there might be a contraction in the secondary market.[46] Regulation of the secondary market might also restrict sales in that arena. Whether transactions between law-abiding citizens or weapons transfers to criminals in the secondary market would be impacted is open to debate. Restricting the latter would clearly reduce homicides, and perhaps other crimes, while restricting the former would have little or no positive impact.

Most public policies have focused on preventing the purchase of firearms by those who have committed felonies in the past. Ideally we would like to restrict ownership among prospective criminals, but we have no effective means of identifying future offenders.[47] Any policy that could accurately identify future offenders and prevent their access to firearms would enjoy virtually unanimous support in legislatures and among the populace. While the Brady Law prevents most felons from purchasing guns in the primary market, it does not regulate the secondary market. There are fewer regulations of the secondary market, and they enjoy less public and legislative support. It is possible to regulate all transactions that take place at gun shows and probably most private sales, but it is not possible to prevent gun theft and the friends and family connections that are popular among criminals.

While it is difficult to estimate with any confidence the number of homicides we can prevent, it is obvious that we can prevent some, and perhaps many. At the same time, though, we need to consider the argument of gun rights scholars who suggest that stricter gun regulations would increase crime overall (and possibly homicide) because criminals would know that their potential victims were unarmed and would be more bold in their attacks.

Overall Costs of Firearms

The costs associated with gun violence go beyond those most commonly considered, such as death and injury. They include medical treatment for gunshot victims and loss of earning power. We might also include the costs associated with preventing gun crime.[48] In a complex analysis, Cook and Ludwig estimate the total costs of gun violence at about $100 billion annually plus the value of avoidance and prevention.[49]

Many of the costs are difficult to quantify, and they rely on survey data to indicate what citizens are willing to pay to avoid gun violence. It is not our purpose here to scrutinize the methodology employed. Other researchers would likely reach figures that are much lower than those of Cook and Ludwig. In addition, they do not attempt to quantify the value associated with gun ownership. Finally, even they admit that their assumptions rest on the elimination of firearms in society, a goal that is not achievable. Nonetheless, they provide a valuable starting point in the discussion of the costs of gun violence.

BENEFITS OF GUN OWNERSHIP

There are three major practical benefits that can be derived from gun ownership.[50] One can use a gun to defend against a potential attacker or prevent a criminal act. This defense may involve protection in the home against an intruder, or it may occur outside the home if one carries a firearm, often concealed. There may be some general crime deterrent benefit that is derived from a criminal's consideration that a potential victim may be armed; that is to say, it may be possible for many to benefit from others carrying guns if criminals are deterred from attacking others for fear of being shot. Finally, many Americans enjoy the use of firearms in sport, either in hunting, target shooting, or collecting.

While these benefits are real, we cannot place a dollar value on them. We do not have tangible evidence that a crime was prevented unless the perpetrator is actually shot, and estimates of the number of crimes deterred are imprecise at best. Still, the number is considerable. The benefit of participating in a sport also defies quantification, but it should be considered a positive outcome of gun ownership. Finally, the deterrent effect of gun ownership is also difficult to measure.

Defensive Gun Use

One of the linchpins in the discussion of the utility of various gun control strategies is the question of defensive gun use. While it is well established that guns are used in the commission of various crimes, the question of how frequently firearms are used to prevent crime and the general deterrent value of firearms is less well known.

There is debate over crime statistics and gun use, but we have data that are generally recognized as valid involving deaths and injuries attributable to firearms. But how often a firearm is used by a potential victim to fend off an attacker is a statistic in tremendous dispute.

The question of the frequency of defensive gun use is one of the most vitriolic debates in the field of criminology. The discussion originated in the public health literature. In 1975 four Cleveland physicians published an article concluding that guns kept in the household were "more dangerous than useful" and that owning a gun was an ineffective way to protect against crime.[51] They found there were six times as many fatal gun accidents in homes that had a gun than criminals killed with those guns. A similar, but more widely cited study was published in 1986 by physicians Arthur Kellerman and Donald Reay, who reached very similar conclusions.[52] Neither study included any calculation of a gun benefit beyond dead intruders.

The debate then expanded to the criminology literature and focused on the annual number of defensive gun uses (DGUs), that is, the number of crimes prevented by firearms. The estimated annual DGUs ranges from a low of sixty-five thousand to a high of 2.5 million.[53] The tremendous disparity in the estimates results from the method used to calculate the estimate.

For David McDowall and Brian Wiersema, as well as for many other pro-control scholars, including Cook and Ludwig,[54] the estimates are based on the National Crime Victimization Survey, a U.S. Bureau of Justice Statistics survey that interviews between forty and sixty thousand households every six months over a three-year period. Respondents who report being the victims of crime are asked if they "did anything" with the idea of protecting themselves while the crime was occurring. Those who do not report being victims are not asked if they prevented a crime from happening. The NCVS data undoubtedly yield a low DGU number and underestimate the number of defensive gun uses. Anyone who prevented a crime from occurring would not report a crime and therefore would not be asked if they did anything to protect themselves. Others, such as a criminal who fought off an attack by a fellow criminal, might have an incentive to lie.

The highest estimate of DGUs was obtained by Gary Kleck and Marc Gertz in a 1993 survey of 4,977 adults that was specifically designed to determine the number of defensive gun uses. They asked if anyone in the household had used a gun, even if it was not fired, for self-protection or to protect property at home, work, or elsewhere.[55] They estimated between 1 and 2.5 million annual DGUs, but they suggest the higher estimate is more accurate because several factors at work might cause underreporting of a defensive gun use.

The debate became more heated in a 1997 exchange in the *Journal of Criminal Law and Criminology*, when some researchers resorted to referring to each other by using initials rather than names. Commenting on the Kleck and Gertz survey, David Hemenway states, "[I]t is clear, however, that its conclusions cannot be accepted as valid."[56] Hemenway criticizes the conclusion of Kleck and Gertz, referring to their work as the K-G survey, arguing that respondents overestimated DGUs because it is a socially desirable response to claim that you thwarted a crime. They found that 1.33 percent of respondents reported a DGU. Hemenway contends that surveys tend to overestimate rare behavior, such as a defensive gun use. Kleck and Gertz defended their work in the same issue.[57]

Smith suggests that the true number of DGUs lies between the high estimate of Kleck and Gertz and the low estimate of Hemenway.[58] He agrees with Kleck and Gertz that the NCVS estimates are low because that survey only includes DGUs as a victim's response to specific crimes. Second, it does not ask directly about DGUs, a survey technique that almost certainly results in underreporting of a behavior. He agrees with Hemenway that the Kleck and Gertz survey overestimates DGUs and that sampling error may be an issue in their work. Smith asserts that making adjustments to both estimates would bring them closer together and yield an estimate somewhere around 1 million annual DGUs.

In a logical, cogent, and reasonable analysis of this work, informed by decades of personal experience in law enforcement, Vizzard, like Smith, states that the actual number of DGUs is most likely somewhere between the low and high estimates.[59]

The National Institute of Justice (NIJ) sponsored a survey in 1994 with a questionnaire designed by Kleck, Cook, and Hemenway.[60] The methodology employed in this survey was slightly different than that used by Kleck and Gertz, and it produced a lower figure. This NIJ survey suggested that the annual number of DGUs is approximately 1.3 million.

While this debate may seem to be little more than a squabble among academics, in fact, the number of defensive gun uses is crucial in calculating the benefits of gun ownership. Thwarting a million crimes annually is an important byproduct of gun ownership. The figure of 1 million seems to be the most reasonable. Not only does it represent a neat compromise figure, it also fits very well with what we know about estimating behaviors from survey research and the best estimates of researchers with actual field experience.

Concealed Carry

Our discussion of concealed-carry laws focuses on the impact of regulations with regard to situations in which an individual may or may not carry a concealed weapon. "May-issue" states restrict concealed carry permits to those who can demonstrate some specific need, while "shall-issue" states issue permits to any citizen who meets the basic requirements, such as passing a criminal background check and a gun safety course.

Concealed-carry laws have become important for both gun rights and gun control groups, and these battles continue to be fought in state legislatures throughout the country. The trend is toward more lenient controls, which generally increase the number of permit holders. The number of shall-issue states is in the thirties, but individual laws can be difficult to categorize.

The wisdom of these laws centers on questions of self-defense and deterrence. Both sides utilize anecdotes to make their point. Pro-control groups focus on crimes committed by citizens who have permits and instances in which people are shot with their own guns, both of which are rare. Pro-gun groups point to situations in which people could not defend themselves or others against attack because they were following the law and not carrying a gun. The most commonly cited example of this is the 1991 Killeen, Texas, restaurant shooting in which more than twenty patrons were killed. Suzanne Gratia Huff, who usually carried a gun in her purse, had left it in her car because she was not legally allowed to bring it into the restaurant. Her parents were killed during the rampage. She argues that she could have and would have shot the killer and saved many lives. Huff used this incident as a springboard for election to the Texas state legislature, and she became a spokesperson for more lenient concealed-carry laws. Examples such as the Killeen shooting are rare.

The first serious academic study of the impact of concealed carry laws was conducted by John R. Lott, Jr.[61] He used complex statistical techniques and examined a large amount of data, concluding that more lenient concealed-carry laws have a deterrent effect, reducing most types of violent crime. Lott's work was immediately attacked by pro-control groups.[62]

Early academic challenges to Lott were numerous and varied.[63] They focused on methodological points and potential coding errors that could have affected the results. Lott responded to these charges with varying degrees of success in the second edition of his book.[64] Other criticism of Lott has focused on his admission that he impersonated a former student who defended him on some weblogs and his claim that survey data he used in some of this work was lost during a computer crash.[65]

Later substantive criticisms of Lott were more serious.[66] These responses also focused on the methodology employed by Lott, and they extended his analysis to include other variables and additional data. They corrected some coding errors and demonstrated that the inclusion or exclusion of a single variable, one that may seem to be unrelated to the crime rate, can affect the results. In a humble, uncommon, and welcome recognition of the limits of quantitative analysis, John J. Donohue, one of Lott's most serious academic critics, concludes that it is not possible, at present, to determine if shall-issue laws increase, decrease, or have no effect on crime rates.[67] There is no question that the work of Ayres and Donohue, Duggan, and Donohue is much more substantive and effective in terms of raising doubts about Lott's conclusions.

David B. Mustard, Lott's coauthor, takes issue with Donohue's criticisms and suggests that we look beyond the methodological debates. Commenting on the paucity of violent crimes committed by those who have a permit to carry a concealed weapon, he suggests that "sometimes the most straightforward evidence, namely, the lack of criminality among law-abiding citizens who carry concealed weapons, is the most convincing and easy to understand."[68]

With a relatively small percentage of the populace having a permit to carry concealed weapons in any state, the deterrent effect of such legislation is probably minimal. There is little doubt that those who have concealed-carry permits are a very law-abiding group of citizens. In an ironic twist, we can argue that we would see a greater deterrent effect if many more people carried firearms, thus increasing a criminal's odds of encountering an armed victim.

General Deterrence

Any deterrent effect of gun ownership, while important in the consideration of gun benefits, is very difficult to measure. Theoretically, this benefit should accrue to all members of society, assuming that (1) criminals have some fear of confronting an armed victim and may avoid a situation in which they believe the potential victim is armed, and (2) criminals know that they cannot accurately predict which potential victim may be armed. As anecdotal evidence, we may point to the relatively low rates of "hot burglaries," that is, burglaries in which someone is in the house, in rural areas and other places where gun ownership is relatively high. Hot-burglary rates are also lower in the United States than in many other countries with lower rates of gun ownership.

Certainly we need to explore this issue more systematically, but that is not a simple task. Some researchers have examined crime rates following passage of various types of gun laws, restrictive or permissive, with mixed results. The crime rate is impacted by many factors, and it is somewhat simplistic to attribute changes to only one factor.

Perhaps the best evidence for deterrence comes from James Wright and Peter Rossi's survey of convicted felons. Among the felons who reported committing a violent crime or a burglary, 42 percent said they had encountered an armed victim; 38 percent claimed they had been scared off, shot at, wounded, or captured by an armed victim; and 43 percent reported not committing a crime they had planned because they knew or thought the victim was carrying a gun.[69]

Still, even pro-gun scholar Kleck can find little direct evidence of a deterrent effect.[70] He does, however, suggest that anecdotal evidence of deterrence does exist and that studies have not disproved the hypothesis.

Sport Shooting

According to a 2001 survey conducted by the U.S. Fish and Wildlife Service, 13 million Americans over the age of sixteen hunt.[71] This represents 6 percent of the population, a decline from the 7 percent who hunted in 1991. The National Shooting Sports Foundation puts the number of hunters at 19 million (including hunters under sixteen) and claims that 23 million people self-identify as target shooters or muzzleloaders.[72] Regardless of which set of figures you use, the number of hunters in the United States is large, although it is declining. The Fish and Wildlife Service estimates that hunters spent $20.6 billion on hunting-related items in 2001.

Not surprisingly, hunting is not evenly distributed across the population. Only 1 percent of females and African Americans hunt, compared with 12 percent of males and 7 percent of whites. While those living in rural areas, defined as living outside a metropolitan statistical area, comprise 19 percent of the U.S. population, they account for 41 percent of hunters. Contrary to many stereotypes, the average hunter has a high school or college education and a slightly above-average income.

On the one hand, the decline of hunting is evidenced by the declining number of hunting licenses being issued by several states. At the same time, hunting is increasing fastest among high-income urban dwellers.[73]

Overall Benefits of Gun Ownership

Unfortunately, we do not have a readily available figure that we can plug in here to say that this is the total dollar value of gun ownership benefits. Studies have tried with very limited success to measure the deterrent effect of gun ownership or of carrying a concealed firearm. We can reasonably estimate that a million or more crimes are prevented annually through defensive gun use.[74]

We also cannot quantify the recreational benefit of gun ownership through various shooting sports activities or the enjoyment derived by gun collectors from their hobby. Those benefits are very real, however, and we must consider them in any analysis of the potential impact of gun control regulations.

Guns Used in Crimes

Much of the focus on guns, obviously, is on those firearms that are used to commit crimes. If we could prevent those guns from being purchased, stolen, or borrowed, or if we could seize firearms possessed by criminals, then we could certainly prevent some crimes. The latter is nearly impossible, except for the seizure of guns that are illegally possessed by convicted felons. Discussion of the former must begin by identifying the sources of those guns possessed and used by criminals.

There are two primary methods of determining the sources of guns used in committing crimes. The first is by tracing guns back to the original seller, and, perhaps, original purchaser. The second is to survey those who have been convicted of using a firearm in the commission of a crime and asking them how they obtained their guns.

The Bureau of Alcohol, Tobacco, and Firearms can use serial numbers to trace crime guns that are seized by police back to the original seller. We must keep in mind that most guns used to commit crimes are never recovered by the police and that most guns that are recovered are not traced, so these statistics have limited value.

The ATF publishes an annual report that summarizes some of the characteristics of the weapons seized during that year. This report includes guns that were seized in forty-four of the cities in the United States with a population of 250,000 or more. In 2000 the ATF conducted traces in 77,250 cases, and 47,478 purchasers were identified.[75]

In 88 percent of the cases, the purchaser was not the possessor; that is, the person who originally purchased the firearm was not the same individual who was arrested for committing a crime with it. There is no way to effectively trace a gun past the initial purchaser, so it cannot be determined whether the gun was transferred through a lawful sale by a private individual or a FFL, illegally transferred by a straw purchaser, borrowed, traded, stolen, or purchased on the black market.

About 15 percent of the guns were used in a crime within a year of purchase, and half had a time-to-crime of six years or less. Semiautomatic pistols had the shortest median time-to-crime, at just over four years, while revolvers had the longest, more than twelve years. The shortest time-to-crime guns were generally cheaper handguns.

The majority of all crime guns were first purchased legally in the state in which they were recovered, although this rate varies significantly from city to city. On the other hand, nearly three-quarters of the guns traced in New York City came from out of state, perhaps because of stringent gun laws in New York City. More than one-third of the guns were traced to 163 dealers, which comprise only 2 percent of the dealers in the study. Each of these dealers had at least twenty-five firearms traced back to them. Again, this pattern varies between cities. Finally, preliminary analysis indicates a possible link between multiple sales (more than one gun at a time), guns used in crime, and those that had serial numbers that had been obliterated.

These data are similar to previous years of the study. While interesting and perhaps indicative, they are not conclusive. The biggest questions are whether guns that are traced are representative of all guns used in crime and how those guns that were transferred from their original owner fell into the hands of criminals.

While the ATF report described the six-year time-to-crime period in which half of the guns were used as "relatively short," the point of comparison was the Police Foundation survey that found the average gun owner had possessed his gun for an average of thirteen years. On the other hand, one could argue that only 15 percent of guns were used in the first year, indicating that most guns were not purchased for the short-term purpose of committing a crime. With regard to the number of dealers with a relatively large number of traces, there is nothing to indicate they are selling guns illegally, although some may be. They may be located near high-crime areas (similar to bars in college towns accounting for a high percentage of underage drinking cases) or they may be high-volume dealers, given that many FFLs are not dealers in the sense of owning a retail shop.[76]

The most recent survey of federal and state offenders and their firearm use was conducted in 1997 by the U.S. Census Bureau.[77] A total of 14,285 state inmates and 4,041 federal inmates were interviewed. A similar survey was conducted in 1991. Overall, in 1997, 18 percent of the state prison inmates and 15 percent of federal inmates reported that they used, carried, or possessed a firearm during the offense for which they were sentenced.

As can be seen in table 2.5, three-quarters or more of the inmates got their weapon from either a friend, family member, or an illegal source. Only 14 percent of state prisoners purchased their weapon from a legal seller. Fewer than 2 percent of those were purchased from a flea market or a gun show.

Table 2.5.   Where State Prisoners Procured Weapon Used in the Commission of Crime of Conviction

Purchased From	1997	1991
Retail shop	8%	15%
Pawn shop	4%	4%
Flea market	1%	1%
Gun show	1%	1%
Friends or family	40%	34%
Street/illegal source	39%	41%

Source: Bureau of Justice Statistics, 2001

The only noticeable difference between the 1997 and 1991 data is the decline in retail shop purchases and increase in the percentage of guns originating with a friend or family member. As we will explore more in the next chapter, this may be an effect of the Brady Bill.

With regard to the type of firearm used, criminal preferences are pretty clear, as can be seen in table 2.6. The handgun is the weapon of choice for criminals. Single-shot and conventional semiautomatic weapons constitute a strong majority of guns used in crime. Military-style semiautomatic and fully automatic weapons comprise about 10 percent of the weapons carried by criminals.

Firearm possession by those convicted of a crime rose slightly among both state and federal inmates from 1991 to 1997. Most of the inmates who possessed a firearm were ineligible to legally purchase a firearm—84 percent of state inmates and 83 percent of federal inmates.

An earlier survey of convicted felons sponsored by the NIJ reached similar conclusions.[78] Almost half (46 percent) of the 1,874 felons interviewed possessed a gun during the offense of conviction. Use of guns in committing

Table 2.6.   Type of Firearm Carried during Current Offense

Type of Firearm	State Inmates	Federal Inmates
Handgun	83%	87%
Rifle	7%	9%
Shotgun	13%	14%
Single-shot	54%	49%
Conventional semiauto	43%	52%
Military-style semiauto	7%	9%
Fully automatic	2%	4%

Source: Bureau of Justice Statistics, 2001

crime was very common among this group. Fully 90 percent said they used a handgun; 27 percent, a sawed-off shotgun; 16 percent, a shotgun; and 10 percent, a rifle, during previous crimes. The most frequently used gun (85 percent) in the current offense was a handgun. The most common reasons for carrying a gun were to scare a victim (70 percent) or to protect themselves (50 percent). Only 36 percent admitted to intending to injure or kill the victim.

They also expressed concern with confronting an armed victim. More than half (56 percent) agreed that a criminal is "not going to mess around with a victim he knows is armed with a gun." A similar number agreed that criminals are more worried about encountering an armed victim than about being confronted by police. Yet they were more regularly or often concerned with being caught (54 percent) or going to prison (50 percent) rather than with being shot at by the police (34 percent) or a victim (34 percent). They also said they were more likely to carry a gun because a victim might be armed than because police are armed. We need to keep in mind that many of their intended victims may also have been criminals, who are more likely than the police to shoot the perpetrator.

Just over one third (37 percent) said they had encountered an armed victim at some time, and 39 percent said they had been deterred from committing a crime at least once because they knew a potential victim was armed. More than two-thirds (69 percent) said they knew a criminal who had been confronted by an armed victim.

The most desirable features in a handgun were accuracy, inability to trace, ease of use, ability to be concealed, ease of acquisition, and firepower. The most recently owned handguns were most likely to be .38 (29 percent) or .357 (20 percent) caliber. This preference for large-caliber guns exceeded their distribution in circulation. The smaller-caliber .22 represents a more commonly owned gun in the United States (34 percent of guns owned), but it represented only 16 percent of the guns carried by felons.

People in this group were likely to purchase their handguns (43 percent), but stealing was the second most common method of procurement (32 percent). Overall, the sources tended to be a friend (40 percent), the street (14 percent), or a gun shop (11 percent). More than half (60 percent) of the felons obtained a handgun within a few hours of deciding to get one.

The question of weapon substitution was also asked of these felons. They indicated it would not be difficult to obtain a gun, but if they could not get the gun they wanted, then they were more likely to get a larger-caliber gun than not to get a gun at all. While these results may be subject to a certain amount of bragging and wishing to appear tough, there may be at least a kernel of truth in them as well. They represent the best data available.

CONCLUSION

There is a large stockpile of firearms in the United States, with most estimates ranging between 200 million and 230 million. While handguns and military-style rifles are more common than in the past, the number of long guns—rifles and shotguns—remains quite large. The number of military-style semi-automatic weapons has increased in the past two decades. The typical gun owner is a middle-aged white male with above-average income.

Firearms were involved in about twenty-nine thousand deaths in 2001, a slight increase from the previous couple of years. More than half of those deaths were suicides, more than eleven thousand were homicides, and accidental shootings accounted for eight hundred deaths. There are other costs associated with firearms—shootings that do not result in death, the costs of medical treatment of gunshot victims, and the economic and social costs of lost wages, and so on.

The question of the potential impact of gun policies on those costs is one that is difficult to answer. The number of accidental shootings and suicides would be difficult to reduce, but it may be easier to reduce the number of homicides. Accidental shooting deaths have been declining in recent years, and the numbers are low. Fewer than one thousand annual deaths is not a large number. Still, all parties in the gun control debate understandably advocate the exercise of safety in the handling and storage of firearms.

Firearms account for the majority of suicide deaths, more than fifteen thousand annually, and there is no doubt that a gun is a very effective means of killing oneself. Designing a policy that protects the privacy rights of individuals and keeps guns away from those who have suicidal tendencies is a difficult task. If we were able to create such a policy, some lives would be saved, although some of the people who use firearms to commit suicide would substitute another method.

Homicides may be the area in which gun regulations could have their greatest impact. There is probably no stopping the individual who is intent upon killing another person; he can and will either procure a firearm on the black market or substitute another weapon. There are policies, however, that would reduce the availability of firearms and prevent some homicides. Many assaults become lethal due to the use of firearms. There would be other consequences to these regulations in terms of inconvenience and additional cost to law-abiding gun owners. There might also be a cost in terms of a citizen's self-defense ability and the loss of a deterrent effect, depending upon the nature of the regulation.

Given that criminals are more likely to obtain their guns in the secondary market, any regulation of the primary market is unlikely to have a significant impact on firearms used in criminal activity. The vast majority of gun owners are law-abiding citizens, and the vast majority of guns purchased will never be used in the commission of a crime. Recent research has suggested that it is the availability of illegal guns, not the overall availability of firearms, that is most strongly related to crime.[79]

Nearly everyone would support a regulation that keeps guns out of the hands of criminals and children while allowing law-abiding citizens to possess firearms. While we can easily identify children and currently have laws in place to prevent them from purchasing firearms, we can identify criminals only after they have been convicted of a crime. We can and do prevent convicted felons from purchasing guns in the primary market, but the secondary market is largely unregulated. Some parts of that market, such as gun shows and private transactions, can be regulated to some extent, while other transfers, such as theft, straw purchases, and trades, are much more difficult to stop.

At the same time, there are significant benefits to gun ownership. Millions of Americans engage in various shooting sports, while others own guns for self-defense purposes. In addition, it is possible that all citizens benefit from those who own guns if criminals are deterred because they think a potential victim might be armed.

At times the debate over statistics can be mind-numbing and appear to be an academic argument between various interest groups and researchers. In fact, it is these statistics that should help us to estimate the potential benefit of various gun control policies.

NOTES

1. A quick look at the literature or websites of the National Rifle Association or the Brady Campaign to Prevent Gun Violence will illustrate this. More authoritative sources can also be misleading. For example, see John Hopkins University, Center for Gun Policy and Research, "Fact Sheet: Guns in the Home" (June 2004). The fact sheet contrasts the health effects and personal safety benefits of gun ownership, citing some studies with questionable methodology, stating a low estimate of defensive gun uses, and failing to consider any benefits of gun ownership except personal protection.

2. George D. Newton and Franklin Zimring, *Firearms and Violence in American Life: A Staff Report Submitted to the National Commission on the Causes and Prevention of Violence* (Washington, D.C.: National Commission on the Causes and Prevention of Violence, 1969).

3. Philip J. Cook and Jens Ludwig, *Guns in America: Results of a Comprehensive National Survey on Firearms Ownership and Use* (Washington, D.C.: Police Foundation, 1996); Gary Kleck, *Targeting Guns: Firearms and Their Control* (New York: Aldine de

Gruyter, 1997), 63–70; and William J. Vizzard, *Shots in the Dark: The Policy, Politics, and Symbolism of Gun Control* (Lanham, MD: Rowman & Littlefield, 2000), 21.

4. Philip J. Cook and Jens Ludwig, "Pragmatic Gun Policy," in *Evaluating Gun Policy,* ed. Philip J. Cook and Jens Ludwig (Washington, D.C.: Brookings Institution, 2003), 3–4; Vizzard, *Shots in the Dark*, 24. According to Department of the Treasury, Bureau of Alcohol, Tobacco, and Firearms, "Firearms Commerce in the United States, 2001/2002" (2003), there were 1.3 million handguns and 2.6 million rifle and shotguns sold in the United States in 1999.

5. Vizzard, *Shots in the Dark*, 24.

6. Vizzard, *Shots in the Dark*, 27.

7. Tom W. Smith, "1999 National Gun Policy Survey of the National Opinion Research Center: Research Findings" (paper presented at the annual meeting of the American Association for Public Opinion Research, Portland, OR, May 2000), 54. More recent Gallup Poll data indicate about the same percentage of households with firearms, but suggest that the decline in household ownership occurred in the early 1990s and was more precipitous than suggested by Smith, The Gallup Brain, "Guns" (October 14, 2003).

8. Smith, "Gun Policy," 52–53.

9. Ludwig and Cook, *Pragmatic Policy*, 4.

10. Smith, "Gun Policy," 14; Ludwig and Cook, *Pragmatic Policy*, 4.

11. Lance Gay, "Number of Hunters Down, but More Rich People Bag Animals," Scripps Howard News Service, January 22, 2004. The author of this book personally knows dozens of hunters, and none of them owns only one firearm. While this is admittedly anecdotal evidence, it is likely to be representative of most hunters, particularly if Gay's contention that hunting is becoming more popular with those in higher income brackets is true.

12. Philip J. Cook, Stephanie Molliconi, and Thomas B. Cole, "Regulating Gun Markets," *Journal of Criminal Law and Criminology* 86, no. 1 (Fall 1995): 59–92.

13. Cook and Ludwig, "Guns in America."

14. James D. Wright and Peter H. Rossi, *Armed and Considered Dangerous: A Survey of Felons and Their Firearms* (New York: Aldine de Gruyter, 1986), chap. 9.

15. Cook and Ludwig "Guns in America," 20–21.

16. All data in this section are from National Center for Injury Prevention and Control, at webapp.cdc.gov/sasweb/ncipc/leadcaus.html.

17. Gun control advocates often cite the overall figure of twenty-nine thousand gun-related deaths. While technically accurate, this may lead the audience to think only of homicides, and perhaps accidental deaths. At the same time we must bear in mind that statistics only include gun-related deaths and exclude shootings that do not result in the loss of life. Of course, the same is true of other causes of death listed here.

18. The Centers for Disease Control and Prevention website provides a variety of data related to firearms-related injuries: www.cdc.gov/ncipc/wisqars/default.htm.

19. Craig Perkins, "Weapons Use and Violent Crime," Bureau of Justice Statistics, September 2003.

20. As we will see later, these data regarding using a firearm to defend against a crime are disputed and most likely underestimate the actual number of defensive gun uses.

21. Don B. Kates, "Comparisons Among Nations and Over Time," in *The Gun Control Debate*, ed. Lee Nisbet (Amherst, NY: Prometheus, 1990), chap. 13.

22. Jens Ludwig and Philip J. Cook, "Homicide and Suicide Rates Associated with the Implementation of the Brady Handgun Violence Protection Act," *Journal of the American Medical Association* 284 (2000): 585–91.

23. Mark Duggan, "Guns and Suicide," in *Evaluating Gun Policy*, ed. Philip J. Cook and Jens Ludwig (Washington, D.C.: Brookings Institution, 2003), 41–73.

24. Arthur Kellerman et al., "Suicide in the Home in Relation to Gun Ownership," *New England Journal of Medicine* 327, no. 7 (1992): 467–72.

25. David A. Brent et al., "Risk Factors for Adolescent Suicide," *Archives of General Psychiatry* 45 (1988): 581–88.

26. Garen Wintemute et al., "Mortality among Recent Purchasers of Handguns," *New England Journal of Medicine* 341, no. 21 (1999): 1583–89.

27. For a summary of these studies, see Andrew J. McClurg, "The Public Health Case for the Safe Storage of Firearms: Adolescent Suicides Add One More 'Smoking Gun,'" *Hastings Law Journal* 51 (2000): 953–1001.

28. Duggan, "Guns and Suicide," 65.

29. McClurg, "Public Health," 999–1000.

30. Kleck, *Targeting Guns*, chap. 8.

31. Duggan, "Guns and Suicide," 53.

32. A more "spirited" discussion of the potential shortcomings of the public health literature may be found in Don B. Kates, "Guns and Public Health: Epidemic of Violence, or Pandemic of Propaganda?" in Gary Kleck and Don B. Kates, *Armed: New Perspectives on Gun Control* (Amherst, NY: Prometheus, 2001), chap. 2.

33. McClurg, "Public Health," 977–82. He suggests that international comparisons in this context are inappropriate due to cultural differences. Because the Unites States has the highest adolescent suicide rate in the world, method substitution is not supported. There is little evidence to support the theory, and firearms reductions would save lives due to the instrumentality effect if for no other reason.

34. As will be discussed in the section dealing with benefits of gun ownership, safe storage can also prevent the use of a gun for self-defense purposes. In order for a firearm to be used in defense or as a deterrent, it must be accessible.

35. Philip J. Cook and Jens Ludwig, *Gun Violence: The Real Costs* (New York: Oxford University Press, 2000), 27, 16–17.

36. Robert J. Spitzer, *The Politics of Gun Control*, 3rd ed. (Washington, D.C.: CQ Press, 2004), 53.

37. Spitzer, *Politics of Gun Control*, 53.

38. Garen J. Wintemute et al., "When Children Shoot Children: 88 Unintended Deaths in California," *Journal of the American Medical Association* 257 (1987): 3107–09.

39. Deborah Azrael et al., "Data on Violent Injury," in *Evaluating Gun Policy*, ed. Philip J. Cook and Jens Ludwig (Washington, D.C.: Brookings Institution, 2003), 412–40.

40. Kates, "Guns and Public Health," 57, 63–66.

41. Kleck, *Targeting Guns*, chap. 9.

42. While we might agree that anyone under eighteen years old should be considered a child, there is no question that the murder of a sixteen-year-old drug dealer by a seventeen-year-old drug dealer is not what we typically think of when someone mentions a child homicide. While the statistics may be technically accurate, they can be misleading.

43. Franklin E. Zimring and Gordon Hawkins, *Crime Is Not the Problem: Lethal Violence in America* (New York: Oxford University Press, 1997), 108.

44. Cook and Ludwig, *Gun Violence*, 34–36.

45. See John R. Lott, Jr., *More Guns, Less Crime: Understanding Crime and Gun Control Laws*, 2nd ed. (Chicago: University of Chicago Press, 2000), chap. 4; and Gary Kleck and Don B. Kates, *Armed: New Perspectives on Gun Control* (Amherst, NY: Prometheus, 2001), chap. 2, 6, and 7.

46. Vizzard, *Shots in the Dark*, 31–33.

47. While it is true that most murderers have a violent criminal history, most violent offenders do not become murderers. While convicted felons are prohibited from legally purchasing firearms by the Brady Law, they could be obtained on the secondary market. Prohibiting anyone with a misdemeanor conviction or a proclivity for violence from purchasing a gun is much more controversial than targeting felons, a policy that enjoys widespread support.

48. Cook and Ludwig, *Gun Violence*, chap. 4.

49. Cook and Ludwig, *Gun Violence*, 115.

50. This section addresses only the practical crime prevention benefits of owning and/ or carrying a firearm. It intentionally ignores the psychological benefit one may experience—safety, power, etc. While those are important considerations, they are generally ignored on both sides of the gun control debate in the policy discussion section of this book. It is my position that my feeling of safety or control, whether it is derived from owning a gun personally or banning all guns in private possession, is irrelevant to a discussion of the relative merits of such policies with regard to saving lives. There is no question, however, that this psychological benefit impacts public opinion, voting behavior, and the decisions of elected officials.

51. Norman Rushforth et al., "Accidental Firearms Deaths in a Metropolitan County (1958–1975)," *American Journal of Epidemiology* 100 (1975): 499–505.

52. Arthur L. Kellerman and Donald T. Reay, "Protection or Peril?: An Analysis of Firearm-Related Deaths in the House," *New England Journal of Medicine* 314 (1986): 1557–60.

53. David McDowall and Brian Wiersema, "The Incidence of Defensive Firearm Use by U.S. Crime Victims, 1987 through 1990," *American Journal of Public Health* 84 (1994): 1982–84; and Gary Kleck and Marc Gertz, "Armed Resistance to Crime: The Prevalence and Nature of Self-Defense with a Gun," *Journal of Criminal Law and Criminology* 86, no. 1 (Fall 1995): 150–87.

54. Cook and Ludwig, *Guns in America*.

55. Follow-up questions determined the number of incidents, if they had occurred in the past year, and excluded cases in which the gun was used to defend against an animal or cases in which the respondent was employed by the police, military, or in private security.

56. David Hemenway, "Survey Research and Self-Defense Gun Use: An Explanation of Extreme Overestimates," *Journal of Criminal Law and Criminology* 87, no. 4 (1997): 1430–45.

57. Gary Kleck and Marc Gertz, "The Illegitimacy of One-Sided Speculation: Getting the Defensive Gun-Use Estimate Down," *Journal of Criminal Law and Criminology* 87, no. 4 (1997): 1446–62.

58. Tom W. Smith, "A Call for a Truce in the DGU War," *Journal of Criminal Law and Criminology* 87, no. 4 (1997): 1462–69. See also Jens Ludwig, "Gun Self-Defense and Deterrence," *Crime and Justice* 27 (2000): 363–417.

59. Vizzard, *Shots in the Dark*, 15–19.

60. Philip J. Cook and Jens Ludwig, "Defensive Gun Uses: New Evidence from a National Survey," *Journal of Quantitative Criminology* 14 (1998): 111–31.

61. John R. Lott, Jr., *More Guns, Less Crime* (Chicago: University of Chicago Press, 1998); John R. Lott, Jr. and David Mustard, "Crime Deterrence and Right-to-Carry Concealed Handguns," *Journal of Legal Studies* 26, no. 1 (January 1997): 1–68.

62. The primary charge was that his work was influenced by the fact that he held the John M. Olin Fellowship at the University of Chicago Law School. The fellowship is funded by the Olin Foundation. The Olin Corporation's Winchester division manufactures ammunition. These charges were without merit.

63. Dan Black and Daniel Nagin, "Do 'Right to Carry' Laws Deter Violent Crime?" *Journal of Legal Studies* 27, no. 1 (January 1998): 209–19; Jens Ludwig, "Concealed-Gun-Carrying Laws and Violent Crime: Evidence from State Panel Data," *International Review of Law and Economics* 18 (1998): 239–54; and Franklin E. Zimring and Gordon Hawkins, "Concealed Handguns: The Counterfeit Deterrent," *Responsive Community* 7 (1997): 46–60.

64. Lott, *More Guns*, 2nd ed.

65. There is no evidence that Lott fabricated any of the data used in the analysis discussed here. In fact, he makes his data available to any researcher who requests it. Nonetheless, the admission that he created a former student to defend him online and the loss of the survey data are an important breach of ethics in the first case and a significant question in the second. There are also questions regarding the sharing of data that have been disputed. The reader can decide whether those incidents call his credibility into such question that none of his research should be trusted. For more information, see Richard Morin, "Scholar Invents Fan to Answer His Critics," *Washington Post*, February 1, 2003; Chris Mooney, "Double Barreled Double Standards," *Mother Jones*, October 2003, at www.motherjones.com/news/feature/2003/10/we_590_01.html; and Donald Kennedy, "Research Fraud and Public Policy," *Science* (April 18, 2003): 393. Lott's response to Kennedy may be found at John R. Lott, Jr., "Research Fraud, Public Policy, and Gun Control," *Science* (June 6, 2003): 1505. Donohue's response to Lott may be found at John J. Donohue, "A Clarification on Data Availability," *Science* (September 26, 2003): 1849.

66. Ian Ayers and John Donohue, "Nondiscretionary Concealed Weapons Law: A Case Study of Statistics, Standards of Proof, and Public Policy," *American Law and Economics Review* 1 (1999): 436–70; Ayers and Donohue, "Shooting Down the More Guns, Less Crime Hypothesis," *Stanford Law Review* 55 (2003) 1193–1312; and Mark Duggan, "More Guns, More Crime," *Journal of Political Economy* 109 (October 2001): 1086–1114.

67. John J. Donohue, "The Impact of Concealed-Carry Laws," in *Evaluating Gun Policy*, edited by Philip J. Cook and Jens Ludwig (Washington, D.C.: Brookings Institution, 2003), 287–325.

68. David B. Mustard, "Comment on Donohue, 'Impact,'" in *Evaluating Gun Policy*, edited by Philip J. Cook and Jens Ludwig (Washington, D.C.: Brookings Institution, 2003), 331.

69. Wright and Rossi, *Armed and Considered Dangerous*, chap. 7.

70. Gary Kleck, "The Nature and Effectiveness of Owning, Carrying, and Using Guns for Self-Protection," in *Armed: New Perspectives on Gun Control*, ed. Gary Kleck and Don B. Kates (Amherst, NY: Prometheus, 2001), 320–28.

71. U.S. Fish and Wildlife Service, at www.census.gov/prod/2002pubs/FHW01.pdf.

72. National Sports Shooting Foundation, at www.nssf.org.

73. Gay, "Number of Hunters."

74. I refrain from counting a person's perceived feeling of greater safety from gun ownership as a benefit in the same way that I did not include perceived feeling of greater danger on the part of some citizens because others own guns in the list of costs of gun ownership. Others would disagree and include both as a cost or benefit. I am more concerned with the actual impact of regulations, not the perceived impact of the laws. I recognize this view is somewhat limited, but it is nearly impossible to quantify those feelings, even in a carefully crafted public opinion survey. The perceived utility of laws and feelings of safety are considered when we examine public opinion.

75. Bureau of Alcohol, Tobacco, and Firearms, "Crime Gun Trace Reports (2000)," *Youth Crime Gun Interdiction Initiative* (July 2002).

76. Many FFLs obtain a license to facilitate personal gun collecting and purchasing firearms out of state. Therefore, many are not gun dealers in the common usage of that term. At the same time, others are very large dealers who sell large numbers of firearms. We would naturally expect that dealers who sell a larger number of firearms would sell more firearms that are used in crimes.

77. Caroline Wolf Harlow, "Firearm Use by Offenders," Bureau of Justice Statistics, November 2001.

78. Wright and Rossi, *Armed and Considered Dangerous.*

79. Lisa Stolzenberg and Stewart J. D'Alession, "Gun Availability and Violent Crime: New Evidence from the National Incident-Based Reporting System," *Social Forces* 78, no. 4. (June 2000): 1461–82.

Chapter Three

Gun Policies

Gun policies exist at all levels of government in the United States—local, state, and federal. The purpose of this chapter is not to chronicle each individual law, which has been done well elsewhere;[1] instead, we focus on the nature of the regulations that can be placed on guns, gun owners, and gun sales in addition to more detailed discussions of the national legislation dealing with firearms.

Regulations regarding firearms come in several different forms. They can be categorized as laws that (1) prevent certain categories of people from purchasing or owning firearms; (2) restrict the types of firearms which may be legally sold; (3) regulate gun safety and carrying; 4) regulate the market; and (5) inform criminal justice system responses.

An important and relatively recent approach to firearm regulation is the use of civil lawsuits that have been filed against gun dealers and gun manufacturers. They are treated separately here because they are a product of the judicial branch of government rather than the result of legislative action. Legislation passed by Congress in 2005 preempted most of these suits.

POLICY MAKING AND GUN CONTROL

There are several models used to describe public policy making. Among the most frequently cited are elite theory, group theory, institutional theory, rational choice theory, political systems theory, and public policy.[2] The models differ in their details, but most include some role for a variety of political actors—elected officials, bureaucrats, interest groups, businesses, and public opinion—and most consider both input and output of the policy process.[3]

The "garbage can model" is most applicable to gun control.[4] This model was adapted by political scientist John W. Kingdon to explain agenda setting in the federal government.[5] Kingdon first discusses policy streams in the government—problem recognition, policy proposal formulation, and politics. Second are policy specialists—bureaucrats, congressional staff, academics, interest groups, and researchers. Third are the policy streams, which include the general national mood, more specific public opinion, elections, partisan politics in Washington, and interest group lobbying.

There are problems and solutions, and it is not always clear which comes first. When the various streams are joined, policy adoption or reform of existing policy usually results. The opportunities for this coupling are not frequent, but they can occur when a policy window opens. Windows sometimes open on a predictable schedule, as with a change in presidential administration. Some open cyclically, as with budgeting, while others are unpredictable, such as an important event or crisis.[6]

Social Security reform is an example of a solution (partial privatization of the system) in search of a problem (an inability to meet long-term commitments). While there is little doubt that the program faces long-term challenges, there is no imminent crisis. President George W. Bush acted as a catalyst to move the topic to the top of the government's agenda. Conversely, intelligence reform was prompted by the terrorist attacks of September 11, 2001. Without that trigger event, it is extremely unlikely that the reforms in intelligence gathering and analysis would have been adopted.

The policy streams in gun control usually converge following a crisis or a precipitating event—a political assassination, school shooting, crime wave, and the like. Because gun policy usually implies increased restrictions on gun purchasing or possession, it is commonly proposed by those in favor of more restrictions. Proposals for increased restrictions on firearms are much more likely to be passed in a time in which a crisis atmosphere exists. During more normal times, the status quo is more likely to triumph. Those periods also provide opportunities for gun rights advocates to roll back gains by the control side or to push for legislation of their own.

Overall, gun policy is less frequently a product of a cyclical or predictable schedule, although the change in administrations from Bill Clinton to George W. Bush had clear implications for gun policy. It is also impacted by public opinion, interest groups, and occasionally academic researchers.

TYPES OF FIREARMS REGULATIONS

Restrictions on Who May Purchase or Own Guns

Some of the earliest gun laws in the United States prohibited African Americans from possessing firearms.[7] By the twentieth century, many states had abandoned race as a means of classification and adopted classifications based on individual status. For example, many states made it illegal for convicted felons to carry concealed weapons.[8] Eventually, most states and the federal government adopted laws that established a minimum age for purchasing a firearm and prohibited possession by convicted felons, those with a history of drug abuse, and those with certain types of mental disabilities.

The primary method of enforcement of these laws is the background check that must be conducted prior to the sale of a firearm by someone who holds a federal firearms license. This background check was mandated nationally with the passage of the Brady Bill in 1993, but many states already had such requirements in place at that time.

These laws restrict only transfers from dealers with FFLs. Private citizens, although they may not legally sell a firearm to someone in a restricted class, are not required to process a background check, whether they sell from their home or at a gun show. This is often referred to as the "gun show loophole." Needless to say, stolen guns that are resold are not accompanied by background checks. As we saw in the previous chapter, most crime guns are not purchased by criminals in retail outlets. Instead, they are usually procured from a friend or family member, stolen, or traded on the black market.

Restrictions on Types of Firearms That May Be Sold or Possessed

Legislatures may pass laws that prohibit anyone from possessing or selling a certain type of firearm. These regulations target the gun, not the gun owner. This prohibition may be retrospective, but it is usually prospective, that is, it applicable only to future sales. Any law that attempts to confiscate firearms already in circulation would be unlikely to pass, very difficult to enforce, and generally ineffective. A recent example of this type of regulation is the 1994 assault weapons ban, which prohibited the sale of new weapons and the manufacture of a large number of semiautomatic firearms. This ban was prospective in that all firearms currently owned were grandfathered into the legislation and remained legal. Some localities have banned other types of weapons, such as Saturday night specials.

The greatest difficulties with such laws lie in defining firearms that are covered and the number of firearms already in the marketplace. The terms that are commonly used, such as assault weapons and Saturday night specials, do not correspond to a particular weapon. They describe broad categories such as military-style semiautomatic rifles or small, inexpensive handguns. These somewhat vague descriptions make it difficult to effectively implement the law because it is not obvious which weapons are included in the ban. For example, the assault weapons ban prohibited the sale of firearms that had certain physical characteristics, but other guns that functioned almost identically but looked slightly different were still legal. In order for a law to be effective, it must be more specific than that.

The number of firearms already in the marketplace may also reduce the potential positive impact of gun restrictions. Again, the assault weapons ban did not touch existing stock, and increased sales between passage of the law and its implementation date meant that there were plenty of such firearms available to those who wanted one, although the price did increase.[9]

The number of firearms that can be purchased at one time may also be restricted. For example, Virginia legislators voted in 1993 to permit citizens to purchase only one handgun per month in response to charges that the state was a haven for gunrunners to Washington, D.C., and New York City.

Gun Safety and Carry Regulations

The category of gun safety and carry regulations includes a large number of regulatory schemes, such as laws that specify safety features that a gun must have. This could be a trigger lock, a light indicator when the firearm is loaded, and fingerprint recognition so the gun can be fired only by its owner. Safe storage of firearms can also be mandated. Requiring that guns be kept unloaded and locked in a gun cabinet or safe and that access by children be restricted are examples of this type of law.

Laws regarding carrying concealed weapons also fall under this heading. The laws of individual states vary from allowing anyone to carry concealed to requiring a permit, which may be relatively easy or difficult to obtain, to outright prohibition. Similarly, gun possession on school property or in public buildings is commonly prohibited.

The largest issues surrounding safety regulations are their effectiveness, ensuring that those who own guns for personal protection can still gain quick access to the firearms, and the added cost to the purchase price. Many gun owners, however, support the addition of such safety devices and willingly pay the additional cost. Gun safety measures target accidental shootings, which are relatively uncommon.

Registration, Licensing, and Other Market Regulations

Another strategy to reduce gun ownership and facilitate criminal investigations is to require that all firearms be registered with the state. Under a registration policy, the state would maintain a list of all legal owners of firearms sold in the state. A crime gun that is recovered could then be traced back to its legal owner. This would be less useful, of course, if the gun had been sold or stolen.

Some control advocates have suggested that owners be licensed, similar to the system we use to certify automobile drivers. Applicants would have to pass a test and would probably have to renew their license and be tested in the future. Advocates argue this would increase gun safety. This policy was advocated by presidential candidate Al Gore in the 2000 campaign.[10]

Other ways to regulate the market include taxes on firearms or ammunition, licensing of firearm dealers, and waiting periods. If taxes are sufficiently high, then they might drive some potential customers out of the market. Licensing of dealers may be strict or lax in terms of defining exactly what constitutes a dealer versus a private seller. Like taxes, high fees can keep some from registering as dealers or renewing their licenses. Waiting periods are designed to prevent spur-of-the moment shootings or decrease the number of firearms sold by increasing the inconvenience to purchasers. All of the strategies mentioned to this point are strongly favored by gun control groups and are almost universally opposed by gun rights groups.

One of the most recent strategies is referred to as ballistic fingerprinting. It is based on the premise that each firearm leaves a unique set of marks on bullets fired from it. This technology is used to compare bullets from different crime scenes to see if the crimes are linked. Anyone who has watched a few crime programs on television is generally familiar with this technique. It is argued that if the government had a bullet from every gun, then the bullets could be traced back to the gun from which they were fired. This type of regulation is tantamount to gun registration in that a governmental agency would have to keep a record of all these markings on file along a record of who owned each gun. The technology, though promising and attractive, is not perfect. The bullet markings may be altered by filing the inside of the gun's barrel. In addition, the reliability of the FBI's ballistics testing has been questioned.[11]

Criminal Justice Responses

There are two primary methods of using the criminal justice system to try to reduce gun violence. The most common is a sentence enhancement for gun-related crimes, in which a set amount of time, usually two or three years, is added to the sentence of any felon who used a firearm in the commission of the crime.

The second method is to use the police to crack down on illegal gun carrying or to increase patrols in high-crime areas. The first tactic increases patrols and also instructs police to be extra vigilant with regard to someone who might be carrying a firearm. The second simply increases the number of patrols in high-crime areas, most often during peak hours for crime.

Criminal justice responses, particularly enhanced sentences, are strongly favored by gun rights groups such as the NRA. They see this as a way of preventing gun crime by punishing those who commit crimes while protecting the rights of law-abiding citizens.

STATE GUN CONTROL LAWS

State gun control laws are as varied as the fifty states themselves. State laws generally fall into the following categories: juvenile possession and ownership, child access prevention, concealed-weapons regulations, gun registration, firearm ownership or purchase permits, owner licensing, safety feature requirements, bans on certain types of firearms, lawsuit immunity for gun manufacturers and dealers, limits on the numbers of guns that can be purchased monthly, waiting periods, and enhanced sentencing laws. This is not an exhaustive list, and, as you might guess, the various permutations and provisions of different laws make a complete categorization very difficult.[12]

There are numerous sources to find a compendium of state laws.[13] Many of these sources are updated quickly to reflect changes in laws. Consulting one or more of the sources will allow you to see the applicable laws in your state.

Several interest groups provide rankings or issue "grades" to individual states. It is not surprising that a recent Brady Campaign "report card" did not issue a single A, and only California, Connecticut, Hawaii, Massachusetts, Maryland, and New Jersey received an A-minus. Alabama, Idaho, Kentucky, Louisiana, Mississippi, Montana, New Mexico, and Wyoming received a grade of F, and another twenty-three states earned a D. Of course, the NRA is all too happy to suggest that there is no correlation between the Brady Campaign grades and the violent crime and murder rates in a particular state. The NRA provides links to Web sites that compile the laws of each state, but the group does not issue rankings or report cards on the states. It does, however, grade candidates in most elections.

Overall, few states ban particular firearms, limit the number of guns that can be purchased, require a permit to purchase a gun, or have gun registration or an owner licensing scheme. Age restrictions, waiting periods (usually for handgun purchases), child access prevention laws, lawsuit immunity, and sentence enhancements are more common policies.

FEDERAL GUN CONTROL LAWS

Most federal laws have regulated the classes of people who may purchase or possess firearms. Prohibition of certain types of weapons has also been implemented at the national level as have enhanced sentences for those convicted of certain gun-related crimes. Most federal legislation has been passed in response to a specific event, set of events, or a recurring crime problem.

Using the terminology of Kingdon, the federal policy window has usually been opened by a triggering event. A problem has been identified, and gun control legislation has been the proposed solution. While it may be true that many gun control advocates have numerous solutions in their minds at all times, the policy arena is more open to passage of those policy prescriptions when there is a perceived threat from crime or criminals.

The first federal legislation was passed in 1927 when Congress voted to prohibit the transfer of handguns via the U.S. Postal Service.[14] Given that other common carriers were not included under this legislation, it is not surprising that it was thought to be ineffective, although it might have made both legislators and citizens feel better because criminals could no longer obtain these weapons through the mail.[15]

National Firearms Act of 1934

Gangster violence, carried out by organized crime groups during the early 1930s, was the major impetus behind the National Firearms Act of 1934 (NFA). The NFA was an attempt to regulate the marketplace through taxes that made certain types of firearms, including sawed-off shotguns and machine guns, quite expensive. Each weapon transfer carried a $200 tax, and importers, manufacturers, and dealers were taxed in addition to the transfer tax. All such weapons had to be registered with the national government.[16] Congress chose to enact heavy taxes rather than ban the firearms outright due to concerns regarding the legislature's authority and the Second Amendment. The NFA was upheld by the U.S. Supreme Court in 1937 in *Sonzinsky v. United States*.[17]

Due to opposition from various sporting groups and the NRA, handguns were excluded from the legislation despite support for their inclusion by the Justice Department. In addition, the definition of a machine gun did not include semiautomatic weapons with a ten-round magazine, a definition that would have included today's assault weapons.[18]

A formal evaluation of the NFA has never been undertaken, and it is difficult to ascertain the effectiveness of the law. Although use of these weapons did decline, it is not clear if that was a consequence of the NFA or a shift in the weapons of choice and the decline of organized crime groups. Nonetheless, the law did establish that there was some limitation on the weapons that could legitimately be possessed by average citizens. Most important, Congress gained, or at least assumed, the power to regulate firearms.

Federal Firearms Act of 1938

By 1937 the Justice Department renewed its efforts to include handguns in the National Firearms Act. While that attempt was not successful, it did result in more legislation being passed by Congress. The bill that eventually became known as the Federal Firearms Act of 1938 (FFA) was a compromise act written largely by the NRA.[19]

The FFA applied to all firearms, but the controls it mandated were relatively modest. It required any interstate dealers to be licensed (the cost of a license was $1), and there were some additional restrictions on the interstate shipment of firearms. Manufacturers and importers were required to purchase licenses. Selling to a restricted class of persons was criminalized, but the enforcement mechanism was weak. Dealers were required to keep records of sales, but penalties for violation of this law were minimal. Dealers were defined as "any person engaged in the business of selling firearms or ammunition . . . at wholesale or retail" as well as gunsmiths and manufacturers. Thus, obtaining a license was neither difficult nor expensive. Over the years, many average citizens became dealers to facilitate purchasing firearms for themselves.

Successful prosecution under the law required proof that sales were made in knowing violation of the law, a standard of proof that is very difficult to meet. Until the 1960s, fewer than one hundred persons per year were arrested under the act.[20] Perhaps the most important impacts of the law were the establishment of the licensing system and the emergence of the NRA as an important player in the legislative arena. Interestingly, while working on the FFA, the NRA developed a model handgun act for states that included a waiting period.[21]

Much of the impetus for gun control had dissipated by the time the FFA was adopted, probably as a result of the declining murder and crime rates. The policy window that had been opened due to concern with organized crime in the early 1930s had closed. The desire for further gun control would not be manifest again until the assassination of President John F. Kennedy in 1963 increased interest in firearms regulation.

According to Vizzard, gun control was dormant during this period because of the strong organizational ability and increasingly widespread support of the NRA and "[t]he deep-seated belief among some members of Congress that unrestricted access to firearms was natural and desirable."[22] In addition, the Treasury Department, which was responsible for enforcement of both the NFA and the FFA, devoted few resources to the task.

Considering the dearth of prosecutions, gun control advocates might point to the FFA as a policy failure. Still, it created new types of regulations for firearms and dealers. The regulations went beyond the taxes imposed by the NFA and created a system of firearms transfers in which the rules were established by the government. That was a very important step. The debates over the FFA were dominated by the groups that would be active in the future—the NRA, sportsmen's organizations, and gun manufacturers aligned against an interested presidential administration, key members of Congress, and a small and disorganized group of private interests.

Gun Control Act of 1968

While the push for stricter gun laws began prior to Kennedy's assassination, final passage of the Gun Control Act (GCA) did not come until 1968.[23] Senator Thomas J. Dodd had proposed further restrictions on mail-order handguns prior to Kennedy's assassination by a man armed with a mail-order surplus military rifle. The Dodd bill died in the Senate Commerce Committee in 1964, but he reintroduced a more restrictive bill in 1965 at the request of the Johnson administration, and the legislative battle was joined. By 1965 Dodd had added long guns to the bill.

The 1965 bill received some support from the NRA, which led to an important split in its membership. A strongly negative response from many of the rank-and-file members of the organization resulted in a change of position by the leadership and stronger opposition to any further controls on firearms. This was a pivotal shift in the position of the NRA.

There was significant political wrangling in 1965 and the following years between the Johnson administration and members of Congress. The logjam broke following the assassinations of Martin Luther King, Jr. and Robert Kennedy in 1968. These murders increased support for gun control in Congress and also served to make the often silent voices of supporters of gun control much more audible, while the cries of control opponents were largely muted.[24] The gun control policy window had opened again.

During debate over the GCA, the Johnson administration backed provisions that provided for registration of all firearms and the licensing of all gun owners. These requirements were deleted from the bill, largely due to the efforts of the NRA and other gun control opponents.

As enacted, the law prohibited interstate firearms sales, added to the categories of persons who could not purchase firearms, added certain "destructive devices" to the NFA list of proscribed weapons, and prohibited the importation of Saturday night specials. The GCA also created the Bureau of Alcohol, Tobacco, and Firearms within the Treasury Department, and this agency was made responsible for the administration of all federal firearms laws.[25]

The definition of a dealer was modified to read someone "dealing in firearms as a regular course of trade or business," and there was a requirement that a federally licensed dealer maintain business premises outside his home. This provision of the bill was rarely enforced, and the number of private citizens who sought and were granted licenses increased to 284,000 by 1992.[26] Perhaps the most effective restrictions of the legislation were those that dealt with interstate commerce. The purchase of out-of-state firearms decreased, although this was probably never a large proportion of firearm sales.

The GCA did not presage the passage of more gun control legislation, and, in fact, the push for further restrictions declined. In the political arena, the forces that opposed gun control were stronger than the forces that supported it. They could be defeated if those who favored control took advantage of a policy window that was open due to a tragic event or concern with increasing crime. In more normal times, however, gun control legislation was unlikely to pass. In addition, the 1970s and early 1980s were characterized by inertia at the federal level and a clear attempt to decentralize power to the states, at least in the first Reagan administration.

Armed Career Criminal Act of 1984

The policy preferences of the Reagan administration were very clear in the legislation that was approved in the 1980s, which reflected Reagan's "get tough with criminals" positions. The major piece of gun-related legislation of the first Reagan administration was the Armed Career Criminal Act of 1984. The major provision of this legislation was a fifteen-year mandatory prison term for any convicted felon who had three previous convictions for robbery or burglary and who was involved in a firearm transfer. In addition, punishment was enhanced for anyone who carried a handgun loaded with armor-piercing ammunition while committing a felony.

The federal sentencing guidelines, passed in 1986, also provided a sentence enhancement for anyone possessing a firearm while committing a crime. Finally, the Drug Abuse Amendments Act of 1988 made it a crime to transfer a firearm to an individual knowing that the gun would be used in criminal activity. While this may reflect a popular wish to punish those who knowingly transfer firearms to criminals, the standard of proof required for conviction is high. All of these bills targeted criminals rather than law-abiding citizens and were passed easily.[27]

Firearms Owners' Protection Act of 1986

Nearly two decades of complaints by the NRA and other gun rights groups about ATF enforcement of the GCA resulted in the passage of the Firearms Owners' Protection Act (FOPA), often referred to as McClure-Volkmer.

As amended and passed, the bill permitted interstate long gun purchases that complied with the laws of both states. Record keeping for ammunition dealers was eliminated. It reduced FFL record-keeping violations from a felony to a misdemeanor and limited the ATF to one unannounced inspection per FFL per year. It prohibited the federal government from centralizing the records of firearms dealers or creating or maintaining any type of registration system. Another provision of the bill redefined the business location of federally licensed dealers to include gun shows, which increased the number of gun shows.

On the pro-control side, FOPA prohibited the manufacture or transfer of machine guns, prohibited the importation of barrels for Saturday night specials, and added to the list of those who are ineligible to purchase firearms.

The bill's passage is seen as both the high point of the NRA's political influence as well as the beginning of its political decline.[28] While the NRA exerted significant influence in the writing of FOPA and worked tirelessly for its passage, the legislation exacerbated a growing rift between the NRA and various police organizations that opposed the bill. This split was quickly exploited by the newly energized Handgun Control, Inc. (HCI) and its leader, Sarah Brady.

The effects of FOPA, like most gun control legislation, were more symbolic than substantive. Still, there was a substantive component in that gun shows and the number of dealers at gun shows did increase. At the same time, a machine-gun market that was in its infancy never developed.[29] Because they were never indexed to inflation or increased, the taxes on those weapons imposed by the NFA were no longer as onerous as they had been in the 1930s, and it is reasonable to assume that a market for machine guns would have developed along with the market for assault weapons.

Symbolically, the rift between the NRA and several law enforcement groups provided a political opportunity for the supporters of gun control. The Democrats tried to seize the moral high ground of being the party that was pro law enforcement, and HCI matured into a force that could at least begin to play on the same field with the NRA. These developments were important in that the NRA had lost a key ally, and it was now opposed by another group that could, to some extent, galvanize and mobilize public opinion. To say that HCI was the equal of the NRA would be a gross overstatement, but it was a legitimate organization that could fight the NRA. That, in and of itself, changed the political landscape.

Cop-Killer Bullets and Plastic Guns

Two pieces of gun control legislation passed in the late 1980s represent the NRA's temporary fall from power and an unusual lack of political savvy on the part of the NRA.

The Law Enforcement Officers' Protection Act, passed in 1986, banned the importation, manufacture, or sale of armor piercing or so-called cop-killer bullets.[30] Promoted by HCI and supported by police and law enforcement organizations, the bill banned bullets that were made from certain hard metals and then coated with Teflon. In some situations, these bullets were capable of penetrating the Kevlar bulletproof vests worn by police officers. The NRA argued that the ammunition had been available for years and that there were no documented cases of bullets penetrating police body armor. The NRA was also concerned about the definition of such bullets because many types of bullets, including some hunting ammunition, could penetrate soft body armor at close range.

While the NRA may have been technically correct on these points, it was clearly on the losing side of the public relations battle. Lining up against what was portrayed as reasonable gun control designed solely to save the lives of police officers was a risky strategy. HCI had created an issue that put the NRA in the position in which it had to choose between supporting a piece of gun control legislation or appear to oppose police safety. The NRA took the bait rather than remaining silent, and there was a political price to pay. The bill was passed, and once again the NRA was on the opposite side from law enforcement groups.

The Undetectable Firearms Act of 1988 (UFA) banned a type of firearm that did not exist. These "plastic guns" were allegedly invisible to metal detectors and x-ray devices. The guns at issue were in fact not made of plastic and were detectable, although not as easily visible as firearms constructed of metal.[31] Still, the prospect of guns being smuggled onto airplanes was a frightening thought even prior to September 11, 2001. Once again, the NRA opposed the legislation and lost in the arena of public opinion as well as on the floor of the Congress.

In both of these cases the issue was more symbolic than real, but both times the NRA lost, politically and substantively.

The Brady Bill

The emergence of HCI and the Bradys as national figures continued after the legislative activity of the late 1980s. White House press secretary James Brady was wounded and partially disabled in the assassination attempt on President Ronald Reagan in 1981. His wife, Sarah, became active in the years after the shooting, and was—and still is—seen as the preeminent spokesperson for gun control groups. As president of HCI, Sarah Brady increased the visibility, political clout, and size of the organization.

In the early 1990s HCI began to lobby Congress to enact a national waiting period for handgun purchases and a background check for firearms purchases. Many states already had some form of background check in place, and it was the waiting period that proved to be the major stumbling block in getting the bill passed. First introduced in 1987, the Brady Bill was finally signed into law in November of 1993.

For political reasons, the bill applied only to handguns, and background checks would be required only for purchases from federally licensed dealers. The secondary market of private sales would remain unregulated. This would reduce the number of purchasers and buyers who would be impacted, a political tactic designed to reduce opposition to the bill. Still, a seven-day waiting period is a "cost" for those purchases that would be covered.

Those who favored passage argued that a background check would help prevent criminals and others who could not legally purchase a firearm from obtaining a gun. The waiting period would serve as a cooling off period for those who would buy a gun in a fit of homicidal passion or rage or during a period of suicidal thoughts.

Those opposed to the legislation were concerned primarily with the background check as a potential first step to gun registration. The waiting period presented a nuisance of varying degrees to law-abiding citizens who simply wished to purchase a legal product. For the buyer who planned ahead and lived fairly close to the dealer, the inconvenience would be no greater than for any special-order purchase. For the person who did not plan ahead or who had to travel some distance to the dealer, the inconvenience would be greater.

The waiting period also presented a larger obstacle to a buyer who was purchasing a firearm to protect herself or a loved one from an immediate threat. Anyone who faces a perceived imminent threat, whether that perception is accurate or not, believes that she needs the protection afforded by a firearm now, not a week from now.

Although proponents of the bill did not officially suggest it, it is reasonable to assume that some sales would be eliminated because of the additional inconvenience. Gun control supporters would view that as a positive, if not fully intended, consequence of the legislation.[32]

In reality, the number of people who purchase a gun and use it immediately in the commission of a crime is relatively small, as is the number who need to purchase a gun immediately for self-defense. There is anecdotal evidence of both types of events, but they constitute a very small percentage of homicides and defensive gun uses.

The bill as introduced would have imposed a seven-day waiting period and a background check only on handgun sales by federally licensed dealers. Long guns and the secondary market were left untouched. Sales reports would be sent to local authorities, not to the federal government, and these reports would have to be destroyed relatively soon after the transaction was completed. This would, in effect, prevent the establishment of gun registration.

The brouhaha that ensued may be best described by Spitzer:

> On its face, such a procedure [waiting period] certainly represents a modest degree of government regulation, for it merely postpones a handgun purchase by a few days and denies handguns only to those who everyone agrees should not have them. Yet the struggle for enactment over a waiting period took on epic proportions as a bitter power struggle between regulation opponents and proponents, where the ground being fought over was far less important than the struggle itself.[33]

While some would dispute that "merely" and "modest" are good descriptions of the inconvenience of a seven-day waiting period, it is difficult to argue that the actual stakes were worth the six-year battle.

The bill was defeated in the House of Representatives in 1988 with the passage of an amendment that mandated a study of instant background checks. Again, it was the waiting period that was the larger political problem. It is politically difficult to oppose an instant background check whose records are not retained by the government. In 1990 both the House and the Senate passed the bill, but the version that made it out of the conference committee was defeated by a Republican-led filibuster in the Senate.[34]

While the election of President Bill Clinton in 1992 meant that the White House now supported the bill, the bill's prospects in Congress were not greatly improved. The bill passed the House again, and much debate, hand-wringing, arm-twisting, and public posturing in the Senate finally resulted in a compromise that was passed in November 1993.

The law created a five-day waiting period for handgun purchases from federally licensed dealers. The dealer was also required to submit information about the buyer to local authorities to confirm the buyer was indeed eligible to purchase the handgun. Authorities could not retain the purchase records. Within five years, the Brady Bill mandated that a National Instant Criminal Background System (NICS) be created to replace the local authorities' check and the waiting period. Those states that already had background checks or handgun licensing were exempted. The bill also increased fees for FFLs.

It is difficult to assess the impact of the Brady Bill. There is no doubt that many potential purchasers have been denied firearms by the background checks. Between 1994 and 2002, more than 976,000, or 2.1 percent, of background check applicants were rejected.[35] About two-thirds of those rejected were felons or had domestic violence convictions or restraining orders. The system is weak with regard to identifying those who are ineligible due to mental illness, drug use, or alien status.[36]

On the other hand, we do not know what happened to these individuals after their purchase was denied. Some may have decided not to purchase, but certainly many turned to straw purchasers or other means of obtaining a gun. Ludwig and Cook found no statistically significant effect of the Brady Bill.[37] Given that the Brady Bill does not deal with the secondary market, it is not surprising that its impact was minimal. Beyond that, many states did not feel any direct impact because they already had background check systems in place.

Politically, the NRA was again cast as the bad guy, opposed to regulations that were supported by public opinion and law enforcement groups. The NRA fared slightly better this time, however, because many gun owners were on their side, not wanting to face the inconvenience of the waiting period. NICS has now been accepted by almost everyone, and the wait that is imposed is usually measured in minutes, not days.[38] Many on both sides of the debate viewed the Brady Bill has a first step toward greater gun control. Those expecting a second step would not have to wait very long.

Assault Weapons Ban of 1994

The impetus for the proposed assault weapons ban was the January 1989 school shooting in Stockton, California, in which five children were killed and twenty-nine wounded by a mentally disturbed drifter using a legally imported Chinese 7.62mm AKM-56S.[39] Led by California, several states subsequently acted to ban certain types of semiautomatic firearms.[40]

The market for these firearms greatly expanded in the late 1970s and early 1980s with the influx of inexpensive Chinese copies of the AK-47 rifle. The relatively high cost of domestically-produced versions of the rifle, such as the Colt AR15, had previously reduced demand for the weapons. These firearms were very similar in appearance to fully automatic machine guns, which were banned. Some manufacturers even created assault pistols by removing the shoulder stocks from rifles. These firearms became popular with many young males who had little interest in hunting or sport shooting. Few were alarmed by this market shift prior to the Stockton shooting, which opened a policy window.[41]

At the national level, President George H. W. Bush reversed his previously stated position and supported federal action. He directed ATF to implement a "suitable for sporting purposes" test for imported rifles as a way of reducing the number of these weapons in the marketplace. The ATF standards, however, focused on appearance rather than function. As a result, manufacturers changed the appearance of their rifles to comply with the standards. In addition, these actions stimulated demand for the rifles amid fears that they would soon be banned.[42]

HCI then moved to attach the assault weapons ban as a companion to the Brady Bill. In 1991 the Senate passed a crime control bill with a version of Brady and a ban on some assault weapons. The House subsequently stripped the assault weapons ban from the bill.

The election of Bill Clinton in 1992 meant that gun control advocates now had a very strong ally in the White House. Once again, the legislation faced an uphill battle in both houses of Congress, but a compromise bill was passed. Political pressure was exerted by Clinton, and Republicans were concerned with appearing to be obstructionist. Thus, an intense lobbying effort by the NRA was overcome.[43]

The final version of the bill banned the manufacture or importation of dozens of specific rifles, pistols, and shotguns, but it left untouched weapons that were nearly identical to those banned. It prohibited magazines with a capacity greater than ten rounds. All currently owned assault rifles and magazines were grandfathered in as legal. Guns were also banned if they possessed two or more of a list of specific physical characteristics that made them appear menacing. A key component was that the law had a sunset provision. If not renewed, it would expire in ten years, which it did in 2004.

The biggest problem with the assault weapons ban was its lack of definition of the term "assault weapon." The choice to use cosmetic appearance to determine which firearms, beyond those specifically listed, would be banned left many copycats on the market as well as many guns that function identically but appear slightly different than a banned gun. The vague definition was the result of the bill's proponents choosing the path of least political resistance. A more specific definition would have included all semiautomatic guns, which would have greatly increased the number of gun owners who were impacted by the law and would likely have doomed it to failure.[44]

The impact of the assault weapons ban was probably minimal. Although Christopher Koper and Jeffrey Roth found a small decline in homicide that might be attributable to the ban, they also acknowledged that the number of banned weapons sold in the months prior to implementation date increased by 120 percent.[45] Kleck argues that the ban could have prevented no more than two homicides annually.[46] Although supporters of the ban like to cite ATF gun trace data, those data have questionable reliability. According to James B. Jacobs, "[L]aws like this reflect and fan the flames of the symbolic conflict between gun owners and gun controllers, with little, if any, relevance to the crime problem."[47] The most extensive research, conducted by Ludwig and Cook, found that the effects of the ban were minimal.[48]

The battle over renewal of the ban began in 2003, but it did not come to the forefront of the political debate until the spring of 2004, when it was amended to include legislation that would have granted gun manufacturers immunity from some lawsuits. The Senate defeated the bill, and the ban expired in 2004.

Lawsuits against Gun Manufacturers and Gun Dealers

It is common in American politics for those who fail in the legislative arena to take the battle into the legal system. In recent history this has been a more common tactic of the political left, primarily on the issues of civil rights, abortion, and women's rights, while in the past it was the more conservative groups that sought relief from economic regulation in the courts.

One frequently employed tactic is the filing of civil liability suits. The burden of proof is lower in civil court than it is in criminal proceedings, requiring only a finding of the preponderance of the evidence as opposed to proof beyond a reasonable doubt. Included among product liability suits are cases against the tobacco industry, asbestos manufacturers, auto companies, breast implant producers, and others.

Suits have been filed against gun manufacturers under several different theories of liability. The theory of strict liability can be used against a party that carries on "an abnormally dangerous activity" even if the party has exercised "the utmost care to prevent the harm."[49] This tact has been unsuccessful insofar as it is difficult to demonstrate that firing a gun is an abnormally dangerous activity. While there is no question that firearms are dangerous, the large majority of owners use them safely.

A second legal approach is that of an unreasonably dangerous or defective product. This approach has also been unsuccessful in the courts. The applied standard is that the product must function in a way that is more dangerous than an ordinary consumer would expect. Consumers expect firearms to be dangerous. Manufacturing defects can make a firearm more dangerous and cause an accident, but very few accidental shootings are the result of manufacturing defects. It is difficult to conceive of a homicide that would be caused by a defective weapon.[50]

A third tactic is to charge the gun manufacturer with negligent distribution and marketing. A finding of liability for negligence requires that the seller did not use reasonable means to prevent the sale of the product to someone who is likely to cause harm to the public or if the product is marketed in such a way as to induce its purchase by someone who will foreseeably misuse the product.[51] These suits have been somewhat more successful.

Public nuisance suits require that the plaintiff have standing to sue as a representative of the general public or as a public official or authority. Public nuisance is defined as an unreasonable interference with a common right of the general public, such as public health, safety, or peace. While this seems to be a promising avenue of litigation for gun control advocates and local governments, there are limits on the type of costs a municipality can recover. For example, police costs are part of the government's basic function and often cannot be recovered from a third party.[52]

The most difficult hurdle for all of these suits is that the harm resulted from the criminal conduct of a third party, except in cases of some accidental shootings. Most juries and judges are reluctant to hold a firearms dealer or manufacturer responsible for the actions of a criminal unless the dealer or manufacturer knew the buyer's criminal record and intent.

The earliest suits were filed by shooting victims based on the theory that the firearms were not defective. With one exception they were unsuccessful. Later suits, filed by cities, counties, and states, alleged that guns can be made safer and that manufacturers have negligently marketed and distributed firearms.[53] The earliest municipal suits were filed by New Orleans and Chicago in 1998. By late 2001 more than thirty municipalities had filed similar suits.[54]

These suits, combined with pressure from the Clinton administration, led Smith & Wesson, the largest firearms manufacturer in the country, to settle with fifteen of the thirty plaintiffs.[55] This settlement received a great deal of media attention, but its actual impact on how firearms are sold is questionable. The company generally agreed to reexamine its marketing practices and to include certain safety devices with its firearms as they became practical.[56] This led to a temporary ostracism of Smith & Wesson by the firearms community.

The question of product safety design is both difficult to answer and disputed. The possibility of greater safety must be balanced with the cost to consumers and society. There is no question that guns are a dangerous product that, when properly used as designed, may cause destruction of property and loss of life. The effectiveness of various gun safety devices, such as the fingerprint recognition software on "smart guns," is questionable. Finally, some safety devices may hamper the use of the firearm for the purpose of self-defense if they delay the owner's ability to access and fire the weapon.

The issue of public nuisance is even thornier. It is claimed that gun manufacturers have marketed their products, especially handguns and military-style firearms, in such a way that they have particular appeal to a younger and more criminally prone audience. While advertising and cosmetic appearance may make certain firearms more attractive to specific markets, how much does that contribute to criminal activity? In other words, is it the marketing that causes the crime? This same logic can be applied to many other types of products. One that readily comes to mind is automobiles. Many television advertisements show a "professional driver" on a "closed course" who appears to be exceeding the speed limit and driving the car in an unsafe manner. Of course, the disclaimer at the bottom of the screen alerts viewers that all safety laws are to be obeyed and that the driving demonstrated in the ad should not be attempted. Even Mazda's advertising jingle "Zoom-Zoom" denotes speed. One could certainly argue that these ads encourage reckless driving. Does that make automobile manufacturers responsible for accidents that result from speeding or reckless driving?

It is also alleged that manufacturers are aware that some of their dealers may be selling illegally or selling many more guns than the legal local market would demand. This assumes that these situations exist, and that manufacturers are aware of them and have not acted on them. It is difficult to argue that those assumptions are supported by a preponderance of the evidence in many cases, although these judgments are subject to individual interpretation. Again, one could ask if any seller of alcohol, including the state, in a college town is guilty of oversupplying the market. That is, any seller must be aware that he is selling much more alcohol than can reasonably be consumed by those of legal age in that market. If so, who should be held accountable? The distiller or brewer? The distributor? The straw purchaser? The consumer?

A Brady Campaign report argues that gun manufacturers are knowingly supplying the illegal gun market and refuse to manufacture safer firearms.[57] Of course, the gun industry denies these allegations, and there is research that suggests that the suits have no basis in law or, perhaps, in reality.[58] The issue has been debated in legal journals as well as between interest groups.[59]

Virtually all of the lawsuits failed, but the cost to the gun manufacturers was significant. Some have suggested that the suits may have contributed to the bankruptcy of several smaller manufacturers.[60] Even if manufacturers were not driven out of business, the cost of firearms inevitably rose to cover the costs of the litigation. In addition, several suits were settled out of court at some cost to the firearms manufacturers.

There are many similarities between suits against gun manufacturers and those against tobacco companies. Although it can be argued that most fire-arms provide only benefits to most gun owners, it is difficult to say the same about tobacco products. Another important distinction is the ability of the industries to survive economic losses. While the tobacco companies survived both some successful suits and their settlement with the government, their pockets are much deeper than those of gun manufacturers. Gun manufactur-ers tend not to be diversified as are tobacco companies, and their revenues are a fraction of those produced by tobacco.

Unable to win significant victories in many state legislatures or in Con-gress, gun control advocates turned to the courts. While the results were neg-ligible, these suits clearly presented a threat to the gun industry, both economically and perceptually. The next step in this dance, then, was for gun manufacturers and their ally, the National Rifle Association, to turn to the legislatures to try to preempt the suits.

STATE LEGISLATIVE ACTION

In 1999 Georgia became the first state to pass legislation preventing any local government from bringing suit against gun manufacturers and dealers, ammunition manufacturers, or trade associations. By 2005 more than thirty states had passed legislation granting immunity to gun manufacturers.[61] While these statutes vary in terms of what is covered, most provide immunity against the suits described above, excepting actual defective-product suits. Some of the acts have been retroactive and halted pending suits.

These bills were frequently sponsored and strongly supported by the NRA and other trade and shooting organizations. While the NRA enjoyed some measure of success at the state level, it also pursued federal legislation.

PROTECTION OF LAWFUL COMMERCE
IN ARMS ACT OF 2005

The Protection of Lawful Commerce in Arms Act passed in the House of Representatives in April of 2003 by better than a 2–1 margin. Although it was a relatively simple measure, the claims and counterclaims between sup-porters and opponents, both legislators and interest groups, obscured the bill's meaning. The bill had 250 cosponsors in the House, and it passed with relatively little fanfare. All parties understood that the real political test would be in the Senate.

S. 1806 was introduced by Senator Larry Craig, also a NRA board member, on October 31, 2003. By early 2004 the bill had fifty-nine cosponsors, one fewer than the sixty votes need to defeat an attempted filibuster. The bill was supported by the Bush administration, which opposed any amendments to the legislation.[62] The *New York Times* weighed in with two editorials opposing immunity and supporting renewal of the assault weapons ban and checks at gun shows and calling Bush to task.[63] There was intense lobbying by both the NRA and the Brady Campaign.[64]

Numerous amendments were introduced during several days of debate in the Senate, and most were rejected. The two critical amendments were offered by Senators John McCain and Dianne Feinstein and included the requirement of background checks on all firearm sales at gun shows and a ten-year extension of the assault weapons ban, respectively. McCain's amendment passed on a 53–46 vote, and Feinstein's amendment passed by a 52–47 margin. The coalitions were slightly different, but several key cosponsors voted in favor of both amendments—Tom Daschle, John Warner, John Breaux, Byron Dorgan, and George Voinovich.

The vote was largely partisan, with forty-one Democrats joined by ten Republicans voting for the Feinstein amendment and eight Republicans and forty-four Democrats voting for the McCain amendment. Still, without those crucial Republican "defections" the amendments would not have passed. Interestingly, both Virginia senators were, in a sense, defectors. George Allen had said he supported extending the assault weapons ban, but voted against the amendment. Warner, who voted against the original assault weapons ban, was a cosponsor of the Feinstein amendment.[65]

These amendments were "poison pills" that were unacceptable to the NRA and supporters of the bill. There was a great deal of pressure from other gun rights groups that suggested that the NRA might be willing to compromise on these items to get the immunity bill passed. The NRA website reassured readers that there would be no accommodation of the other side.[66] The organization was true to its word, and it asked its supporters in the Senate to vote against the measure. As a result, the bill was overwhelmingly defeated on a 90–8 vote by a strange coalition of pro-gun control and pro-gun rights senators. Neither side was willing to accept the compromise.

As a result, gun control and the assault weapons ban became issues in the presidential election of 2004. Democratic presidential nominee and Massachusetts senator John F. Kerry voted in favor of both amendments and against the overall bill. Wayne LaPierre, executive vice president of the NRA, predicted the votes would come back to haunt those senators who backed the amendments, including Daschle.[67] LaPierre's statement proved prophetic when Daschle was defeated in November.

Not surprisingly, the *New York Times* editorial page lamented the influence of the NRA: "In the end the Senate killed a disastrous bill that would have compromised justice and public safety by gutting the rights of crime victims to sue irresponsible gun makers and shady weapons dealers. Lawmakers whose votes against the bill were dictated by the National Rifle Association's display of raw power deserve no praise."[68] Even Feinstein recognized the power of the NRA: "They had the power to turn around at least 60 votes in the Senate. That's amazing to me."[69] Both the NRA and the Brady Campaign claimed victory in the vote, although it was the NRA that had the power to have its legislation reintroduced the next year.[70]

With the outcome of the 2004 elections seemingly favoring the gun rights side, the immunity bill was reintroduced as S. 397 and H.R. 800 in 2005. It was essentially the same legislation as that introduced in 2004. It prohibits lawsuits against third parties unless those parties have violated criminal law in the transfer of the firearm. It also allows civil actions for negligent entrustment, defective products, breach of contract, or some actions of the attorney general. As amended and passed by the Senate, the bill provides that all handguns transferred by a federally licensed dealer must be accompanied by a trigger lock, and it directs the attorney general to study the feasibility of a national standard for armor-piercing ammunition.

S. 397 passed on a 65–31 vote on July 29, 2005.[71] The bill was carefully managed by Craig and the Republican leadership in that Craig introduced the two amendments that passed and only three other amendments were brought to a vote. These amendments would have exempted lawsuits resulting from injuries to children, expanded the definition of armor-piercing ammunition, and significantly rewritten the bill. All three were easily defeated. There were no "poison pill" amendments this time. The bill garnered the support of fifty Republicans, fourteen Democrats, and the Senate's lone Independent. It was opposed by twenty-nine Democrats and two Republicans.

It would be easy to characterize the vote as partisan, but it was more than that. We need to bear in mind that the partisan split in the Senate to a large extent reflects that of the country as a whole—the red states and blue states. None of the Democrats who voted for the bill represented states in the Northeast or the Midwest, and no southern Democrat voted against it. The only Republicans voting against S. 397 were Mike DeWine and Lincoln Chafee. The Republicans who supported amendments opposed by the NRA in 2004, namely McCain and Warner, introduced no amendments and voted for the bill.

The passage of S. 397 was a major victory for the NRA as well as firearms dealers and manufacturers. This was the consensus of major news media, legislators, and the interest groups, with the exception of Gun Owners of America, which objected to the Craig amendments requiring trigger locks and mandating the study of armor-piercing ammo.[72] The NRA hailed the passage of S. 397 as a "MAJOR first step toward ending the anti-gun lobby's reign of extortion through reckless law suits against the firearm industry," a sentiment that was echoed by the Citizens Committee for the Right to Keep and Bear Arms.[73] The Brady Campaign said the Senate had voted "to strip the legal rights of innocent victims of gun violence and give sweeping legal immunity to reckless and unsavory gun dealers."[74]

The *New York Times* described the bill as "long sought by the gun lobby," and the *Washington Post* used similar language in describing the legislation.[75] An early indication of the importance attached by the NRA was an alert posted during the August recess stating, "[I]t is critical that you once again contact your U.S. Representative and urge him/her to pass S. 397, as passed by the Senate."[76] If this was anything but a strong victory, the NRA could have asked its supporters to lobby for the removal of the amendments.

The House of Representatives substituted S. 397 as it was passed by the Senate for its own version of the bill. It passed by a 283–144 margin on October 20, 2005. Although only four Republicans voted against the legislation, fifty Democrats voted for it.[77] By passing the legislation in the same form as the Senate, the House ensured that it would not go to a conference committee, which could have weakened the measure, and then back to the Senate where it could have been voted down. Rather it went directly to Bush for his signature.

Although the major hurdle was cleared in the Senate, the final passage of the bill was described as "handing the nation's gun lobby a paramount victory it has sought for years."[78] The support of the fifty-nine Democrats in the House "reflected the changing politics of gun control, an issue many Democrats began shying away from after Al Gore, who promoted it, was defeated in the 2000 presidential race."[79]

The NRA and the Brady Campaign reacted predictably to the passage of the bill, the former calling it a "historic victory," and the latter decrying the "tragic capitulation to the gun lobby" and promising suits challenging the constitutionality of the law.[80] The rhetoric of the interest groups notwithstanding, final passage of the bill can only be interpreted as a major victory for gun rights groups in general and the NRA in particular. The NRA fought for the legislation for several years and turned down the opportunity to have it pass in 2004 in exchange for extending the assault weapons ban. Their success in the 2004 elections ensured passage without any "poison pill" amendments in 2005. The Protection of Lawful Commerce in Arms Act clearly indicated that gun control supporters were losing the legislative battle among many Democrats as well as the strong majority of Republicans.

The impact of this legislation will be felt more in terms of what did not happen. If some of the lawsuits had been successful, then the ripple effects could have been felt by average gun owners through higher prices and, perhaps, reduced availability of firearms. This victory was also symbolic insofar as the NRA reestablished itself as the major force in gun-related legislation.

Although the political winds can change direction quickly and unexpectedly, the gun rights forces are in national ascendance, at least until a gun-related tragedy opens a policy window. The future goals of the gun rights groups are uncertain, but they had significant political momentum following the expiration of the assault weapons ban and the passage of the manufacturers' liability bill.

CONCLUSION

Much of the national gun control legislation that has been passed has, not surprisingly, had little effect on gun owning or crime. The legislation can generally be described as tinkering at the edges. Few weapons have been banned, and most of those were neither popular crime guns nor were they firearms commonly owned by law-abiding citizens. The legislation passed because relatively few gun owners were directly impacted. Much of the legislation was designed by the sponsoring legislators and interest groups with that in mind. They understand that regulations that affect large numbers of gun owners are likely to engender strong and deep opposition that cannot be overcome.

Because legislation is often the product of compromise, we would not expect to see sweeping gun control legislation pass in Congress or in most state legislatures, and that is largely what we have seen. The slippery slope fear so often vocalized by gun control opponents has not materialized. That may indicate that gun control supporters do not really want to move as far or as fast as is suggested by opponents. It is more likely, though, that the sustained efforts of the opposition have prevented the passage of all but the relatively innocuous legislation.

Most of the gun control legislation has passed because of a triggering event—a crime wave, political assassination, or school shooting. In more typical times, gun control is not high on the list of priorities for the public and, therefore, it is not a high priority for elected officials. For example, the assault weapons ban was passed on the heels of a tragic school shooting, but there was relatively little fanfare when it expired in the absence of such an event.

Much of the legislation has focused on restricting the types of people who can own or possess firearms—primarily criminals, the mentally unstable, and children. These bills tend to be popular with a wide cross-section of the population, including gun owners. At other times, certain types of guns have been targeted, such as machine guns, assault weapons, and small, inexpensive handguns.

In addition, gun dealers and manufacturers are required to be licensed by the federal government. Attempts have been made to enact more comprehensive regulations, such as gun registration and owner licensing, but those policies have failed to come even close to passage. Gun safety has also become more important in the regulatory schemes proposed by gun control advocates.

More recently, those who favor gun control have turned to the courts by suing dealers and gun manufacturers for selling and marketing practices. Most of the lawsuits were unsuccessful, although their defense has been costly for the gun dealers and producers. In response, they, along with their ally the NRA, have urged their friends in Congress to pass legislation that would preempt current suits and prevent future suits from being filed. The NRA and its allies gambled in 2004 that they could get a bill passed in Congress that would limit the liability of gun dealers and manufacturers without accepting an extension of the assault weapons ban as a tradeoff. The midterm elections of 2004 went in their favor, and the gamble paid off in 2005. Gun rights forces are once again on the offensive in Congress as well as in many state legislatures. Supporters of stronger gun control laws are playing defense, and they need a big play to turn the game around.

For much of the legislative history of gun control, the gun rights forces were unchallenged, but that changed in the 1980s with the emergence of the Brady Campaign. Effective lobbying by interest groups on both sides of the issue has made the playing field more level. The balance of power is likely to shift in response to triggering events that open a policy window and the outcome of elections that change the legislative balance of power or install a new party in the White House.

While the political stakes are very high on issues such as background checks, assault weapons bans, concealed-carry laws, and gun safety mandates, the reality is that these regulations have little effect on the average law-abiding gun owner or the average criminal gun owner. Limiting the liability of gun manufacturers and dealers defeated a tactic that had the potential to take a serious toll on the gun industry. At its core, gun control is a truly substantive issue, but as it has been addressed in legislatures in the United States, it has been more symbolic. Given public opinion on the issue, the intense lobbying of interest groups, and the nature of elections and the political process, the battle over gun control will continue for some time. It is to these forces that we now turn our attention.

NOTES

1. An excellent summary of federal and state legislation may be found in Jon S. Vernick and Lisa M. Hepburn, "State and Federal Gun Laws," in *Evaluating Gun Policy,* eds. Philip J. Cook and Jens Ludwig (Washington, D.C.: Brookings Institution, 2003), 348–58. Both the NRA and Brady Center websites also have links to summary of laws in effect in different states.

2. Michael E. Kraft and Scott R. Furlong, *Public Policy: Politics, Analysis and Alternatives,* 10th ed. (Washington, D.C.: CQ Press, 2004), chap. 3. Thomas R. Dye, *Understanding Public Policy* (Upper Saddle River, NJ: Prentice-Hall, 2002), chap. 2, defines the models as Institutional, Process, Rational, Incremental, Group, Elite, Public Choice, and Game Theory.

3. Charles E. Lindblom and Edward J. Woodhouse, *The Policy-Making Process,* 3rd ed. (Upper Saddle River, NJ: Prentice-Hall, 1993).

4. Michael Cohen, James March, and John Olsen, "A Garbage Can Model of Organizational Choice," *Administrative Science Quarterly* 17 (March 1972): 1–25.

5. John W. Kingdon, *Agendas, Alternatives, and Public Policies,* 2nd ed. (New York: Longman, 2003), 83–89.

6. Kingdon, *Agendas,* chap. 8.

7. Robert J. Cottroll and Raymond T. Diamond, "The Second Amendment: Toward an Afro-Americanist Reconsideration," *Georgetown Law Journal* 80 (1991): 309–61.

8. William J. Vizzard, *Shots in the Dark: The Policy, Politics, and Symbolism of Gun Control* (Lanham, MD: Rowman & Littlefield, 2000), 87–88.

9. Jens Ludwig and Philip J. Cook, "Homicide and Suicide Rates Associated with the Implementation of the Brady Handgun Violence Protection Act," *Journal of the American Medical Association* 284 (2000): 585–91.

10. The statement was made during a debate held in Winston-Salem, North Carolina, and moderated by Jim Lehrer of PBS *NewsHour.* For a transcript, see web.lexis-nexis .com/universe/document?_m = a55b3b65f73c7f17ea3e6bc2f98d370b.

11. Eric Lichtblau, "Report Questions the Reliability of an F.B.I. Ballistics Test," *New York Times,* February 11, 2004.

12. Vernick and Hepburn, "Gun Laws."

13. These sources include Vernick and Hepburn, "Gun Laws," (also includes a list of laws for some U.S. cities); Bureau of Justice Statistics, "Survey of State Procedures Related to Firearm Sales, Midyear 2002," April 2003; Open Society Institute, "Gun Control in the United States: A Comparative Survey of State Firearm Laws," April 2000; "The Brady Campaign to Prevent Gun Violence 2003 Report Card," at www.bradycampaign .org/facts/reportcards/2003/; www.nraila.org/GunLaws/Default.aspx# (includes text and explanation of state laws), and see www.nraila.org/Issues/FactSheets/Read.aspx?ID = 155 for the NRA response to the Brady report card; and Gunlaws.com, at www.bloomfield press.com/links/index.htm.

14. Franklin E. Zimring and Gordon Hawkins, *The Citizen's Guide to Gun Control* (New York: Macmillan, 1987).

15. James B. Jacobs, *Can Gun Control Work?* (New York: Oxford University Press, 2002), 20; Robert J. Spitzer, *The Politics of Gun Control,* 3rd ed. (Washington, D.C.: CQ Press, 2004), 110–11.

16. Jacobs, *Gun Control*, 20–21.

17. *Sonzinsky v. United States*, 300 U.S. 506 (1937).

18. Vizzard, *Shots in the Dark*, 89–90.

19. Vizzard, *Shots in the Dark*, 90–91; Spitzer, *Politics of Gun Control*, 111–12.

20. Spitzer, *Politics of Gun Control*, 112.

21. Vizzard, *Shots in the Dark*, 90.

22. Vizzard, *Shots in the Dark*, 91.

23. An excellent and more detailed discussion of the Gun Control Act of 1968 may be found in Vizzard, *Shots in the Dark*, chap. 7.

24. Vizzard, *Shots in the Dark*, 95–97.

25. Jacobs, *Gun Control*, 24.

26. Bureau of Alcohol, Tobacco, and Firearms, "Commerce in Firearms in the United States," February 2000.

27. Jacobs, *Gun Control*, 26–27.

28. Spitzer, *Politics of Gun Control*, 119–20; Vizzard, *Shots in the Dark*, 131–32.

29. Vizzard, *Shots in the Dark*, 130.

30. A brief but thorough discussion of the details of how bullets can penetrate body armor can be found in Vizzard, *Shots in the Dark*, 129–30.

31. Jacobs, *Gun Control*, 29; Osha Gray Davidson, *Under Fire: The NRA and the Battle for Gun Control* (Iowa City: University of Iowa Press, 1998), 98–99.

32. These arguments are remarkably similar to those advanced when discussing waiting periods for abortions. Those who argue for them suggest they merely allow considered reflection and impose a minor inconvenience. Opponents suggest that the intent is to stop some women from having abortions.

33. Spitzer, *Politics of Gun Control*, 126. The fact that Spitzer would describe the legislation in this way suggests that he supported the legislation.

34. While Republicans led the filibuster, political party was not the only factor that influenced an elected officials' vote. This is true of all gun control legislation. The strongest support for gun control comes from urban legislators, while those from the South, the West, and those who represent rural areas constitute the strongest opponents. This is true at both the national and state levels See Spitzer, *Politics of Gun Control*, 131 and chap. 9.

35. Michael Bowling et al., "Background Checks for Firearms, 2002," Bureau of Justice Statistics, U.S. Department of Justice, September 2003.

36. Jacobs, *Gun Control*, 95–96. The problems with regard to mental disqualifications are varied. It is difficult to identify those we wish not to purchase a firearm, that is, which illnesses make one ineligible—any psychological treatment, confinement in a facility, voluntary or involuntary, etc. It is also difficult to determine if or when that person's rights should be restored. Finally, those records are almost always confidential and are not available to the public and, many argue, should not be.

37. Ludwig and Cook, "Homicide and Suicide."

38. At the outset, there were more frequent delays in getting the background check completed in some localities. This was largely due to the inefficiency of various law enforcement groups, often due to personnel shortages, in getting data entered into the system in timely fashion and performing the check when requested. Sometimes the delays were caused by computer glitches. These delays have been reduced over time, both in number and the time required. In addition, there are statutory limits on the maximum length of the delay before a purchaser must be permitted to buy the firearm.

39. As explained by Vizzard, *Shots in the Dark*, 138, this semiautomatic rifle externally looks virtually identical to the automatic AK-47. Spitzer, *Politics of Gun Control*, 42, 120, identifies the Stockton weapon as an AK-47. Spitzer also mentions the Killeen, Texas, restaurant shooting as another event that spurred interest in the assault weapons ban. Interestingly, the Killeen shooting is often used by gun rights groups to argue in favor of lenient concealed carry laws because one of the patrons argued she would have shot the gunmen if she had been allowed to carry the handgun she left in her car into the restaurant.

40. Vizzard, *Shots in the Dark*, 139.

41. Vizzard, *Shots in the Dark*, 138.

42. Vizzard, *Shots in the Dark*, 140.

43. For a more detailed discussion, see Vizzard, *Shots in the Dark*, 140–42.

44. Vizzard, *Shots in the Dark*, 142.

45. Christopher S. Koper and Jeffrey A. Roth, "The Impact of the 1994 Assault Weapons Ban on Gun Violence Outcomes: An Assessment of Multiple Outcome Measures and Some Lessons for Policy Evaluation," *Journal of Quantitative Criminology* 17, no. 1 (March 2001): 33–74.

46. Gary Kleck, "Impossible Policy Evaluations and Impossible Conclusions: A Comment on Koper and Roth," *Journal of Quantitative Criminology* 17, no. 1 (March 2001): 75–80.

47. Jacobs, *Gun Control*, 32.

48. Ludwig and Cook, "Homicide and Suicide."

49. Scott R. Preston, "Targeting the Gun Industry: Municipalities Aim to Hold Manufacturers Liable for Their Products and Actions," *Southern Illinois Law Journal* 24 (Spring 2000): 596.

50. Preston, "Gun Industry," 598.

51. Preston, "Gun Industry," 601.

52. Preston, "Gun Industry," 603.

53. Andrew J. McClurg, David B. Kopel, and Brannon P. Denning, *Gun Control and Gun Rights* (New York: New York University Press, 2002), 288–89.

54. Summaries of most of these cases and their current disposition may be found at www.gunlawsuits.org/docket/docket.php, which is the website of the Legal Action Project (LAP) of the Brady Center, or in NRA-ILA, "Taxpayer Funded Reckless Lawsuits Against the Firearms Industry," April 25, 2004, which can be found by clicking on the fact sheet link on the NRA-ILA website. The NRA-ILA fact sheet simply lists actions, while the LAP site provides information regarding the facts of the case and interpretation of actions from the LAP perspective, of course.

55. An excellent summary of the contents of the Smith & Wesson settlement may be found in McClurg, Kopel, and Denning, *Gun Control*, 347–52.

56. Jacobs, *Gun Control*, 182–83.

57. Allen Rostron, *Smoking Guns: Exposing the Gun Industry's Complicity in the Illegal Gun Market* (Washington, D.C.: Brady Center to Prevent Gun Violence Legal Action Project, 2003).

58. Michael I. Kraus, *Fire & Smoke: Government, Lawsuits, and the Rule of Law* (Oakland, CA: Independent Institute, 2000).

59. For example, see Edward Winter Trapolin, "Comments: Sued Into Submission: Judicial Creation of Standards in the Manufacture and Distribution of Lawful Products—

The New Orleans Lawsuit against Gun Manufacturers," *Loyola Law Review* 46 (Winter 2000): 1285; and Frank J. Vandall, "Article: O.K. Corral II: Policy Issues in Municipal Suits against Gun Manufacturers," *Villanova Law Review* 44 (1999): 575.

60. Jacobs, *Gun Control*, 184.

61. As is so often the case, the exact number here depends upon how you count. According to NRA-ILA, "Courts Reject Lawsuits against Gun Makers," October 16, 2003, at www.nraila.org/Issues/FactSheets/Read.aspx?ID = 37, thirty-three states "have enacted NRA-backed legislation that does just that [prohibiting localities from filing these suits]." The Brady Campaign, in "Special Protection for the Gun Industry: State Bill," 2005, at www.bradycampaign.org/facts/issues/?page = immun_state, claims that twenty-one states "do not grant special immunity to the gun industry," twelve states prohibit localities from filing suits, and seventeen states prohibit municipal lawsuits and some individual suits as well.

62. Helen Dewar, "Bush Opposes Additions to Gun Bill," *Washington Post*, February 26, 2004.

63. "The Gun Lobby's Bull's-Eye," *New York Times*, February 25, 2004; "Down and Dirty in the Gun Debate," *New York Times*, February 27, 2004.

64. The NRA mailed at least two "Legislative Alert" postcards urging members to contact their senators. The Brady Center posted notices almost daily on the website urging supporters to contact their senators.

65. Spender S. Hsu, "Warner, Allen Split Over Assault Weapons," *Washington Post*, March 3, 2004.

66. NRA-ILA, "Statement on S. 1805," at www.nraila.org/Issues/Articles/Read.aspx? ID = 139.

67. Sheryl Gay Stolberg, "Looking Back and Ahead after Senate's Votes on Guns," *New York Times*, March 4, 2004, at www.nytimes.com/2004/03/04/politics/04GUNS.html.

68. "Congress and the Gun Lobby," *New York Times*, March 3, 2004, at www.nytimes .com/2004/03/03/opinion/03WED2.html.

69. Sheryl Gay Stolberg, "Senate Leaders Scuttle Gun Bill Over Changes," *New York Times*, March 3, 2004, at www.nytimes.com/2004/03/03/politics/03GUNS.html.

70. See Brady Campaign to Prevent Gun Violence, "Senate Votes Down Immunity for Gun Industry," March 2, 2004, and "The Morning After: Police, Victims, Democrats and Republicans Stood Up to an Extremist Agenda, Forced It Down," March 3, 2004, both of which claim victory. While the NRA did not claim victory in its official statement on S. 1805, the release does note that the NRA withdrew its support and the amended bill was "successfully defeated" and that "the U.S. Senate had its vote today; law-abiding gun owners will have their turn to vote in November."

71. Protection of Lawful Commerce in Arms Act: (Sec. 3) Prohibits a qualified civil liability action from being brought in any state or federal court against a manufacturer or seller of a firearm, ammunition, or a component of a firearm that has been shipped or transported in interstate or foreign commerce, or against a trade association of such manufacturers or sellers, for damages, punitive damages, injunctive or declaratory relief, abatement, restitution, fines, penalties, or other relief resulting from the criminal or unlawful misuse of a firearm. Requires pending actions to be dismissed.

Excludes from such prohibition actions: (1) brought by a directly harmed party against a person who transfers a firearm knowing that it will be used to commit a crime of violence or a drug trafficking crime; (2) brought against a seller for negligent entrustment or negligence per se; (3) in which a manufacturer or seller of a firearm knowingly violated a state or federal statute applicable to the sale or marketing of the firearm and the violation was a proximate cause of the harm for which relief is sought; (4) for breach of contract or warranty in connection with the purchase of the firearm; (5) for death, physical injuries, or property damage resulting directly from a defect in design or manufacture of the firearm when used as intended or in a reasonably foreseeable manner, except that where the discharge was caused by a volitional act that constituted a criminal offense, such act shall be considered the sole proximate cause of any resulting death, personal injuries, or property damage; or (6) commenced by the Attorney General to enforce firearms provisions under the federal criminal code or the Internal Revenue Code. Permits a person under age seventeen to recover damages authorized under federal or state law in a civil action that meets specified requirements.

(Sec. 5) Child Safety Lock Act of 2005—Prohibits the sale, delivery, or transfer by a licensed importer, manufacturer, or dealer of a handgun to any person other than a person with a firearms license unless the transferee is provided with a secure gun storage or safety device. Lists exceptions, including for U.S. and state agencies and for law enforcement. Grants immunity from a qualified civil liability action for a person who has lawful possession and control of a handgun and who uses a secure gun storage or safety device. Establishes as penalties for violations: (1) license revocation or suspension for up to six months; or (2) a civil penalty of up to $2,500.

(Sec. 6) Sets penalties for using or carrying armor piercing ammunition during and in relation to a crime of violence or a drug trafficking crime, and for possessing armor piercing ammunition in furtherance of any such crime, that shall be in addition to the punishment otherwise provided for such crime.

Directs the Attorney General to conduct and report to the chairman and ranking member of the House and Senate Judiciary Committees on a study to determine whether a uniform standard for the testing of projectiles against body armor is feasible.

72. Gun Owners of America, "Senate Passes Gun Control Amidst Protection for Gun Makers—Now the House Has to Clean Up the Senate's Mess," July 29, 2005, at www.gunowners.org/a072905.htm.

73. NRA-ILA, "S. 397 Passes U.S. Senate!!!" *NRA-ILA Grassroots Alert* 12, no. 30 (July 29, 2005); CCRKBA, "CCRKBA Hails Passage of Industry Lawsuit Protection Bill in Senate," at www.ccrkba.org/pub/rkba/press-releases/CC_Senate_Passes_Gun_Lawsuit_Reform.

74. Brady Campaign to Prevent Gun Violence, "Majority of the US Senate in 'Unholy Alliance' with NRA," July 30, 2005, at www.bradycampaign.org.

75. Carl Hulse, "Senate Approves Bill Protecting Gun Businesses," *New York Times*, July 30, 2005, at www.nytimes.com/2005/07/30/politics/30cong.html; Shailagh Murray, "Senate Passes Bill Barring Gun Suits," *Washington Post*, July 30, 2005.

76. NRA-ILA, "Continue to Attend Town Hall Meetings—Urge Passage of S. 397 in the U.S. House," *NRA-ILA Grassroots Alert* 12, no. 33 (August 19, 2005).

77. U.S. House of Representatives website, at clerk.house.gov/evs/2005/roll534.xml.

78. Amy Goldstein, "House Passes Ban on Gun Industry Lawsuits," *Washington Post*, October 21, 2005.

79. Sheryl Gay Stolberg, "Congress Passes New Legal Shield for Gun Industry," *New York Times*, October 21, 2005, at www.nytimes.com/2005/10/21/politics/21guns.html.

80. NRA-ILA, "Historic Victory for NRA U.S. House of Representatives Passes the 'Protection of Lawful Commerce in Arms Act,'" October 20, 2005, at www.nraila.org /News/Read/Releases.aspx?ID = 6682; Brady Campaign to Prevent Gun Violence, "Congress Ignores Rights of Victims of Gun Violence and Grants Gun Industry Sweeping Legal Immunity President Bush Urged to Reject Bill," October 20, 2005, at www.brady campaign.org/press/release.php?release = 697.

Chapter Four

Public Opinion

What do the American people think about guns and gun control? How do citizens view current laws, and what policies would they like to see implemented in the future? What, if anything, do they think will be effective in controlling or reducing gun violence? The answers to these questions are critical to the discussion of gun control. Elected officials respond to interest groups, but, more importantly, they also respond to the clearly expressed wishes of voters.

Democratic theory argues that the recorded votes and other actions of elected officials should reflect the will of the people. Practical election politics requires that representatives vote in accord with the wishes of their constituents when those preferences can be determined. Most of us would agree that a pure democracy in which all important issues are decided by "the will of the people," however expressed, is not an ideal form of government. Our republican form of government tempers the idea of direct democracy by having us elect representatives who make those decisions for us.

While many of us support direct democracy in theory, the reality of having citizens, whose knowledge and interest may be limited, deciding public policy is generally not appealing. Few of us would feel reassured if the citizens who are deciding policy for us were unaware of the ramifications of those policies or were uninterested in the issues, especially if they enact policies with which we disagree. While the importance of knowledge for decision making is largely unquestioned, its relevance for the formation of opinions is more debated. For example, does one need to know the details of how a gun works to understand that a firearm is dangerous? Or does one need to be familiar with guns to understand the potential benefits of firearms ownership and use? Is knowledge of current laws necessary to form a judgment regarding the wisdom and likely impact of other policy proposals?

Majority rule is an attractive concept as well as an important tenet of our political culture, but both the Constitution and our traditions provide protections for political minorities. While expressing a desire for majority rule, we make allowances for the will of an impassioned minority to override the opinion of a less interested majority. Whether we agree or disagree with this concept, this model has accurately described gun control policy in the United States for at least several decades. An intensely interested minority (those who are usually opposed to gun control measures) has generally thwarted attempts to enact policies that are favored by the majority.

The most accurate way to determine the will of the people with regard to specific issues is through the use of public opinion polls.[1] Using constituent phone calls, letters, or e-mails to gauge public sentiment can be misleading because it is usually those people who are intensely interested in or directly affected by an issue who take the time to contact elected officials. They may be representative of the broader public, but they probably are not. And while winning candidates often claim to have a mandate from the people to enact certain policies, it is usually inaccurate to interpret an electoral outcome as dependent upon a single issue.

Polling itself is as much an art as it is a science. The accuracy of any poll depends upon the nature of the sample, that is, which people are asked the questions (the sample must be representative of the population with regard to certain characteristics), what specific questions are asked (question wording can impact the results), and how those results are interpreted (what constitutes a high or low level of support for an idea).[2]

This chapter examines the public's view of guns and gun control. We review national surveys as well as the results from surveys conducted in Virginia, and we examine some aspects of the issue and polling that are often overlooked.

THE PUBLIC'S VIEW OF GUNS
AND GUN CONTROL

As you already know, proponents and opponents of gun control measures have very few areas of agreement. These disagreements are evident in the views of average citizens and in the research conducted by academics who write about gun control.[3] Despite these differences in opinion, many researchers have noted an apparent consensus in favor of the general concept of gun control.[4] Spitzer argues that the support for various gun control policies is strong and consistent and that the long-term trend is toward increasing support for gun regulations.[5] Even Kleck, who takes issue with many of the general findings, is forced to admit that "there are a large number and wide range of weak-to-moderate regulatory controls that solid majorities of Americans will endorse if asked."[6]

One of the most comprehensive analyses of longitudinal data was conducted by Smith, who found support for many different types of gun regulations. With regard to both general attitudes and opinions regarding specific gun policies, he found that support was relatively constant over time: "Public support for the regulation of firearms is high, deep and widespread."[7] A majority of citizens supported sixteen of the nineteen gun control measures included in several surveys conducted by the National Opinion Research Center (NORC) between 1972 and 1999. Support ranged from a high of 90 percent for placing tamper-resistant serial numbers on guns to a low of 13 percent for a total ban on handguns. Other measures garnering majority support included obtaining a police permit before a gun may be purchased, mandatory background checks for sales by both firearms dealers and private citizens, a five-day waiting period, and mandatory registration of all guns.[8]

Smith's study found even stronger support for safety measures, including mandating handgun trigger locks, safe storage laws, and requiring gun purchasers to take a gun safety course. In all, fourteen of sixteen gun safety measures garnered majority support. Support for requiring current gun owners who do not take a gun safety course to turn in their weapons fell just short of a majority at 49 percent.[9] It should be noted that support for various safety measures generally runs fairly high. Most commonly, however, there is no negative consequence associated with the safety measure. For example, the "smart gun" technology has not yet been perfected, and a safely stored firearm may not be readily available if needed for self-defense. These possibilities are rarely mentioned in survey questions, so respondents are often expressing a preference for safety in a veritable vacuum, which is an easy position to take.

Finally, Smith concluded that these attitudes tend to be stable.[10] Even the

Table 4.1. Public Support for Various Gun Regulations

Regulation	1998	1999
Background check and five-day waiting period	85%	81%
Handgun registration	85%	80%
Checks on private gun sales	80%	79%
Rifle/shotgun registration	72%	61%
Handgun ban	16%	13%
Manufacturer liability	40%	40%
Home less safe with handgun	46%	43%

Source: National Opinion Research Center surveys, 1998 and 1999.

shootings at Columbine High School in Littleton, Colorado, did not significantly change opinion, though Smith did find the shootings may have briefly
increased the salience of crime in general and gun violence in particular.[11]
Other research has suggested that there is at least a short-term impact of
events like the Columbine shootings on public opinion.[12]

One apparent exception to the trend of stable opinion was uncovered by
the Gallup Poll's surveys regarding support for the assault weapons ban. In
1996 Gallup found 57 percent support for banning assault rifles. Support
climbed slightly to 59 percent in 2000, but it dropped to 50 percent in 2004
while opposition rose from 39 percent to 46 percent.[13] Many different surveys
have contained a few gun-related questions, and some of these questions have
been repeated in different surveys to permit comparisons over time. Most
results support the stability hypothesis.[14]

In summarizing public opinion on gun control, Vizzard wrote, "[T]here
can be little question that a large majority of the American public gives at
least tacit support to more comprehensive gun control. But opinion-poll
results do not reflect the depth of commitment, degree of interest, or depth of
knowledge regarding a policy area."[15]

Vizzard raises some very important points. First, given that less than half
the population owns a firearm, it is relatively easy for a majority of citizens
to support additional regulation of guns. Any perceived benefit they derive
from the law will accrue to them at no direct cost. Because they do not own
a gun and are unlikely to purchase one in the future, they will not have to pay
for additional safety devices. They will not be inconvenienced by a waiting
period to purchase a handgun, nor do they need to be concerned with having
to register their firearms.

Smith's research found that more than two-thirds of the people felt they
had little (33 percent) or only some (36 percent) of the information they
needed to understand the issue. At the same time, an even higher percentage
said they were very unlikely (57 percent) or somewhat unlikely (25 percent)
to change their position on gun control.[16]

This is not to say that nonowners should neither have nor express an opinion regarding gun control, nor that they should not influence gun policy. It
simply recognizes that it is relatively easy for any group of citizens to
approve of a policy when another group of citizens will bear the cost for that
policy. This is referred to as a free-rider problem. Free riders are those people
who can use a service without paying for it. An example of this would be if
several families lived on a jointly owned private road, but only the household
at the end of the street paid to have it maintained. The others would benefit
from the road, but they would not pay. Perhaps a better analogy would be

nonsmokers supporting higher cigarette taxes or teetotalers supporting higher taxes on alcoholic beverages.

Second, even if we assume that a majority of the public supports various regulations or restrictions, should that be all that is required for legislators to enact such policies? Should policy simply follow the wishes of the majority, or should policy makers consider the vehemence with which the minority opposes regulations? Finally, should we weight the importance of opinion according to the basis for that opinion? In other words, should we follow the wishes of people who may know little or nothing about firearms when we regulate those items? This argument can be made about a large number of issues unrelated to firearms and gun control.

THE PERCEIVED IMPACT OF GUN
CONTROL LAWS AND LINKING PUBLIC
OPINION AND PUBLIC POLICY

Public opinion impacts governing largely through its influence on agenda setting by defining the issues that are important to citizens, and thus to elected officials. Polls can be used to shape policy to fit the will of the people or they can be used by less ethical leaders to "govern by poll," that is, to do whatever is popular regardless of the wisdom of the policy or its impact.[17]

Robert Erikson and Kent Tedin outline five models describing how public opinion may be reflected in policy making. The rational-activist model assumes that an informed electorate holds elected officials accountable for their actions. The political parties and interest groups models suggest that those organizations play a mediating role in presenting opinion to decision makers. The role-playing model refers to elected officials who attempt to act in accord with opinion for fear of electoral loss, while the sharing model argues that elected officials are, in terms of attitudes and beliefs, often very much like those they represent.[18] Regardless of the model or whether the effect is direct or indirect, public opinion plays a role in governmental decision making.

Examining both elite and mass public opinion of the gun control issue, Kara Lindaman and Donald Haider-Markel found that between 1970 and 1990 elite opinion became more polarized and more in favor of gun control.[19] Democratic support for gun control increased at a much greater rate than support among Republicans. At the same time, mass support for gun control remained relatively stable, though at a higher level than elite support. Support for gun control among the Democratic elites and masses mutually reinforce one another, while it seems that the Republican elite opinion influences mass opinion, but not vice versa. It is possible, then, to conclude that policy preference may follow from public opinion for Democrats, but that policy and elite opinion lead public opinion among Republicans.

The impact of gun control laws is an important consideration when legislators are considering laws regarding firearms. As has been argued throughout this book, the benefit of any law should be discounted by its costs when determining a law's effectiveness and its wisdom. It is foolish to enact a law that will have little or no effect on the behavior we are trying to regulate, unless the costs are negligible. On the other hand, it would be foolhardy not to enact legislation that will achieve the intended goals at a very low cost. Public opinion polls rarely measure the perceived benefit the public expects to derive from gun control laws.

While not directly addressing the efficacy of various gun control regulations, Kellerman and colleagues did ask respondents on three different surveys about the potential costs and benefits of gun ownership. In each wave, the plurality or majority of respondents agreed that the presence of a gun in the home made the home less safe. Not surprisingly, gun owners were much more positive regarding the impact of having a gun in the home, with a plurality or majority saying that a gun made the home generally more safe.[20]

Gun owners and nonowners also disagreed over the effectiveness of several home security measures, including having a dog in the home and installing a burglar alarm system, bright exterior lights, or metal security doors. While gun owners rated owning a gun as more effective than nonowners did, they still felt that an alarm, bright lights, or a dog would be a more effective deterrent.

Other research has also revealed significant differences in opinion between gun owners and nonowners. Robin M. Wolpert and James G. Gimpel found that gun owners generally held opinions that coincided with their self-interest. They were more likely than nonowners to oppose banning handguns, assault weapons, and waiting periods.[21] The authors suggest that gun owners are influenced by the NRA's activities that raise the salience of the issue and provide information on candidates' positions on the issues. The NRA also argues that gun laws will restrict access to firearms by law-abiding citizens and that gun ownership deters crime. Gun owners are likely to think that their opinions are legitimized by the Second Amendment and that their ability to exercise their rights is determined by the government rather than themselves.

The results of two surveys conducted for the Harvard Injury Control Research Center in 1996 and 1999 indicated that people generally thought that their community would be less safe if more people carried guns (a reference to concealed-carry laws) and large majorities did not think that "regular citizens" should be allowed to carry guns into various public venues, including restaurants, government buildings, sports stadiums, and college campuses.[22] Again, gun owners were less concerned about others carrying firearms, and a plurality of those who reported carrying a gun in the past month for protection thought that more people carrying guns would make their community safer.

Edward L. Glaeser and Spencer Glendon's survey analysis suggests that ownership of handguns is more likely to be instrumental than ownership of rifles or shotguns insofar as handgun owners are more likely to identify protection as a reason for owning the firearm.[23] While not calling it a gun culture, they conclude that ownership is related to belonging to a peer group in which gun ownership is the norm, and they also correlate ownership with a mistrust of the police or courts and a belief in private retribution.

It is important to examine the factors that determine or help us to predict what types of people are more or less likely to support gun control. Several different characteristics, attributes, or beliefs can be employed to help us predict a person's opinion regarding gun control. These explanatory variables range from gun ownership to a respondent's sex, area of residence, or trust in government. There is a consensus that attitudes toward gun control are influenced by gun ownership, political party, and political ideology. Most researchers agree that men, those who live in the South, those who live in rural areas, those who mistrust the government, and self-described conservatives or Republicans are less likely to support a variety of gun control measures.[24]

The importance of these characteristics and their impact on attitudes toward firearms was summed up by the director of the New York State Rifle and Pistol Association in a 2003 *New York Times* article that discussed attempts to toughen gun control laws in New York City.

Brophy . . . said the city's seeming intolerance for firearms reflected the social and political culture in Manhattan and other parts of the city where relatively few residents hunted, shot or owned guns.

"They don't have a day-to-day familiarity with guns anymore like they have with, say, cars," he said. "Guns are a useful tool, but many people have no understanding of that tool anymore, and what they don't know, they fear."[25]

Familiarity with firearms, then, is an important consideration in the discussion of public opinion regarding guns and gun control. As we will see shortly, familiarity is an important determinate of attitudes toward gun control.

The question of how important gun control is to the respondent, what we call issue salience, has not been settled.[26] Smith found that a majority of respondents considered gun control to be one of the most important (26 percent) or an important issue (57 percent).[27] Conventional wisdom holds that the issue is more important to those who support gun rights than it is to those who are more supportive of gun regulations. However, Smith's research indicates that those who favor gun control are less likely to change their opinions in the face of possible negative impacts of the policy than those who oppose gun control.[28] This is not a direct measure of salience, but it is a good measure of issue consistency. Other researchers have pointed to the vehemence of those who oppose gun control as a reason that policy has not always followed opinion. For example, Howard Schuman and Stanley Presser found relatively equal salience among individuals on both sides of the issue.[29]

Salience has frequently been measured by asking the respondent to name the most important issue currently facing the country. The economy typically is at the top of the list, and crime is often named as one of the most important, but gun control is rarely mentioned. This probably underestimates the importance of gun control as an electoral issue, while specifically asking about the importance of gun control may overstate its importance. Still, the effectiveness of the NRA in impacting elections is a testament to the importance of the gun issue to at least a small percentage of voters. That small percentage can be enough to sway many close elections in one direction or the other.

Surveys commonly ask respondents if they favor or oppose certain policies, but they rarely ask respondents if they think various policies will impact violent crime, suicides, or accidental shootings. Two independent surveys found that support for gun control policies does not necessarily depend upon an evaluation that the policies would reduce crime or violence.[30] Other research indicates that about equal numbers of respondents say that the presence of guns in the house would make them more or less safe, but, in what appears to be a contradiction, they were more likely to think negative consequences would result than positive outcomes when a firearm is present in the household. In addition, Smith found less support for the idea that gun control measures would be helpful in reducing violent crime than he found for various other policies.[31] In other words, some citizens favor more regulations on firearms, but they do not think those measures will decrease gun violence. At the least, asking why legislators should pass ineffective laws is a reasonable question. Allaying citizens' fears may be a reasonable response to that question. Spitzer agrees that this discrepancy exists, although he suggests it simply means that support for gun control rests on other factors in addition to the impact on crime.[32]

Several Gallup surveys examined attitudes toward guns and other factors and their impact on school violence. They asked what could be done to prevent school shootings such as Columbine. "Better gun control laws" was the third most frequently cited item (12 percent in 1999, 11 percent in 2001), following increased parental involvement and responsibility (32 percent, 31 percent), and more security at schools (16 percent, 14 percent). When asked how important various issues were as a cause of school violence, the availability of guns (46 percent, extremely important; 31 percent, very important) ranked second behind the students' home life, including their relationship with their parents (57 percent, 35 percent). Other factors ranked lower, included the portrayal of guns and violence in entertainment and music (38 percent, 30 percent) and coverage of school shootings by the news media (32 percent, 32 percent).[33]

It should be evident at this point that the surveys regarding public opinion and gun control agree in some areas and disagree in others. There is a general consensus that the public supports many gun safety measures and some other firearm regulations, while rejecting a ban on firearms. With regard to issue salience and the impact of gun laws, the results are mixed. We will now attempt to explain some of these disparate findings.

Surveys conducted by the Center for Community Research at Roanoke College have tested some of the conventional wisdom regarding public opinion and gun control, and they have utilized some innovative ways to measure and explain various aspects of opinion.

Gun control is a multifaceted issue, which makes measurement quite difficult. Asking a common and basic question such as "Do you think current gun control laws are too strict, about right, or not strict enough?" may be an effective way to gauge a respondent's overall view of the issue, but it provides relatively little understanding of what people truly think. Asked alone, it is not obvious exactly what that question measures because of most respondents' unfamiliarity with current laws. If someone is not familiar with current laws, then how can they reasonably judge whether those laws are strict or lenient? It is more likely that this question is a surrogate for the respondent's perception of the seriousness of gun violence insofar as many of those citizens who see gun violence as a serious problem are likely to think that gun laws are too weak.

Thus far, we have noted several problems with most efforts to measure opinion regarding gun control. First, many people and pollsters are not aware of current state or national laws.[34] Second, many people are not familiar with the guns they are trying to regulate.[35] Third, we often do not measure expectations of various policies or ask respondents to follow them to their conclusion, which creates problems for any legislator trying to follow the will of the people.[36] Finally, we are not very effective at measuring issue salience.[37]

The consumer of survey results must always consider who conducted and who sponsored the poll. We would expect that a survey conducted for the NRA would reach different conclusions than one conducted for the Brady Campaign. However, some research indicates that the results of surveys conducted for competing interest groups may not be as divergent as one might anticipate.[38] On the other hand, a poll conducted by the firm Penn, Schoen & Berland Associates, Inc. and distributed by the firm and the Brady Campaign during the 2004 presidential campaign showed that the expiration of the assault weapons ban would hurt the Bush candidacy, but it suffered from biased question wording.[39] The NRA often includes "surveys" in its mailings to members, but most of those mailings are really designed to raise funds, not to measure opinion. The group rarely cites survey results in its communications with members, citizens, or legislators.

The surveys discussed below deal with each of these problems with varying degrees of success. The focus is on the perceived utility of gun control laws and the types of people who support such proposals. Several questions deal with the issue of respondents' self-assessment of their familiarity with guns and, to a lesser extent, with the issue's salience.

The findings presented here are taken from several surveys conducted by the Center for Community Research. Several of the same questions were included in each survey, so we can compare results at different times and from one state with two national samples.

MEASURING SUPPORT
FOR GUN CONTROL

As noted above, most surveys on gun control ask those people who are interviewed whether they favor or oppose current laws and those policies that might be considered in the future. They also ask whether current laws are too strict, about right, or too lenient. While this provides a very general idea of the public's attitude toward guns and gun control, our thought process and opinions are often more complex than can be measured in one question. In addition, this does not remedy the problem that we are asking the majority of respondents to posit an opinion regarding something with which they are not familiar—gun laws.

The problem of question wording is ubiquitous in survey research, and polling with regard to gun control is not immune. While it is true that most major polling firms do their best to accurately and fairly measure public opinion, that does not mean they are always successful. Two of the most important scholarly critics of gun control criticize various polls for routinely biasing their results by omitting response alternatives that gun control policies might *increase* crime. According to Lott, "[T]he notion that gun control laws could primarily reduce legitimate gun ownership and therefore increase crime apparently never entered the pollsters' minds."[40] There are also problems associated with including undefined terms such as "military-style assault weapons" and "Saturday night specials" in survey questions. If it is not clear what those terms mean, then interpretation of the results may be ambiguous or misleading.[41] Still, the practice of asking opinions without regard for the amount of information possessed by the respondent or the accuracy of that information is relatively common in public opinion surveys. Terms used in surveys are often undefined by interviewers because defining the term can lead to question bias. Those who write survey questions prefer that respondents provide their own definition and context to most terms for that reason.

The Roanoke College surveys included some of the commonly asked questions and provided some responses not commonly offered, but they focused more on the expected utility of various regulations. The purpose was to ascertain the impact people think certain laws will have on gun violence, accidents, and suicides.

Because both attitudes toward guns and gun control and the factors that influence those attitudes are more complex than can be measured in one question, we asked multiple questions related to each topic. We also combined several of those questions in indices that measure more of the breadth of the topic.[42]

An index is a single measure that combines the answers to several questions. We created indices to measure attitudes toward gun control and to combine various demographic characteristics and other attributes that are related to those attitudes. This facilitates the ranking of those persons interviewed from most to least likely to think that gun laws can impact behavior and from those most familiar to least familiar with guns. The indices are different for the Virginia and national samples because those questionnaires included some identical and some unique questions, but they are quite similar in terms of what they measure.

THE VIRGINIA SURVEY

The first survey to be discussed is a statewide poll conducted in Virginia in October 2001 in which 593 randomly selected persons were interviewed. While Virginia is thought to be a gun-friendly state, the reality is more complex than that. There is clearly a diversity of opinion reflected by the Commonwealth's residents and in its laws.[43]

There were eleven questions that specifically dealt with gun control. One was the general question regarding the perceived strictness of existing law.[44] The others were related to the perceived utility of gun laws or asked respondents to choose between possible scenarios of how a gun in the home might be used. We included questions regarding attitudes toward the National Rifle Association and the Brady Campaign to Prevent Gun Violence (then known as Handgun Control, Inc.). We also asked about the perceived utility of laws and possible consequences of having a gun in the household.

A series of questions tapped into the respondent's "interactions" with guns from childhood through the present. As stated above, we know that those who own guns are more opposed to gun control policies than those who do not own guns. It is likely that it is not just owning a gun, but rather a respondent's familiarity (in the sense of being accustomed to having guns in the house) with guns that influences her views.

These questions also gauge respondents' familiarity with guns without asking them to identify various parts of a gun or explain how one works. Being around guns certainly does not make someone a firearms expert, but owning, firing, or even seeing others fire a weapon provides some rudimentary understanding of how guns work. In addition, being raised in a household in which guns were present might make a person more comfortable with firearms.[45] Returning to the Brophy quote, people fear that which is unknown to them.

We created two indices to measure familiarity with firearms and attitudes toward the expected utility of gun control policies. The following questions are included in the KNOWGUN-VA index: familiarity with how a gun works, presence of handguns in the residence, presence of rifles or shotguns in the residence, respondent's experience with firing a firearm, and presence of guns in the respondent's childhood residence.[46]

The UTILITY-VA index is comprised of the general items regarding the respondent's views on gun control laws as well as their views of the NRA and HCI. It also includes specific items regarding the perceived utility of stricter gun control laws, such as whether they would reduce the number of crimes, accidental shootings, and suicides; keep guns away from children; and make the respondent more or less safe.

Each of the two new variables is normally distributed. Scores on KNOWGUN-VA, with a range of 5 to 12, include five separate items, has a mean of 8.15, and a standard deviation of 2.18. Scores on UTILITY-VA range between 11 and 33. It includes eleven individual questions, has a mean of 22.65, and a standard deviation of 5.79.

Both distributions demonstrate a diversity of opinion in that relatively equal numbers of respondents are more or less familiar with guns (although it is skewed slightly toward the more familiar side), and the attitude index also features a wide dispersion, making them useful indices. For those more familiar with statistics, we would say the distributions form a normal curve.

Virginia Survey Summary

Respondents distinguished between the potential utility of various gun control laws. A plurality (44 percent) thought that current gun control laws were about right, while many more felt they are not strict enough (39 percent) than said they are too strict (12 percent). Yet a majority (51 percent) of those interviewed said that enforcing current laws would be more likely than passing new laws to decrease gun violence (32 percent). Perhaps surprisingly, nearly twice as many people thought that a gun in the home would be used for self-defense (48 percent) than thought it would accidentally kill or injure another person (28 percent).[47]

A majority (57 percent) of respondents said that stricter laws would help keep guns out of the hands of children, while fewer thought they would reduce the number of accidental shootings (51 percent), would reduce the number of crimes committed (50 percent), would make the respondent personally more safe (31 percent), or would reduce the number of suicides (26 percent). A large majority (75 percent) felt that a five-day waiting period for handgun purchases would prevent shootings.

Despite the gun control sentiment expressed in many of the responses, the NRA was viewed favorably by a larger number of respondents (36 percent) than was HCI (25 percent). To be fair, the NRA was also seen in an unfavorable light by a higher percentage of respondents than HCI (27 percent, 20 percent).

While these numbers indicate that a majority of Virginia residents see some benefits to stricter gun control laws, there is a sizable minority that does not. Only 9 percent thought stricter laws would make them less safe, and 13 percent said that a waiting period would endanger potential victims of violence who needed a firearm for defense, but many respondents thought that stricter laws would make no difference in many areas. Still, more than half thought that laws could reduce at least some type(s) of gun violence.

The only approximate measure of salience was a question that asked the most important issue in the gubernatorial election for the respondent.[48] Gun control did not make the top ten issues, but Governor Mark Warner's courtship of the NRA was covered in the news media, and many observers attributed his victory, at least in part, to his "Sportsmen for Warner" campaign.[49]

Explaining Perceived Utility in Virginia

Most of the variables we would expect to be related to attitudes toward firearms had statistically significant relationships with UTILITY-VA, including sex (men were more likely than women to favor gun rights); political party

(Republicans were more pro-rights than Independents, who were more pro-rights than Democrats); political ideology (liberals were more in favor of gun control than moderates, who were more pro-control than conservatives); gun ownership (gun owners were more pro-rights than nonowners); and using a gun for personal protection, having ever fired a gun, familiarity with guns, and presence of a gun in childhood household (those less familiar with guns were more in favor of gun control). The insignificant relationships with trust in government and using a gun for hunting were somewhat surprising.

Regression Results—Virginia Survey

One of the difficulties presented by the independent variables in this topic is multi-colinearity. That is, there are strong relationships among all of those variables that had significant relationships with UTILITY-VA, so it is difficult to determine which of the variables are most strongly related to attitudes toward firearms. We used stepwise multiple regression to control for this problem. This statistical procedure helps us to decide which of the variables is more important in predicting a respondent's attitude. For example, is it being female, being a Democrat, or holding a liberal political ideology that makes one more likely to favor gun control measures? All independent variables were run separately first and decisions were made as to which variables to include in the analysis. The results can be seen in table 4.2.

Seven independent variables were selected for inclusion in the regression model. The results indicate that there are four different models that should be examined. Two of the variables—trust in government and if any guns were used for hunting—were not statistically significant in the bivariate relation-

Table 4.2.   Variables Related to Perceived Gun Law Utility in Virginia

Variables Included	R	R Square	Standardized Beta	Significance
KNOWGUN-VA	.479	.230	.479	.000
KNOWGUN-VA	.427	.000		
Political party	.573	.328	−.318	.000
KNOWGUN-VA			.417	.000
Political party			−.234	.000
Political ideology	.588	.346	−.157	.007
KNOWGUN-VA			.372	.000
Political party			−.227	.000
Political ideology			−.160	.005
Sex	.602	.362	−.136	.007

ship, and they were not included in the multiple regression models. The third—type of area in which the respondent was reared—was significant in the bivariate situation, but it had little explanatory power.

The other variables—the KNOWGUN-VA index, political party, political ideology, and sex—were significant in the multivariate model. It is clear that the KNOWGUN-VA index is a powerful explanatory variable. To some extent, however, this should not be surprising, because a person's familiarity and experience with firearms is magnified by the five variables included in the index.[50] Still, it is the most powerful variable in the models shown above, and its power is weakened only slightly when combined with a separately created POLITICS index that includes political party and political ideology.

NATIONAL SURVEYS

The Center for Community Research conducted two national surveys, one in the fall of 2002 (N = 343) and the other in the spring of 2003 (N = 234). Some of the interviews in the 2002 survey were completed during the sniper shootings in the Washington, D.C. area that made national news for more than a month. Shortly after calling began in 2003, President Bush made the decision to commence the war in Iraq.

These events could skew the results on the surveys. The sniper shootings might increase support for gun control, while a war may increase enthusiasm for the right to self-defense. In fact, the results from the two surveys reveal that opinion on several of the issues related to gun control had shifted somewhat from the fall to the spring. The results discussed here are a combined data set consisting of questions that were asked in both surveys. While it cannot be empirically demonstrated that this merging of data creates a true snapshot of opinion, it clearly levels out some of the opinion shifts that may occur temporarily in exceptional circumstances. Indeed, it is difficult to establish what would be a normal or typical time in which to measure attitudes toward guns and gun control, although as noted earlier, some research has found opinion regarding gun control to be stable and not subject to major fluctuations due to current events.

Some of the questions have been included on other national surveys. Others differ in that they ask the respondent to choose what they think is the most likely potential outcome from various gun policy proposals that could be enacted. In each case, respondents were provided with two competing scenarios and asked to choose the one they thought was most likely to result from the policy. In each question the alternatives were balanced in that one presented a more favorable outcome if a gun regulation were enacted, while the other suggested a negative outcome.[51]

National Surveys Summary

Our discussion begins with the fundamental question of how we should interpret the Second Amendment. An overwhelming percentage of respondents believe that the Second Amendment confers an individual right to own firearms. To be sure, nearly as many believe that this right is conditional and must be balanced against other rights (42 percent) as believe that this right is absolute (44 percent), but only 10 percent believe that it is a collective right.[52]

We then asked if a gun owned by a law-abiding citizen would be more likely to be used for self-defense or to be involved in an accidental shooting. Respondents were almost twice as likely to think the gun would be used for self-defense (56 percent) than to be involved in an accidental shooting (30 percent). In general, the findings were similar, but slightly less favorable toward gun control and its impact, than the Virginia survey.

Table 4.3 outlines the public's perceptions of the likely impact of various gun control proposals. A majority of respondents thought a mandatory five-

Table 4.3.   Perceived Impact of Gun Control Laws

Policy	Percent	Number
Stricter gun control laws will . . .		
Reduce violent crime	43%	249
Reduce gun accidents	45%	258
Reduce suicides	20%	116
Keep guns away from children	51%	292
Make respondent more safe	32%	182
Make respondent less safe	18%	101
Five-day waiting period will . . .		
Prevent shootings	74%	423
Hamper self-defense	16%	93
Mandatory gun registration will . . .		
Reduce crime	36%	206
Make no difference in crime	60%	346
Making it more difficult to purchase a gun will . . .		
Reduce crime	44%	254
Increase crime	38%	215
Policy most likely to decrease violent crime . . .		
Longer prison sentences	39%	222
Stricter gun laws	19%	110
Educate society to be less violent	37%	213

day waiting period to purchase a gun would prevent spur-of-the-moment shootings and that stricter gun laws would help keep guns out of the hands of children.

Less than half said that stricter gun laws would reduce violent crime (43 percent), accidents (45 percent), or suicides (20 percent). They were also not very optimistic about the potential impact of gun registration. Three in five (60 percent) said they thought that registration would make no difference, while just over one-third (36 percent) said it would reduce crime.

Respondents were slightly more likely to think that making it more difficult to purchase a gun would reduce crime (44 percent) than that it would increase crime because criminals would be more bold if they knew that potential victims were unarmed (38 percent). Still, this is an important finding because it points to the ambivalence of the public toward the effects of gun control measures.

In general, people thought that either longer prison sentences (39 percent) or educating society to be less violent (37 percent) would be more effective ways to decrease violent crime than enacting stricter gun laws (19 percent). As with the Virginia sample, the nation was more likely to hold either a positive or negative view of the NRA than the Brady Campaign, although views of both were slightly more positive than negative.

We also included several questions that dealt with actual and potential lawsuits as well as child access laws dealing with firearms and other items. The purpose of including the other items, unrelated to guns, was to differentiate between people who simply favor holding someone responsible for events and those who think that gun manufacturers are important offenders that should be punished. In other words, some people may prefer to hold some entity—government, businesses, society, or other entities perceived to be negligent—responsible for third-party actions, whether related to a firearm, a dangerous substance such as tobacco or alcohol, or a household poison. Others might hold the individual responsible—the smoker, the drinker, the shooter, and so forth. It is also possible that respondents would make different judgments in different situations.[53]

Table 4.4 shows that relatively few people responded positively to governmental lawsuits against either gun manufacturers or cigarette makers. Only 17 percent of the respondents thought gun manufacturers should be held liable for negligently marketing their guns.[54] Even fewer respondents (15 percent) favored governments suing gun manufacturers to recover medical costs incurred in treating gunshot wounds. There was more, but still relatively low, support (26 percent) for suing tobacco companies for the medical treatment of smokers, but virtually no support (6 percent) for the hypothetical suit

Table 4.4.   Percent Who Favor Various Lawsuits or Child Access Laws

Policy	Percent	Number
Gun manufacturers should be liable for marketing negligence	17%	98
Gun manufacturers should be sued for medical costs	15%	87
Cigarette makers should be sued for medical costs	26%	149
Fast food restaurants should be sued for medical costs	6%	36
Favor child access laws for firearm storage negligence	76%	433
Favor child access laws for household poison negligence	59%	337

against fast-food restaurants to recover medical costs associated with eating too much junk food.[55]

Child access laws received much greater support in the surveys. Fully three-quarters (76 percent) supported holding parents or other adults responsible, criminally and civilly, if they negligently stored a firearm and a child used that gun. Fewer, but still a majority (59 percent), favored a hypothetical child access law that would deal with poisons commonly found in the household, such as mouse poison and drain openers.

There are several indicators in the survey dealing with a respondent's familiarity with firearms, summarized in table 4.5. Nearly two-thirds of the respondents said they were at least somewhat familiar with how guns work (35 percent very familiar; 30 percent somewhat familiar). Slightly more (71 percent) reported having fired a gun at some time in their lives. Just fewer than one in three (31 percent) said that they currently own a handgun or a long gun.

There are other ways that one might be familiar with, or comfortable with, the presence of guns. These include if there were guns in the household when one was a child (58 percent), or if there are currently guns in the household but one is not the owner (13 percent).[56]

Finally, regarding the question of issue salience, 19 percent of those sur-

Table 4.5.   Familiarity with Firearms

Condition	Percent	Number
Self-reported familiarity with firearms	66%	374
Ever fired a gun	71%	404
Currently own a handgun or long gun	31%	180
Ever carry a gun for protection	11%	59
Reported gun in household as child	58%	325
Currently gun in household	44%	255

veyed said that gun control was the most important issue for them in voting in national elections, and 55 percent said it was an issue they considered when voting. The responses regarding state elections were nearly identical. While this figure is almost certainly inflated, it is consistent throughout the surveys, and the question was asked in the beginning of the interview, so the responses were not influenced by all the other gun-related questions that might create a perception that the issue is more important than the respondent might think. It is likely, however, that responses were influenced by the power of suggestion; that is, we asked how important this specific issue is to respondents rather than ask them the open-ended question of what issue is most important to them. Even with these caveats, we can say that gun control is very important to some voters, and is important to more than half.

Explaining Perceived Utility in the Nation

Using a similar methodology to that employed in the Virginia survey, indices were created to measure familiarity with firearms, perceived utility of gun control measures, and demographic characteristics related to attitudes toward firearms.

Different combinations of variables were tested, and the most parsimonious led to the following indices.[57] KNOWGUN-US includes the respondent's self-rating regarding familiarity with firearms, if there was a gun in the household when he was a child, and if the respondent currently owns a gun or lives in a household where a gun is present.[58] It has a range of 3 to 10, with a mean of 6.18 and a standard deviation of 2.32. DEMOPOL-US is an index composed of sex, political party, and political ideology.[59] Its range is 3 to 8, and it has a mean of 5.23 and a standard deviation of 1.57. The UTILITY-US index includes whether the respondent thinks that stricter gun control laws would reduce the number of violent crimes committed, accidental shootings, and suicides; keep guns away from children; or make the respondent more or less safe; whether a five-day waiting period would reduce shootings; whether gun registration would reduce shootings; and whether making it more difficult to purchase a firearm would reduce crime.[60] It ranges from 8 to 24 with a mean of 15.94 and a standard deviation of 4.76. Each index has a normal distribution.

Each of the component variables in the KNOWGUN-US and DEMOPOL-US indices was related to UTILITY-US in the expected direction, as were the indices themselves. Those with higher scores on each index were more likely to think that gun control laws would reduce gun violence. Regression analysis was utilized to determine the relative impact of the variables.

Regression Results—National Surveys

Again, we used stepwise multiple regression, in which all independent variables were run separately first and decisions were made as to which variables to include in the analysis. The results can be seen in table 4.6 below.

In the national surveys, familiarity with firearms was a more powerful predictor of perceived utility of gun control regulations than was the demographic index. To some extent this coincides with the findings of Smith, who noted that "exposure to guns strongly influences one's assessment of the usefulness of gun control laws in reducing crime," although Smith did not conduct a multivariate analysis. He also found that sex, political party, political ideology, and whether one lived in a rural, suburban, or urban environment had an impact on attitudes toward gun control, all in the expected direction.[61]

SUMMARY

The results from the Virginia and national surveys indicate the ambivalence of the American public with regard to gun control. Similar to the findings of most previous research, majorities supported a variety of gun control regulations, but they were somewhat skeptical with regard to expected outcomes. When presented with competing scenarios, those surveyed were only slightly more likely to choose the positive outcome of gun regulations over the potential negative outcome.

Respondents in the national surveys clearly indicated that they believe that the Second Amendment confers an individual right to own firearms, but fewer than half believe that the right is absolute. Nearly as many believe that the right must be balanced against others, but only one in ten said they think the right is a collective or societal right.

With regard to reducing gun violence, strong pluralities said that some regulations could reduce gun crime and accidental shootings, but less than one-fourth thought that gun laws could impact suicides. A majority thought that stronger laws could keep guns away from children and that a five-day waiting

Table 4.6.   Variables Related to Perceived Gun Law Utility in the United States

Variables Included	R	R Square	Standardized Beta	Significance
KNOWGUN-US	.508	.258	.508	.000
KNOWGUN-US			.382	.000
DEMOPOL-US	.574	.329	.295	.000

period was more likely to prevent shootings than to hamper a potential victim attempting to defend themselves.

On the other hand, by an almost 2–1 margin, respondents thought that a gun in the home was more likely to be used for self-defense than to be involved in an accidental shooting. By about the same margin, longer prison sentences or education were thought to be better preventatives of gun violence than stricter gun laws. And respondents were almost as likely to say that making purchasing a gun more difficult would increase crime by disarming potential victims as they were to say it would reduce crime.

Focusing on the results of any one question may provide the ammunition, so to speak, that one can use to defend her point of view, but it would not be an accurate representation of public opinion regarding guns and gun control. The results here provide some ammunition to each side. It might be more accurate, though, to say the public has mixed feelings regarding gun control.

Explaining why a respondent holds a particular view on gun control issues is, to some extent, dependent upon how the issues are framed, the structure of the questions, and how those questions may be combined. The "truth" may be "out there," but our definition of the truth determines where we will find it.

It is clear that a person's familiarity with firearms and his political beliefs strongly impact his views on gun control. Regardless of how we combine those variables and indices, they remain the strongest explanatory variables in the analysis. Which is the most influential depends upon which variables are included in the analysis.

While one may quibble with the variables that were included in any or all of the indices discussed in this analysis, it is clear that we cannot ignore a person's familiarity with firearms, beyond simple ownership, as an important factor in determining views on gun control. It is, of course, possible to compute indices with other variables included or without some of those included here, which could lead to slightly different results.

When we consider familiarity with guns and political beliefs, sex assumes less importance in the analysis and other variables often thought to influence opinion disappear from the regression analysis completely. One could argue that sex should be eliminated from the model because it adds so little to the explanatory power of the model (1.6 percent additional explained variance with KNOWGUN-US, party and ideology; 1.5 percent additional explained variance with POLITICS and KNOWGUN-US) when the other variables are considered. If we eliminate sex, then what remains are the variables, in whatever combination, that measure political beliefs and familiarity with firearms.

The importance of gun familiarity in determining views of gun control combined with indicators that gun ownership may be declining and that the number of hunters is definitely decreasing may indicate a slow trend toward greater support for gun control over time.

CONCLUSION

There is no doubt that the issues surrounding gun control are and will continue to be important, and that groups on all sides of the issues will continue to tout poll results to indicate that the public is on their side. In general, those who favor gun control constitute the majority opinion, while those who are opposed to gun control win in terms of intensity.

While we have been measuring the public's view on these issues for decades, we have not exhausted either the analysis of existing data or new information that we gather. We need to continue to be sensitive to the issues of question wording and how we conceptualize the gun control issue. At the same time, we should continue to search for the demographic, social, and cultural factors that influence these opinions. We can attach our own interpretation to the data, but there are clear indications that those citizens who most strongly support gun control measures are those who are the most unfamiliar with firearms. Obviously, those who are more familiar with firearms see them as less dangerous and as less of a threat. The reader may think of that as evidence of a gun culture or simply that those who are more familiar with any object are often less likely to fear it. This may not be too surprising, but it should have implications for citizens and the elected officials who are considering gun-related legislation.

This chapter has suggested a variation in the measurement of gun control opinion. Certainly there are many more possible variations that should be explored. Examples might include probing more deeply regarding respondents' knowledge of current national and state laws, their understanding of how guns work, and the reasons why people own guns (important for new technologies that purport to make firearms "safer").

Another question we might ask is: Why is it that those who do not own firearms and are less familiar with guns are more in favor of gun control measures? Part of the reason, obviously, is that it is easy to say an item should be regulated if it does not directly affect you, but may be due in part to other reasons—fear of the unknown, a different understanding of the nature of crime and human behavior, and so on. These are important considerations for us as we explore the issues surrounding guns and gun control, and for legislators who are considering bills that increase or decrease the regulation of fire-arms.

NOTES

1. For a discussion of public opinion and democratic theory, see Barbara A. Bardes and Robert W. Oldendick, *Public Opinion: Measuring the American Mind* (Belmont, CA: Wadsworth, 2000), chap. 1.

2. Extended discussions of various aspects of polling may be found in Herbert F. Weisberg, Jon A. Krosnick, and Bruce D. Bowen, *An Introduction to Survey Research, Polling, and Data Analysis*, 3rd ed. (Thousand Oaks, CA: Sage, 1996); and Floyd J. Fowler Jr., *Survey Research Methods*, 3rd ed. (Thousand Oaks, CA: Sage, 2002).

3. For example, Philip J. Cook and Jens Ludwig, *Gun Violence: The Real Costs* (New York: Oxford University Press, 2000); and Gary Kleck and Don B. Kates, *Armed: New Perspectives on Gun Control* (Amherst, NY: Prometheus, 2001) both examine the issue of gun control, but adopt different perspectives and reach very different conclusions.

4. Robert J Spitzer, *The Politics of Gun Control*, 3rd ed. (Washington, D.C.: CQ Press, 2004), 104; David R. Harding Jr., "Public Opinion and Gun Control: Appearance and Transparence in Support and Opposition," in *The Changing Politics of Gun Control*, ed. John M. Bruce and Clyde Wilcox (Lanham, MD: Rowman & Littlefield, 1998), 196–223.

5. Spitzer, *Politics of Gun Control*, 99–102.

6. Gary Kleck, *Targeting Guns: Firearms and Their Control* (New York: Aldine de Gruyter, 1997), 337.

7. Tom W. Smith, "1999 National Gun Policy Survey of the National Opinion Research Center: Research Findings" (paper presented at the annual meeting of the American Association for Public Opinion Research, Portland, OR, May 2000), 2. A brief and easily accessible summary of these data may be found in Tom W. Smith, "Public Opinion about Gun Policies (Public Perspective)," *Future of Children* 12 (Summer–Fall 2002): 155.

8. Smith, "Gun Survey," 34.

9. Smith, "Gun Survey," 37.

10. Smith, "Gun Survey," 8.

11. Smith, "Gun Survey," 10.

12. Donald P. Haider-Markel and Mark R. Joslyn, "Gun Policy, Opinion, Tragedy, and Blame Attribution: The Conditional Influences of Issue Frames," *Journal of Politics* 63, no. 2 (May 2001): 520–43.

13. The Gallup Brain, "Guns," October 14, 2004.

14. John T. Young et al., "The Polls—Trends: Guns," *Public Opinion Quarterly* 60 (1996): 634–49.

15. William J. Vizzard, *Shots in the Dark: The Policy, Politics, and Symbolism of Gun Control* (Lanham, MD: Rowman & Littlefield, 2000), 69.

16. Smith, "Gun Survey," 11.

17. For a discussion of the impact of polls and agenda setting, see Albert H. Cantril, *The Opinion Connection* (Washington, D.C.: CQ Press, 1991), 222–28; and Herbert

Asher, *Polling and the Public: What Every Citizen Should Know*, 2nd ed. (Washington, D.C.: CQ Press, 1992), 17–20.

18. Robert S. Erikson and Kent L. Tedin, *American Public Opinion*, 6th ed. (New York: Longman, 2001).

19. Kara Lindaman and Donald P. Haider-Markel, "Issue Evolution, Political Parties, and the Culture Wars," *Political Research Quarterly* 55, no. 1 (March 2002): 91–110.

20. Arthur R. Kellerman et al., "Public Opinion about Guns in the Home," *Injury Prevention* 6 (2000): 189–94.

21. Robin M. Wolpert and James G. Gimpel, "Self-Interest, Symbolic Politics, and Public Attitudes toward Gun Control," *Political Behavior* 20, no. 3 (1998): 241–62.

22. David Hemenway, Deborah Azrael, and Matthew Miller, "National Attitudes Concerning Gun Carrying in the United States," *Injury Prevention* 7 (2001): 282–85.

23. Edward L. Glaeser and Spencer Glendon, "Who Owns Guns? Criminals, Victims, and the Culture of Violence," *American Economic Review* 88, no. 2 (May 1998): 458–62.

24. Spitzer, *Politics of Gun Control*, 102.

25. Winnie Hu, "Council Seeks to Toughen Gun Laws," *New York Times*, August 23, 2003.

26. The salience of the gun control issue is also discussed in chapter 5.

27. Smith, "Gun Survey," 11.

28. Smith's conclusions are based on two different tests. First, those who favored gun control were more likely to consider the issue as one of the most important and to be very unlikely to change their opinion. At the same time, they were less likely to say they had all the information they needed on the issue. This self-assessment held true when tested by counterarguments depending upon the respondent's answer to an initial question. Those who said they favored a regulation were presented with an argument opposing that regulation, while those who opposed it were given an argument in favor of it. Those who favored gun control were less likely to change their view when presented with the counterargument. See Smith, *Gun Survey*, 11–13.

29. Howard Schuman and Stanley Presser, "The Attitude-Action Connection and the Issue of Gun Control," *Annals of the American Academy of Political and Social Science* 455 (May 1981): 40–47.

30. Gary Kleck, "Crime, Culture Conflict and the Sources of Support for Gun Control," *American Behavioral Scientist* 39, no. 4 (February 1996): 387–404; Young et al., "The Polls."

31. Smith, "Gun Survey," 8.

32. Spitzer, *Politics of Gun Control*, 102–103.

33. The Gallup Brain, "Children and Violence," August 11, 2003.

34. Vizzard, *Shots in the Dark*, 69–70.

35. David B. Kopel, "Assault Weapons," in *Guns: Who Should Have Them*, ed. David B. Kopel (Amherst, NY: Prometheus, 1995), 159–232.

36. Harding, "Public Opinion." Kleck's analysis of General Social Survey data discussed the utilitarian view of support for gun control laws, but it found little evidence for it. See Kleck, "Culture Conflict."

37. David J. Bordua, "Adversary Polling and the Construction of Social Meaning: Implications in Gun Control Elections in Massachusetts and California," *Law and Policy Quarterly* 5, no. 3 (1983): 347–48.

38. James D. Wright, "Public Opinion and Gun Control: A Comparison of Results From Two Recent National Surveys," *Annals of The American Academy of Political and Social Science* 455 (1981): 24–39.

39. Penn, Schoen & Berland Associates, "New National Polls Show Assault Weapons Ban Wedge Factor in Election—Moves Key Swing States Into 'Kerry' Column as Voters Perceive Ban as Key 'Homeland Security' Leadership Issue," October 9, 2004. The wording of the presidential preference question follows. "If the election for President were being held today, for whom would you vote? Democrat John Kerry, who is a hunter and a sportsman. Kerry believes that Congress and the White House must renew the ban on military style assault weapons when it expires in several weeks. Four years ago, Republican George W. Bush, as a candidate for President, pledged to support the renewal of the assault weapons ban. Yet, as President, Bush has broken his promise and has not asked Congressional leaders to extend the ban. The ban is now set to expire."

40. John R. Lott, Jr., *The Bias against Guns* (Washington, D.C.: Regnery, 2003), 34.

41. See Kleck, *Targeting Guns*, chap. 10; and Lott, *Bias*, 33–37.

42. There are many different concepts that are multidimensional and cannot be measured with one question. An example of this is measuring racist attitudes. The concept of racism is complex, and it cannot be measured with one question, nor can it be measured directly. Therefore, researchers will typically use indices when measuring racism. Because of the wide variety of positions, opinion regarding abortion could also be measured using an index.

43. This is discussed in detail in chapter 7.

44. This question was included, despite the criticism previously directed toward that question, because it so commonly asked on questionnaires dealing with gun control.

45. A piece of personal anecdotal evidence may help to illustrate this point. A few years ago I attended a large outdoor flea market with my wife. This annual event attracts tens of thousands of visitors and includes antique dealers, people who make crafts, etc. It began as a gun show and it retains that component, although the gun show is now a relatively small part of the event. Nevertheless, one can see people carrying firearms as they walk through the crowds of browsers on their way to and from the building that houses the gun show. I asked my wife if she was uncomfortable among strangers carrying guns. She responded, "No, there were guns in the house when I was a kid, and my dad had guns, so they don't bother me."

46. While slight additional weight is given to the self-assessment question, making the weight of all the variables equal had very little effect on the variables' distribution.

47. Using different question wording—"Do you think having a gun in the house makes it a safer place to be or a more dangerous place to be?"—the Gallup Poll found that 35 percent of those surveyed in 2000 thought it would make it safer, and that percentage increased to 42 percent in 2004. Those thinking it would make the house more dangerous fell from 51 percent, in 2000 to 36 percent in 2004. See The Gallup Brain, "Guns."

48. As mentioned earlier, this type of question may underestimate the importance of the gun control issue. It was asked prior to any questions regarding gun control. Asking it later in the questionnaire would have almost certainly led to some mentions of it as the most important issue.

49. See the discussion of this election and Governor Warner in chapter 7.

50. As a check, political party and political ideology were combined into a POLITICS

index. When entered into the regression model in place of the separate variables, POLITICS became the most powerful variable (R = .512, Sig. = .000). In the multivariate models, this was also true (POLITICS [Beta = −.425] and KNOWGUN-VA [Beta = .383]), R = .634; (POLITICS [Beta = −.421], KNOWGUN-VA [Beta = .340], and Sex [Beta = −.132]), R = .646.

51. In this way we go beyond simply asking those interviewed if they favor a particular policy and force them to consider potential outcomes of the policy. For example, our question dealing with the impact of gun registration reads as follows: "Some people think that mandatory registration of all guns will help reduce violent crime and help police solve crimes by tracking guns. Others believe that gun registration will not impact crime because criminals won't register their guns and will either purchase illegal guns or steal guns they use when committing crimes. Which of these is closer to your view?" This question states two distinct points of view and asks the respondent to choose the one closest to theirs. It is typical of the types of questions we asked. In some cases, we did ask if they favored a particular policy.

52. In comparison, a 2003 Gallup Poll found that 68 percent of respondents indicated that the Second Amendment conferred an individual "right to keep and bear arms for their own defense" in addition to the need to maintain a militia. A large majority (82 percent) of those who believed in an individual right also said that the government could impose some restrictions on that right. See The Gallup Brain, "Guns."

53. Another example of this in political science literature is trying to differentiate trust in government from more general trust in institutions. To do this, you might ask about trust in governmental officials, clergy, doctors, teachers, etc.

54. As you may recall, these suits allege that the manufacturers knowingly sell more guns to dealers in particular geographic areas than they "know" can be sold to residents of that area. The excess guns are then sold to people who live in jurisdictions where laws would not permit them to buy guns or they are sold to straw purchasers. Another charge is that the manufacturers market firearms to crime-prone youth in a fashion that glorifies violence and crime.

55. Although the inclusion of fast food may be thought by some to inappropriate, it should be noted that several lawsuits have been filed against fast food outlets for the effects of their products, and states have begun to pass preemptive legislation to stop these lawsuits.

56. The figure of 44 percent of respondents reporting that they currently live in a household in which there is a firearm is comparable to other surveys discussed earlier in the chapter.

57. The criterion used for inclusion in the KNOWGUN-US and DEMOPOL-US indices was the indices' ability to explain variation in UTILITY-US. Adding additional variables in the KNOWGUN-US index (ever fired a gun; currently carry a gun) added very little to the explanatory power, and their inclusion would have weighted owning a gun too heavily. With regard to DEMOPOL-US, the variable if the respondent was reared in an urban, suburban, or rural environment added little to the explanatory power of the index. UTILITY-US was constructed from all of those variables included in the surveys that dealt with the perceived utility of gun regulations. Other questions and combinations are certainly possible.

58. The items included are a four-point scale for self-assessed familiarity with guns

(very, somewhat, not very, or not all familiar), if there was gun in the household as a child (yes, unsure, no), and if there is a gun in the current household (respondent owns, other household member owns, or none).

59. The items included are sex (male, female), political ideology (conservative, moderate, liberal), and political party (Republican, Independent, Democrat).

60. Each item included has a three-point scale (yes, unsure, no), so all items are weighted equally in the index.

61. Smith, "Gun Survey," 8.

Chapter Five

Interest Groups, Gun Control, and Elections

Although their political power may not be as great as many Americans believe, interest groups play an important role in public policy making. From the elections that determine who will be the lawmakers to helping shape the legislation that is passed and influencing its implementation, interest groups are a critical part of the process.[1]

Groups help to define issues, influence public opinion, and provide information to the elected officials who decide which bills will be passed into law. While we commonly think of interest groups being active in the halls of Congress, many are also involved at the state and local levels of government. Interest group activity is primarily focused on lobbying and electioneering, although those roles may be defined broadly to include a host of activities.

Lobbying is generally thought of as providing information to elected officials to facilitate their decision making. This information may take the form of a draft of legislation, a memo indicating problems with current laws or bills that are being considered, the results of public opinion polls, or communications from constituents who were prodded into action by the group. Clearly this information is designed and shaped to bolster the position of the group. Information to the contrary is frequently omitted.

Interest group activity in elections can take the form of direct contributions to specific candidates' campaigns; independent expenditures, which is money spent to support or oppose a candidate that is not funneled through the candidate's campaign organization; or communications with the interest group's members in a particular district that encourage support or opposition for a candidate.

In this chapter, we explore the role of interest groups in gun control policy. We identify the major groups on both sides of the issue and examine their

141

lobbying and electoral activities. We assess their impact in shaping gun control policy, and we evaluate the importance of the gun control issue in determining who wins and who loses elections.

PRO GUN CONTROL GROUPS

Brady Campaign to Prevent Gun Violence

The Brady Campaign traces its roots to the establishment of the National Council to Control Handguns (NCCH) in 1974.[2] The NCCH, originally a member of the National Council to Ban Handguns, was founded by Mark Borinsky, a victim of gun violence. He was joined by retired CIA agent Ed Welles and DuPont executive Pete Shields, whose son had been killed in a random shooting. Prior to this time, there was no significant *organized* gun control movement. An organization devoted to gun control was welcomed by many in Congress and by some staffers within the Department of Justice.[3] Borinksy and Shields were able to translate their personal tragedies into a public policy issue:

> In short, within the confines of a small but critically important group, there occurred a *collective attribution that a social problem existed* and a collective sense of what needed to be done to correct it. In the simplest possible terms, this framing of the problem—this collective attribution, this ideology that the gun control movement now promulgates—became "guns destroy, guns must be controlled."[4]

In 1980 the NCCH was renamed Handgun Control, Inc. A fissure within the organization resulted in a change of philosophy from banning to controlling handguns. The shift was a pragmatic choice, not a philosophical epiphany. It was clear that neither the public nor Congress supported an outright ban and that pursuit of such a policy would be fruitless and possibly detrimental to the organization.

HCI, under the leadership of Shields, expanded its membership, attracted national publicity, and became active in lobbying and in political campaigns. By 1981, membership was over one hundred thousand, and HCI had contributed $75,000 to congressional campaigns in the 1980 cycle.[5] Much of the increase in membership was due to the 1980 murder of John Lennon and the 1981 assassination attempt on President Ronald Reagan.[6] Both of these shooters used cheap handguns in their attacks, heightening awareness of the issue.

Building on increasing membership and political clout, the Center to Prevent Handgun Violence (CPHV), an outreach organization, was founded as a companion to HCI in 1983. Two years later, Sarah Brady, the wife of Jim

Brady, Reagan's press secretary who was wounded in the assassination attempt on Reagan, became active in gun control issues.

Brady's decision to the join the gun control debate and HCI brought another injection of publicity and membership to the movement and the organization. Brady was an eloquent spokesperson and put a recognizable face on HCI. Often appearing with her husband, who was confined to a wheelchair and whose speech was slurred as a result of the wounds he sustained, Brady raised the profile of the group and opened doors that had previously been closed. Her credentials, as the daughter of a Republican activist and an FBI agent, as well as her husband's, as the press secretary to the conservative Republican President Reagan, added significantly to the clout of HCI. In 1989 the CPHV established the Legal Action Project to become active in the courts.

Throughout the late 1980s and 1990s, the Brady Campaign correctly claimed some credit for the gun control measures that were passed in the Congress and in many states. It became the preeminent gun control advocate in the country, although its size and resources were (and still are) about one-tenth of those of its opponent, the National Rifle Association.[7] Working with President Clinton and an amenable Congress, the Brady Campaign lobbied tirelessly—and ultimately successfully—for congressional support of the Brady Bill, which was passed in 1993.

Despite the characterization of the Brady Bill as not signifying a major policy change and Clinton's support as more political than substantive, there is no doubt that the bill was passed due to the tenacity of Sarah Brady and the relatively modest goals of the legislation and HCI.[8] "By seeking incremental gun laws, HCI has erased a perception of political ineptitude and shaken its loser image."[9] More important, passage of the Brady Bill indicated that the NRA could be defeated.

Flush with that success, HCI went to work with congressional allies on what was dubbed Brady II. This comprehensive legislation would establish a national licensing requirement for handgun possession, require that all firearms be registered, increase the federal firearms license annual fee from $200 to $1,000, and require that ammunition dealers be licensed. Brady II has been described as "the gun control movement's *piece de resistance*."[10] It would have been systematic gun control comparable to that of most European nations, far beyond anything ever passed in the United States.

HCI may have overestimated its influence, however, and the NRA helped defeat many gun control supporters in the 1994 congressional elections. The Republicans gained a majority of the seats, and new House Majority Leader Newt Gingrich said that he would not move any gun control legislation.[11] Even without such a significant turnover in Congress, it is doubtful that HCI and its allies would have been able to shepherd Brady II through the legislative process. The bill was too far-reaching in its goals. With the tortuous path taken to the passage of the Brady Bill, it seems that Brady II was doomed from the start.

Yet HCI had not lost all of its power. Another testament to Sarah Brady's influence was her speech at the 1996 Democratic National Convention in which she asked that anyone convicted of misdemeanor domestic abuse be added to the list of those who are ineligible to purchase firearms. In September of that year Congress included an amendment to the FY 1997 Omnibus Consolidated Appropriations Act that prohibits gun ownership or possession by anyone convicted of domestic abuse.[12]

In June 2001, HCI was renamed the Brady Campaign to Prevent Gun Violence and the CPHV was renamed the Brady Center to Prevent Gun Violence, maintaining its legal action and educational mission. Later that year, the Brady Campaign merged with the Million Mom March. Although there have been no national legislative victories in recent years, the Brady Campaign remains the preeminent gun control organization, and it has won some battles at the state legislative level. In addition, it was instrumental in the filing of civil lawsuits against gun dealers and manufacturers.

The Brady Campaign solicits contributions on its website, but there are no membership dues. Visitors are invited to sign up for e-mail updates, and one can become a member of the Brady Leadership Council with an appropriate contribution. Council members get special updates and are invited to policy briefings, appearances, and the like.

Violence Policy Center

> The Violence Policy Center (VPC) is a national non-profit organization working to fight firearms violence through research, education, and advocacy. As a gun control think tank, the VPC analyzes a wide range of current firearm issues and provides information to policymakers, journalists, public health professionals, grassroots activists, and members of the general public.[13]

The VPC was founded in 1988 and engages primarily in research and advocacy. It produces up to twenty studies per year, and the organization is frequently used as a media resource on gun-related issues. While there is no membership dues structure, the VPC solicits contributions and encourages individuals to sign up for e-mail alerts. The organization publishes its research and actively distributes its press releases.

It has been suggested that the VPC feels that the Brady Campaign has been "accommodationist" in its agenda and its tactics. At the same time, Brady views the VPC as one of the more militant voices in the gun control movement.[14] Unlike the Brady Campaign, the VPC expressly advocates the prohibition of private handgun ownership in the United States.

The VPC is not mentioned frequently or in much detail in most works that discuss gun control groups, but it is quite effective in terms of getting media attention. While it does not stage events, it disseminates research, and its leadership is an important resource for journalists. The VPC is viewed as an authority in the field. It would not be inaccurate to say that a journalist searching for a quote about a specific piece of legislation will call the Brady Campaign, but a journalist looking for research on gun policies will call the Violence Policy Center.

Coalition to Stop Gun Violence

The Coalition to Stop Gun Violence (CSGV) emerged from the civil rights movement in the early 1970s and pushes a progressive agenda to reduce firearm death and injury. We were founded on the principle of collaboration, meaning that we work closely with other organizations to achieve our common goals.

Our organizational structure is unique among national gun violence prevention organizations. CSGV is comprised of 45 national organizations working to reduce gun violence. Our coalition members include religious organizations, child welfare advocates, public health professionals, and social justice organizations. This diversity of member organizations allows us to reach a wide variety of grassroots constituencies who share our vision of non-violence.[15]

The CSGV was founded in 1974 as the National Coalition to Ban Handguns, an organization created by the United Methodist General Board of Church and Society to unite various church groups in support of banning handguns. Today, its member organizations include the American Psychiatric Association, Americans for Democratic Action, the YWCA USA, and several churches. The group also claims one hundred thousand individual members. The coalition is the political wing of the group, and the education fund is educational in nature. They are involved in grassroots training; electoral activity, particularly get-out-the-vote efforts; and litigation support. Like the VPC, there are no official membership dues, but the CSGV accepts contributions.

While the coalition changed its name, its mission remains the same—the elimination of various types of firearms—from Saturday night specials to larger-caliber handguns and assault weapons. The CSGV spends more resources working with member organizations than lobbying. It also helps to disseminate the research of the VPC, whose goals it shares.

Despite the coalition's more extreme positions, its strategy of attacking the issue on multiple fronts, and its call for the elimination of private ownership of handguns, there is a fairly congenial relationship between the group and the Brady Campaign. The coalition has been described as the second most influential group in the gun control movement.[16]

Million Mom March

> In August 1999, Donna Dees-Thomases, a New Jersey mother, read with horror about a gunman who randomly shot at a group of children in Granada Hills, California. Seven days later, on August 17, Donna decided to apply for a permit to march on Washington to protest this country's lack of meaningful gun laws. After nine months of organizing, mobilizing, advertising, and energizing, the day finally came. On May 14, 2000, approximately 750,000 mothers and others gathered on the National Mall in Washington, D.C., to demand sensible gun laws. An additional 150,000 to 200,000 people marched in support events across the country. Following the event, the Million Mom March participants became a chapter-based organization to promote sensible gun laws in state legislatures. . . . On October 1, 2001, the Million Mom March merged with the Brady Campaign to Prevent Gun Violence.[17]

Although it no longer exists as a separate entity, the Million Mom March (MMM) is considered here because it received a great deal of publicity during its relatively brief independent existence. The similar agendas made the union with the Brady Campaign relatively easy. MMM called for handgun registration and licensing, but not for prohibition, gun safety measures, a waiting period, and a one-gun-per-month limit, nearly echoing the policy prescriptions of the Brady Campaign.

While the inaugural Million Mom March was very successful, later events were not. The group's membership grew dramatically after the initial march, and it opened almost 250 offices in forty-six states. The momentum quickly waned, however, and within a year the group had laid off thirty of thirty-five employees, closed offices, and had great difficulty mustering a fraction of the number of initial marchers for an anniversary event.[18]

MMM is perhaps the best example of the problems the gun control movement has in sustaining intensity over a period of time. Despite significant national publicity, support from organizations such as the League of Women Voters and the National Parent Teacher Association, the Million Mom March survived for only one year.

GUN RIGHTS GROUPS

National Rifle Association

The National Rifle Association is the largest and most influential gun rights organization, and it is one of the most effective interest groups in the country.

Boasting more than 4 million members, the group dwarfs other pro-gun rights groups, and it is exponentially larger than its primary opponent, the Brady Campaign.

There are several branches to the organization. The National Rifle Association is the trunk of the tree, while the NRA-Institute for Legislative Action (NRA-ILA) and the NRA-Political Victory Fund (NRA-PVF) are the largest branches.

The organization is involved in lobbying, all types of electoral work, and legal actions, and it has a vast network of grassroots outreach programs. Annual dues are $35, but the NRA offers discount programs, magazine subscriptions, financial services, insurance, and so on. The discount program covers a wide array of services and products including car rental and hotel discounts, a prescription drug card, and discounts from numerous merchants across the country. Of course, hunting and fishing companies also participate. The NRA offers a large number of programs for law enforcement officers and groups, hunters, sport shooters, women, and youth. They sponsor shooting competitions, educational and training programs, and local clubs. In short, the member benefits package comes close to rivaling that of the American Association of Retired Persons (AARP).[19]

Established in 1975, the Institute for Legislative Action (ILA) is the "lobbying" arm of the National Rifle Association of America. ILA is committed to preserving the right of all law-abiding individuals to purchase, possess and use firearms for legitimate purposes as guaranteed by the Second Amendment to the U.S. Constitution.

ILA's ability to fight successfully for the rights of America's law-abiding gun owners directly reflects the support of NRA's more than 4 million members—a number that has more than tripled since 1978. When restrictive "gun control" legislation is proposed at the local, state or federal level, NRA members and supporters are alerted and respond with individual letters, faxes, e-mails and calls to their elected representatives to make their views known.

Through the distribution of millions of printed fact sheets, brochures and articles annually and the posting of information and the latest news daily on its Internet site (www.nraila.org), the Institute provides facts about responsible firearms ownership, the Second Amendment and other topics.[20]

NRA-ILA has a staff of more than eighty people, and it lobbies at the national, state, and local levels. Like other interest groups, the NRA works primarily with its supporters and those who can be persuaded to vote with it. Political campaigns are the purview of the NRA-PVF.

The NRA-PVF ranks political candidates—irrespective of party affiliation—based on voting records, public statements and their responses to an NRA-PVF questionnaire. In 2002, NRA-PVF was involved in 271 campaigns for the U.S. House and Senate, winning in 253 of those races. These victories represent the election of pro-gun majorities in both the U.S. House and Senate.

NRA-PVF endorsed thousands of candidates running in state legislative races and achieved an 85% success rate in those elections.[21]

This is not to say that the NRA wins all of its battles—it does not. However, if we assume that the organization can count 253 "friends" in a legislative body of 345, then it is indeed relatively successful.

The NRA was founded in 1871 as a small shooting association. It soon began to strengthen its ties with the government, first by being commissioned to help train members of the New York National Guard. In 1903, Congress created the National Board for the Promotion of Rifle Practice to ensure the population was militia-ready. Several members of the NBPRP board were also on the NRA board and helped secure passage of Public Law 149, which authorized the sale of military surplus weapons through NRA-sponsored clubs. This helped to resuscitate the organization, which had been in decline. Soon Congress was giving away the surplus weapons and funding NRA shooting matches. As a result, NRA membership grew significantly.[22]

The NRA became active in national legislation during the 1930s. Its opposition to sections of the National Firearms Act of 1934 led to the deletion of national gun registration from the bill, and its success in shaping that legislation led to a more active role in developing the Federal Firearms Act of 1938. While the NRA accepted some regulation in both instances, it resisted more extensive regulation and weakened the enforcement mechanisms included in the bills.[23]

Its tactics then foreshadowed the strategies of today. It distributed editorials, and press releases, and communicated with shooters and gun owners, urging them to write or send telegrams to their congressional representatives. This strategy was successful, in part because the NRA was the only game in town—there was no organized opposition.

The NRA continued its involvement with shooting sports and hunting, and returning soldiers from World War II increased its membership. These new members had more interest in hunting than gun control, and that, combined with a Congress that was not pushing gun control legislation, led the NRA to devote more attention to that pursuit in the pages of its magazine the *American Rifleman*.[24] In 1958, the NRA's main entrance bore the slogan "Firearms Safety Education, Marksmanship Training, Shooting for Recreation."[25]

The 1960s brought a stronger push for gun control legislation in Congress, and the NRA responded in opposition. Still, resistance to the passage of the Gun Control Act of 1968 was tepid by today's standards. The NRA even endorsed banning Saturday night specials—at least for a period of time.

The 1970s saw a schism develop within the ranks of the NRA. The passage of the GCA exacerbated the differences in goals advocated by the two factions within the organization. One group was primarily interested in promoting shooting sports and the like, while another was becoming increasingly interested in opposing gun control legislation and protecting Second Amendment rights. The latter group gained both followers and intensity following the 1971 search for illegal firearms in which ATF agents shot a Maryland man after breaking down his door. No firearms were found, and the man, a NRA life member and *Washington Post* employee, was paralyzed.[26]

The *American Rifleman* published a series of articles and editorials discussing the dangers to gun owners from the GCA and criticizing the tactics employed by the ATF. Still, most of the NRA leadership and membership was moderate on the gun control issue: "Although the leadership did not favor gun control and was committed to opposing most gun-control proposals, it did not operate on an assumption that the Infidels were at the gates or that gun prohibition was imminent."[27] The planned move of NRA headquarters to Colorado Springs from Washington, D.C., and the construction of an outdoor recreational complex in New Mexico indicated a lack of interest in political affairs, and it spurred an organized coup.

The more political wing of the organization, although constituting perhaps only 25 percent of the membership, was very well organized. Several of the group's leaders had been fired by the moderate leadership in 1976, ostensibly due to budget cuts, but it is more likely that the firings were the result of statements and publications critical of the leadership and its lukewarm opposition to gun control. They organized the Federation for the NRA in response to the leadership's agenda of working with groups such as the Sierra Club and Greenpeace on various conservation and wilderness protection initiatives.[28]

The takeover was led by former executive committee member and Border Patrol director Harlon Carter and firearms publisher Neil Knox and was carried out at the 1977 convention. The group took control of the board of directors by having Carter elected to chief operating officer. Carter, in turn, appointed Knox as director of the ILA. The coup was relatively easily accomplished because only life members who were present at the convention could vote in the board elections, and supporters of the Federation for the NRA were the members most highly motivated to attend the convention. Of course, the ability of the coup leaders to rally and organize their followers was essential to the takeover.[29] The new NRA had been born.

The group then embarked on recruiting new members to enhance its clout on Capitol Hill. Membership incentives were created, and the NRA became very successful in self-promotion. Although some of the old guard left, many more new members were added to the rolls. Prior to the 1977 convention, there were just over 1 million members. By 1983, that number had grown to 2.6 million. It had increased to more than 3.5 million by the early 1990s, when it lost some members, but it has rebounded and now stands at more than 4 million.[30] The NRA has also benefited from its relationship with the gun manufacturing industry. While the NRA has at times done the political bidding of the gun industry, such as in its support for lawsuit immunity for gun manufacturers, it has also benefited from the relationship. It has gained advertising revenues from the industry, and it has likely gained members from inserts in product packaging.[31]

To be sure, there were some missteps in the 1990s with the "cop-killer bullets" and "plastic guns" issues that found the NRA in opposition to many law enforcement groups. There was also the infamous Wayne LaPierre reference to ATF agents as "jackbooted thugs," which cost the group members, most prominently George H. W. Bush, and some prestige as well.[32] Nonetheless, the NRA rebounded effectively from those setbacks, and LaPierre emerged as a strong and skillful leader.

With the eventual replacement of the Knox-Carter faction with the Wayne LaPierre–James Baker–Chris Cox–Charlton Heston group, the NRA maintained its strong anti-gun control positions, and it added a more polished image. Heston, a former actor, was instrumental in portraying a more positive and mainstream image for the group.

In the early 1990s, the NRA become more active in state politics when it became evident that the national-level pendulum might be swinging toward gun control advocates.[33] It focused successfully on right-to-carry laws and preemptive laws, which prevent local governments from passing gun control regulations. The NRA also began to focus more on alternative means of communication (Internet, e-mail, and now its own radio station) because it believed it was not being treated equally by the news media. Finally, the group began to push for laws protecting gun dealers and manufacturers against certain lawsuits. That effort began at the state level, but the groups focused more attention on Congress as it made electoral gains and its chances of success increased. With the passage of that legislation, the NRA reestablished itself as one of the most powerful interest groups in the country.

Gun Owners of America

Gun Owners of America (GOA) is a non-profit lobbying organization formed in 1975 to preserve and defend the Second Amendment rights of gun owners. GOA sees firearms ownership as a freedom issue.

From state legislatures and city councils to the United States Congress and the White House, GOA represents the views of gun owners whenever their rights are threatened.[34]

GOA is affiliated with Gun Owners of America Political Victory Fund, the political wing of the organization; Gun Owners of California, which operates only in that state; and Gun Owners Foundation, the research component of the group.

GOA members receive a newsletter, e-mail alerts, and a candidate rating guide. GOA also has a legal defense program, which is involved in gun-related legal issues. Annual membership dues are $20.

Dwarfed by the NRA, both in numbers and power, GOA's members are more militant than those who belong to the NRA. GOA serves to keep the NRA consistent in its approach. It will occasionally attempt to siphon members from the NRA by suggesting that the NRA is willing to compromise on gun control. For example, during the 2004 Senate debate over limiting liability for gun manufacturers, GOA suggested on its website that the NRA might be willing to accept amendments to the legislation that would renew the assault weapons ban or require background checks for all firearms sales at gun shows. The NRA was forced to immediately stake out a no-compromise position on the bill.

If the media paid more attention to GOA, then it could work to the advantage of the NRA by making the NRA appear to be more mainstream. The charges of NRA-backed extremism often leveled by gun control advocates might not ring as true with the public if GOA was providing an even more extreme and publicized position.

Citizens Committee for the Right to Keep and Bear Arms

With more than 650,000 members and supporters nationwide, the Citizens Committee for the Right to Keep and Bear Arms is one of the nation's premier gun rights organizations. As a non-profit organization, the Citizens Committee is dedicated to preserving firearms freedoms through active lobbying of elected officials and facilitating grass-roots organization of gun rights activists in local communities throughout the United States.[35]

Citizens Committee for the Right to Keep and Bear Arms (CCRKBA) is headquartered in Bellevue, Washington, and its website provides gun-related news, press releases, and links to related sites. It is affiliated with the Second

Amendment Foundation (SAF) inasmuch as CCRKBA chairman Alan Gottlieb was the founder of the SAF. While the CCRKBA is not prominently mentioned in the media, it lobbies extensively. It has a $15 membership fee. While the SAF focuses more specifically on awareness of Second Amendment issues, the CCRKBA is more concerned with specific gun control policies and legislation.

Second Amendment Foundation

> The Second Amendment Foundation (SAF) is dedicated to promoting a better understanding about our Constitutional heritage to privately own and possess firearms. To that end, we carry on many educational and legal action programs designed to better inform the public about the gun control debate.[36]

The SAF was formed in 1974 and is also headquartered in Bellevue, Washington. The organization has several publications, including the *New Gun Week* newspaper, *Women & Guns* and *Gun News Digest* magazines, and two newsletters. The SAF sponsors an annual conference, has a media outreach program, and is involved in legal actions. Its annual dues are $15.

The SAF is similar to GOA in that its views are less frequently sought by journalists, and hence it is less well known than the NRA. Obviously, its membership is much smaller, and its focus is more on the Second Amendment itself, although the group expends many resources on research and the dissemination of research on gun policy and the Constitution. The academic literature on gun control often fails to mention the SAF, the CCRKBA, or GOA, helping to add the relative anonymity of the groups.

THE STRUGGLE FOR POWER

The primary combatants in the struggle over gun control today are the NRA and the Brady Campaign. Each has strengths and weaknesses that it brings to the battle. The NRA has its membership, organization, and reputation. The Brady Campaign brings its political savvy, emotional appeals, and positive media relations.

Although it has been described as an "invincibility myth," the NRA does enjoy the status of being the big boy on the block in the shaping of gun policy.[37] First, the NRA has a membership in excess of 4 million. Regardless of how one looks at it, that translates into political power. Those members are not evenly distributed across the country, which works both in favor of and against the NRA. It gives the group more power in states where there are more members, less power in states with fewer members. The NRA is able to concentrate its lobbying efforts in those states, and, of course, on those national legislators who represent those states in which they have a strong presence. So while the group is unlikely to be a major political player in Massachusetts, it is influential in West Virginia.

The NRA-PVF communicates its candidate ratings and endorsements quite effectively. That information is published in the NRA's magazines, and communicated through e-mails and sometimes get-out-the-vote phone calls and postcards. Any NRA member who is paying even minimal attention to a campaign is very likely to be aware of which candidate is the choice of the NRA.

In addition, NRA members are strongly motivated to heed the call of the leadership. While we do not have direct evidence of this, it is generally assumed that the NRA has the ability to turn out voters in its strongholds. That perception, accurate or not, is sufficient to guide the voting behavior of elected officials in those areas. While many would argue that "money is the mother's milk of politics," those funds are used to attract voters. A group that can deliver voters possesses power because it can directly supply candidates with what they need. This is the modus operandi of the AARP, which neither makes campaign contributions nor endorses candidates. It simply tells its membership of more than 20 million where the candidates stand on issues of importance to senior citizens. Much empirical evidence indicates that older Americans are more likely to vote, and everyone "knows" that AARP helps to shape that vote. Similarly, while labor unions provide both money and organization for candidates, it is the loyalty of their members that has given them their power, although labor's solidarity and its power seem to be in decline. In the gun control arena, it is the NRA that has the advantage in terms of numbers and in terms of commitment.

The NRA also has a very strong lobbying organization at the national level and in many states. The NRA-ILA has a comparatively large staff (more than eighty persons), and it is far more sophisticated than a bunch of good ol' boys sitting around the truck and chewing the fat . . . or tobacco! They are professionals, with many having significant Capitol Hill experience, and in some cases, law degrees. For these reasons and more, the NRA's access to elected officials is famous.[38]

The Brady Campaign's primary strengths are its ability to appeal to emotion, the personal appeal of the Bradys, and its relationships with law enforcement, the medical community, educational groups, celebrities, and the media. It is much easier to appeal to the emotion of the average citizen when drawing attention to the societal costs of firearms. Accidental shootings (particularly if they involve children), school shootings, and homicides are all tragic events and stir much stronger emotions than a hunter or skeet shooter enjoying their sport. Defensive gun uses are less gut-wrenching than many of the homicides and accidental shootings, and they are rarely covered by the media.[39] Almost every shooting that involves a child is covered in the media, and there is no doubt about the sympathy that is evoked. All pro-gun control groups have learned to use those events to generate support for their cause and to open a policy window to push for more gun regulations.

They have also learned to use statistics to their advantage. For example, references to the number of children involved in shootings may include any-one under the age of twenty-one, which will include many of the victims and perpetrators of gang violence, a group most of us do not consider children in the traditional sense. This allows the Brady Campaign to expand the signifi-cance of the issue beyond those who are directly involved. It is difficult for the NRA to expand the issue beyond those who are gun owners or who already see the need to use a gun to protect themselves or their families. While the Constitution is a broadly revered document, Second Amendment appeals are clearly strongest for those who own firearms. In comparison, free-dom of speech and religion are generally viewed as almost universally appli-cable.

In addition, the background of Jim and Sarah Brady make them ideal rep-resentatives for the cause. Their Republican credentials and the courage they have displayed in the aftermath of Jim's shooting evoke admiration and com-passion. Any attack on their cause has to be carefully calculated so it does not appear to be a personal attack. Conversely, attacking the "gun lobby" is a pastime for gun control groups and legislators.

The Brady Campaign has cultivated strong alliances with organizations that are sympathetic to their goals. Through its 1995 Campaign to Protect Sane Gun Laws, Handgun Control, Inc. contacted 108 national organizations, including the AARP, the American Medical Association, the National Associ-ation for the Advancement of Colored People (NAACP), the United States Catholic Conference, and the Conference of Mayors, securing pledges to fight the gun lobby's effort to repeal "sensible gun laws."[40]

More recently the Brady Campaign has taken advantage of what it calls "the NRA blacklist."[41] This is a list of individuals, organizations, and compa-nies that have contributed resources in support of gun control. While the NRA has maintained the list for years, it has not publicized it heavily, even within its own ranks, nor has it called for a boycott of entities on the list, although it seems likely that the NRA would hope to have some economic impact on those companies and persons on the list. A boycott is a common, although often unsuccessful, interest group tactic. The Brady Campaign scrolls the names of persons, mostly celebrities, on the list on its website with a link to a separate site to solicit contributions "to ensure that their voices will not be silenced." It also ran full-page ads in the *New York Times* and other newspapers publicizing the list.[42]

Both the NRA and the Brady Campaign benefit from the presence of the other groups on their side who have more extreme agendas. While both of the giants have to maintain a degree of ideological purity, they appear moderate when compared with some of the other groups.

SPENDING ON THE ISSUES

Money is an important indicator of relative political strength, and there is little doubt that power follows money. Having said that, it is both common and far too easy to look only at money spent on lobbying activities and campaign contributions when measuring the relative importance of an interest group.[43]

Not surprisingly, the NRA spends far more than the Brady Campaign on lobbying activities. More interesting are the totals for Gun Owners of America and the Citizens Committee for the Right to Keep and Bear Arms. Lobbying amounts spent from 1998 through 2000 can be seen in table 5.1.

These figures alone do not indicate dominance by the gun rights lobby, but they suggest that the gun rights groups have more resources to put into the effort and that those resources are spread among several different groups. On the gun control side, the Coalition to Stop Gun Violence spent $80,000 on lobbying in each of those years. While the gun control groups did not spend more than $800,000 in any of these years, gun rights groups did not spend less than $4 million. A spending advantage of five to one is indeed significant. It bears repeating that spending alone does not guarantee results. It does, however, indicate that these groups have access to decision makers, and access is half of the battle.

Table 5.1. Lobbying Expenditures, 1998–2000

Year	1998	1999	2000
Brady Campaign	$80,000	$720,000	$340,000
NRA	$2,250,000	$1,600,000	$1,150,000
GOA	$1,150,000	$3,040,000	$4,150,000
CCRKBA	$698,393	$808,395	$1,020,759

Source: www.Opensecrets.org

THE GUN ISSUE AND ELECTIONS

It is nearly impossible to pinpoint a specific issue that determines the outcome of any particular election, but that does not stop pundits, talking heads, party officials, academics, and journalists from offering their opinions. Gun control is never thought to be *the most important* issue, except perhaps by the NRA or the Brady Campaign, but it has been a key issue in several elections.

In most elections the economy is the overarching issue. "It's the economy, stupid" was the mantra of the Clinton campaign in 1992, and it is usually good advice for anyone running for president, or many other offices, to focus on the state of the economy. At other times, the specific issue might be unemployment, inflation, the budget deficit, or even interest rates.

During peacetime, foreign policy is relatively unimportant, but that obviously changes during a war or international crisis. Other issues tend to be less important for most voters, but many issues are important, even critical, for a small number of voters. One such issue is abortion; another is gun control.

Conventional wisdom holds that the intensity of the gun control issue is greater for supporters of gun rights than it is for proponents of gun control; they are more likely to vote for or against a candidate based solely on their position on gun control. In one study, voters in nineteen of twenty-five states in which surveys were conducted were found to be more strongly committed to the NRA than to the Republican or Democratic parties. That core constituency was above 10 percent in only eight of those states, but 10 percent is a significant share of voters.[44]

Everyone would agree that the number of single-issue voters is small, but many more voters include gun control as one of a group of issues that they use to evaluate candidates. The number of voters in this category would probably not constitute a majority or even a sizeable plurality. We need to keep in mind, however, that many elections are close, and the difference between winning and losing is often just a few percentage points. In elections that are very close, one can point to any number of issues that could have been a determining factor. Post-election analyses often shine a light on one particular group, such as soccer moms, angry white men, or social conservatives, that might have tilted an election in the winner's direction. Gun rights advocates are not commonly placed in this category, but it would not be unreasonable to do so, at least in some elections.

Those elections in which the gun issue may have an impact can be either national or statewide. Gun control is less likely to be an issue in municipal elections, although that is certainly possible. Gun control can be thought of as a partisan issue, a regional issue, or a rural versus urban and suburban issue. At the national level, partisan differences have become more important as the Democratic Party has lost some support in the South and the West, the two regions that most strongly support gun rights.[45]

Still, it may be more accurate to classify the issue as regional or rural/urban because the partisan shifts have been caused by a series of issues, of which gun control is only one. More important, many Democratic legislators who represent states strongly supportive of gun rights tend to vote in favor of gun rights. At the same time, Republican legislators who represent states in favor of gun control tend to favor that position. One piece of research indicates that "party influence . . . *never* occurs on gun control" in congressional roll call voting.[46] The rural/urban split is much more easily understood, as it is a reflection of different cultures and differing crime rates. For many people who live and were raised in rural areas, guns are a part of their lives. They are used for hunting, recreation, and perhaps as a defense against certain wild animals. That is a very different perception of firearms than would be held by someone raised in an urban environment.

MONEY SPENT IN CAMPAIGNS

The NRA claims a very high rate of success in influencing elections. That success rate is, to some extent, inflated by the fact that the organization does not endorse a candidate in every contest. A nonendorsement could reflect a judgment that both candidates are acceptable, that neither is acceptable, or that the preferred candidate is not capable of winning. Taking all of that into account, the NRA's winning percentage is still high. As mentioned previously, the NRA enjoys a strong loyalty in its membership and a substantial advantage in financial resources.

The total money spent on electoral activities by the various gun-related interest groups is demonstrated in tables 5.2 through 5.5. In tables 5.2 and 5.3, we see the totals for the Brady Campaign and the National Rifle Association. The comparison here is stark. The NRA outpaces the Brady Campaign by a very large margin in terms of receipts, money spent, and independent

Table 5.2.   Brady Campaign PAC Campaign Spending

Year	1998	2000	2002	2004
Receipts	$90,755	$1,721,519	$241,626	$200,523
Spent	$178,430	$1,663,060	$255,640	$166,108
Independent expenditures	$5,301	$1,243,567	$90,678	

Source: www.Opensecrets.org

Table 5.3. National Rifle Association PAC Campaign Spending

Year	1998	2000	2002	2004
Receipts	$7,773,471	$17,884,202	$10,486,283	$12,605,089
Spent	$7,978,499	$16,821,436	$10,933,890	$12,695,683
Independent expenditures	$1,676,808	$6,464,283	$1,306,882	$1,381,415

Source: www.Opensecrets.org

expenditures. This advantage was consistent in the 2000 and 2004 presidential election years as well as the 1998 and 2002 midterm elections. As with lobbying, money alone does not bring victory, but the differences are so great in this instance that it would be foolish to argue there was no impact. The amount of money spent by the NRA, even if it was not spent wisely, would still have some effect. And we have no indication that the NRA is not wise in its investments.

Considering only campaign contributions and including other groups in the analysis does not change the results. Tables 5.4 and 5.5 show the trends from 1990 to 2004 for gun control organizations and gun rights organizations. Again, the latter have a sizeable advantage in terms of contributions. We can also see the partisan split in that more than 90 percent of contributions made since 1994 by gun control groups have gone to Democrats. Gun rights groups are only slightly less partisan in their preference for Republican candidates. Both were more bipartisan, but not close to fifty-fifty, prior to 1994.

What is the payoff for the money spent in campaigns? That depends upon whom you ask. The interest groups claim success, but never enough success to eliminate the threat, whatever the threat may be. They are also reluctant to admit they did not fare well. Of course, much of that rhetoric is aimed at keeping their supporters in a state of sufficient anxiety so that monetary contributions continue to roll in.

We have already examined in some detail the NRA's success rate in congressional elections. The NRA also suggests that it was instrumental in the 2000 and 2004 Bush victories, but it does not invite blame for Clinton's victories in 1992 and 1996. In either case, it is very difficult to say who should receive credit or blame, but there is a logical argument that the NRA did help Bush win in 2000 and perhaps again in 2004.

The 1998 congressional elections saw the Republicans lose seats in Congress, although that had little impact on gun control. That same year brought victory to gun control advocates in California, which resulted in policy changes.[47] In the 1970s and 1980s, when the NRA was even more dominant at the national level, its record in congressional elections has been described

Table 5.4. Gun Control Organization Contribution Trends

Election Cycle	Total Contributions	Contributions from Individuals	Contributions from PACs	Soft Money Contributions	Donations to Democrats	Donations to Republicans	% to Dems.	% to Repubs.
2004	$62,700	$6,050	$56,650	N/A	$62,200	$500	99%	1%
2002	$136,256	$17,900	$118,356	$0	$137,125	($869)	100%	0%
2000	$503,799	$99,985	$403,814	$0	$489,299	$14,500	97%	3%
1998	$166,296	$11,550	$154,746	$0	$156,796	$9,500	94%	6%
1996	$231,274	$15,540	$214,984	$750	$217,454	$13,820	94%	6%
1994	$226,191	$6,000	$220,191	$0	$211,941	$14,250	94%	6%
1992	$174,012	$12,400	$160,612	$1,000	$148,862	$25,150	86%	14%
1990	$158,168	$750	$157,418	N/A	$136,268	$22,400	86%	14%
Total	$1,658,696	$170,175	$1,486,771	$1,750	$1,559,945	$99,251	94%	6%

Source: www.Opensecrets.org

Table 5.5. Gun Rights Organization Contribution Trends

Election Cycle	Total Contributions	Contributions from Individuals	Contributions from PACs	Soft Money Contributions	Donations to Democrats	Donations to Republicans	% to Dems.	% to Repubs.
2004	$879,620	$37,494	$842,126	N/A	$112,750	$766,870	13%	87%
2002	$2,790,045	$263,040	$1,462,282	$1,064,723	$174,250	$2,613,49	76%	94%
2000	$4,086,245	$508,947	$1,752,776	$1,824,522	$284,200	$3,802,045	7%	93%
1998	$2,505,000	$317,628	$1,837,372	$350,000	$320,115	$2,194,903	13%	88%
1996	$1,949,277	$129,596	$1,731,956	$87,725	$294,690	$1,676,837	15%	86%
1994	$2,387,499	$77,242	$2,006,757	$303,500	$457,288	$1,965,047	19%	82%
1992	$1,871,226	$52,375	$1,818,851	$0	$670,292	$1,222,284	36%	65%
1990	$909,887	$20,700	$889,187	N/A	$314,752	$607,335	35%	67%
Total	$17,378,799	$1,407,022	$12,341,307	$3,630,470	$2,628,337	$14,848,818	15%	85%

Source: www.Opensecrets.org

as "spotty" and its role in at least some of its "victories" has been questioned.[48] Having considered all of that, few elected officials in districts with significant numbers of NRA members would choose to run afoul of the NRA and test its electoral clout.

Often more valuable than money is the NRA's grassroots communications. The NRA's members are motivated voters and often respond to the appeals from the leadership. We have only recently become more aware of how important these communications can be for interest groups and how extensive they are.

Beyond the campaign contributions and independent expenditures, interest groups expend many resources in issue advocacy and membership contacts. Issue advocacy was done through ads that largely circumvented the old campaign finance laws by avoiding the use of the so-called magic words such as "vote for," "vote against," "elect," or "defeat," but they clearly advocated casting a ballot for or against a particular candidate. These ads were largely eliminated by the McCain–Feingold reform legislation. In addition, interest groups contact their members, and select nonmembers they believe will be sympathetic to their message, through direct-mail appeals, telephone calls, and personal contacts. While the exact amount of money groups spend on these activities is difficult to determine, we have begun to see that these efforts are very extensive. The NRA is one of the groups heavily involved in this type of campaign activity.[49]

Two Tennessee contests for the U.S. Senate in 1994 demonstrate how the NRA can be effective even when its financial impact is minimal.[50] The NRA is credited with contributing to the victories by Republicans Fred Thompson and current Senate Majority Leader Bill Frist. Each candidate won a seat that had been held by a Democrat. In Thompson's case it was an open seat, while Frist defeated incumbent Jim Sasser. Both races were expensive ($12 million in the Frist–Sasser race, and just under $8 million in the Thompson–Jim Cooper contest), and the victories were decisive (Frist won 56 percent and Thompson 60 percent of the votes cast). NRA contributions accounted for less than 0.5 percent of PAC contributions and less than 0.2 percent of total spending. The independent expenditures were helpful in defining the candidates' positions on gun control, "but the grassroots support from NRA members across the state proved to be the most decisive element in the NRA strategy. . . . The NRA grassroots efforts on Election Day delivered voters to the polls."[51]

Similarly, in 2004 the NRA played a role in the defeat of Senator Tom Daschle in South Dakota. Daschle ran into trouble with the NRA due to his position as minority leader and the tightrope he tried to walk in 2004 regarding the gun manufacturers immunity legislation and amendments attached to it. He was targeted by the NRA, and he lost a close election. The defeat of such a high-ranking party official who is not tainted with scandal is relatively uncommon. It is reasonable to think that the NRA had a hand in the defeat of Daschle.

There are much less reliable data on statewide elections, although we explore one case study in chapter 7, which examines Virginia in depth. Even the NRA does not keep score at this level, except for governor's races, but it is clear that the group is involved with many campaigns for statewide office and even some for the state legislature.[52] A logical assumption would be that the NRA is more successful in districts in which membership is high.

ELECTION 2000

Gun control was thought to be an important issue in the 2000 presidential campaign because of the closeness of the outcome in states such as West Virginia, Tennessee, and Arkansas, which were carried by George W. Bush. West Virginia is a traditionally Democratic state, and certainly Al Gore could have reasonably been expected to carry his home state of Tennessee and Clinton's home state of Arkansas.

Although gun control was not prominently featured during the campaign, the candidates had different positions. During Bush's tenure as Texas governor he signed a permissive concealed-carry law and supported tougher penalties on criminals who use firearms as well as lawsuit immunity for gun manufacturers—positions in line with the NRA.

Gore's positions were clearly anathema to the NRA and other gun rights groups. Earlier in his political career, Gore had been more congenial toward gun rights, but his position shifted as he became a more national figure in the Democratic Party.[53] He became supportive of many of Clinton's gun control initiatives, and during the 2000 presidential campaign he proposed a licensing system for those who wanted to purchase a firearm, requiring background checks of all firearm sales at gun shows, banning Saturday night specials, and limiting handgun sales to one per month. In short, Gore was no friend of the NRA.

The candidates' differences were made very clear during the October 11, 2000, presidential debate.[54] Gore made no secret of his support for more gun control legislation even as he tried to reassure gun owners:

> I will not do anything to affect the rights of hunters or sportsmen. I think that home-owners have to be respected in their right to have a gun if they wish to. . . . I think these assault weapons are a problem. So I favor closing the gun-show loophole. . . .

I think we ought to restore the three-day waiting period under the Brady Law . . .
child trigger locks on a mandatory basis and others. . . . I am for licensing by states
of new handgun purchases . . . a photo license I.D. like a driver's license for new
handguns.

For his part, Bush supported stronger enforcement of existing gun laws,
stiffer penalties for criminals, background checks at gun shows, voluntary
distribution of trigger locks, and working to change the broader culture that
may foster violence.

In the immediate aftermath of the 2000 election, so much attention was
focused on Florida that little space and time was devoted to gun control or
other issues that may have influenced the outcome. The result in Florida,
however, would have been moot had Gore carried West Virginia, Tennessee,
or Arkansas. The NRA is strong in all three of those states, and it made a
strong push for support for Bush in all three, including sending Charlton Heston on tour. In an odd twist, it was noted after Bush's inauguration that he
"ran poorly in states that favor gun control."[55] It could just as easily have
been said that Gore did not do well in states that are opposed to gun control.
The NRA was happy to take credit for Gore's defeat, and by 2004, many
analysts had picked up on the importance of the gun issue.

One analysis of the 2000 election found that Gore got the support of about
two-thirds of the voters who thought it should be much more difficult to purchase guns, a slight majority of those who thought it should be harder, and
less than one-third of the rest.[56]

THE AFTERMATH OF THE 2000 ELECTION

The issue was raised in some congressional races in 2002, and the media were
beginning to note that the Democrats were losing votes over gun control.[57]
Pro-gun rights representative John Dingell held off a primary challenge from
an opponent who was supported by Sarah Brady and other gun control advocates.[58]

By 2004, Doug Hattaway, Gore's 2000 campaign spokesman, was relating
a story about overhearing fellow travelers in a plane over Tennessee discussing how Gore would take their guns away. He realized then that the issue was
beginning to hurt Democrats among voters who were gun owners, but not
necessarily staunch NRA supporters.[59]

Hattaway, later a consultant to Americans for Gun Safety, a pro-control
group, urged the Democrats to approach the issue with "a moderate rights
and responsibilities" message "rather than throwing away elections on policies that are going nowhere."[60] The point was not that Democrats should

ignore the issue or run on a gun rights platform. Rather, they should learn from the mistakes of the Gore campaign and not advocate policies that would not be adopted by Congress.

Senator Jon Corzine said that Democrats should support the assault weapons ban and background checks, both of which are supported by a majority of the public, but oppose handgun registration, which is not as popular.[61] That was largely the strategy of John Kerry, but it was not successful. It was probably an overstatement, but one newspaper opined that "aside from same-sex 'marriage,' there is at least one other cultural issue no Democrat running against President Bush wants to touch: gun control."[62]

Several of the Democratic presidential hopefuls in 2004 took this advice perhaps a step further. The issue was raised in the first candidate debate on May 2, 2003, in Columbia, South Carolina. Moderator George Stephanopoulos asked Senator Joe Lieberman, Gore's vice-presidential running mate in 2000, if he still supported Gore's handgun owner licensing plan. "I have never supported such a proposal," Lieberman replied. "The American citizens have a right to own firearms. . . . The laws ought to concentrate . . . on stopping criminals and children and others who shouldn't have guns from getting them." When other candidates were asked if they supported gun-owner licensing, only the Reverend Al Sharpton said he did.[63]

Still, Lieberman supported "common sense gun control" measures like background checks, mandatory trigger locks on new handguns, the assault weapons ban, and closing the gun show loophole. He claimed an 86 percent lifetime rating from the Brady Campaign.[64]

Former Vermont governor Howard Dean was more circumspect. He supported the assault weapons ban and instant background checks on all retail and gun show sales. Anything else would be left up to individual states:

> If you say "gun control" in Vermont or Wyoming, people think it means taking away their hunting rifle. If you say "gun control" in New York City or Los Angeles, people are relieved at the prospect of having Uzis or illegal handguns taken off the streets. They're both right. That's why I think Vermont ought to be able to have a different set of laws than California.[65]

In response to another question about gun control, Dean responded, "[I]n Vermont gun control laws would have no effect whatsoever. They certainly don't seem to have much effect in New York, although my position is New Yorkers can have as much [gun control] as they want."[66] Still, Dean, easily the most pro-rights Democratic candidate, understandably downplayed his position during the primary season.[67]

General Wesley Clark was endorsed by filmmaker and political activist Michael Moore, director of *Bowling for Columbine* and *Fahrenheit 911*, who said Clark was "not afraid, as many Democrats are, of the NRA," and that he supported, among other measures, a federal ballistic-fingerprinting database.[68]

ELECTION 2004

Given the importance of terrorism and the war in Iraq, gun control was not a crucial issue in the presidential election of 2004, but it was not unimportant either. Many pundits and the National Election Pool exit poll suggested that "moral values" was the most important issue for a significant number of voters.[69]

While the meaning of moral values was not entirely clear, it seemed that most analysts felt that it meant religion, abortion, and gay marriage. It could also refer to a host of other issues that go beyond religion, including gun control. It is reasonable to assume that if you believe that one candidate is closer to your "values," then he may share your views on specific issues as well. At the very least, that belief will make you more comfortable with that candidate.[70] As Bush campaign manager Ken Mehlman said when describing how the Republicans had targeted specific voters, "If you drive a Lincoln or a BMW and you own a gun, you're voting for George Bush."[71] Republican research after the 2000 campaign allowed them to target very specific audiences with unique appeals by segmenting the electorate, especially Republican supporters, into numerous demographic categories. For example, they found that Republicans were much more likely than Democrats to drive a Porsche, watch auto racing, water-ski, and hunt.[72]

Many Democrats and their supporters in their election postmortems agreed with Mehlman's assessment. There was a significant outcry that the Democrats had lost touch with average America on a range of cultural issues that extended beyond gay marriage and abortion. Reacting to a suggestion that the party needed to reestablish its liberal roots, Virginia's Democratic governor, Mark Warner, said, "That's not a recipe for winning. That's a recipe for disaster."[73] Harold M. Ickes, a former Clinton adviser who headed the 527 group MoveOn.org, suggested, "I think we [Democrats] ignored in large measure the three big cultural issues of this election: guns, abortion and gay rights. . . . These are very, very big issues. They really, really motivate people."[74]

Democratic National Committee chairman Terry McAuliffe said that Kerry's support of gun control had hurt the Democratic Party's appeal in union households.[75] Wellington E. Webb, former Denver mayor and a candidate to succeed McAuliffe as chairman, spoke of how the Republicans had tactically defeated the Democrats in states like West Virginia: "In West Virginia, the issues are the three g's: God, guns and gays."[76]

This theme was referenced even earlier in the news media. The *Washington Post* included guns, God, and gays as part of the moral-values group of issues.[77] A *New York Times* columnist suggested that the Democratic Party was in danger of being defined by "bicoastal, tree-hugging, gun-banning, French-speaking, Bordeaux-sipping, *Times*-toting liberals" who motivate the party's base but turn off swing voters.[78] One of his four recommendations to the party was to "accept that today, gun control is a nonstarter. Instead of trying to curb guns, try to reduce gun deaths through better rules on licensing and storage, and on safety devices like trigger locks." A *Washington Post* columnist wrote that the Democrats might fare better if they nominated a more moderate candidate such as Virginia Governor Warner in 2008.[79]

National Review Online columnist Dave Kopel, a well-known gun rights supporter, wrote that "the Second Amendment triumphed on Election Day."[80] According to his scorecard, the pro-rights position picked up three seats in the Senate; lost one in the House of Representatives, where it maintained a solid majority; and broke even in governors' races. Of course, the reelection of Bush was counted as a victory as well.

During the campaign, gun control was seen as a potentially important issue in states like West Virginia.[81] Democrats were keenly aware that the state's five electoral votes could be crucial and that the NRA would be active in the state.[82] The assault weapons ban expired during the campaign, and Democratic presidential candidate John Kerry briefly attempted to spotlight the issue, but, with the exception of the Brady Campaign, there was virtually no mention of the ban by Kerry or his supporters for the remainder of the campaign.[83] At the same time, Kerry said he would release a Sportsmen's Bill of Rights that included the right to bear arms, but it also was apparently absent for the remainder of the campaign. Kerry did outline his positions on gun control and crime on his website.[84]

Gun control was mentioned once and only briefly in the third of the series of presidential debates. The question focused on the assault weapons ban. Bush defended his "tepid" support for extending the ban, but he said that enforcement of existing laws was the best way to stop gun violence. Kerry referred to the expiration of the ban as "a failure of presidential leadership."[85]

CBS Evening News included hunting and fishing as part of its "What Does It Mean to You?" series of reports on issues in the 2004 campaign.[86] The report focused more on environmental issues than gun control, and correspondent Bob McNamara suggested that Kerry might make inroads into what he described as the "hook and bullet" crowd that usually votes Republican because of gun control. "But this time around, there are signs that the . . .

bloc is not as one-dimensional as it used to be. In fact, a recent poll of licensed fisherman and hunters says they're worried the Bush administration is risking the nation's water and air to suit oil and gas interests." He then discussed policy on wetlands, the Clean Water Act, forests, and endangered species, issues on which Kerry's positions were portrayed as more environmentally friendly than the president's.[87]

Each of the candidates for president was interviewed by *Field & Stream* magazine.[88] One reporter described it as the "the key interview of this year's presidential campaign."[89] Most of Bush's interview focused on fishing and conservation, but he did reiterate his support for extending the assault weapons ban, and he said that instant background checks "ought to be extended to all places guns are sold." With regard to further gun control laws, his response was "they (gun owners) should not be concerned as long as I'm the president." While Bush said he had done some hunting, it was clear that his passion was for fishing.

Kerry emphasized that he fishes and hunts and that he favors conservation of land and water. It seems that he hunted more than Bush (at least he had more stories to tell). He defended his "F" rating from the NRA, calling its rating system "silly." He voted for "reasonable" measures and said he would protect the right of the people to bear arms. He claimed that the laws he supported would not take away anyone's guns. Kerry also spent a great deal of time touting his support of various conservation measures.

Both presidential candidates were also interviewed in *Outdoor Life* magazine.[90] Like the *Field & Stream* interview, many of the questions focused on conservation and land use questions. The candidates generally agreed on extending the assault weapons ban and expressed a belief in an individual Second Amendment right to bear arms. They clearly disagreed on holding gun manufacturers responsible for criminal misuse of their firearms.

The response that created some controversy was to the question of the candidates' favorite gun. For Bush it was a shotgun. Kerry's response was that his favorite gun was a M-16 that saved his life and the lives of his crew during the Vietnam War. He said he did not own one at present, but that he did have a Chinese assault rifle.

That comment was deemed newsworthy by the *New York Times*, which raised the question of the gun's legality.[91] The following day the Kerry campaign said that Kerry did not own an assault rifle, and that an aide who filled out the questionnaire had made a mistake. Kerry did reportedly own a double-barreled twelve-gauge shotgun and a "single-bolt-action military rifle" that was "a relic" and had never been fired. Kerry had received the rifle from a friend, and it had no manufacturing markings.[92]

During the general election, Kerry made several attempts to court the vote of hunters. Early in the fall campaign, Kerry referred to his hunting and fishing hobbies in the swing states of Pennsylvania and Ohio, which contain many hunters.[93] Later, he reiterated his commitment to the sport of hunting in the magazine interviews, and Kerry went on a goose hunt and photo op in the battleground state of Ohio.[94] A Kerry aide said it was more important that voters "get a better sense of John Kerry, the guy" than that he shot a goose. Kerry's hunt also led to a NRA ad that spoofed the outing.[95] The photograph chosen to be included with the ad, not surprisingly, was reminiscent of the famous Michael Dukakis in a tank photograph from the 1988 presidential campaign. Kerry's facial expression in the NRA ad rivaled the silliness of the look of Dukakis in the tank.[96] Kerry's hunting trip was also treated with disdain by one *New York Times* columnist.[97]

The interest groups were also active in the campaign, although they were not as visible as in 2000. Their ads were mostly limited to the battleground states, but their websites were full of activity. The NRA began communicating its preferences to its members at an early date.[98] The October issue of *America's 1st Freedom*, the NRA's more political magazine, shouted: "John Kerry Will Take Your Guns!" The November issue included an interview with Bush, an article entitled "John Kerry's Newest Scheme to Ban Your Guns," and photos of each candidate—Bush in a field wearing a hunting vest and Kerry clasping hands with Senator Edward Kennedy.[99] The groundwork for this was laid earlier when the battle over the assault weapons ban heated up and Kerry and his running mate, John Edwards, both headed back to Washington to cast votes to extend the ban.

Even before then, the organization's website had posted sixteen footnoted "facts" indicating that Kerry was "the most anti-gun presidential nominee in history!"[100] The NRA unveiled its "That Dog Don't Hunt" ad, both as a thirty-second television advertisement and as a print ad. The print ad featured a photo of a nicely groomed poodle sporting a sweater emblazoned with "Kerry" and a waving American flag. The text cited Kerry's votes in favor of various gun control measures.

It was expected that the NRA would take on the "radical left" of Hollywood, CBS, George Soros, and the 527 groups such as MoveOn.org. "This untold story of leftwing zealots' (like Michael Moore) stealth plans to undermine a presidential election should inspire all NRA members to vote—and to make sure every like-minded friend and family member also cast their ballot."[101] On October 13, the NRA took the expected step of officially endorsing Bush.[102]

The Brady Campaign was also active in the presidential campaign. Like the NRA, most of its activity involved communication with members and those who visited its website. On October 1, 2004, the Brady Campaign and

Million Mom March officially endorsed Kerry.[103] Most of the press release focused on the actions of the Bush administration in adopting an individual-right view of the Second Amendment, its support for the destruction of background check documents, its failure to renew the assault weapons ban, its support for immunity for gun manufacturers, and for "time and time again . . . cav[ing] in to the gun lobby . . . and choos[ing] the extreme ideological positions of the National Rifle Association over the need to protect American citizens from gun violence every single time." The release suggested that "Mr. Bush should seek to be the President of the National Rifle Association. He has earned that job."

One paragraph argued that "Senator Kerry has consistently supported sensible gun laws . . . to reduce gun violence. . . . As a hunter and a war hero, Senator Kerry knows that sportsmen do not need military-style assault weapons, and that measures to keep guns away from criminals, terrorists and children are just common sense."

Likewise, the Brady Campaign's response to the NRA's endorsement of Bush was expected: "President George W. Bush earned the National Rifle Association's endorsement, which he received today, by selling out America's police."[104] The reference was to the expiration of the assault weapons ban, although the release also mentioned the requirement that background check records be destroyed after the check was completed. The release also announced a Brady Campaign TV ad attacking Bush for "turning his back on the victims of violent crime, on police officers gunned down on our streets, on the fight against terrorists."

The Brady Campaign commissioned the national public opinion polling firm Penn, Schoen & Berland Associates, Inc. to conduct a survey on the importance of the assault weapons ban as an issue in the campaign.[105] The firm interviewed five hundred likely voters in each of three battleground states—Florida, Ohio, and Pennsylvania. The report concluded that support for Bush declined in each state when respondents were told the candidates' positions on the assault weapons ban. The results of this survey are, at best, questionable given the nature of the question posed.[106]

Both the NRA and Brady Campaign reacted to the election outcome as would be expected. The Brady Campaign's initial response was to note that Bush had "avoided being identified with the views of NRA partisans" and referred to his debate response that he favored extending the assault weapons ban and his belief in background checks at gun shows.[107] Brady Campaign president Michael Barnes called on Bush to keep those promises. A later press release argued that the "gun lobby [is] losing clout in key states," pointing to Kerry's victories in Maine, New Hampshire, Minnesota, Wisconsin, Michigan, and Pennsylvania, "six states supposedly among the leaders in NRA membership."[108] It also noted the election of pro-gun control Ken Salazar in the Colorado Senate race. When you tout *one* Senate victory and the states your presidential candidate carried *while losing the election*, it could be said that you are making lemonade from your lemons.

For its part, the NRA claimed a 95 percent success rate among endorsed congressional candidates, improving upon 89 percent in 2002 and 85 percent in 2000.[109] NRA-backed candidates won in 241 of 251 races in the House of Representatives and 14 of 18 in the U.S. Senate. NRA executive vice president Wayne LaPierre called on "national Democratic leaders [to] stop taking this party off the cliff and look at the heartland and the wreckage this issue has caused. They have to start putting up candidates who support gun rights and have a voting record to match their photo-ops."

The Brady Campaign viewed the NRA endorsements through a different prism, noting that the NRA's victory in half the Senate races could be attributed to the fact that the organization did not endorse anyone in thirteen races because both either both candidates were pro-control or the NRA candidate was "sure to lose."[110] The high percentage in the House was achieved through endorsing incumbents and, again, not endorsing when their candidate was weaker.

Overall, the NRA mailed out 6.5 million endorsement postcards and letters and 4.6 endorsement "bags" in 107 newspapers in twelve states; distributed 4 million "That Dog Don't Hunt" fliers; made 2.4 million phone calls; handed out 1.6 million bumper stickers; ran 28,000 television ads, 20,000 radio ads, and 1,700 newspaper ads; and posted 510 billboards in eleven states, at a cost of about $20 million.[111] The January 2005 issue of *America's 1st Freedom* shouted: "Freedom Finishes First!"[112] If the proof is in the pudding, then the passage of the Protection of Lawful Commerce in Arms Act in 2005 signals that it was the NRA that was the victor in the election.

While the election may not have been a landslide for the gun rights side, it clearly tilted in their favor. They picked up a few seats in the Senate, where they most needed them. More important, if the Democrats decide that gun control is one of the issues on which they can compromise to try to win back some of the swing states and Southern states they have lost recently, then the political landscape on the issue may be changed significantly for some time to come. While it is unlikely that most Democrats would back too far off their support of gun control, they may implicitly agree not to push for any gun control legislation, and they may ratchet down their opposition to some gun rights bills. The selection of former Vermont governor Howard Dean as party chairman was a signal that the party might downplay the gun control issue. Its opposition to the manufacturers' liability bill in 2005 was also somewhat muted.

CONCLUSION

There are several interest groups involved in the gun control issue, although the two major adversaries are the National Rifle Association and the Brady Campaign to Prevent Gun Violence. The NRA has a long history. The organization has been involved with gun control legislation since the 1930s, but it was transformed to become the preeminent supporter of gun rights in the 1970s. The group was taken over by a faction that felt it had been too accommodationist with regard to gun control. The "new" NRA was more clearly and more narrowly focused on protecting Second Amendment rights. The group has grown significantly since then, in terms of both membership and political influence. A couple of tactical missteps in the 1980s cost the group some support, but it recovered nicely and reemerged even stronger. With more than 4 million members and millions of campaign dollars, the NRA is a serious political force.

The Brady Campaign traces its roots to 1974, and it has undergone both superficial and, to some extent, substantive changes. Its transformation, in contrast to that of the NRA, was to morph into a more mainstream organization, and it abandoned its overt calls for banning firearms to lobby for less strong restrictions on both guns and gun owners. The Brady Campaign began to emerge as a true counterforce to the NRA in the 1980s, and it experienced several legislative victories during that time. Most significant, of course, was the adoption of the Brady Bill.

Other groups on both sides of the issue have smaller memberships, but are important nonetheless. They tend to be more radical in their views and their rhetoric, smaller in membership, and largely invisible to the media. They are overshadowed by the larger groups, but several of the pro-gun rights groups, like Gun Owners of American and Citizens Committee for the Right to Keep and Bear Arms, are well financed and are active in political campaigns.

The NRA and the gun rights lobby as a whole are much larger and better financed than the groups that support gun control. This is true if we look at memberships, the amount of money spent on lobbying activities, or involvement in elections. Once again, the NRA is the leader in all three categories. With more than 4 million members and tens of millions of dollars spent in national elections, the NRA is still the most powerful gun-related interest group. The Brady Campaign only recently emerged as a challenger to the NRA's position, after decades in which the NRA was largely unopposed. The Brady Campaign has won some legislative victories and used its political savvy to establish good media relations, and maintains relationships with organizations in the medical and educational fields. The NRA has focused more on motivating its supporters to vote and contact elected officials. All of these activities influence the decisions officials make after they win election.

Elections themselves can be affected by the gun control issue and the groups that promote their ideas. Although it is a relatively small number of voters for whom gun control is a critical issue or the most important issue in the voting decision, those voters can make the difference in close elections. Those voters tend to be opposed to gun control. There is no doubt that the gun control issue is an important one that captures the attention of candidates for public office, from local municipal elections to presidential elections. Whether the issue is treated individually or included within a set of cultural issues, gun control is important to a group of voters who are capable of swinging an election.

Gun control influenced the 2000 presidential election by shifting states such as West Virginia, Tennessee, and Arkansas in favor of Bush. Although overshadowed by the continuing debate regarding the vote in Florida, these states were critical in that had Gore carried any of the three, his loss in Florida would have been irrelevant and he would have been elected president. The electoral impact of gun control in 2004 may not have been as important, but many Democratic consultants now suggest that the party should moderate its positions on many social issues, including gun control. Evidence of the importance of the issue in congressional and statewide elections is clear, if not pervasive. Overall, while not the most important issue in any single election, gun control is an issue that is important in many races.

NOTES

1. Anthony J. Nownes, *Pressure and Power: Organized Interests in American Politics* (Boston: Houghton Mifflin, 2001).

2. The organizational history may be found at www.bradycampaign.org/press/?page = history.

3. Gregg Lee Carter, *The Gun Control Movement* (New York: Twayne, 1997), 74.

4. Carter, *Gun Control Movement*, 75.

5. Robert J. Spitzer, *The Politics of Gun Control*, 3rd ed. (Washington, D.C.: CQ Press, 2004), 95.

6. Carter, *Gun Control Movement*, 83; Diana Lambert, "Trying to Stop the Craziness of This Business," in *The Changing Politics of Gun Control*, ed. John M. Bruce and Clyde Wilcox (Lanham, MD: Rowman & Littlefield, 1998), 184.

7. Spitzer, *Politics of Gun Control*, 95.

8. William J. Vizzard, *Shots in the Dark: The Policy, Politics, and Symbolism of Gun Control* (Lanham, MD: Rowman & Littlefield, 2000), 135–36. The Brady Bill is discussed in more detail in chapter 3 of this book. It is true that the bill was modified significantly from what was originally introduced and that the waiting period provision was rendered impotent by the introduction of the instant background check.

9. Lambert, "Stop the Craziness," 184.

10. Carter, *Gun Control Movement*, 84.

11. Carter, *Gun Control Movement*, 85–86.

12. Lambert, "Stop the Craziness," 184.

13. Violence Policy Center, at www.vpc.org/.

14. Vizzard, *Shots in the Dark*, 66.

15. Coalition to Stop Gun Violence, at www.csgv.org/who_we_are/.

16. Vizzard, *Shots in the Dark*, 66.

17. Million Mom March, at www.millionmommarch.org/about/.

18. Spitzer, *Politics of Gun Control*, 97.

19. A relatively concise description of NRA activities that help make the group a powerful force in politics can be found in Ronald G. Shaiko and Marc A. Wallace, "Going Hunting Where the Ducks Are: The National Rifle Association and the Grass Roots," in *The Changing Politics of Gun Control*, ed. John M. Bruce and Clyde Wilcox.

20. National Rifle Association, Institute for Legislative Action, at www.nraila.org/About/NRAILA.aspx.

21. National Rifle Association, Political Victory Fund, at www.nrapvf.org/About/Default.aspx.

22. Carter, *Gun Control Movement*, 66.

23. Carter, *Gun Control Movement*, 68; Vizzard, *Shots in the Dark*, 59.

24. Edward F. Leddy, *Magnum Force Lobby* (Lanham, MD: University Press of America, 1987), 197.

25. Carter, *Gun Control Movement*, 71.

26. Vizzard, *Shots in the Dark*, 60.

27. Vizzard, *Shots in the Dark*, 60–61.

28. Carter, *Gun Control Movement*, 79–80.

29. Vizzard, *Shots in the Dark*, 61; Carter, *Gun Control Movement*, 80.

30. Carter, *Gun Control Movement*, 81.

31. Spitzer, *Politics of Gun Control*, 79–80.

32. For a more detailed discussion of this incident and other NRA gaffes, see Spitzer, *Politics of Gun Control*, 89–94.

33. Carter, *Gun Control Movement*, 108–109.

34. Gun Owners of America, at www.gunowners.org/protect.htm.

35. Citizens Committee for the Right to Keep and Bear Arms, at www.ccrkba.org/.

36. Second Amendment Foundation, at www.saf.org/default.asp?p = mission.

37. Spitzer, *Politics of Gun Control*, 97–99.

38. Spitzer, *Politics of Gun Control*, 86–89.

39. See chap. 6.

40. Carter, *Gun Control Movement*, 101.

41. The list scrolls on the Brady Campaign website, at www.bradycampaign.org.

42. The Brady Campaign frequently runs such ads. Another example is the "Hate Has Found a Home in the National Rifle Association" ad, which was comprised of a compilation of unflattering quotes from NRA officials and board members. *New York Times*, February 25, 2004. Given the Brady Campaign's proclivity to advertise in these arenas and the NRA's dearth of such ads, it seems likely that readers of the *Times* and the *Post* are more likely to be pro-control.

43. For a discussion of the importance of both money and skill in the NRA's lobbying efforts, see "In the Cross-Hairs: The National Rifle Association's Main Strength as a Lobbying Group Has Often Been the Weakness of Its Opponents; Not Any Longer," *Economist* 356 (July 8, 2000): 27–29.

44. Shaiko and Wallace, "Going Hunting," 167–69.

45. Vizzard, *Shots in the Dark*, 73.

46. James M. Snyder and Tim Groseclose, "Estimating Party Influence in Congressional Roll-Call Voting," *American Journal of Political Science* 44, no. 2 (April 2000): 203.

47. Vizzard, *Shots in the Dark*, 78.

48. Osha Gray Davidson, *Under Fire: The NRA and the Battle for Gun Control* (Iowa City: University of Iowa Press, 1998), 145; Carter, *Gun Control Movement*, 110–11.

49. See Anna Nibley Baker and David B. Magleby, "Interest Groups in the 2000 Congressional Elections," in *The Other Campaign: Soft Money and Issue Advocacy in the 2000 Congressional Elections*, ed. David B. Magleby (Lanham, MD: Rowman & Littlefield, 2003), 51–78. Other chapters in that book describe in detail interest groups activities in individual races.

50. A lengthy discussion of these races and the NRA's grassroots efforts may be found in Shaiko and Wallace, "Going Hunting," 165–69.

51. Shaiko and Wallace, "Going Hunting," 166–67.

52. The NRA began sending e-mail alerts to members in Virginia in March regarding the November 2005 gubernatorial election. This was a race of some importance to the NRA and gun control because it featured two candidates with very different positions on the issue.

53. "The Election: Issues 2000: A Special Briefing; The Economy, Trade, Foreign Policy, Social Security, Health, Education, Death Penalty, Gun Control, Poverty, Race, Campaign Finance, Environment, New Technology, Values," *Economist* 356 (September 30, 2000): 59–102.

54. The debate was held in Winston-Salem, North Carolina on October 11, 2000, and was moderated by Jim Lehrer of the *PBS NewsHour*. For a transcript, see www.web.lexis -nexis.com/universe/document?_m = a55b3b65f73c7f17ea3e6bc2f98d370b.

55. R. W. Apple Jr., "A Road Not Traveled: The New Era of G.O.P. Control," *New York Times*, January 21, 2001.

56. Paul R. Abramson, John H. Aldrich, and David W. Rohde, *Change and Continuity in the 2000 and 2002 Elections* (Washington, D.C.: CQ Press, 2003), 144–48.

57. Frank Rich, "It's the War, Stupid," *New York Times*, October 12, 2002; Katharine Q. Seelye, "Hammering on the 'L' Word," *New York Times*, December 6, 2002. See also Abramson, Aldrich, and Rohde, *Change and Continuity*, 260.

58. Jodi Wilgoren, "Dingell Holds Off Challenger to Win Primary in Michigan," *New York Times*, August 7, 2002, at www.nytimes.com/2002/08/07/politics/07MICH.html.

59. Associated Press, "Democrats Play It Safe on Gun Issues," MSNBC Online, March 1, 2004, at www.msnbc.com/id/4420922.

60. Sheryl Gay Stolberg, "A Swing to the Middle on Gun Control," *New York Times*, March 7, 2004, at www.nytimes.com/2004/03/07/weekinreview/07stol.html.

61. Stolberg, "Swing to Middle."

62. "Democrats and Guns," *Washington Times*, February 12, 2004, at www.washing tontimesonline.com/op-ed/20040212-081232-1419r.htm.

63. Democratic Presidential Candidate Debate, George Stephanopoulos, moderator, Columbia, SC, May 2, 2003.

64. "Joe Lieberman: Fighting Crime and Keeping Communities Safe," at www.joe 2004.com.

65. "Sensible Gun Laws," Howard Dean for America, at www.DeanForAmeri ca.com.

66. Roger Simon, "The Doctor is In," *U.S. News & World Report*, August 8, 2003, 5.

67. Adam Nagourney, "Dean's Challenge: Turn Enthusiasm Into Votes," *New York Times*, July 7, 2003.

68. Michael Moore, "I'll Be Voting for Wesley Clark/Good-Bye Mr. Bush," January 14, 2004, at www.clark04.com/moore.

69. According to the NEP, 22 percent of the voters said that "moral values" was the most important issue in the voting decision. It was not clear, however, exactly what was meant by moral values. Still, over 80 percent of those who cited moral values as the most important issue voted for President Bush. www.msnbc.com/id/5297138.

70. This phenomenon was noted by Rutgers University anthropologist Helen Fisher who suggested that people have a "primal need to know that a candidate is a member of their tribe." If you share various activities, then "you're not only in intellectual sync, you're probably in some biological sync on some level." Quoted in Kate Zernike, "Kerry's Lesson: Lambeau Rhymes with Rambo," *New York Times*, September 19, 2004, at www.nytimes.com/2004/09/19/weekinreview/19zernike.html.

71. Quoted in Adam Nagourney, "Bush Campaign Manager Views the Electoral Divide," *New York Times*, November 19, 2004.

72. Katherine Q. Seelye, "How to Sell a Candidate to a Porsche-Driving, Leno-Loving Nascar Fan," *New York Times*, December 6, 2004.

73. Adam Nagourney, "Baffled in Loss, Democrats Seek Road Forward," *New York Times*, November 7, 2004, at www.nytimes.com/2004/11/07/politics/campaign/07dems .html.

74. Nagourney, "Baffled in Loss."

75. Adam Nagourney, "Democratic Leader Analyzes Bush Victory," *New York Times*, December 11, 2004, at www.nytimes.com/2004/12/11/politics/11dems.html.

76. Adam Nagourney, "Democrats Hear from 8 Who Want to Lead Party," *New York Times*, December 12, 2004, at www.nytimes.com/2004/12/12/politics/12dems.html.

77. Terry M. Neal, "Election Reflections," *Washington Post*, November 4, 2004, at www.washingtonpost.com/ac2/wp-dyn/A24733-2004Nov4.

78. Nicholas D. Kristof, "Time to Get Religion," *New York Times*, November 6, 2004.

79. George Will, "Virginia's Democratic Contender," *Washington Post*, December 19, 2004.

80. Dave Kopel, "Arms Alive," *National Review*, November 3, 2004, at www .nationalreview.com/script/kopel/kopel200411031134.asp.

81. James Dao, "Where Kerry Is Trying to Avoid Gore's Pitfalls," *New York Times*, October 13, 2004.

82. Dan Balz and Jim VandeHei, "Candidates Narrow Focus to 18 States," *Washington Post*, March 15, 2004.

83. Jodi Wilgoren, "Kerry Faults Bush for Failing to Press Assault Weapons Ban," *New York Times*, September 14, 2004. See also Jodi Wilgoren, "G.O.P. Draws Criticism

from Kerry on Assault Weapons Ban," *New York Times*, September 11, 2004, at www.ny times.com/2004/09/11/politics/campaign/11kerry.html.

84. Kerry for President, "Kerry Stands Up to NRA's Divisive Agenda in Letter to Blacklisted Americans," at www.johnkerry.com/pressroom/releases/pr_2003_1030.html and www.johnkerry.com/issues/crime.

85. Debate transcript, at www.nytimes.com/2004/10/13/politics/campaign/14D TEXT-FULL.html.

86. Bob McNamara, "The Issues: Hunting and Fishing," *CBS Evening News*, October 28, 2004.

87. If this report had been included in the content analysis of CBS News coverage, it would have been coded as pro-gun control because it made no mention of the NRA's strong support for Bush or of gun control at all, except in passing. It is not unreasonable to include environmental issues in a discussion of fishing and hunting, but access to public lands and gun control must also be included in a balanced report.

88. Sid Evans and Bob Marshall, "A Sporting Debate: George Bush vs. John Kerry: The *Field & Stream* Interviews," *Field & Stream* (October 2004), at www.fieldand stream.com/fieldstream/columnists/article/0,13199,702716,00.html#.

89. Zernike, "Kerry's Lesson."

90. "Bush vs. Kerry," *Outdoor Life* (October 2004), at www.outdoorlife.com/out door/news.article/0,19912,696240,00,html. It is not clear that these were personal interviews. The transcript reads like the responses were prepared in advance, and the flap over Kerry's possession of an "assault rifle" was later explained as a misstatement by an aide. Although it was not an official endorsement, *Outdoor Life* made its preference clear in its August issue. See www.outdoorlife.com/outdoor/news/article/0,19912,688083,00.html.

91. Jodi Wilgoren, "In Magazine Interview, Kerry Says He Owns Assault Rifle," *New York Times*, September 26, 2004, at www.nytimes.com/2004/09/26/politics/campaign /26guns.html. In the article, a Kerry aide said he did not know the rifle model, but that Kerry was a registered gun owner in Massachusetts.

92. "No Assault Rifle for Kerry, After All," *New York Times*, September 27, 2004.

93. Associated Press, "Kerry Talks Faith, Firearms as He Tries to Lure Key Voters," *Roanoke Times*, August 2, 2004.

94. Associated Press, "Kerry Goes Hunting; Bush Meets Archbishop," *Roanoke Times*, October 22, 2004.

95. NRA-PVF, "If John Kerry Thinks the Second Amendment is about Photo-Ops, He's Daffy" [print advertisement] at www.nrapvf.org.

96. Of course, photographs can be chosen for the message they convey, which may or may not reflect reality.

97. Maureen Dowd, "Cooking His Own Goose," *New York Times*, October 24, 2004, at www.nytimes.com/2004/10/24/opinion/24dowd.html. Dowd stated that Kerry "made an animal sacrifice to the political gods" in an effort to prove he is man enough to run the country. "Democrats have been panting to get a gun into their nominee's hands for a month now." She also noted that, according to a Kerry aide, "two of the birds would soon be sent back to Mr. Kerry for consumption."

98. Wayne LaPierre, "The Case against Kerry," *America's 1st Freedom* (October 2004): 34–38. Kerry's positions were attacked at the NRA Convention in Pittsburgh in April by both Vice President Dick Cheney and NRA officials. See James Dao, "N.R.A.

Lashes Out at Kerry over Terror and Gun Issues," *New York Times*, April 18, 2004, at www.nytimes.com/2004/04/18/politics/campaign/18NRA.html.

99. James O. E. Norell, "John Kerry's Newest Scheme to Ban Your Guns," *America's 1st Freedom* (November 2004): 42–46.

100. NRA-PVF, "John Kerry Wants to Ban Guns in America," at www.nrapvf.org /Kerry/default.apsx.

101. James O. E. Norell, "Why You Can't Stay Home This Election Day," *America's 1st Freedom* (October 2004): 28–33.

102. NRA-PVF, "NRA Endorses George W. Bush for President," at www.nrapvf.org /News/read.apsx?ID = 4614.

103. Brady Campaign to Prevent Gun Violence, "To Restore Sanity on Gun Issue, Brady Campaign, Million Mom March Endorse John Kerry for President," October 1, 2004, at www.bradycampaign.org/press/release.php?release = 594.

104. Brady Campaign to Prevent Gun Violence, "After Selling Out Police, Bush Takes Delivery of the Payoff," October 13, 2004, at www.bradycampaign.org/press/release .php?release = 598.

105. Penn, Schoen & Berland Associates, "New National Polls Show Assault Weapons Ban Wedge Factor in Election—Moves Key Swing States into 'Kerry' Column as Voters Perceive Ban as Key 'Homeland Security' Leadership Issue," October 9, 2004.

106. The question read: "If the election for President were being held today for whom would you vote? Democrat John Kerry, who is a hunter and a sportsman. Kerry believes that Congress and the White House must renew the ban on military style assault weapons when it expires in several weeks. Four years ago, Republican George W. Bush, as a candidate for President, pledged to support the renewal of the assault weapons ban. Bush has broken his promise and has not asked Congressional leaders to extend the ban. The ban is now soon set to expire." The report noted that Kerry's support rose from 46 percent to 48 percent and Bush's support declined from 50 percent to 44 percent when likely voters in Florida were presented with the positions. The results were similar in Ohio and Pennsylvania, and, not surprisingly, Bush's support as the candidate with the best plan to deal with terrorism declined. The poll also found that support for renewing the ban was lower in the three swing states than nationwide, and that respondents viewed assault weapons as different from other types of firearms and separate from other gun control laws.

107. Michael D. Barnes, "How Bush Neutralized the Gun Issue as Part of His Winning Strategy," November 4, 2004, at www.bradycampaign.org. See also Brady Campaign to Prevent Gun Violence, "President Bush Supported Sensible Gun Policy on Campaign Trail—Now It's Time for Action," November 5, 2004, at www.bradycampaign.org/press /release.php?release = 606.

108. Brady Campaign to Prevent Gun Violence, "No Mandate for Gun Extremism," November 9, 2004, as www.bradycampaign.org/press/release.php?release = 607.

109. NRA-PVF, "NRA: Freedom Prevails across the Country; George Bush Re-Elected, Daschle Defeated; Overwhelming 95% Success Rate Nationwide," November 4, 2004, at www.nrapvf.org/news/read.aspx?id = 4843&t.

110. Brady Campaign, "No Mandate."

111. Chris W. Cox, "Your Tools for Victory," National Rifle Association Institute for Legislative Action, at nraila.org/Issues/Articles/Read.aspx?ID = 154.

112. *America's 1st Freedom* (January 2005): cover.

Chapter Six

Guns in the Media

The mass media's portrayal of events, individuals, and groups influences the public's perceptions in a variety of ways. The news media are, without question, the primary source of political information for most Americans.[1] Less settled are questions regarding precisely what we learn from the media, how that learning occurs, and the political and social effects of what we learn. We examine those questions in this chapter and present evidence indicating that the media's presentation of the gun control issue is not, to borrow a phrase from Fox News, "fair and balanced."

Defining the term "news" is not nearly as simple as it may appear. Even listing the characteristics of news can be a challenge because many of them—timeliness, spontaneity, social or political importance—are found in some news stories but not in others. The definition of news largely determines which events are defined as newsworthy and which events are not. David L. Paletz writes, "[N]ews is composed of reports and accounts by journalists of what is going on in the world."[2] While this description is accurate, there are many things going on in the world that are not considered newsworthy. Decisions regarding which events are worth covering are made by newspaper editors and television news producers. Those decisions are often based on evaluations of the story's impact on the audience, and the impact is a function of precisely what happened and to whom.

Doris A. Graber has outlined five criteria that are used in selecting news stories. These include: a strong impact on readers or listeners; natural or man-made violence, conflict, disaster, or scandal; the familiarity of either the person involved in the event or the nature of the situation; proximity in terms of location; and the timeliness or novelty of the event.[3] News reports usually rely on the words of others—governmental officials, interest groups representatives, academic experts, and average citizens. Stories often include the reactions of those who are affected by or involved in the events as well as those of "experts."

News is also defined as unusual as opposed to the commonplace events. I recall being told by a journalism school professor that "it isn't news when a dog bites a man, but it is news when a man bites a dog."[4] A snowstorm in Brownsville, Texas, is news; a snowstorm in Minneapolis, Minnesota, is not news unless it is a very big storm. At the same time, a hurricane in Florida is news even if it occurs during the hurricane season, and almost anything the president does is considered newsworthy.

The definition of news impacts the media's coverage of guns and guns control. For example, a shooting that occurs in an elementary school is news. A homeowner who uses a firearm to scare off a potential robber is not news. The emotional impact of a school shooting is undeniable and significant. The tragedy of one child accidentally shooting another is the type of story that begs for coverage. An intentional child shooting packs even more of an emotional wallop. In a typical defensive gun use, a potential crime is thwarted, a perpetrator is chased away, and no one is injured. There is little news value in that story unless it involves a famous person.

All news media are complicit in giving greater coverage to events that have more conflict and drama and involve influential leaders or celebrities. For example, a sexual assault charge against a well-known basketball player receives more coverage than a trade bill being considered by Congress. News is often reported in ways that make it more personal or understandable to the average person in the audience. W. Lance Bennett describes how reporters shape the news to be interesting to the audience and to fit their preconceptions—to personalize, dramatize, and normalize the news so that it is interesting, suspenseful, and yet not too threatening.[5] So, news can be defined by the event itself (a tsunami that kills more than 150,000 people), who is involved (the results of the president's annual physical), or where it happened (New York versus Peoria). Therefore, many events that would help swing opinion in favor of gun rights are not defined as news, not only because of possible political bias but also because of the way the term "news" is defined. At the same time, there seem to be some biases at work with regard to how certain types of news stories are covered. The sparse existing research suggests that news reports are more likely to be reported either objectively or in a way that favors the gun control position. Gun rights positions are rarely treated positively in the news media.

THE POLITICAL IMPACT OF THE NEWS

One of the most important impacts of the media is agenda setting for both elected officials and the public.[6] The best way to understand this phenomenon is through the adage "The media don't tell us what to think. They tell us what to think about." They help identify those issues that are important at any given point in time, and, in so doing, they help prod elected officials to action. Agenda setting often takes place after a trigger event focuses the attention of the public and elected officials on a specific issue or a problem. For example, child abuse in one daycare center may spur a local, regional, or even state-wide investigation into the practices of all daycare centers. On a larger scale, the tragic events of September 11, 2001, placed terrorism on the agenda of all governments in the United States. News coverage of a school shooting raises concerns regarding the safety of schools and the children who attend them among parents, the public, and elected officials. Agenda setting is rarely intentional on the part of the media. They simply cover the news, and the audience reacts to it. Of course, their decisions regarding what news to present and how that news is presented influence audience reaction. Just as the Patriot Act and the war on terror resulted from the events of September 11, the installation of metal detectors in some schools and the call for more gun control resulted from events such as the shooting at Columbine High School.

The media are crucial in helping to define political, social, and economic reality for consumers. Learning occurs in the day-to-day coverage of various events, people, and issues. If the picture of the world, or any part of it, presented by the news media is consistent in its description, tone, and outlook, then it may lead the audience to adopt a vision of reality in concert with that image.[7] Like agenda setting, the creation of these stereotypes is not intentional on the part of the media. They simply present images and information that comport with a widely held view. Like his father, George W. Bush is sometimes grammatically challenged. Baseball superstar Barry Bonds is surly. Russian women are old and overweight. The streets of many major cities are unsafe, and guns are dangerous weapons to be avoided. While all of these depictions are true in some situations, we do not know if they are generally accurate descriptions.

One of the traditional canons of journalism is that the media should cover issues fairly and accurately. For journalists, this is most often expressed by the term "objectivity." Objectivity is operationalized as presenting both sides of the issue to the news consumer and allowing the consumer to decide which view is correct. Reporters exclude their personal opinion, get the facts right, and strive to be impartial so as to avoid intentional bias.[8] This paradigm has been largely dominant in American journalism since technological advances in the nineteenth and twentieth centuries made truly mass media possible. A mass media required more balanced news, which the newly invented wire services could sell to many different news organizations. Prior to this time, most news media in the United States were either partisan or ideological. Many were also sensational in nature.[9]

By framing an issue in a particular way, the media can influence public opinion. Framing implies a specific definition of the issue that may include the cause, the nature of the problem, possible solutions, and impact.[10] Framing can lead to other definitions of the issue, other solutions, and consequences being ignored or treated unequally. Paletz views framing as a factor which can "undermine" objectivity. For Paletz, framing is a central idea that provides context for the facts of the story; both which facts to include and exclude, as well as any interpretation given to those facts; the language that journalists use in relating the news story; and the pictures that accompany the story.[11] While we tend to think that facts "speak for themselves," in reality facts have to be placed in a context and interpreted in order for them to have meaning. While issue framing is important and can have social and political repercussions, we must bear in mind that we can and do think independently of the media and that brainwashing exists largely in science fiction or in films like *The Manchurian Candidate*.

Research indicates, however, that issue framing can influence citizens' opinions regarding gun policy. Two separate studies conducted by Donald Haider-Markel and Mark R. Joslyn examined framing of a concealed-handgun law and the Columbine High School shootings and concluded that issue frames did influence opinion, although the impact was tempered by the individual's predisposition or susceptibility to the frame. That is, frames that agree with your existing view will be more readily adopted. Framing may also contribute to partisan polarization and issue salience, the importance we attach to an issue.[12]

Interest groups and elected officials attempt to persuade the media to adopt their definition or framing of a particular issue. Karen Callaghan and Frauke Schnell describe the jockeying that takes place between the news media, interest groups, and elected officials during the framing of a political issue. The final news product, then, may reflect the view of one side of the debate, some combination of views from two or more actors, or a "purely media-generated version" of the issue.[13]

BIAS IN THE NEWS?

Charges of bias against the media have been leveled by both the left and the right for several decades. The theories are relatively simple. For the liberals, the conservative bias results from the fact that most media are owned by large corporations, which we know tend to be more politically conservative. The privately owned media, then, reflect the views of the owners. This bias is evident in the type of stories that are covered (weighted toward politics) and the sources that are referenced (most commonly governmental officials). In addition, the media focus coverage on more mainstream political actors and interest groups, thus freezing out—intentionally or not—legitimate dissenters.

On the other side, conservatives charge that reporters, who tend to be more liberal than their readers or viewers, inject some of their own biases—intentionally or not—into their news judgments. Thus, we see a liberal slant to the news. This bias is most evident in how the news is presented, how various individuals and groups are portrayed, and the terms that are used to describe events or people.

Bias, then, can creep into the news in two separate ways. First, reporters and editors may produce news coverage that generally favors one side of the debate. This can be a function of news sources that are used, the descriptions of events, and even the specific language employed. Second, bias may be present in the choices that are made with regard to which events are covered.

The first type of bias is usually investigated through use of content analysis, which systematically examines the specific language that is used in a news story, the sources that are used, and the presence or absence of certain issue frames. The second type of bias is much more difficult to detect. Events that are not covered by the media frequently remain unknown to us for the very reason that they were not. Unless we have personal knowledge of the event or know someone who does, we are likely to remain uninformed. If a tree falls in the forest, but it is not covered on the evening news, did it really fall?

Most academics agree that there are relatively few ideological biases in the news.[14] Still, there is some evidence that there are biases on a few issues, most notably abortion and gay rights.[15] In addition, some studies have concluded that there are biases in news coverage of presidential campaigns.[16] Other researchers have argued that the injection of the media's own views into the news may be more common than generally thought.[17]

However, conventional wisdom suggests that most biases in America's news media tend to be less ideological and more commercial. Because most news media in the United States are privately owned (with the exception of the high-quality, low-ratings PBS *NewsHour* and National Public Radio's *Morning Edition* and *All Things Considered*), they must be profitable unless the owners are willing to lose money to provide a public service. Few, if any, owners are. Higher circulation figures for newspapers and better ratings for television stations translate into higher revenues. In the past decade or two, television news has become a revenue producer, as compared to the 1960s when the networks were willing to lose money on the news.

As a result, the search for revenue is as strong as, if not stronger than ever.

This leads to news coverage that maximizes the audience, what many people refer to as "infotainment," or the blurring of the line between news and entertainment. The slide down that slippery slope can be seen in some television news-magazines, tabloid newspapers, and even in the more elite media in how a news broadcast is put together (quick edits, few talking heads) and the layout of the newspaper (more color photos and bold headlines). The type of stories that are covered is also affected by these economic pressures. The phrase "If it bleeds, it leads" has been used frequently to describe the tendency to focus on the more unusual or controversial aspects of events that are thought to be more attractive to the audience. Television news must be influenced, to some extent, by the film that can be shown to accompany a story. While some would charge this is elevating style over content, others would say it simply recognizes the importance of the visual aspects of television news. Newspapers are not immune to these economic pressures, either, as is evidenced by the emphasis on "soft news" in many papers and an increase in the percentage of the daily paper devoted to advertising.[18]

The news media's emphasis on and misrepresentation of crime and criminal justice news is well documented. According to Ray Surette, "examination of the content of crime news reveals a . . . distorted, inverted image."[19] Crime is overemphasized as a news topic, and violent crime receives a disproportionate share of the coverage. Crime news is also more highly attended by readers and viewers than most other subjects. The media's coverage of crime and criminals has been found to influence public opinion, although the effect is neither direct nor dramatic.[20] Many Americans exaggerate their chances of being the victim of a crime, and it appears that those who watch more television are more likely to overestimate their chance of victimization.

Many books that focus on gun control (usually from the gun rights perspective) contain some discussion of the role of the media, but the discussion usually focuses on anecdotal evidence of bias.[21] Critics often point to specific stories with charges of bias, but there is a dearth of long-term, methodologically sound analyses.

A thoughtful article by former *U.S. News & World Report* senior editor Ted Gest suggests that "America's news media consistently display a mixture of bias, carelessness and plain error in reporting issues involving guns."[22] Gest believes that the media's emphasis of crime coverage is inevitable and the presence of guns in many crimes makes gun coverage a fait accompli due to the definition of news.

Reporters are more likely than their readers to favor stricter gun control laws and believe that those laws would impact crime.[23] Gest argues that reporters who cover crime and guns have no special training and receive little guidance from editors, colleagues, or style manuals that are deficient in their discussion of firearms. However, in 1999 the *Columbia Journalism Review* published a list of sources reporters could consult with regard to lawsuits against firearms manufacturers and regulating guns as consumer products. The list included interest groups, think tanks, and a few academic researchers.[24]

Conversely, Thomas Winship, a former editor of the *Boston Globe*, argues that the media are too timid in their coverage of guns and control: "The press has failed to take a strong stand against gun proliferation. Newspapers should inaugurate a sustained crusade against gun distribution and use."[25] Although he might be accused of engaging in hyperbole, Winship's position is clear:

> Statistics . . . are convincing, horrifying and a desperately urgent issue everywhere, except on our front pages. So are the cynical excuses editors give about not doing more. We are talking about guns, guns, guns, gunning down infants on the streets, teen-agers and teachers in classrooms, and adults at high noon and at midnight.[26]

The anti-gun bias is further supported, at least anecdotally, by Michael Bane, a writer who is supported in part by the National Shooting Sports Federation and has joined with shooting-sports champions to offer hands-on firearms seminars to journalists: "I believe the media—print and electronic—may be the single biggest casualty in the three decades of this 'shooting war.'"[27] Bane describes how many journalists come to see sport shooters as normal people during the course of the seminars.

Bane relates the case of a "veteran national political correspondent, whose name you would recognize, working for one of the most prestigious national news outlets in the country" who was forbidden by his producers from attending a seminar. The reporter claimed that his producers were "unwilling to present any positive firearms stories," so they did not assign journalists to cover stories that might have a pro-gun slant.[28] This is disturbing behavior that not only implicates a broadcast network in blatant news bias, but also violates several canons of journalism.

While many accounts suggest that the media are biased in favor of gun control, it is difficult, if not impossible, to find even anecdotal evidence that the media favor the pro-gun stance.[29] In one of the most comprehensive analyses of media coverage, Callaghan and Schnell analyzed network news coverage of the Brady Bill and the assault weapons ban from 1988 to 1996. The networks generally adopted the "culture of violence" frame, which was the second most common frame used by the Brady Campaign (then Handgun Control, Inc.) and pro-gun control elected officials. The frame most commonly used by the NRA, "feel-good laws," was conveyed by the media much less frequently.[30]

In a different study of issue framing, Dhavan Shah found that gun control was more frequently discussed by the media in material rather than ethical terms. The ethical considerations usually consisted of the opposition to gun rights and societal violence and violence against children. The material coverage included discussion of gun control proposals.[31] Either a material or an ethical issue frame could be biased in favor of gun rights or in favor of gun control.

A study of media habits and gun control conducted by Kenneth Dowler concluded that watching crime dramas on television or relying primarily on television news for information was associated with lower levels of support for gun control. Greater reliance on print news sources was correlated with higher levels of support for gun control.[32]

In another large study, Brian Anse Patrick examined elite newspaper coverage of five nationally prominent interest groups—the American Association of Retired Persons, the American Civil Liberties Union (ACLU), the National Association for the Advancement of Colored People, Handgun Control, Inc., and the National Rifle Association. After examining 1,474 articles in the *New York Times*, the *Washington Post*, the *Christian Science Monitor*, *The Wall Street Journal*, and the *Los Angeles Times*, Patrick found "these data strongly support a conclusion of systematic marginalization of the NRA in elite newspaper coverage, as compared with other interest groups."[33]

According to Patrick,

> [T]hose articles discussing the NRA tend on average toward fewer paragraphs with direct quotations or attributed viewpoints, less utilization of group pseudo-events, less favorable use of personalization techniques, and more use of joking or punning headlines. They also have higher levels of satire or mockery directed at the group, more negative use of verbs of attribution. . . . Tone and semantics also tend more toward the negative for the NRA in editorial and op-ed coverage than for other groups.[34]

Former reporter Tamryn Etten analyzed 117 randomly selected gun-related news stories published in newspapers from around the country. Etten found that while 70 percent of the stories were reported in neutral or near-neutral fashion, stories that were biased toward the pro-gun control view outnumbered those biased in favor of gun rights by an almost four-to-one margin.[35]

Finally, the generally conservative Media Research Center examined network news coverage of gun policy and found that anti-gun stories outnumbered pro-gun stories by an eight-to-one ratio. ABC News was the most biased, while NBC News was the least.[36]

While there are relatively few studies of media coverage of gun control, none of them has found a bias in favor of gun rights. In addition, complaints from those who favor gun control regarding media coverage of the topic are virtually nonexistent.[37] At the same time, discussion of media coverage of the issue is minimal in the work of the scholars who seem to favor the gun control position.

The research presented in the remainder of this chapter analyzes the coverage of gun control by *CBS Evening News* and the *New York Times* for a three-year period, as well as the final passage of the Brady Bill, the Columbine High School shooting, and the Washington, D.C., sniper shootings. It examines both the events that were covered and how those events were reported.

METHODOLOGY

This study examines elite media coverage of guns and gun control in *CBS Evening News* and the *New York Times* between January 1, 2000, and December 31, 2002, in addition to coverage of the final passage of the Brady Bill in 1993, the Columbine High School shooting in 1999, and the Washington, D.C., sniper shootings. Tapes of CBS News stories were obtained from the Vanderbilt News Archive at Vanderbilt University.[38] A total of 129 television news segments were included.[39]

CBS was selected because that network covered more gun control stories than any of its competitors, and it had the plurality of stories related to guns and gun control in the 2000 election. The *New York Times* is generally considered to be the country's leading newspaper, "the lion whom the jackals follow,"[40] or at least one of the few elite news media.[41]

For the *New York Times,* a LexisNexis academic search was conducted using the search term "gun control."[42] There were 252 total news stories dealing with gun control, 142 covering the Washington, D.C. sniper shootings, 88 that featured the events at Columbine High School, and 15 dealing with the final passage of the Brady Bill.

The unit of analysis is the story. Each of the stories was coded for the following variables: news anchor (CBS), length, reporter(s), topic(s), type of story, content bias, correspondent/reporter tone bias, video topics or photograph subjects, experts interviewed, interest groups mentioned, how those groups were portrayed, whether any statistics were used in the story, whether the story included children, and whether there was any mention of defensive gun use.[43]

Coverage of defensive gun use is an important topic because of the centrality of those events to those who tout the positive benefits of firearms. While there is debate over the actual number of times that a gun is used to thwart a criminal, John R. Lott's analysis of *New York Times* coverage in 2001 found

104 gun-related crime articles and one story that featured a defensive gun use.[44]

Coding for bias in terms of content, tone, and interest group coverage are the more subjective variables in this analysis. The judgment was made on the story as a whole, and there were no "magic" words. That is to say, the use of a particular word would not cause a story to be coded as biased. Content was judged to be biased if there was little or no information presented to counterbalance claims from either side in the debate. Tone was judged to be biased if the presentation used language that clearly favored one side or the other.[45]

Judgments regarding coverage of interest groups were made in similar fashion to content.[46] When there was any doubt regarding possible bias, the judgment was made to code the story as neutral or mixed. The percentage of stories labeled as biased is also reduced by the inclusion of some stories in the analysis (primarily those regarding Columbine and the Washington snipers) that did not deal in any way with guns or gun control. These stories were included because of the potential for discussion of gun control in the coverage of those topics, and they were judged to be neutral if they did not mention gun control.

CBS EVENING NEWS RESULTS

Due to the smaller number of stories on CBS, both objectively and in comparison with the *Times,* all stories are included in some of the tables below. In some cases statistics for all stories and only "pure" gun control news stories—excluding those stories that reported on Columbine, the Washington, D.C. snipers, or the Brady Bill—are reported.

There were thirty-three different correspondents, but only eight reported on five or more stories. The most frequently used reporters were Jim Stewart (nineteen; 15 percent), Bill Whitaker (fourteen; 11 percent), Bob McNamara and Dan Rather (nine; 7 percent each), Bob Schieffer (eight; 6 percent), Vince Gonzales and Jerry Bowen (six; 5 percent each), and Jim Axelrod (five; 4 percent). The relatively small number of stories reported by various correspondents makes meaningful comparisons difficult, but there were some significant differences among the journalists with the largest number of stories.

The topic covered most frequently was the Columbine High School shootings (thirty-six; 28 percent) followed by gun control or gun control legislation (thirty-five; 27 percent), the Washington, D.C. snipers (fifteen; 12 percent), the Brady Bill (twelve; 9 percent), and interest groups involved with gun control (twelve; 9 percent. See table 6.1). No other topic was the primary subject

Table 6.1. *CBS Evening News* **Story Topics (All Stories)**

Topic	Number	Percent of Topics
Columbine shootings	36	28%
Gun control/legislation	35	27%
D.C. snipers	15	12%
Brady Bill	12	9%
Interest group	12	9%
School shooting	9	7%
Guns/ammunition/dealer	8	7%
Political campaign	6	5%
Gun violence	5	4%
Arrest/suspect	5	4%
Lawsuits	5	4%
Second Amendment/Ashcroft	4	4%
Other	8	6%

Note: Percents do not add to 100% because a story may have had more than one topic.

more than ten times, although school shootings (nine; 7 percent) were close to that figure. While there is nothing too surprising in these results, the large number of stories on the Columbine shootings and the Washington, D.C. snipers indicates disproportionate coverage of those events.

The National Rifle Association was, by far, the interest group most frequently referenced in the *CBS Evening News* stories (twenty-seven; 69 percent) of stories that referred to an interest group), followed by other gun rights groups and the Million Mom March (five; 13 percent each), the Brady Campaign (three; 8 percent), the Violence Policy Center and other gun control groups (two; 4 percent each). No other group was mentioned more than once. Looking only at the "pure" gun control stories in the three-year period makes little difference in this table. The attention paid to the NRA declined slightly, but the NRA remained in the dominant position as "spokesgroup" for the gun control issue. This suggests that the *CBS Evening News* often refers to the NRA, and, as we shall see shortly, the NRA is willing to provide comments for most stories.

While the NRA received the lion's share of the interest group coverage, it also received the most negative coverage (see table 6.2). The NRA was mentioned in a positive light in three stories (11 percent), but it was treated negatively in eleven stories (41 percent). The pro-control groups were mentioned less often on the *CBS Evening News*, but they generally received neutral or even positive coverage. Four of the negative portrayals of the NRA were in stories reported by Jim Stewart. Two of the positive references were stories covering the NRA convention reported by Randall Pinkston. How each group was covered by the *CBS Evening News* changes very little if the Columbine,

Table 6.2.   *CBS Evening News* Interest Group Bias

Interest Group	Positive (All Stories)	Negative (All Stories)	Neutral (All Stories)	Positive (Gun Control Only)	Negative (Gun Control Only)	Neutral (Gun Control Only)
National Rifle Assoc.	11% (3)	41% (11)	48% (13)	14% (3)	36% (8)	50% (11)
Brady Campaign	33% (1)	0% (0)	67% (2)	100% (1)	0% (0)	0% (0)
Million Mom March	80% (4)	20% (1)	0% (0)	80% (4)	20% (1)	0% (0)
Violence Policy Center	0% (0)	0% (0)	100% (2)	0% (0)	0% (0)	100% (1)

snipers, and Brady Bill stories are excluded from the analysis. Coverage of the NRA by the *CBS Evening News* is both quantitatively and qualitatively different from the attention given to other interest groups in the gun control debate. The NRA is mentioned more often but more frequently in negative terms.

Experts cited in the stories included law enforcement officers or prosecutors (forty-eight; 38 percent); family, friends, or victims themselves (forty-six; 36 percent); elected officials (thirty; 24 percent); NRA officials (eighteen; 14 percent); President Bill Clinton (fifteen; 12 percent); and other pro-gun rights groups (ten; 7 percent). No other experts were cited ten times or more (see table 6.3). Other notable experts were Brady Campaign officials (nine; 7 percent), gun shop owners (nine; 7 percent), Violence Policy Center representatives (six; 5 percent), and gun control experts from academia (three; 2 percent).

If one includes only the gun control stories from 2000 through 2002, then law enforcement and family and friends decline in frequency of use while the NRA and Clinton increase in frequency. Most other experts remain about the same in terms of usage. We would expect the media to rely heavily on elected officials as experts on gun control, given that politicians are often thought of, by others as well as by themselves, as experts on a variety of topics. Similarly, Clinton's support of gun control and his willingness to speak out, as well as his position as president, make him an excellent source. Law enforcement personnel are also obvious experts, while friends and family help make the story more interesting and add to the emotional impact.

Use of the NRA as an expert voice may be surprising, but it allows the correspondents to achieve objectivity (real or imagined) in their reports.

The most frequently aired video clips were so-called talking heads (seventy-six; 59 percent); guns (thirty-three; 26 percent); the crime scene (twenty-nine; 23 percent); Columbine victims, usually students running from

Table 6.3. *CBS Evening News* **Experts**

Expert	Number (All stories)	Percent (All stories)	Number (Gun control only)	Percent (Gun control only)
Law enforcement, prosecutor	48	38%	17	26%
Victim, family, friend	46	36%	17	26%
Elected official	30	24%	19	29%
National Rifle Association	18	14%	16	25%
President Clinton	15	12%	13	20%
Other pro-gun	10	7%	9	15%
Brady Campaign	9	7%	2	3%
Gun shop owner	9	7%	5	8%
Bureaucrat	8	6%	3	5%
Doctor	7	6%	3	5%
Violence Policy Center	6	5%	5	8%
School official	5	4%	3	5%
Other gun control	5	4%	4	6%
Clergy	5	4%	0	0%
George W. Bush	4	3%	4	6%
Lawyer	4	3%	3	5%
Tom Mauser—Columbine parent/activist	4	3%	4	6%
John Ashcroft	4	3%	3	5%
Academic—gun control	3	2%	2	3%
Academic—not gun control	3	2%	1	2%
Al Gore	2	2%	2	3%
Other	21	16%	13	21%

Note: Percents do not add to 100% because a story may have included more than one expert.

the school following the shooting (twenty-one; 16 percent); other crime or shooting victims (fifteen; 12 percent); and gun shops or gun shows (eleven; 8 percent. See table 6.4) No other video clips were shown more than ten times, but other notable clips included Clinton (seven; 5 percent) and the wounded Columbine student who jumped or fell from a window (six; 5 percent).[47] The frequency of Columbine video declines when those stories are eliminated from the analysis, but it is also clear that Columbine video was used in stories that did not deal explicitly with Columbine. The use of guns and crime scenes may seem obvious to us because we are conditioned to seeing those images. Both contribute significantly to the emotion of the story. Guns can appear menacing, depending upon how they are shown. Very interesting here is the use of Columbine victims in stories that did not deal with the Columbine shootings. Again, the emotion of those video clips is undeniable. One could also argue that those images create or reinforce the idea that

Table 6.4. *CBS Evening News* **Video Subject**

Video Clip	Number (All Stories)	Percent (All Stories)	Number (Gun Control Only)	Percent (Gun Control Only)
Talking head	76	59%	41	62%
Guns	33	26%	24	36%
Crime scene	29	23%	16	24%
Columbine victims	21	16%	5	8%
Victim	15	12%	8	12%
Gun shop/gun show	11	8%	5	8%
President Clinton	7	5%	5	8%
Columbine jumper	6	5%	3	5%
Police	5	4%	0	0%
Funeral	5	4%	0	0%
Other	33	26%	20	30%

Note: Percents do not add to 100% because a story may have included more than one video clip.

gun control is necessary. The evidence presented here does not confirm or deny that possibility.

More than two-thirds (68 percent) of the stories, not surprisingly, contained neutral or mixed content (see table 6.5). The information in the story was either neutral with regard to gun control, balanced between gun control and gun rights, or gun control was not mentioned. For example, many of the stories that dealt with the Columbine shootings and the Washington snipers did not discuss gun control. Very few stories (4 percent) had pro-gun rights content, while more than one-quarter (28 percent) had pro-gun control content.

When we eliminate the Columbine, snipers, and Brady Bill stories, the coverage becomes more biased in the pro-control direction. While half of the stories are neutral or mixed, nearly as many (46 percent) are pro-control in terms of content, and only 5 percent are slanted toward the gun rights position. It is clear that the story content is biased in favor of the gun control

Table 6.5. *CBS Evening News* **Story Content Bias**

Story Content Bias	Number (All Stories)	Percent (All Stories)	Number (Gun Control Only)	Percent (Gun Control Only)
Pro-gun control	36	28%	30	46%
Pro-gun rights	5	4%	3	5%
Neutral/Mixed	88	68%	33	50%

position. The tone of the story, however, is more crucial to any assessment of media or reporter bias.

With regard to the reporter's tone, the results were quite similar to those that dealt with story content (see table 6.6). While the findings appear to be almost identical, the overall results mask the fact that there were eight stories with neutral or mixed content and a pro-gun control tone. At the same time, there were eight stories with pro-gun control content and neutral or mixed tone. There were also three stories in which the content was pro-gun rights and the tone was neutral or mixed.

Examining only the pure gun control stories with regard to correspondent tone, we see that the coverage becomes more biased in favor of the pro-gun control position. The majority of stories were still neutral or mixed, but 41 percent were judged to be pro-control in terms of tone, and none were judged to be pro-gun rights. These results are the most important thus far. They indicate that objectivity is not as common as we would like in the reporting on CBS.

Less than one-fourth (23 percent) of the stories contained any reference to statistics (see table 6.7). Just over half (50 percent) mentioned a child in the story. If the Columbine, sniper, and Brady Bill stories are removed from the analysis, the percentage of stories that referred to children declines somewhat, and the percentage of stories citing statistics increases.

Only two of the stories reported by CBS referred in any way to defensive gun use. One of these was an "Eye on America" segment reported by Dan Rather, which focused on the 1991 Killeen, Texas, restaurant massacre and interviewed State Representative Suzanne Gratia Huff. Huff argued that had she been permitted to carry her concealed gun into the restaurant she would have shot the murderer before he got a chance to kill her parents and twenty other people. Her position was balanced by the president of the International Association of Chiefs of Police, who noted that putting more guns on the street is not the answer to gun violence and that possession of a gun does not make society safer.

Table 6.6. *CBS Evening News* Story Tone Bias

Story Tone Bias	Number (All Stories)	Percent (All Stories)	Number (Gun Control Only)	Percent (Gun Control Only)
Pro-gun control	36	28%	27	41%
Pro-gun rights	1	1%	0	0%
Neutral/Mixed	92	71%	39	59%

The second story focused on a *Los Angeles Times* article which reported that "hundreds of Texans with histories of violence, mental illness or prior convictions for serious crimes such as rape and armed robbery" had been issued concealed-carry licenses under a bill signed by then-governor George W. Bush. The story included an excerpt from "a member of the Banshees, a violent motorcycle gang," who had been convicted of a double murder for shootings he claimed were self-defense in spite of evidence that both victims were shot in the back. The shootings occurred after he obtained a carry permit.

While table 6.6 suggests bias in how CBS reports the news, table 6.7 indicates that there is also bias in terms of which stories are covered. It was mentioned earlier that defensive gun uses often do not meet the criteria used to define an event as newsworthy, but CBS failed to even mention self-defense or personal protection as possible reasons for owning a firearm. Putting the evidence together at this point, it is easy to accuse the *CBS Evening News* of both sins of omission and sins of commission.

Different stories were covered in different ways (see table 6.8). In some cases, the type of coverage was dramatically different. For example, the Washington, D.C. snipers stories were all neutral or mixed in terms of content and tone. Most of those stories did not deal with the weapon used at all, although several did.

Somewhat surprisingly, only two of the stories that focused on Columbine were judged to be pro-gun control in their content, and the same number were pro-control in terms of tone. One Columbine story was pro-gun rights (a victim's parent suggesting that gun control would not have prevented the tragedy). Many of the Columbine stories did not deal with gun control at all. As a result, 92 percent of those stories were neutral in content, and 94 percent were neutral in tone.

Coverage of the Brady Bill was not as balanced. The content in one-third (33 percent) of the stories was pro-control, while the tone in 58 percent (seven of twelve stories) was pro-control. Fewer than half (42 percent) were neutral in content, and just one third (33 percent) were neutral in tone. One Brady

Table 6.7. *CBS Evening News* Items in Stories

Item Mentioned	Number (All Stories)	Percent (All Stories)	Number (Gun Control Only)	Percent (Gun Control Only)
Statistics cited	30	23%	21	32%
Child in story	65	50%	29	44%
Defensive gun use mentioned	2	2%	2	3%

Table 6.8. *CBS Evening News* Story Content and Tone Bias

Story Topic—Content	Pro-Gun Control	Pro-Gun Rights	Neutral/Mixed
Columbine	6% (2)	3% (1)	92% (33)
Brady Bill	33% (4)	8% (1)	58% (7)
D.C. snipers	0	0	100% (15)
Gun control/gun legislation	46% (16)	3% (1)	51% (18)
Other	37% (23)	6% (4)	57% (35)
Story Topic—Tone	Pro-Gun Control	Pro-Gun Rights	Neutral/Mixed
Columbine	6% (2)	0	94% (34)
Brady Bill	58% (7)	8% (1)	33% (4)
D.C. snipers	0	0	100% (15)
Gun control/gun legislation	49% (17)	3% (1)	50% (17)
Other	34% (21)	2% (1)	65% (40)

Bill story was pro-rights in content and tone. The relatively small number of stories in this section can, however, make the use of percentages misleading. General gun control or gun legislation stories (46 percent; sixteen of thirty-five) were more likely to reflect the gun control view.[48] Results with regard to tone were quite similar, with the exception of the campaign stories, where only one of six stories was pro-gun control.

Reporters also make a significant difference (see table 6.9). While the number of stories covered by any single reporter is small and makes any conclusion somewhat tentative, there are clear differences in how various correspondents reported their stories. Jim Stewart had the largest number of stories (nineteen), and his coverage, in content and especially tone, was the most pro-gun control. In comparison, both Bob McNamara and Jerry Bowen covered fewer gun-related stories, but their coverage was neutral. Stewart and Dan Rather were the only correspondents who had more bias in the tone than the content of their stories. Again, in comparison, Bill Whitaker (who had the second-highest total number of stories) had one report classified as having pro-control content and two as having pro-gun rights content, but all of his stories were neutral in tone. Bob Schieffer seems to "spin" a story in accord with its content. Half of his eight stories had bias in content and tone, three pro-control and one pro-rights.

Discussion

It would be relatively easy to paint with a broad brush and claim that the *CBS Evening News* is biased in favor of the gun control position in its coverage of the issue, but that would be both simplistic and somewhat misleading. The

Table 6.9. *CBS Evening News* Correspondent Bias

Reporter	Pro-Gun Control	Pro-Gun Rights	Neutral/Mixed
Stewart—Content	37% (7)	0	63% (12)
Stewart—Tone	58% (11)	0	42% (8)
Whitaker—Content	7% (1)	14% (2)	79% (11)
Whitaker—Tone	0	0	100% (14)
Rather—Content	33% (3)	11% (1)	56% (5)
Rather—Tone	44% (4)	0	56% (5)
McNamara—Content	0	0	100% (9)
McNamara—Tone	11% (1)	0	89% (8)
Schieffer—Content	38% (3)	13% (1)	50% (4)
Schieffer—Tone	38% (3)	13% (1)	50% (4)
Bowen—Content	0	0	100% (6)
Bowen—Tone	0	0	100% (6)
Gonzales—Content	50% (3)	0	50% (3)
Gonzales—Tone	50% (3)	0	50% (3)
Axelrod—Content	60% (3)	0	40% (2)
Axelrod—Tone	60% (3)	0	40% (2)
Andrews—Content	25% (1)	0	75% (3)
Andrews—Tone	25% (1)	0	75% (3)
Blackstone—Content	50% (2)	0	50% (2)
Blackstone—Tone	50% (2)	0	50% (2)
Other—Content	27% (14)	2% (1)	71% (36)
Other—Tone	22% (11)	0	78% (40)

reality is more complex. Still, the data clearly indicate that the pro-gun control position is presented on the *CBS Evening News* much more frequently than is the pro-gun rights position, and the percentage of stories that are neutral or balanced is smaller than we would expect if the *CBS Evening News* adheres to an objective model of journalism.

Overall, 68 percent of the reports were neutral or mixed in their coverage. Yet the number of stories with a pro-gun control bias outnumbered those with a pro-gun rights bias by a seven-to-one margin. The results regarding story tone were even more lopsided, with thirty-six being judged pro-control and only one pro-rights. When the Columbine, Washington, D.C. snipers, and Brady Bill stories are removed from the analysis, the coverage is even more biased in favor of the gun control position.

It is also clear that the correspondent assigned to the story influences the story frame. Most notable for a pro-control bias were Jim Stewart, Bob Schieffer, and Dan Rather. Jim Axelrod, Vince Gonzales, and John Blackstone reported fewer stories, but they also had high percentages of pro-control bias. On the other hand, several reporters, notably, Bill Whitaker, Bob McNamara, and Jerry Bowen, were more balanced in their coverage of gun-related stories.

Also of interest is the decision which stories to cover. It is self-evident that final passage of the Brady Bill was worthy of national news coverage. It is less clear that the Columbine shootings and Washington, D.C. snipers stories warranted *as much* national coverage as they received. It is also noteworthy that nine stories were devoted to coverage of school shootings other than Columbine. Remember that school shootings was *not* a topic included in the online search of the archives.

The use of experts, or at least individuals familiar with the topic, is also worthy of consideration. Not surprisingly, elected officials and representatives from interest groups were the most frequently cited experts. Academic experts were cited much less frequently. This pattern might be expected given the willingness of both politicians and interest groups to use the media to disseminate their views and the relative inability of many academics to speak in sound bites.

The National Rifle Association can not possibly complain regarding its *visibility* on CBS. The NRA is *the* authority on matters pertaining to the gun rights position, and its representatives were cited almost as often as all pro-control groups combined. All told, gun rights groups' experts outnumbered gun control groups' experts twenty-eight to twenty, dropping to twenty-five to eleven when the Columbine, snipers, and Brady Bill stories were excluded. Of course, many of the lawmakers, particularly Clinton, who was quoted fifteen times, were pro-control. Still, gun rights groups can not reasonably claim they are excluded from the discussion on CBS.

The NRA also dominated in terms of interest groups that were mentioned in stories, being included in 69 percent of the stories that referred to an interest group when the Columbine, snipers, and Brady Bill stories are included, and 58 percent when they are not. All pro-control groups accounted for 44 percent and 37 percent, respectively, of the interest group references.

The NRA was much more likely than other groups to receive negative coverage on the *CBS Evening News*. The NRA was portrayed negatively in eleven stories and positively in only four stories, while the Brady Campaign, Million Mom March, and Violence Policy Center together were covered positively in four stories and negatively in only one story.

While the video clips shown on CBS primarily featured the individual talking head, other topics such as guns, the crime scene, clips from the Columbine shootings, and victims were prominently featured as well. And while about one-third of the stories included some mention of statistics, almost half included a reference to children. That overrepresents the number of children involved in shootings. Finally, even the *possibility* that one might use a gun to prevent a crime is rarely mentioned on the *CBS Evening News.*[49]

THE *NEW YORK TIMES* RESULTS

The analysis of the *New York Times* coverage of guns and gun control is divided into separate topic areas because of the large number of articles on certain topics. The Columbine shootings; the Washington, D.C. snipers; and coverage of the passage of the Brady Bill are dealt with individually. The bulk of the section deals with gun control articles published in the three-year period.

The *New York Times* published 252 articles dealing with gun control during this period—138 in 2000, 60 in 2001, and 54 in 2002. The disparity in coverage from year to year is due in part to the 2000 elections and the increased involvement of Clinton with the issue. The Bush administration proposed no significant legislation in the policy area, and few bills were introduced in Congress because it was generally understood that significant legislation would be defeated by a Republican majority in the House of Representatives and the Senate. Only 15 percent of the articles appeared on the front page of the *Times*, but 76 percent were five hundred words or longer.

Only three reporters wrote ten or more gun control-related news stories for the *Times* in the time period between 2000 and 2002. Fox Butterfield (thirty-one articles) reported on general gun control issues during the time. James Dao (twenty-five) covered the 2000 presidential election and wrote some gun control articles in the earlier part of the period, while Michael Janofsky (fourteen) wrote numerous articles covering state gun laws, primarily proposed legislation in Colorado following the Columbine shootings.

Nationally, gun control (forty-three articles) was the most frequently covered topic, but state laws (thirty-two), the 2000 presidential campaign (twenty-nine), and lawsuits dealing with guns (twenty-six) also received significant attention from the *Times* (see table 6.10). The National Rifle Association itself was the subject of fifteen articles during this time. The only other topic that was the subject of ten or more articles was the school shooting at Santee High School near San Diego.

The *Times*, like the *CBS Evening News*, mentioned the National Rifle Association in its news stories much more frequently than any other interest group active in the gun control debate. NRA references alone outnumbered

Table 6.10. *New York Times* **Story Topics**

Topic	Number	Percent
Gun control/legislation	43	17%
State laws	32	13%
Campaign 2000	29	12%
Lawsuit—guns	26	10%
NRA/Heston	15	6%
Santee school shooting	10	4%
School shooting	8	3%
Gun safety	8	3%
Second Amendment	8	3%
Interest group	8	3%
Million Mom March	8	3%
Smith & Wesson agreement	7	3%
John Ashcroft/Justice Dept.	7	3%
Gun traces	7	3%
Gun violence/crime	7	3%
Other	107	42%

Note: Percents do not add to 100% because a story may have had more than one topic.

all mentions of pro-control groups by ninety-five to seventy-five. The Brady Campaign was the most frequently mentioned pro-control group (twenty-eight), followed by the Violence Policy Center (sixteen). In most of the articles, spokespersons from the various groups were asked to comment on the news event.

It is not the case, however, that the NRA's coverage was positive (see table 6.11). The large majority of the articles mentioned the NRA in a neutral fashion (87 percent), but the negative references of the group outnumbered the positive by eleven to one. The only other groups ever portrayed negatively were other pro-rights groups, usually state organizations. No pro-control group was mentioned in a negative way in a news story during this time; most

Table 6.11. *New York Times* **Interest Group Bias**

Interest Group	Positive	Negative	Neutral
NRA	1% (1)	12% (11)	87% (82)
National Sports Shooting Federation	0% (0)	0% (0)	100% (17)
Brady Campaign	0% (0)	0% (0)	100% (28)
Violence Policy Center	0% (0)	0% (0)	100% (15)
Other pro-control group	3% (1)	0% (0)	97% (30)
Other pro-rights group	0% (0)	31% (4)	69% (9)

of them were treated in a neutral fashion. This was also true of the National Shooting Sports Federation, the group that represents gun manufacturers and frequently was invited to comment on lawsuits that had been filed against gun dealers or manufacturers.

The *Times* was most likely to use either interest groups (41 percent) or elected officials (32 percent) as expert sources for their stories (see table 6.12). It is worth noting that gun control scholars were cited in twenty-five articles, or 10 percent of the cases. The *Times*'s use of "official" sources, like that of CBS, is not surprising, although its heavy reliance on interest group representatives, who do not even feign objectivity, might be questioned. Still, almost all of the articles in the *Times* balanced interest groups or balanced the NRA with a pro-control politician.

Overall, a large majority of the *New York Times* articles provided a neutral or balanced perspective in those stories analyzed (see table 6.13). In terms of content, 80 percent of the *Times*'s news articles were judged to be neutral or balanced. That said, articles that were pro-gun control in content outnumbered those that favored gun rights by a margin of thirty-nine to eleven (16 percent to 4 percent).

An even higher percentage (87 percent) of the articles were neutral or bal-

Table 6.12.   *New York Times* Experts

Expert	Number	Percent
Interest group	100	41%
Elected official	78	32%
Police	30	12%
Academic—gun control	25	10%
Court/official document	25	10%
Bureaucrat/Justice Dept.	18	7%
Political campaign	13	5%
School official	11	5%
Gun dealer/shop owner	10	4%
President Clinton	9	4%
Other	85	34%

Note: Percents do not add to 100% because a story may have included references to more than one expert.

Table 6.13.   *New York Times* Story Content Bias

Story Content Bias	Number	Percent
Pro-gun control	39	16%
Pro-gun rights	11	4%
Neutral/Mixed	202	80%

anced in their tone (see table 6.14). Only 13 percent had a pro-control bias, but only one article (1 percent) was judged to have a gun-rights bias. When compared to the analysis of CBS, coverage in the *Times* was much more neutral or balanced in terms of both news content and reporter tone. In both cases, the *Times*'s score for objectivity is about 30 percent higher than that for the *CBS Evening News*. Still, the coverage in the *Times* was also more likely to favor gun control over gun rights.

The *Times* cited statistics in 20 percent of its stories, while children were mentioned in 30 percent.[50] A defensive gun use reference was included in eleven (2 percent) of the articles (see table 6.15). Those articles did not refer to an incident in which a gun was used defensively; rather they included some reference to the possibility that a gun *might* be used to defend against a crime or that personal protection is a possible reason for owning a firearm. The overemphasis on children and underrepresentation of defensive gun uses are not statistics to be held up as models of journalism.

Closer analysis of individual reporters' stories reveals substantial differences, or, more accurately, a substantial difference (see table 6.16). Fox Butterfield, who wrote more gun control stories than any other reporter, was also the least objective reporter. More than half of his articles were neutral or balanced in content (65 percent) and tone (55 percent), but his reporting was the most likely to be biased. None of Butterfield's articles favored the gun-rights position, but more than one-third (36 percent) favored gun control in content, and almost half (45 percent) were pro-control in tone. In contrast, James Dao wrote twenty-five gun-related articles, the second largest number on the *Times* staff, but only one was pro-control in content, while five favored the gun rights position. All twenty-five of his stories were neutral or balanced in

Table 6.14. *New York Times* **Story Tone Bias**

Story Content Bias	Number	Percent
Pro-gun control	33	13%
Pro-gun rights	1	0%
Neutral/Mixed	218	87%

Table 6.15. *New York Times* **Items in Stories**

Topic Mentioned	Number	Percent
Statistics cited	51	20%
Child in story	75	30%
Defensive gun use mentioned	11	2%

Table 6.16. *New York Times* Reporter Bias (News Stories, Gun Control Only)

Reporter	Neutral/Balanced	Pro-Control	Pro-Rights
Butterfield—Content	65% (20)	36% (11)	0% (0)
Butterfield—Tone	55% (17)	45% (14)	0% (0)
Dao—Content	76% (19)	4% (1)	20% (5)
Dao—Tone	100% (25)	0% (0)	0% (0)
New York Times—Content	84% (16)	16% (3)	0% (0)
New York Times—Tone	90% (17)	11% (2)	0% (0)
Janofsky—Content	93% (13)	7% (1)	0% (0)
Janofsky—Tone	93% (13)	7% (1)	0% (0)
Associated Press—Content	88% (7)	12% (1)	0% (0)
Associated Press—Tone	100% (8)	0% (0)	0% (0)
Clines—Content	33% (2)	50% (3)	17% (1)
Clines—Tone	83% (5)	17% (1)	0% (0)
Lacey—Content	100% (6)	0% (0)	0% (0)
Lacey—Tone	83% (5)	17% (1)	0% (0)
Glaberson—Content	80% (4)	20% (1)	0% (0)
Glaberson—Tone	100% (5)	0% (0)	0% (0)
Toner—Content	80% (4)	20% (1)	0% (0)
Toner—Tone	100% (5)	0% (0)	0% (0)
Other—Content	82% (120)	14% (21)	2% (6)
Other—Tone	89% (131)	10% (15)	1% (1)

tone. This is not the first time that Butterfield's coverage of gun control has been criticized.[51] If Butterfield's articles are removed from the analysis, objectivity in the *Times*'s coverage of gun control increases significantly.

Brady Bill Passage

The *New York Times* ran fifteen articles during the final passage of the Brady Bill in 1993. The primary reporter was Clifford Krauss, who wrote eight of the articles. All of his stories were neutral or balanced in both content and tone. Overall, three of the articles were pro-control in content, and two were pro-control in tone. The rest were neutral or balanced. The NRA was mentioned in six of the articles, and all of those were neutral references, while the Brady Campaign (then known as Handgun Control, Inc.) had three neutral and two positive references. One of the articles mentioned defensive gun use. The coverage of the Brady Bill was prominent, with 27 percent of the articles appearing on the front page.

The Washington, D.C. Snipers

There were 142 articles covering the Washington, D.C. snipers. Most of these stories focused on the details of the crimes, the investigation, and the prosecution of the suspects. It is not surprising that 95 percent (135) of the articles were neutral or balanced in content, while 4 percent were pro-control and 1 percent favored gun rights. In terms of tone, 96 percent (136) were neutral or balanced, with 4 percent favoring gun control and 1 percent favoring gun rights. Six of the articles focused on ballistic fingerprinting technology; none mentioned defensive gun use. Fully 16 percent (22) of the articles referred to children. Almost one-fourth (24 percent) were front-page stories, and 89 percent were five hundred words or longer. In simple terms, the coverage was extensive by any measure.

Seven articles mentioned the NRA (four neutral, three negative), while the Brady Campaign was included in five and the Violence Policy Center in four (all neutral). Four of the articles that referenced the NRA were written by Butterfield; three of those references were negative.

The Columbine High School Shootings

The *Times* extensively covered the tragedy at Columbine High School. There were eighty-eight stories about the events written by numerous reporters (six reporters wrote five or more articles, but none wrote ten or more). Almost one-fourth (22 percent) were on the front page, and 85 percent were five hundred words or longer. The large majority (90 percent) was neutral or balanced in terms of content (8 percent pro-control; 1 percent pro-rights), and every story (100 percent) was judged to be neutral or balanced in tone. There was one reference to defensive gun use. The NRA was included in eleven stories (seven neutral, four negative), while the Brady Campaign, Violence Policy Center, and National Shooting Sports Federation were all mentioned once. Frank Bruni wrote six of the articles—three were pro-control and one pro-gun rights in content, and he referred to the NRA negatively twice.

Gun control was the topic in 10 percent of the stories, more than the investigation, the suspects, or the students (4 percent each). Students were the most frequently cited sources (17 percent), followed by elected officials (14 percent), police (12 percent), and friends and family (12 percent).

Editorials

The editorial pages are the part of the newspaper designated for opinions. While the editorial position of a paper may well be biased, that is clearly not a violation of any of the canons of journalism. On the contrary, it is standard, expected, and respected.

It is obvious that the editorial position of the *New York Times* favors gun control. During the 2000–2002 period, there were twenty-six editorials in the *Times* that focused on gun control. In addition, there were four columns on the topic and eight op-ed pieces. About three-fourths of the commentary pieces were pro-control. With regard to content, 77 percent favored gun control, 18 percent were neutral, and 5 percent favored the gun rights position. In terms of tone, the results were almost the same (79 percent pro-control, 16 percent neutral, and 5 percent pro-gun rights). Examining only the editorials, twenty-four of twenty-six favored gun control in both content and tone. None of the commentary pieces discussed defensive gun use, but 40 percent included a reference to children. The NRA was mentioned in eighteen of the articles (fifteen negative, five neutral, and two positive), while all other groups combined were mentioned a total of ten times.

There were nine commentary pieces published during the period in which the Washington, D.C. snipers story was covered. Five of those were pro-control in content and tone; four were neutral in content and tone. Three mentioned the NRA, and all of those references were negative.

The Columbine tragedy produced eleven commentary pieces. Seven of them favored gun control, and four were neutral. Six of seven Columbine editorials were pro-control in content, and five of seven were pro-control in tone.

Does the editorial position of the newspaper influence the news pages? Although it is important, that question is difficult to answer, and the data contained here do not provide us with an answer. We can say, however, that the *Times* editorial pages are clearly biased in favor of gun control, while its news coverage is more balanced, though still slanted toward the gun control position.

Discussion

Coverage of guns and gun control issues in the *New York Times* was generally balanced, although there were some exceptions. The *Times* covered the issue both nationally and at the state level. The National Rifle Association was mentioned more frequently in *Times* articles than all other interest groups combined. Although references to the NRA were overwhelmingly neutral, negative references outnumbered positive references by eleven to one.

In terms of story content and reporter tone, *Times* coverage of gun control was predominantly neutral or balanced (80 percent and 87 percent, respectively). Still, a pro-gun control bias was much more likely than a gun rights bias in these articles (16 percent to 4 percent in content; 13 percent to 0 percent in tone). Much of this bias is attributable to the articles authored by Fox Butterfield. While Butterfield accounted for 12 percent of the articles analyzed, he wrote 28 percent of the articles with pro-control content and 42 percent of the articles with pro-control tone. The contrast in the writing of Butterfield and that of James Dao, the second most prolific reporter, is stark. Dao's articles were much more likely to be to be neutral (100 percent) in tone, and, while 76 percent were neutral in content, a gun rights slant was found in five of his articles, and a gun control stance was found in only one. An observer might raise the question why the *Times* so frequently assigned stories to Butterfield.

Overall, the *Times* included references to children in disproportion to their victimization rates, and there were relatively few references to defensive gun use. The *Times* coverage of the debate over gun control in Colorado following the Columbine tragedy can be seen as either a follow-up on an important issue or as an overemphasis on the high school shootings.

There is little doubt that the coverage afforded to the Columbine shootings and the Washington, D.C. snipers was both extensive and disproportionate. That coverage was, however, largely neutral (but still more likely to favor control than gun rights). This is important because the sheer amount of coverage indicates that the editors at the *Times* felt these were very important stories. The presence of conflict, drama, and tragedy make them ideal news stories. Yet it is possible that extensive coverage magnifies the importance of the events for the audience.

The editorial position of the *New York Times* is obvious. The editorial board appears to have rarely, if ever, seen a piece of gun control legislation that it did not like and sees few legitimate reasons for owning a firearm. Again, it should be emphasized that the editorial position is clearly not an infringement on journalistic objectivity.

CONCLUSION

In some important ways, the coverage of guns and the issue of gun control by the *CBS Evening News* and the *New York Times* was similar, but in other ways it was different. While the majority of the news stories in both media were neutral in terms of content and reporter tone, more of the news reports had a bias in favor of gun control rather than a bias in favor of gun rights.

The standard against which the coverage is judged is critical to the conclusion. If one argues that news coverage should be 100 percent objective, then both media fail. If the standard is somewhat less than that, then how fairly these media deal with the issue of guns and gun control is debatable.

The 100 percent standard is almost certainly unrealistically high and certainly subject to observer error. Still, the media should strive for that mark, and the ratio of gun control bias to gun rights bias in both news media is telling.

The coverage in the *New York Times* was more balanced or neutral than the coverage by the *CBS Evening News*. In addition, much of the bias that is found in the *Times* is attributable to one reporter—Fox Butterfield. While the *CBS Evening News* correspondents were certainly different in terms of their objectivity, the slant in the *CBS Evening News* was more pervasive.

Looking beyond the analysis of how stories were covered to examine which stories were covered reveals more bias. Neither news medium paid much attention to the possibility, to say nothing of the reality, that guns can be used to prevent crime. While part of this is due to how news is defined, it is virtually impossible to say that is the only reason. In most defensive gun uses, no one is injured, and only a few result in death. Therefore, the media are not likely to cover these events using a generally agreed-upon standard of newsworthiness. Not including the justification for owning a firearm is, however, a separate issue, and one that can not be explained by journalistic practices.

Both media focus on children in their coverage to a much greater degree than children are actual shooting victims. For example, CBS often included film of the Columbine shootings in stories that did not deal with Columbine. They also covered several school shootings, with no apparent consideration of the number of victims. Their age appeared to be more relevant. This standard appears to be different from that employed in judging defensive gun uses as not newsworthy. It also differs from the standard used when determining whether to grant national news coverage to the shooting of an adult.

The National Rifle Association received a disproportionate share of the attention given by both CBS and the *Times* to interest groups involved in the gun control debate, but that coverage was more negative in both media. References to the NRA were not always balanced by references to pro-control groups, but the negative light in which the NRA was shown more than accomplished any balancing we might expect to see by including other groups in the story.

In summary, while it may be unrealistic to expect any medium to achieve 100 percent in terms of neutrality or objectivity on any particular issue, it is not unreasonable to expect that these two well-respected national news outlets would do better than the results here indicate. Questions regarding the assignment of the least objective reporters to cover gun control stories should be raised within the news organizations.

The data reported here demonstrate nothing with regard to the impact of the coverage. However, it would be naive to suggest that there is no impact. The data show that consumers of information provided by the *CBS Evening News* and the *New York Times* are receiving a view of the issue that favors the gun control side of the debate. It is logical to assume that those consumers would be more likely to adopt a position that favors that position more than they might if the news presentation were more balanced or tipped to the gun rights side.

NOTES

1. Several studies have found relatively weak correlations between attention to the mass media and political knowledge. For example, see John P. Robinson and Mark R. Levy, *The Main Source: Learning from Television News* (Thousand Oaks, CA: Sage, 1986); and Dan Drew and David Weaver, "Voter Learning in the 1988 Presidential Election: Did the Debates and the Media Matter?" *Journalism Quarterly* 68 (1991): 27–37. Michael X. Delli Carpini and Scott Keeter, *What Americans Know about Politics and Why It Matters* (New Haven, CT: Yale University Press, 1996), 185, suggest that "this finding is unsatisfying, given that much of one's observed knowledge about politics must come, at least initially, from the mass media." They assert that poor survey indicators for media attention may be responsible.

2. David L. Paletz, *The Media in American Politics: Contents and Consequences*, 2nd ed. (New York: Longman, 2002), 57.

3. Doris A. Graber, *Mass Media & American Politics*, 6th ed. (Washington, D.C.: CQ Press, 2002), 108–09.

4. This was noted in a reporting class by Professor Eugene Goodwin at Penn State University. While I do not recall the exact date, the quote has always stuck with me. It is possible that this phrase was coined by someone else before Goodwin.

5. W. Lance Bennett, *News: The Politics of Illusion*, 2nd ed. (New York: Longman, 1988).

6. Maxwell E. McCombs and Donald L. Shaw, "The Agenda-Setting Function of Mass Media," *Public Opinion Quarterly* 36 (1972): 176–87; and Roger W. Cobb and Charles Elder, *Participation in American Politics: The Dynamics of Agenda Building* (Baltimore: Johns Hopkins University Press, 1983).

7. Denis McQuail, "The Influence and Effects of the Mass Media," in *Media Power in Politics*, ed. Doris A. Graber, 4th ed. (Washington, D.C.: CQ Press, 2000), 7–23.

8. Paletz, *The Media*, 65.

9. The evolution of the American press is thoroughly and concisely explained in Larry J. Sabato, *Feeding Frenzy: How Attack Journalism Has Transformed American Politics* (New York: Free Press, 1991), chap. 2.

10. Robert M. Entman, "Framing: Toward Clarification of a Fractured Paradigm," *Journal of Communication* 43 (1993): 51–58.

11. Paletz, *The Media,* 66–67.

12. Donald P. Haider-Markel and Mark R. Joslyn, "Gun Policy, Opinion, Tragedy, and Blame Attribution: The Conditional Influence of Issue Frames," *Journal of Politics* 63, no. 2 (May 2001): 520–43.

13. Karen Callaghan and Frauke Schnell, "Assessing the Democratic Debate: How the News Media Frame Elite Policy Discourse," *Political Communication* 18 (2001): 183–212.

14. Graber, *Mass Media,* 128, 253–54.

15. David Shaw, "Abortion Bias Seeps into News," *Los Angeles Times,* July 1, 1990, 1. Anecdotally, the author recalls watching reports of a gay rights march that took place in Washington several years ago. The *CBS Evening News* coverage included film of several of the marchers. Their appearance was very typical in that they looked like citizens one might expect to see at any political rally. Coverage of the event by Pat Robertson's CBN (certainly not a major news network or one that would be generally categorized as "objective") broadcast included film of marchers from the same event, but their appearance and behavior were significantly different than those who were on CBS. While it is impossible to say if either broadcast specifically chose which marchers to spotlight, there is no doubt that the impact on the viewers was significantly different.

16. S. Robert Lichter and Richard E. Noyes, *Good Intentions Make Bad News: Why Americans Hate Campaign Journalism,* 2nd ed. (Lanham, MD: Rowman & Littlefield, 1995); and Stephen J. Farnsworth and S. Robert Lichter, *The Nightly News Nightmare: Network Television's Coverage of U.S. Presidential Elections, 1988–2000* (Lanham, MD: Rowman & Littlefield, 2003).

17. Timothy E. Cook, *Governing with the News: The News Media as a Political Institution* (Chicago: University of Chicago Press, 1998); and Thomas E. Patterson, "Political Roles of Journalists," in *The Politics of News, The News of Politics,* eds. Doris Graber, Denis McQuail, and Pippa Norris (Washington, D.C.: CQ Press, 1998), 17–32.

18. Of course, public ownership of the media can bring its own set of biases if the government attempts to control news content and presentation.

19. Ray Surette, *Media, Crime, and Criminal Justice: Images and Realities* (Pacific Grove, CA: Brooks/Cole, 1992), 62.

20. Surette, *Media, Crime,* chap. 4.

21. Gary Kleck and Don B. Kates, *Armed: New Perspectives on Gun Control* (Amherst, NY: Prometheus, 2001); and John R. Lott, Jr., *The Bias against Guns* (Washington, D.C.: Regnery, 2003). Although Lott's work is based on an extensive content analysis of print and broadcast media coverage of gun control, many of the results are recounted in anecdotal form. To be fair, he cites statistics with regard to coverage of defensive gun uses and the use of academics who study gun control as sources by the media. In addition, his conversations with several reporters are also enlightening.

22. Ted Gest, "Firearms Follies: How the News Media Cover Gun Control," *Media Studies Journal* 6, no. 1 (1992): 140. Charges of ignorance, misinformation, and bias against guns and gun owners are also leveled against the media in William R. Tonso, "Shooting Blind," *Reason* 27, no. 9 (Nov. 1995): 30. Tonso's article deals mainly with coverage of assault weapons and how that coverage helped create support for the assault weapons ban. For a discussion of earlier coverage of gun control, see William R. Tonso, "Calling the Shots," *Reason* 17 (March 1985): 42.

23. Gest, "Firearms Follies," 144.

24. "Guns," *Columbia Journalism Review*, February 15, 1999, 6–8.

25. Thomas Winship, "Step Up the War against Guns," *Editor & Publisher* 127, no. 17 (April 24, 1993): 24.

26. Winship, "Step Up the War," 24.

27. Michael Bane, "Targeting the Media's Anti-Gun Bias," *American Journalism Review* 23, no. 6, (July 2001): 18.

28. Bane, "Targeting," 18.

29. For anecdotes from a variety of sources, see Kenneth Smith, "Loaded Coverage," *Reason* 32, no. 2 (June 2000): 39.

30. Callaghan and Schnell, "Assessing the Debate."

31. Dhavan Vinod Shah, "Value Judgments: News Framing and Individual Processing of Political Issues" (PhD diss., University of Minnesota, 1999).

32. Kenneth Dowler, "Media Influence on Attitudes toward Guns and Gun Control," *American Journal of Criminal Justice* 26, no. 2 (2002): 235–47.

33. Brian Anse Patrick, *The National Rifle Association and the Media* (New York: Peter Lang, 2002), 53.

34. Patrick, *The National Rifle Association*, 52.

35. Tamryn Etten, "Gun Control and the Press: A Content Analysis of Newspaper Bias," (paper presented at the annual meeting of the American Society of Criminology, San Francisco, November 20–23, 1991).

36. Geoffrey Dickens, "Outgunned: How the Network News Media Are Spinning the Gun Control Debate," Media Research Center, January 5, 2000, at www.mediaresearch.org/specialreports/2000/rep01052000.asp. While the report does not specify the methodology employed, the findings reflect those of other academic studies, although they are more pronounced in the MRC report.

37. Kleck and Kates, *Armed*, 203.

38. The Vanderbilt News Archive was searched with the following terms: gun control, gun violence, gun legislation, gun safety, gun laws, guns and polls, defensive gun use, campaign 2000 and guns, Brady Bill, Columbine, sniper, Second Amendment, National Rifle Association, Brady Campaign (and Handgun Control), and Million Mom March.

39. The news archive counted only ninety-seven news segments. The difference is almost exclusively due to counting coverage of the Brady Bill, Columbine High School shootings, and the Washington, D.C. snipers. While the archive counted continuous coverage as one segment that could be eight or nine minutes in length, this study counted those as individual stories when different reporters covered different aspects of the story.

40. Graber, *Mass Media*, 46.

41. Paletz. *The Media*, 72.

42. In addition, numerous articles were clipped by the author as part of the daily reading of the newspaper. Searches were also conducted for a one-month period around the passage of the Brady Bill and a two-month period following the Columbine shootings and the initial Washington, D.C. snipers shooting to coincide with the time frame of news segments on CBS. Gun control articles were included if they dealt with national legislation or events or state laws from outside the New York tri-state area. Some articles dealing with New York, Connecticut, or New Jersey were included if the subject was more national than local. Although these criteria were somewhat subjective, they did not affect the

results. The stories that were judged to be biased were not of local origin. Editorials, columns, and op-ed pieces were included if they dealt with gun control, but they were analyzed separately.

43. A defensive gun use could be mentioned in theory as a potential reason for purchasing or owning a firearm. No specific incident had to be mentioned for a story to be coded as including a reference to defensive gun use.

44. John R. Lott, Jr., "Media Bias against Guns," *Imprimis*, 33, no. 9 (September 2004). Lott's search of *USA Today*, *The Wall Street Journal*, and the *New York Times* for 2001 revealed only that one article mentioned a defensive gun use. Widening the search revealed that the *Los Angeles Times*, the *Washington Post*, and the *Chicago Tribune* each reported three such stories in 2001.

45. Following are examples of two stories from the *CBS Evening News* and the *New York Times* that were judged to be biased in content and tone. For illustrative purposes one is obvious on its face, and the other is subtler.

On April 6, 2000, Dan Rather interviewed President Bill Clinton. The introduction referred to gun violence as "another health-related issue" (adopts the issue framing of gun control advocates) and Clinton's "battle with Congress over laws aimed at reducing gun crimes" (again, it is debatable if the laws would reduce gun crimes) "and the prospects for passing even *modest* new measures" (emphasis in original; there is a question about what constitutes a modest measure). Rather went on to describe a "fierce fight to get additional gun safety legislation passed." This story was pro-control in content because there was no rebuttal to the points made by Clinton. The tone was pro-control because of Rather's commentary in the story.

A February 27, 1995, "Eye on America" update on the anniversary of the implementation of the Brady Law was introduced by Connie Chung: "CBS News has learned the law *is* having an impact. . . . Jim Stewart has the surprising results." Stewart: "On the first anniversary of gun control, two things are clear. More handguns were sold last year than any time in history and more criminals than anyone ever dreamed of tried to do the buying." Stewart claimed that the *CBS Evening News* documented 2,356,376 handgun applications nationwide and 44,788 denials, which he described as the "big news." While he could not say the number of crimes prevented, "what we did find is that an amazing number of Americans, with serious criminal records aren't going to the black market trying to buy a gun. They're first coming here, to a gun store, and trying to buy one like anyone else." There are several issues here. A denial does not necessarily indicate that someone has a serious criminal record. It's also not clear what constitutes an amazing number of Americans. There is no mention that many of those denied a purchase could have gotten a gun on the black market, and the report may mislead the viewer into thinking that gun shop purchases are a common way for criminals to obtain guns. That was not true, even prior to the Brady Bill.

Fox Butterfield wrote an article on October 7, 2002, that discussed ballistics tests. The article begins, "The technology exists to create a national ballistic fingerprint system that would enable law enforcement officials to trace bullets recovered from shootings, like those fired by the Washington-area sniper, to a suspect. Such a system would have been of great use in the Washington case, in which six people were shot to death, because so far bullet fragments are virtually the only evidence. But because of opposition by the gun industry and the National Rifle Association, only two states have moved to set up a ballistic fingerprint system, and Congress has prohibited a national program, experts say." Butterfield does not attribute his first two sentences, which were separate paragraphs in the article. This reads more like an editorial. He goes on to discuss the benefits of the system, without a single reference to technological problems or the fact that the gun could only be traced if all guns were tested and all sales recorded. Even then, a bullet fired from a stolen gun would not lead police to the shooter. He does mention that the NRA opposes the idea because it has called it tantamount to a national gun registry. He does not quote a NRA official, but a Brady Campaign official is quoted as referring to the NRA's position as "paranoia . . . which prevents effective law enforcement."

On December 6, 2001, Butterfield wrote an article regarding the Justice Department prohibiting the FBI from looking at gun background check records to determine if any of the people detained after the September 11 attacks had bought a gun. He states that the policy "has frustrated some FBI and other law enforcement officials" and that the department is "being unusually solicitous of foreigners' gun rights." There is no attribution for that statement, although the police chief of Los Gatos, California, is quoted later in the article. Someone at the FBI had already gotten two "hits" on the system. Unnamed FBI officials said the checks had been allowed in the past. He does quote a NRA spokesman who said that the two hits obtained indicated that the Clinton administration had not enforced the checks properly. There is no mention that the destruction of the records are to protect the privacy of the purchasers, a point the NRA spokesman almost certainly would have raised. The implication of the story is that the September 11 investigation was hindered to protect the rights of gun owners and "foreigners." The statements to that effect clearly overwhelm any evidence to the contrary.

46. As an example of the latter, both CNN and CBS stories regarding the Million Mom March on Washington were analyzed. The CNN story included mention of a "competing" group of women who were protesting the march as a way of arguing for gun rights. The CBS stories made no mention of this other group. Instead, they focused on how MMM was promoting legislation that would reduce gun violence against children. The CNN coverage was neutral, while the CBS coverage was positive toward MMM. No CNN stories are included in this analysis.

47. This clip shows a student who had been shot in the head leaning out a window. As rescuers reach up for him, he appears to fall or jump from the window.

48. The most biased stories were those that dealt with guns or ammunition (63 percent; five of eight), school shootings (56 percent; five of nine), or political campaigns (50 percent; three of six).

49. Although it was not considered in this analysis, the reader is encouraged to go to www.cbsnews.com and click on the link to "Interactive Guns in America." There you will find a firearms timeline, which traces the passage of gun control laws, lawsuits, and safety requirements. There is another link to "Gun Deaths and Laws," which provides state-by-state information from the National Center for Health Statistics and the Brady Campaign. Other links connect to "Who's At Risk" and "Kids and Guns." The latter link contains data from the Johns Hopkins Center for Gun Policy and Research that reveals the dangers of guns. Two final links are "U.S. School Shootings" and "U.S. Workplace Shootings." These are interactive maps in which clicking on a point reveals the date, place, and number of deaths in the shooting.

50. If the Columbine news articles were included here, as they were in the table for the

CBS Evening News, the percentage of articles that included a reference to children would be significantly higher.

51. Dave Kopel and Paul H. Blackman, "Gray Gun Stories," *National Review*, June 9, 2003, at www.nationalreview.com/script/kopel/kopel060903.asp. Kopel and Blackman describe a series of factual errors in Butterfield's writings. While that was a concern in the present analysis, the purpose in this research is to look only at the manner in which the information is presented. The factual accuracy of the information was not considered in the coding. Of course, factual errors are at least as serious, if not more so, than biased presentation. That is particularly true, when, as Kopel and Blackman assert, the factual errors are consistently in favor of one side of the debate.

Chapter Seven

A View from a State:
Gun Policy in Virginia

As federalism is defined in the United States, the individual states are often regarded as laboratories for the national government. Various policies are adopted and implemented in the states, and we can see which policies are successful to help ensure wiser decisions at the national level.[1] This experimentation may be deliberate, such as in the case of welfare reform, in which several states were granted waivers by the federal government to establish their own rules regarding programs designed to help the poor.

Another interpretation of federalism simply promotes greater state autonomy. It recognizes the fact that there is a great deal of diversity among the states and that a single program may not be equally effective in different states. States benefit because they can create, enact, and implement policies that will be of greater value to them.[2]

In the case of gun control, it is a situation of pure federalism, in that states often wish to follow their own path with regard to guns and gun control legislation. This is more a matter of political culture and public opinion than it is an attempt to have the states experiment with gun control policy making. It recognizes that circumstances regarding firearms are very different in California than they are in North Dakota.

Virginia is uniquely situated to serve as a bellwether for gun control legislation. Its proximity to Washington, D.C., and its cultural, economic, and geographic diversity make it a state with a variety of views. While Virginia may be categorized as one of the conservative, southern, Republican-leaning "red states," it is not as simple as that.

The people, opinions, and politics of northern Virginia, Tidewater, Richmond, Southside, the Shenandoah Valley, and southwest Virginia are distinctly different. The bulk of Virginia's population lives in the northern part of the state and along the east coast. Those areas also have a higher percentage of immigrants from other states due to the presence of the federal government and high-tech industry in northern Virginia and military bases in Tidewater. Central, south, and southwest Virginia are areas of slower growth, both economic and population, less transient populations, and a more traditionally southern culture. Politically, Virginia remains the only state with a one-term limit on its governor. The legislature, known as the General Assembly, meets for a six- or eight-week session in alternate years. The "long session" is in even-numbered years, when the biennial state budget plan is adopted. Legislative and statewide elections are held in odd-numbered years.

Virginia is important to the gun control debate, in part, because it is the home of the national headquarters of the National Rifle Association. Former NRA lobbyist Todd Adkins describes Virginia as "generally pro-gun. Virginia would be about a 7 on a 1 to 10 scale."[3] Many gun control bills are introduced, but defeated in the General Assembly. For example, a bill that would ban .50 caliber ammunition was defeated rather easily in Virginia in 2003, but it was not introduced in any other state. California became the first state to ban .50 caliber rifles in 2004.[4]

The plethora of bills in Virginia is partly due to the nature of the General Assembly. Adkins describes it as an "honest system in that committees allow bills to come up for a vote." This is true as a legislative norm, not a partisan practice, he notes. Many of the bills that are killed easily in committee in Virginia would never "see the light of day in other states."

While Virginia currently leans more toward gun rights, its laws place it somewhere in the middle of the pack in terms of state gun control laws. The state received a C-minus on its 2005 report card issued by the Brady Campaign.[5] While that grade may seem low, thirty-one states earned a D or F.

Virginia has a child access prevention law, regulates the possession and sale of firearms to juveniles, and has a one-handgun-per-month limit on most purchasers. On the other hand, no permit is required to purchase firearms in the Commonwealth, there is no registration or licensing policy, and it is a shall-issue state with regard to concealed-carry permits.[6]

Gun control is an important issue in many elections within Virginia, and the NRA is relatively active in statewide elections. Pro-gun control groups are less active, in terms of both elections and lobbying elected officials in Richmond. A study of the 2000 U.S. Senate campaign in Virginia found that the NRA was one of the most active interest groups in terms of contact with its membership, and it was estimated that the group spent almost $700,000 in that campaign—more than any other interest group.[7]

This chapter focuses on the issue of gun control in the Virginia General Assembly, examines the important gun legislation introduced in the General

Assembly, explores the role of interest groups in the legislative process, and discusses the importance of Governor Mark Warner's successful campaign outreach to the Commonwealth's sportsmen.

THE 2003 GENERAL ASSEMBLY

Several gun-related bills were introduced in the Virginia General Assembly's 2003 session. Many of them were "dead on arrival," and had no chance of passage, while others were more seriously considered. The 2003 session featured legislation introduced on both sides of the debate, ranging from requiring background checks of gun purchasers at gun shows to banning the sale of a certain type of ammunition to permitting those who have a permit to carry a concealed weapon to carry their guns in restaurants. At present, it is generally agreed that most pro-control measures stand little or no chance of passage in Virginia because key committees in the House of Delegates are controlled by Republicans who support gun rights. The real debate in the Commonwealth, therefore, is over the pro-gun rights measures.

House Bill 1997

H.B. 1997 was introduced by Republican delegate Lee Ware, one of the legislature's staunch supporters of Second Amendment rights. The bill would have modified the current prohibition against carrying a concealed weapon into a restaurant by creating and defining "entertainment establishments." The bill "defines an entertainment establishment as an establishment . . . whose sale of alcohol constitutes more than 30 percent of total sales . . . and removes the prohibition on taking an otherwise legally concealed handgun into a restaurant, replacing it with a prohibition on taking an otherwise legally concealed handgun into an entertainment establishment."[8]

Depending upon one's position on the gun control issue, this bill was known as "guns in bars" or "guns in restaurants." Similar bills had died in previous years, but 2003 was seen by many observers as the year in which it stood a strong chance of passage. More legislative support had been lined up, and the primary interest groups, particularly the NRA, were prepared to make this their signature legislation of the session. H.B. 1997 was considered to be the most important gun-related measure in the 2003 session, and it was seen as a test of the increasing strength of the gun rights forces in the state.

Ware's legislation was strongly supported by the NRA and several other hunters' associations in the state. It was opposed by gun control groups such as Virginians Against Handgun Violence (VAHV); the Virginia Hospitality &

Travel Association (VHTA) which was representing restaurant owners; and the more radical pro-gun groups Virginia Citizens Defense League (VCDL) and Virginia Gun Owners Coalition (VGOC). A careful reading of that list of opponents proves the old adage "Politics makes strange bedfellows." Gun control advocates, the staunchest defenders of gun rights, and restaurant owners indeed comprise an unusual combination of groups to be aligned together on any piece of legislation.

The gun rights groups were the most vocal opponents. The VCDL organized a postcard and e-mail campaign that generated more than five hundred e-mails and scores of postcards in the offices of several key legislators.[9] The VCDL opposed the legislation as too concessionary and contrary to its demands for repeal of all restrictions on carrying licensed concealed handguns.

The restaurant owners' opposition was grounded in a belief that permitting concealed handguns in any establishment that serves alcohol is a recipe for disaster. The risk that someone carrying a gun would consume alcohol and have his judgment impaired would be too great. Restaurant owners think this would result in shootings and deaths. The opposition of Virginians Against Handgun Violence is both predictable and self-explanatory.

According to the NRA's memo to members of the House of Delegates Militia, Police, and Public Safety Committee (Militia and Police), the change in the law would bring Virginia more in line with other states that issue concealed-carry permits. In addition, permit holders can be trusted with this responsibility: "These men and women have proven to be one of the most law-abiding segments of the citizenry at large, not only here in Virginia, but throughout the country. There is nothing to suggest that their law-abiding behavior will somehow change upon entering a restaurant that has been licensed by the ABC to serve alcohol."[10]

The bill easily passed through the sympathetic Militia and Police Committee on a 15–7 vote.[11] This committee was dominated by Republicans from the gun-favoring regions—thirteen of the fifteen Republicans voted in favor of the bill, and one of the opponents apparently agreed with the VCDL and VGOC that it did not go far enough. Only one of the Republicans on the committee hailed from northern Virginia, and he is a strong supporter of gun rights and personally has a permit to carry a concealed firearm, according to discussion in committee. Two Democrats, one from southwest Virginia and one from Southside, voted in favor of the bill, while five (three from northern Virginia and two from the Richmond area) opposed it.

The bill faced a tougher time on the floor of the House, but it prevailed in a 52–48 vote. While the vote fell to some extent along party lines, twenty-one Republicans voted against it, and nine Democrats voted in favor of the bill. Eight of the nine Democrats who supported the bill were from southwest Virginia or Southside, while the other was from Tidewater. Only one of the defecting Republicans was from Southside; none was from southwest.

The bill faced an uphill battle in the Senate. While both sides acknowledged that the vote on the floor would be close, the NRA believed that it would prevail. The difficulty would be to get the bill out of committee. While it may seem more logical that the bill would be referred to Courts of Justice, which deals with most gun control bills, it was assigned to the Rehabilitation and Social Services Committee because it redefined the section of the state code that deals with Alcohol Beverage Control (ABC) laws.

Either road was difficult for the bill's supporters. First, Republicans only held a one seat advantage on Senate committees. Second, neither of those committees was stacked in favor of gun legislation, like the Militia and Police Committee on the House side.

The Senate committee officially carried the bill over, effectively killing it, without taking a formal vote.[12] Chairman Emmett Hanger announced that the committee was deadlocked on the bill 7–7 (one senator was not present due to a death in the family). The bill's fate was sealed several days before, however, when the VHTA successfully captured the vote of Republican Nick Rerras, from the Tidewater region.

In an interview the day before the Senate Rehabilitation and Social Services Committee killed the concealed-carry bill, NRA lobbyist Adkins discussed the implications of the vote.[13] Adkins said he had discussed the vote with Rerras, who was cross-pressured by the restaurant lobby, which included some of his prominent supporters. While Adkins understood Rerras's position, he noted that Rerras said he expected the NRA would target him in the next election, and Adkins anticipated that as well.

Rerras did not face a primary election opponent, although the NRA had the option of finding and supporting a sympathetic Democratic candidate for the November election. The NRA simply withdrew its support from Rerras, but he was reelected anyway, demonstrating the limits of the NRA's influence. The NRA ran a risk if it allowed Rerras to cast his vote without repercussions. This is true even with a legislator who is usually on the side of gun rights. The organization believed it needed to send a message to other legislators—your support has to be 100 percent or else you may face the wrath of the NRA. Conversely, the failure to defeat Rerras indicates that the NRA is not omnipotent.

It was generally accepted that all seven Democrats on the Social Services Committee were strongly opposed to the legislation. All of them were African Americans and/or females from northern Virginia or the Richmond area. Two of the eight Republicans represented northern Virginia, and three were from

Tidewater. Several days prior to the vote, a couple of the Republicans were thought to be wavering in their support, one due to media and constituent pressure and the other due to pressure from and sympathy toward the more radical gun groups. The support of the wavering Republicans was gained, but Rerras's vote was irretrievably lost.

Tom Lisk of the VHTA would not discuss the specifics of lobbying Rerras, but he did not disagree that it was his group which influenced Rerras. According to Lisk, the group "tried to avoid making this a gun control issue."[14] He noted that they do not have a position on gun control, but they opposed this bill because of its potential impact on restaurants. While more traditional gun control groups such as VAHV and the Million Mom March also opposed H.B. 1997, the Restaurant Association took the lead "because we're better organized."

Obviously, Lisk was able to convince Rerras that reelection was more likely with the VHTA in his corner than the NRA, and his assessment was correct. Rerras received the support of the VHTA and won reelection. This was clearly a case of an interest group influencing a legislator's vote.

When asked about Rerras's reelection campaign, Lisk noted that "they're [NRA] astute enough to know he's good [on most of their issues]. It's tough to find a single-issue candidate." Of course, Lisk had a vested interest in minimizing the chances of Rerras being defeated in a Republican primary, and he did not say there was no chance. Still, Lisk noted that Rerras's constituency was somewhat split on the issue of gun control.

During the committee session, Hanger announced that the group was deadlocked and that it would be counterproductive to debate the bill any further. With that said, debate was stifled, and the bill died. At the same time, Rerras did not have to cast a formal vote. None was taken, and none was recorded. Hanger was attempting to provide political cover for Rerras by not holding a formal vote and silencing the groups in the room. Although all those present knew what had happened, there was no paper trail to trace back to Rerras.

Interestingly, prior to this nonvote, Hanger asked for Ware's support for a committee amendment that substituted a .02 blood alcohol content (BAC) standard for carrying a concealed weapon. Anyone at or above that level would not be legally permitted to carry a concealed firearm. This would have eliminated all restaurant restrictions on concealed-carry permitees, but it would have established a virtual zero-tolerance for drinking while carrying a concealed weapon. This is the position promoted by the VCDL and VGOC.[15] No vote was taken on that amendment, but it was accepted by Ware. Presumably it would have passed 8–7 on a party-line vote, then Rerras would have voted to defeat the amended bill. This amendment may have been a concession to Senator Ken Cuccinelli, one of the more hard-line committee members, the VCDL, and VGOC.

Senate Bill 698

The only significant pro-gun control measure introduced in the General Assembly's 2003 session was Senator Henry Marsh's bill, which would have required that all firearms transfers that take place at gun shows include a background check of the purchaser. This would be required of all sellers, not only licensed dealers.

While this would close the "gun show loophole," it would have left private gun sales that are not conducted at gun shows unregulated. Marsh said he viewed it as a first step toward the goal of regulating the secondary gun market.[16]

S.B. 698 was referred to the Senate Courts of Justice Committee, where it was quickly killed.[17] While the bill had no chance of passage in the House of Delegates and probably would not have passed on the floor of the Senate, many legislators and lobbyists were surprised that it was defeated by a lopsided 11–3 vote in committee.

Committee debate featured a battle of statistics. The Virginia Firearms Dealers Association's veteran lobbyist Tom Evans cited a Bureau of Justice Statistics study that found fewer than 1 percent of convicted offenders said they purchased their gun at a gun show. Marsh cited an ATF trace of seized weapons that found that one-third of the guns came from gun shows.[18] Several members of the committee expressed skepticism at the effectiveness of such a bill. It was suggested by opponents that many sales would simply move from inside the gun show to the parking lot, where the sales would not be regulated.

At the conclusion of the debate, only three Democrats voted for the measure, while all eight Republicans and three Democrats opposed it. Several of the senators who voted against the bill were not thought to be friends of gun rights groups.

Marsh attributed the bill's defeat to the strength of the NRA and criticized some of his colleagues for siding with the NRA. Marsh was surprised by the "tepid nature of the opposition" to his bill. The pro-gun forces offered only "token opposition," he said. What appeared to be weak opposition may have been confidence that the bill would ultimately be defeated. Gun rights lobbyists Adkins and Evans noted that they were certain that the bill would ultimately be killed, so they intentionally kept a low profile so as not to excite gun control advocates.

Evans said he had four votes when the meeting began, and he eventually

won 11–3. He said he felt that the bill would have made it out of the committee if the other side had been less strident.[19] Testimony at the Senate committee hearing was heated, according to Evans, at least on the other side. "They
have so much invested and have rarely realized anything from it [recently]
that their rhetoric gets more fiery." He noted that a minister called to testify
ended up "preaching" to the committee, a lobbying taboo. "They killed
themselves," Evans claimed. He felt that he was better off not strongly opposing the bill, a sentiment echoed by Adkins.

Evans felt that the supporters of S.B. 698 relied almost exclusively on
anecdotal evidence and emotional stories that do not reflect reality: "They
[gun control groups] know that few crime guns come out of gun shows. They
see this as the first step to the final kill [banning guns]."

H.B. 2798: The Omnibus Gun Bill

Many other less important bills that dealt with the concealed carry law were
merged into the House of Delegates' Omnibus Bill. The bill sailed through
the House Militia and Police Committee on a 18–1 vote, and it passed the
House by a 82–18 margin. The measure was killed by the Senate Courts of
Justice Committee on a 9–5 vote after several court clerks from around the
Commonwealth objected to the additional burden placed on them. Committee
chairman Ken Stolle, who voted against the bill, expressed concern over the
unfunded mandate, and Senate Minority Leader Richard Saslaw was worried
that this was just another way of chipping away at the concealed-carry law.
Both Stolle and Saslaw had voted to kill S.B. 698 earlier in the session.

"I have no doubt that if this bill were to make it to the floor [of the Senate],
it would pick up one more piece of luggage, which the sponsor said he would
readily welcome, and that's guns in bars," Saslaw said.[20] There had been a
rumor in the General Assembly that if H.B. 1997 were killed, which it was,
then it would be added to the Omnibus Bill on the floor of the Senate. The
veracity of the rumor was never tested.

Summary of the 2003 General Assembly
Session

The 2003 session of Virginia's General Assembly can be interpreted in at
least three different ways. It can be seen as an indicator of the strength of the
gun lobby and its legislative influence, as a stalemate between the opposing
sides of the gun issue, or as a testament to the ability of the gun control supporters, even in a period of relative weakness, to stymie the other side's initiatives. A strong case can be made for any of those scenarios.

There is little doubt that the gun rights forces enjoy a position of strength in the Virginia legislature. The fact that the only serious firearms-related bills were those introduced by gun rights supporters indicates that the agenda is being set by that group. H.B. 1997 was defeated, but not by gun control supporters as much as it was a casualty of lobbying by the restaurant industry. At present, support for gun rights is strong, deep, and entrenched in the House's committee system. No gun control measure will get passed in that body, and most gun rights bills will garner sufficient support to move on the Senate. Support in the Senate is weaker, but with the right combination of lobbying and bill craftsmanship, it could be overcome.

Yet 2003 can also be seen as a stalemate. Despite the advantages outlined above, the supporters of H.B. 1997 were unable to get the bill passed. They easily defeated S.B. 698, so it is clear that serious gun control measures are dead on arrival in the House of Delegates, but no significant gun rights legislation was produced in 2003 either. H.B. 1997 may be seen as a watered-down attempt to incrementally chip away at restrictions on those who carry concealed weapons. In that sense, the bill itself was a compromise for the gun lobby, a compromise that was defeated.

The most difficult case to make is that 2003 was a victory for gun control advocates. They managed to stop the strongest initiative of the opposition, and they garnered some support for their own bill, though less than they might have hoped for. They also worked successfully with other groups to defeat legislation they opposed. They are weak, but not so weak that they are unable muster the support when they really need it.

THE 2004 GENERAL ASSEMBLY

The 2004 session of the General Assembly was dominated by the budget issue. Gun control, and every other issue, took a backseat to questions regarding the biennial budget and taxes. Early in the session, the budget created clear lines of demarcation between Democratic governor Mark Warner and the Republican legislature. It later caused a rift between Republicans in the House and the Senate, and ultimately resulted in a split in the Republicans in the House of Delegates. While this issue received the lion's share of media and public attention in 2004, many bills related to firearms were also on the legislature's agenda.

Gun control advocates viewed 2004 as an opportunity to again stalemate those who wanted to loosen Virginia's firearms laws and a chance, albeit a small one, to push their own legislation forward. There were plans to attack on several fronts, including closing the gun show loophole, banning all firearms in restaurants and bars, adding restrictions on obtaining a concealed carry permit, and increasing regulations regarding guns on school property.[21]

Marsh revived his bill to require background checks for all gun show transactions. The bill, to the surprise of many, cleared hurdles in both the Senate Courts of Justice and Finance committees, before it was defeated by the full Senate. It passed Courts of Justice on an 8–7 vote, with support falling generally along regional lines. Three Republicans, including Floor Leader Thomas Norment, supported the bill, and two southwestern Virginia Democrats opposed it.[22]

In a vote that split the parties, the Senate voted against Marsh's bill by a 24–15 vote. Six of the fifteen votes in favor of the bill were cast by Republicans.[23] Floor debate was highlighted by a heated exchange over the use of statistics regarding the number of crimes committed annually with firearms purchased at gun shows.[24] Although Marsh's bill was again defeated, in 2004 the NRA felt it sufficiently important to send out an e-mail alert to Virginia members, a step not taken in 2003.[25] Still, the NRA maintained a relatively low profile on the bill. For example, a *Washington Times* article on the measure contained quotes from the president of the VCDL, but it did not mention the NRA.[26]

Two bills related to carrying guns in restaurants that serve alcohol were also introduced in the 2004 session. Senator Janet Howell proposed legislation that would have banned all guns from such establishments (current law allows carrying if the firearm is in plain view). On the other side, Cuccinelli's bill would have permitted concealed firearms in alcohol-serving establishments if the holder did not have a blood alcohol content of .02 or higher. Both were killed in the Courts of Justice Committee.[27] In both votes, there were defections on both sides of the aisle, along regional lines.

With much less media attention than was garnered by the pro-control bills, gun rights supporters won several small but significant victories in 2004. One bill created exceptions to the one-handgun-a-month limit for gun collectors and concealed-carry permit holders. Several other law changes dealt with issues related to concealed-carry permits, including reciprocity agreements with other states and temporary permits that may be issued by the state police. Several measures restricting localities' ability to preempt state legislation on firearms were also passed. In all, the gun rights forces counted as victories fifteen separate measures that were passed by the General Assembly.[28]

An omnibus product liability bill that would have limited suits against firearms dealers and manufacturers as well as cigarette makers and fast-food restaurants passed in the House, but was killed on a 14–1 vote in the Senate

Courts of Justice Committee, with even the always-reliable Cuccinelli voting against it.

REGIONAL AND POLITICAL PARTY
INFLUENCE ON GUN CONTROL

In both Virginia and national politics, political party and geography influence positions on the issue of gun control. In the past decade or so, the national Republican Party has come to be more identified as the party of gun rights, while the Democrats have become the party of gun control.

While there is some truth in that partisan alignment, it is too simple to think of gun control as a partisan issue the same way that we think of abortion or social welfare as partisan issues. Gun control often cuts across party lines and becomes a rural versus urban debate.[29] Both factors clearly influence the politics of gun control in Virginia. The shape of the votes in both the Senate and the House on the important gun legislation of the 2003 session demonstrates this clearly. While Republicans were more supportive of gun rights than Democrats, at least part of that is attributable to greater Democratic strength in the urban areas of the state and a Republican advantage in the rural areas. In addition, the key votes were cast by urban Republicans breaking from the party line to vote against gun rights, while some rural Democrats were lined up on the other side.

Ware recognizes that gun control in Virginia has historically been more of a regional issue than a partisan debate, but he feels that is changing with the loss of rural Democrats in the Commonwealth. The suburbs of Washington, D.C. and the Tidewater area tend to favor gun control, and he feels the newspapers in those markets share that position.[30]

The issue became modestly more partisan in Virginia when Republicans gained the majority in the General Assembly. Several legislators noted that when Vance Wilkins, a Republican from the Shenandoah Valley, became Speaker of the House, he reshaped the Militia and Police Committee. Democratic delegate Jim Scott, a gun control supporter, said that Wilkins stacked the committee to be sure than "no gun control legislation would ever make it to the floor."[31] The NRA's Adkins described Wilkins as an "important figure" in building the Republican majority in the House of Delegates and in aiding the gun rights position.

House Majority Leader Morgan Griffith referred to the 2000–2001 committee as "a work of art" fashioned by Wilkins.[32] Several senior Republicans later asked to be replaced, and Wilkins accommodated them by substituting several freshmen in 2002–2003. As a result, the current committee is less supportive of gun rights, according to Griffith, but it remains solid. Still, Scott said that introducing gun control legislation in the House was an exercise in futility, largely due to the Militia and Police Committee.

Adkins also noted that the Democratic Party is now controlled by more urban representatives, and so it is more hostile to guns than it has been in the past. With the retirement of former Majority Leader Dick Cranwell, there is no strong gun rights spokesman in the Democratic Party.[33]

Ware also agrees that prior to Wilkins's ascendance to Majority Leader and Republican control of the House, Cranwell was very supportive of gun rights. With the departure of Wilkins and the election of William Howell to the position of Speaker, the commitment was more uncertain. Still, Ware described the House as "a bulwark for Second Amendment rights."

It is interesting to note that in the NRA's 2001 endorsements, Wilkins and Griffith received two of the six A-plus grades given by the NRA in the one hundred House of Delegates races.[34] Howell earned an A, and his picture was one of only eight delegates' photos featured in the flyer. Overall, the NRA endorsed forty-five Republicans, ten Democrats, and three Independents in that election. It did not make an endorsement in any race in which no candidate received a grade of at least a B, and there were six races in which at least two candidates were graded A and no endorsement was made. This pattern of endorsements is similar to what we see from the NRA in congressional races.

Even the Senate, which is more receptive to gun control legislation than the House, has regional as well as partisan differences. Most of the senators from southwest Virginia, the Shenandoah Valley, and Southside are supporters of gun rights, regardless of political party. Similarly, many Republicans from northern Virginia and Tidewater are more supportive of gun control. The Senate does not and has not had leadership that is strongly committed to gun rights, and, as a result, the Senate is more amenable to gun control legislation. According to Griffith, Republican Senators Stolle or Norment would be the most natural leaders on the issue, but both represent districts in which there is significant sentiment in favor of gun control. Both Stolle and Norment were "defectors" on some of the gun control votes in the 2004 session. On the other hand, Senator John Edwards of Roanoke is a fairly consistent supporter of the gun rights. Recently retired Bo Trumbo, from southwest Virginia, was frequently seen as the NRA's point man in the Senate.

An excellent example of the cross-pressured rural Democrat is Delegate Jim Shuler. He represented a district that is both liberal and conservative. It includes Blacksburg, the home of Virginia Tech, and the surrounding areas that are more rural. Blacksburg comprises about 52 percent of the district. "It is a challenge to represent all of my constituents," he said.[35]

That may be particularly true on the issue of gun control. "The extremes on both sides make it difficult to reach a reasonable decision," Shuler said. Yet Shuler is a consistent supporter of gun rights, which he believes is the predominant opinion in his district. He voted for Ware's "guns in restaurants" bill in spite of a shooting in a Blacksburg bar a few years before. Discussing the issue with Shuler, one does not get the idea that he is a "true believer" in the cause, but he clearly understands the importance of the issue to many of his constituents, and he responds to those constituents with his votes.

Shuler was defeated in the 2001 election by Republican Dave Nutter in a race that may have turned on the gun issue. Majority Leader Griffith's PAC helped finance Nutter's campaign and featured Nutter's support of gun rights. A Post-it note in that campaign mentioned twice that Nutter was endorsed by the NRA, described him as "the only candidate who will protect our gun rights," and noted, "[Y]ou can trust Republican Dave Nutter to protect your freedoms."[36] According to Griffith, there was a sixteen-point swing in that race during the month after gun control was featured as a prominent issue. The NRA gave Nutter an A-minus and Shuler a C-plus in that race.

Despite the loss, Shuler won election in a new district created by the redistricting following the 2000 census. With a seat on the Militia and Police Committee, Shuler is once again under the watchful eyes of the NRA and its allies.

Despite the importance of region, partisanship plays a significant role in gun control in Virginia. One of the important reasons for this may be the commitment of some party leaders to the issue. The influence of former Speaker Wilkins was previously discussed. At present, while the jury is still out on Speaker Howell, gun rights advocates are relying more heavily on the leadership of Majority Leader Griffith.[37]

Finally, this highlights the importance of the support of key members of the leadership. Whether influenced by regional biases, the hard work of gun lobbyists, or some combination, gun rights have enjoyed the support of influential members of the House of Delegates for decades under first Democratic and then Republican control. The House has become increasingly pro-gun rights in the past decade because of the support of Wilkins, who was willing and able to shape the relevant committees to support his position. Still, Wilkins solidified a coalition that was in place, to some extent, under Cranwell. Supporters of gun rights in Virginia have clearly benefited from bipartisan support in the leadership in the House of Delegates, based primarily on region.

INTEREST GROUPS IN VIRGINIA

National Rifle Association

Although it may be a surprise to many citizens and political observers, the NRA is a moderate gun rights group in Virginia. That was noted by several legislators on both sides of the issue. The NRA is willing to compromise on some issues and to move incrementally, while some of the other gun rights groups are more militant. For example, while the goals of the NRA include repealing Virginia's one-gun-a-month law and eliminating all restrictions on the rights of those who have been issued a concealed-weapon permit, they are aware that the first goal is not attainable at present, and they are willing to move toward the latter incrementally.

The NRA lobbyist in Virginia in 2003 was Todd Adkins, an attorney by training and deputy director of the NRA Institute for Legal Action. The NRA organizes in the fall to determine which bills it will push in the spring legislative session. Adkins spent more time doing hands-on work in Virginia than other states in his territory because Virginia is home to NRA headquarters, and it is therefore seen as a very important state.

Adkins was more interested in winning votes than in winning minds or hearts: "I don't care why they (legislators) vote with us. I just care how they vote." The focus is on winning the legislative battles. He frequently spoke in opposition to gun control bills in committee hearings, but he rarely spoke in favor of gun rights bills. Like many lobbyists, he commonly knew the outcome of a vote before it was taken; usually he had known for days. And he would say little once the vote was lost. "It does more harm than good," he said. "VCDL hasn't figured that out yet." When lobbying, Adkins focused much of his time on the legislators in the middle on gun issues. At present, those tend to be the Republicans from northern Virginia and Tidewater.

Adkins believes there are three ways that a lobbyist can approach an issue—political, logical, and emotional. "In order to win, we [the NRA] have to get two out of those three. The other side almost always has the emotion with them." He thinks the NRA usually has the logical, so the fight is for the political aspect. His approach is to ask for a legislator's vote or help. He says he rarely has to threaten a legislator, even implicitly. They know their districts, and they know how powerful the gun lobby is in their district. Threats are not necessary and might even be counterproductive. Adkins's approach is much more low-key. Personal observation and interviews with legislators confirmed Adkins's description of his lobbying style.

Adkins hopes to sway the swing votes by establishing what he describes as "an open and honest relationship. I don't scream and yell. I don't ask for a vote that I believe will hurt them [electorally]. I've never seen a politician lose [an election] because they voted with us. They lose because they vote against us. The NRA is about membership. It's not about money or fancy lobbyists. They [NRA members] listen to us and trust us."

Adkins advises Republicans to adhere to their core constituencies' issues—anti-taxes, pro-guns, and anti-abortion—and to ignore the media and the polls. His advice to Democrats is to vote to protect gun rights and neutralize the Republican advantage on that issue.

Virginia Firearms Dealers Association and Virginia Shooting Sports Association

Tom Evans has been lobbying in the Virginia General Assembly for nearly thirty years, and he says his basic lobbying strategy is to treat the legislators with respect. In 2003 he was working for the Virginia Firearms Dealers Association, the Virginia Shooting Sports Association, and several other sportsmen's groups.

A former police officer, Evans is in some ways both the stereotype and the antithesis of what you would expect in a Virginia gun lobbyist. He is very soft-spoken, with a distinct Southern accent, and his testimony in committee hearings is concise and to the point. In that sense he appears to be the stereotypical Virginia gentleman. At the same time, as his years of experience would indicate, he is older than the typical lobbyist, and he walks with the help of a cane and a brace because, as he says, his knee gives out on occasion. Still, he stands when he testifies in committee, and it is obvious that there is mutual respect between him and the legislators. "A lot of them [legislators] will respond favorably to my requests, and I'm proud of that," he says.[38]

That is not to say that he is not strongly committed to his issues or that he does not lobby intensely. While the NRA can "stir up the troops" and activate their "huge" membership, Evans has to be more low-key because his constituency is not nearly that large. He often works closely with the NRA. "I'm careful where I spend their [his groups'] money," Evans said. He will not spend much time on a bill that he knows has no chance to pass.

He worked with Democratic State Senator Virgil Goode (now a Republican member of the U.S. House of Representatives) when he sponsored the concealed-carry legislation in the General Assembly. He says he helped Goode craft the bill, although he disavows the amendments that may have helped the bill pass but complicated its implementation.

Evans has interesting views of the other lobbyists on both sides of the issue. He respects the NRA, which he describes as a "moderate lobbying organization. The NRA is highly principled, extremely ethical, and highly competent." He is less complimentary of the other groups who lobby for gun rights, noting that the more radical gun rights groups do more harm than good because they refuse to compromise. The Virginia Citizens Defense League is similar to the old Gun Owners of America–Virginia. Evans says: "They apply pressure, set up newcomers [in the General Assembly] to fail, then berate them." He feels that the VCDL and the Virginia Gun Owners Coalition operate as much as entrepreneurs as they do as lobbyists. They are working to build their organizations, and that often means losing on an issue to excite current members and attract new members. This means they frequently lose votes on legislation, and they may antagonize legislators who support gun rights. This assessment was confirmed in interviews with legislators who said that some gun rights lobbyists (not Adkins or Evans) had been banned from some legislative offices, including offices of "friendly" legislators. Evans is also not fond of most of the gun control lobbyists, although he clearly respects Tom Lisk of the VHTA. He feels they rely almost exclusively on anecdotal evidence and emotional stories that do not reflect the reality.

Virginia Citizens Defense League and Virginia Gun Owners Coalition

While these are separate groups with separate lobbyists, they take similar positions on issues, and they often work together, as they did to oppose H.B. 1997. Both are no-compromise gun rights groups that oppose all restrictions on gun ownership, except criminal checks.

The VCDL is headed by Phillip VanCleave, and Mike McHugh is president of the VGOC. Both groups were very active in their opposition to H.B. 1997, and they won a moral victory in that their amendment was adopted by the Senate Rehabilitation and Social Services Committee before the bill was defeated. In a postcard mailing, McHugh notified his members that with the help of Gun Owners of America executive director Larry Pratt, "Senator [Ken] Cuccinelli is drafting a comprehensive amendment to fix HB 1997. . . . It will repeal the unconstitutional ban on self-defense in restaurants by *banning alcohol consumption while carrying concealed—not concealed carry.*"[39]

These groups, however, do not measure success only in terms of moral victories. Both McHugh and VanCleave were quite vocal with their dismay in media interviews after the committee killed the bill and the amendment. They were pleased that the bill was stopped, but they had not achieved their goal. By contrast, both Adkins and Evans were silent.

It is difficult to get McHugh, who frequently carries his concealed gun in the Capitol, to talk about his lobbying tactics.[40] It is obvious that the VGOC and the VCDL both rely more on the media to get out their message than do the other gun groups. Undoubtedly, much of this is due to their smaller membership numbers. One of the other lobbyists referred to the VGOC as "a coalition of two." And, as Tom Evans noted above, they rely heavily on being very vocal to attract more members to their organizations, and losing is not such a bad thing.[41]

The VCDL organized several events around Virginia in 2004. About thirty members protested a Falls Church policy requiring city workers to notify police if they saw someone carrying a gun on city property by carrying hand-guns into a city council meeting.[42] The VCDL also challenged a Metropolitan Washington Airports Authority regulation that banned guns on its property, including some highways and the Reagan National Airport metro station.[43] The group protested a sign in a Radford park that read, in part, "No fire-arms," and they celebrated the implementation of some relaxed statutes by having about thirty members openly carry firearms into a northern Virginia restaurant.[44] Given these tactics, it is not surprising that the groups are gener-ally shunned by the NRA and VSSA.

Virginia Hospitality & Travel Association

Tom Lisk is the chief lobbyist for the Virginia Hospitality & Travel Associa-tion. While this group is not one of the usual suspects in gun lobbying, it was an important and decisive opponent of H.B. 1997. It was their pressure on Rerras that convinced or coerced him to oppose the bill in committee.

As discussed above, the VHTA took the lead in opposing H.B. 1997, partly because it is better organized than the gun control groups in Virginia and it was more likely to be successful. No gun control groups would have been able to persuade Rerras to oppose the bill, but the VHTA persuaded him to vote against it.

Lisk demonstrated great familiarity with the issue at hand and with the NRA's arguments. He noted several weaknesses of the statistics used by the NRA (borrowing a favorite NRA tactic), expressed concern over potential shootings in restaurants, and was able to mention the two specific bar or res-taurant shootings in the previous several years in Virginia.[45]

It was obvious from conversations with Adkins and Evans that Lisk was respected by the gun lobbyists. In contrast, representatives from the VCDL and the VGOC, the pro-gun groups opposed to H.B. 1997, were not "invited" to a group meeting of gun rights proponents when the House was considering killing a bill that would have banned the sale of .50 caliber ammunition.[46]

Virginians Against Handgun Violence

Virginians Against Handgun Violence, in conjunction with the Million Mom March, was present in support of S.B. 698 during the committee hearing.

While VAHV has an enduring presence in Richmond, it is not currently one of the more influential groups on the issue of gun control. This is evidenced by their show of support for S.B. 698, a bill that all agree was doomed to failure, and their backseat approach to H.B. 1997, which was the real gun measure of importance in the 2003 session. At the same time, the organization should be credited with being willing to play second fiddle when it was understood that the restaurant owners' coalition stood a better chance of defeating the measure. VAHV distributed a folder of materials to legislative offices, including a fact sheet on background checks and gun shows, a question-and-answer sheet, and a list of statewide organizations that supported S.B. 698.[47]

As mentioned above, VAHV has been active in Virginia for several years, but recently it has not been nearly as influential as its opponents. When asked about interest groups on this issue, no legislator mentioned VAHV, although VAHV helped persuade Marsh to sponsor S.B. 698. In fact, legislators did not discuss gun control groups at all, reflecting the relative level of recent activity of these groups in the General Assembly.

VIRGINIA GOVERNOR MARK WARNER, THE "NEW" DEMOCRAT?

Even at the conclusion of his term, Governor Mark Warner remained an enigma on the issue of gun control, due in part to the fact that the General Assembly failed to pass important gun control legislation during his tenure. His 2001 campaign may have been a watershed for Democrats, both in the Commonwealth and across the country. The Warner campaign, with his Sportsmen for Warner group, reached out to gun owners and gun groups, particularly in southwest Virginia. Southwest Virginia has traditionally been a Democratic stronghold due to the presence of mining and, of course, the United Mine Workers' Union. Recent conventional wisdom holds that Democrats have ignored this part of the state to concentrate on the more voter-rich Democratic strongholds of northern Virginia and Tidewater. Warner's campaign was determined not to make that mistake. He made numerous campaign stops in southwest Virginia, and Sportsmen for Warner was part of that regional push. Warner even went hunting at one point to prove his credentials. Although his hunting photo op was staged, it was generally accepted as more credible than the hunting exploits of John Kerry in 2004.

Warner campaign manager Steve Jarding recruited political activist Sherry Crumley, who was about to sign up for Republican Mark Earley's gubernatorial campaign, to lead the Sportsmen for Warner group. With her help, the group distributed thousands of yard signs across the region. The Warner campaign also created a direct-mail piece that was sent to a list of gun owners culled from lists from various hunting and sportsmen's groups. That mailer provided a side-by-side comparison of Earley and Warner on various gun-related issues. Jarding estimated that the mailer reached about 90 percent of NRA members in the area.[48]

Sportsmen for Warner also helped coordinate a traveling exhibition of trophy buck mounts that appeared at several gun shows around the Commonwealth. The exhibit was accompanied by a banner noting that it was sponsored by Sportsmen for Warner. All of this, according to Jarding, was to ensure that any attacks by Earley and the NRA would be blunted.

Adkins said the Warner campaign was in contact with the NRA throughout the campaign, and he was quick to point out that the letter mailed to NRA members in the last week of the campaign, while stating that Republican Mark Earley was a better candidate, was not an endorsement. Warner responded to the NRA's questionnaire, and Adkins characterized his responses as "OK." According to Jarding, Warner scored much better than "OK."

In the end, the NRA did not endorse a candidate. **"The NRA Political Victory Fund has issued a grade of A − to Republican Mark Earley and a grade of C to Democrat Mark Warner. In our judgment, Mark Earley is clearly a better candidate for Virginia's NRA members, gun owners and sportsmen."**[49] Yet Earley's name did not appear on a separate flyer of NRA endorsements in the 2001 General Election in Virginia, while those of the Republican candidates for lieutenant governor (Jay Katzen, who lost) and attorney general (Jerry Kilgore, who won) did appear. It is true that the Democratic candidates for the down-ticket offices were more strongly supportive of gun control than Warner was.[50] Still, Jarding argued that Warner should have graded much higher than a C, and he questioned Earley's grade as well.

Early in the campaign, Earley's support of gun rights was perceived by some as tepid, but he asserted more effort in that area as the campaign wore on. In an early October debate, Earley called the NRA "a very positive influence," while Warner described the NRA as "basically an organization that adequately and well represents sportsmen."[51] In that same debate, Warner said he would oppose any new firearms restrictions other than banning guns in recreation centers.

In a debate the following week, both candidates expressed views more strongly in favor of gun rights. Warner said, "I agree the NRA plays a responsible role in Virginia, does a good job educating young people, especially on gun safety," while Earley cited critical remarks about the NRA made by Warner in 1995 when he was the Democratic Party's state chairman.[52]

With no endorsement by mid-October, the *Roanoke Times* opined that "the National Rifle Association's silence has become deafening in the Virginia governor's race."[53] Earley had voted for Virginia's one-gun-a-month law, a regulation that is anathema to the NRA. According to reporter Michael Sluss, Warner "has recognized that gun-related issues have hurt his party's state-wide candidates in rural areas. He carefully cultivated a base among rural hunting and fishing enthusiasts by promising to oppose new gun restrictions."[54]

Jarding said that Warner's strategy was to neutralize the NRA "as much as they can be neutralized." He assumed that the NRA would not endorse a Democrat, even one who was stronger on opposing gun control than his opponent, but Jarding wanted the NRA to remain neutral.[55]

Jarding said that he spoke with the NRA state liaison and told him that Warner was prepared to mount a $3 million national campaign demonstrating the NRA was not nonpartisan if the group endorsed Earley. Jarding also said he would contact acquaintances in the news media and try to plant similar stories. His argument was that Earley had voted for one-gun-a-month and that his law firm had represented People for the Ethical Treatment of Animals (PETA), a nemesis of the NRA. Jarding believes that Democratic candidates need to appeal directly to hunters and sportsmen, arguing that they are often stronger on issues such as habitat and opening land for hunting.

Warner's strategy proved successful, as he was the first victorious Democratic candidate for governor in Virginia in the previous three elections, a long dry spell for Democrats in the Old Dominion state. Jarding noted that Warner carried 51 percent of the rural vote, about 15 percent better than what had been typical for Democrats. Warner's positions on guns and gun control also did not hurt him in northern Virginia. According to Jarding, Warner's numbers in that area were what they had expected.

The following spring, Warner began to repay his debt when he signed legislation that prohibits cities and counties from establishing new restrictions on guns. He described the bill as preserving "important public safety protections without infringing on the rights of those legally permitted to carry a gun."[56] A week later, the NRA Institute for Legislative Action mailed a postcard to members recognizing Warner's support of the legislation and asking members to "thank him" by phone, e-mail, or mail.[57]

Adkins called Warner "a poster child" for other Democrats. He won election in a state that had been trending Republican in a year when there were few other elections to steal the spotlight. Democrats in other states mention Warner's campaign as a model to victory without being prompted by his name, according to Adkins. Adkins believes this is a recipe for electoral success for Democrats and, of course, great for his organization. He argues that the Democrats could win back many of those voters in key states who have defected to the Republicans for gun issues, but are more likely to support Democrats on economic issues.

Although Warner was still a lame-duck Virginia governor in 2005, his star was rising nationally. A Democratic Party that was questioning its liberal leanings was looking for a fresh and more moderate face. He had impressed many of his partisan brethren at the 2004 Democratic National Convention in Boston.[58] By early 2005 he was being mentioned as a possible presidential candidate in 2008.[59] Although that speculation may have been premature, a one-term former governor of Georgia won the Democratic presidential nomination in 1976, and a few months later Jimmy Carter was elected president of the United States. When asked if he spoken with Warner regarding his political future, Jarding replied that he had spoken with Warner more in the past several months than he had in several years.

CONCLUSION

The initial assessment of gun-related legislation in Virginia might be that the chances of any pro-control legislation being passed in the near future are slim and none. While that is probably accurate, it is only part of the story. Gun rights supporters may have an easier time playing defense in Virginia at present, but they are not scoring major victories. As former NRA lobbyist Adkins said, the number of pro-control bills he had to fight had shrunk considerably in the past couple of years: "I have many fewer headaches than two years ago." Elected officials understand that they cannot come after guns: "Now we have to push legislation through, and test these folks to see where they really are." He made that statement in 2003, but the following session was one of relatively minor victories for gun rights. While the gun control forces made some headway in the Senate on adding restrictions on gun shows, the chances of passage in the House are negligible. Stalemate is the order of the day.

Unless the partisan composition of the House of Delegates changes dramatically, it is unlikely that any significant gun control measure will be passed in the General Assembly in the next decade at least. There is no reason to believe that the Democrats will gain significant numbers of seats in the next several elections. And unless the membership of the House of Delegates Militia, Police, and Public Safety Committee changes significantly, which is also unlikely, no meaningful gun control measure will make it out of that committee.

Still, the Senate is much less supportive of gun rights legislation. While it is doubtful that the Senate will produce any meaningful gun control measure in the short term, it is not much more likely that it will pass meaningful gun rights legislation or, more important, repeal any existing laws.

Ware's attempt to chip away at the concealed carry law may ultimately be successful, but it is doubtful that all restrictions on those who have been issued permits will be eliminated. Similarly, repealing the one-gun-a-month law, the holy grail for gun rights groups, is still little more than wishful thinking. Small exceptions were carved into each of these areas in 2004, but the basic restrictions remain. Ware has vowed to bring back his bill, as has Marsh. Certainly Ware's legislation has a much greater chance of being passed. If it is a war of attrition, then the gun rights forces have the advantage at the present time.

Democrats in Virginia are on notice regarding the gun issue, according to Jim Scott: "Democrats talk openly about staying away from that issue [gun control]. They don't think it's a winnable battle." They feel they cannot win in the General Assembly, and it may cost them elections. Scott noted Mark Warner's open courting of gun groups, and he believes that gun control was a major reason that former U.S. senator Chuck Robb was defeated by George Allen. Scott sees little benefit in sponsoring gun control legislation in the current political climate: "[Preventing a concealed carry permitee from] Brandishing a gun in a public building may pass, but that's a small victory."

Overall, Virginia remains a "moderate" state with regard to its gun control regulations. The Commonwealth has joined a majority of states in banning suits against gun manufacturers, even while it maintains its child access prevention law. Its concealed-carry law is moderate for those types of laws. It is a shall-issue state, but there are still restrictions on where permitees may carry their concealed weapons.

Perhaps the most far-reaching change in the Commonwealth will be the legacy of Governor Warner. If the Democratic Party moves to at least a status quo position on the issue of gun control—if not outright support of gun rights—then the prospect of gun control legislation being passed in Virginia is quite dim. Most Republican governors would veto any such bill, and if opposed by Warner and future Democratic governors, then there is no chance that any new gun control measures will become law in Virginia.

The nominees for governor in the 2005 election, Democratic Lieutenant Governor Tim Kaine and Republican Attorney General Jerry Kilgore presented significantly different views on gun control. Kaine, a former mayor of Richmond who had supported gun control, defeated Kilgore, a delegate from far southwest Virginia and a vociferous supporter of gun rights. The campaign was acrimonious in its early stages, and gun control was one issue that Kilgore seemed intent on emphasizing.[60] Still, Kaine emphasized his support for the Second Amendment and organized a Sportsmen for Kaine group, taking a page from Warner's playbook, although the campaign focused more on taxes and the death penalty.

If Warner is a true harbinger of change for the national Democratic Party, then Virginia's importance on the issue of gun control may well be magnified. Combined with the impact of firearms issues in the 2000 and 2004 presidential campaigns the importance of Warner's 2001 campaign may be critical to the future of the Democratic Party. NRA lobbyist Adkins expressed hope of a trend of Democrats at least backing off the gun issue if not moving toward the pro-gun rights side. On the other hand, he suggested that many Republicans in Virginia and nationally could be hurt by a shift of the party toward gun control: "If the Republicans are no different from the Democrats on guns, and they [voters] agree with the Democrats on other issues, they will vote for Democrats."

Although this gun control "realignment" is possible, it is not a strong possibility. A Democratic move to the middle on the issue still would not necessarily mean that gun laws would be relaxed or repealed. In Virginia the battles around the fringes are likely to continue, but it seems that the basic boundaries of the debate will remain unchanged for quite some time.

NOTES

1. Daniel J. Elazar, *American Federalism: A View from the States* (New York: Crowell, 1966), 216.

2. James Q. Wilson and John J. DiIulio, Jr., *American Government: The Essentials*, 8th ed. (Boston: Houghton Mifflin, 2001), 51–52.

3. Todd Adkins, interview with the author, Richmond, VA, January 24, 2003.

4. Carolyn Marshall, "California Bans a Large-Caliber Gun, and the Battle Is On," *New York Times*, January 4, 2005, at www.nytimes.com/2005/01/04.national/04guns.html.

5. Brady Campaign to Prevent Gun Violence, "Virginia Receives Grade of "C − " on Laws Shielding Families from Gun Violence," January 12, 2005.

6. A more extended synopsis of the state's firearms laws may be found at the NRA-ILA, "Firearms Laws for Virginia," at www.nraila.org/GunLaws/StateLaws.aspx?ST = VA.

7. Robert Holsworth et al., "The 2000 Virginia Senate Race," in *The Other Campaign: Soft Money and Issue Advocacy in the 2000 Congressional Elections*, ed. David B. Magleby (Lanham, MD: Rowman & Littlefield, 2003), 111–28.

8. R. Lee Ware, "Concealed Handguns in 'Entertainment Establishments,'" summary, H.B. 1997, Virginia General Assembly, 2003 session.

9. Mike McHugh, "Your Immediate Action Needed" [postcard], Virginia Gun Owners Coalition, February 2003.

10. Todd A. Adkins, "Memorandum of Support RE: House Bill 1997," National Rifle Association Institute for Legislative Action, January 24, 2003.

11. Pamela Stallsmith, "Guns Allowed in Bars?" *Richmond Times-Dispatch*, February 1, 2003, at www.richmondtimesdispatch.com/news/politics/MGBWQFZMBD.html.

12. Pamela Stallsmith, "Hidden Gun Law Defeated," *Richmond Times-Dispatch*, February 15, 2003, at www.richmondtimesdispatch.com/news/politics/MGBETF2PSBD .html.

13. Todd Adkins, interview with the author, Richmond, VA, February 13, 2003.

14. Thomas Lisk, interview with the author, Richmond, VA, February 14, 2003.

15. It is also the preferred position of the NRA, but Adkins realized it would never pass, and he pushed for the more viable H.B. 1997 option.

16. Henry Marsh, interview with the author, Richmond, VA, February 13, 2003.

17. Michael Sluss, "Guns Show Bill Gets Shot Down in Committee," *Roanoke Times*, January 16, 2003; Tyler Whitley, "Extension of background checks rejected," *Richmond Times-Dispatch*, January 16, 2003, at www.timesdispatch.com/news/politics/MGB70YY 30BD.html.

18. Marsh's office did not respond to a request for a copy of this study. I was unable to find the study.

19. Tom Evans, interview with the author, Richmond, VA, February 14, 2003.

20. Associated Press, "Panel Defeats Concealed Weapons Bill," *Roanoke Times*, February 18, 2003.

21. Associated Press, "Gun-Control Advocates Push to Keep Guns Worn in Plain Sight Out of Bars," *Roanoke Times*, January 14, 2004. The issue of guns on school property is a volatile one. What may appear to be a "no-brainer" for citizens of urban areas is a completely different issue in rural areas where students might drive directly from school to catch an hour or so before sunset in which to hunt. It is as much a cultural issue as a gun control issue and has been contested in Virginia for many years.

22. Kevin Miller, "Background-Check Gun Bill Clears Panel," *Roanoke Times*, January 22, 2004.

23. Justin Bergman, "Senate Rejects Gun Show Bill," *Free Lance-Star*, February 12, 2004, www.fredericksburg.com/News/apmethods/apstory?urlfeed = D80LCCRO0.xml.

24. Kevin Miller, "Bill Pushing for Broader Background Checks Dies," *Roanoke Times*, February 12, 2004.

25. NRA-ILA, "Virginia—Urge Your Senator to Oppose Gun Show Bill (SB 48) Today" [e-mail communication], January 22, 2004, www.nraila.org/CurrentLegislation /Read.aspx?ID = 927.

26. Christina Bellantoni, "Lawmakers Seek to Close Loophole in Gun Sales," *Washington Times*, February 1, 2004, washingtontimes.com/metro/20040201- 10511506716r.htm.

27. Jeff E. Schapiro, "Extended gun checks are rejected," *Richmond Times-Dispatch*, February 12, 2004.

28. Michael N. Graff, "Virginia Tops Nation in New Pro-Gun Laws," *Winchester Star*, July 16, 2004, at www.winchesterstar.com/TheWinchesterStar/040716/Area_VIRgin.asp. The NRA counted sixteen new pro-gun laws; NRA-ILA, "July 1 Marks Vast Improvements for Virginia Gun Laws," at www.nraila.org/News/Read/Releases.aspx?ID = 3943.

29. Harry L. Wilson and Mark J. Rozell, "Virginia: The Politics of Concealed Weapons," in *The Changing Politics of Gun Control*, ed. John M. Bruce and Clyde Wilcox (Lanham, MD: Rowman & Littlefield, 1998), 125–38.

30. R. Lee Ware, interview with the author, Richmond, VA, January 23, 2003.

31. James Scott, interview with the author, Richmond, VA, January 23, 2003.

32. H. Morgan Griffith, interview with the author, Salem, VA, April 7, 2003.

33. Cranwell represented southwest Virginia in the House of Delegates for many years. He was a champion of gun rights and served as a counterweight to others in the Democratic Party who were more in favor of gun control.

34. National Rifle Association, "Virginia 2001 General Election Candidate Endorsement" [mail flyer], October 2001.

35. James Shuler, interview with the author, Richmond, VA, February 13, 2003.

36. Friends of Morgan Griffith, "You Can Trust Republican Dave Nutter to Protect Your Freedoms" [Post-it advertisement], October 2001.

37. It is interesting that supporters of gun rights have found strong advocates in Griffith and his predecessor on the other side of the aisle, Dick Cranwell. Both hail from the Roanoke Valley, and both supported gun rights (Wayne LaPierre got his start in politics as the legislative aide to Cranwell's ally and fellow Democrat in the House of Delegates, Vic Thomas. All three were from Roanoke, VA), but the two leaders agree on almost nothing else and were fierce adversaries when they served together in the House. Not surprisingly, both are very strong partisans.

38. Evans, interview with author.

39. McHugh, "Immediate Action."

40. Mike McHugh, interview with the author, Richmond, VA, February 14, 2003.

41. To be fair, losing helps all groups galvanize support and solidify their base because of the imminent threat. Even Adkins noted that it is much easier for the NRA to raise money when they are losing than when they are winning.

42. "Anti-Gun Ordinance Backfires on Falls Church," *Roanoke Times*, October 11, 2004.

43. Associated Press, "Airport Gun Ban Stirs up Opposition," *Roanoke Times*, February 2, 2004.

44. Paul Dellinger, "Group: Sign That Bans Guns Is Off Mark," *Roanoke Times*, May 23, 2004; Knight Ridder Newspapers, "Virginians Tote Guns to Celebrate New Freedoms," *Roanoke Times*, September 12, 2004.

45. Lisk, interview with author.

46. I was even permitted to sit in on that meeting, but the VCDL and VGOC representatives were not allowed in the room.

47. Virginians Against Handgun Violence, "Lobbying Materials," February 2003.

48. Steve Jarding, interview with the author, Salem, VA, January 27, 1995.

49. James Jay Baker, "NRA Issues Grades in Race for Virginia Governor, Earley Earns A−, Warner C" [letter], October 2001.

50. National Rifle Association, "Virginia 2001 General Election Candidate Endorsement" [postcard], November 2001.

51. Michael Sluss, "Candidates Focus on Taxes, but Lobby for NRA Support," *Roanoke Times*, October 4, 2001.

52. Michael Sluss and Isak Howell, "Earley, Warner Have Final Say at Roanoke Debate," *Roanoke Times*, October 11, 2001.

53. Michael Sluss, "NRA Stays Very Quiet on Earley, Warner," *Roanoke Times*, October 17, 2001.

54. Sluss, "NRA Stays Quiet."

55. Jarding, interview with the author.

56. Michael Sluss, "Late-Term Abortions, Gun Restrictions Vetoed," *Roanoke Times*, April 5, 2002.

57. NRA-ILA, "Legislative Alert" [postcard], April 11, 2002.

58. Michael Sluss, "Warner Impresses Democratic Leaders," *Roanoke Times*, July 29, 2004.

59. Michael Sluss, "Warner Downplays National Attention," *Roanoke Times*, January 16, 2005.

60. Michael D. Shear, "Governor Hopefuls Hit Hard and Often," *Washington Post*, December 9, 2004.

Chapter Eight

Politics and Gun Control Policy—Present and Future

GUNS IN AMERICA

While we may all agree that gun violence in America is a problem, we may disagree on the nature of the problem and what we can do to alleviate it. We should begin the discussion by asking whether the source of the problem is guns themselves, or some of the people who possess them. Do guns kill people, or do people use guns to kill people? Existing laws should be evaluated; then we should consider the feasibility of any meaningful restrictions on firearms and the potential impact of those regulations.

The argument in this book is that guns are a tool. They can be a tool for recreation, for personal or family protection, or for crime, unwarranted and unjustified violence, or death. Like any tool, a firearm's use is largely determined by its owner. Everyone agrees that most owners use their firearms responsibly and legally. A small percentage of those who possess guns use them recklessly or with malicious intent. Identifying this relatively small group of irresponsible owners and criminals and preventing them from obtaining weapons is a goal shared by all. The means to that end are what are in debate.

Although it is obvious that a firearm is a potentially deadly tool, that can also be said of other legal products such as automobiles. Similarly, alcohol may be consumed responsibly or the consumer can behave recklessly, thereby endangering herself and others. But is a gun qualitatively different? The purpose of a firearm—unless it is for collecting only—is to destroy something, while automobiles are not designed to cause damage. Alcohol can also be used recreationally, although its purpose is less benign than that of a car.

A firearm in the hands of a young or unsupervised child or someone with suicidal intentions is a tragedy waiting to happen. A firearm in the hands of a criminal presents a clear danger to society. A firearm in the hands of a law-abiding citizen is a source of pleasure and can provide a sense of well-being and safety.

Still, guns in and of themselves do not kill people any more than cars kill people. Both are inanimate objects. When either is possessed by a person who disregards the laws and basic safety rules, there is a risk of a crime or an accident that may result in serious injury or death. The question of the violent nature of humans, or at least Americans, is beyond the scope of this work, but it is certainly worth considering when contemplating the nature of crime and violence in the United States.

The number of firearms in the country exceeds 200 million. The existing political climate does not support either prohibiting production of more firearms or the confiscation of those already in circulation. Therefore, the number of firearms in circulation will only grow. While both the percentage of households owning a gun and the number of hunters are declining, it is also true that the average number of firearms owned is increasing. In addition, it is possible that the decline in households owning a gun is related more to an increasing number of single-female-headed households than it is to a decreasing attraction to firearms. The decline in hunters is real, and it may have political consequences in the future if the trend continues. Still, it is likely that general support for hunting and hunters will continue, much as support for the small farmer remains high despite a decline in the number of small family-owned farms. Many people see hunting as a tie with our past and a way of bringing families, particularly fathers and sons, together.

The gun market has changed in the past several decades. Handguns and military-style assault rifles have become more popular, while more traditional long guns comprise a smaller segment of the market.[1] This is reflective of a shift in emphasis from hunting to gun collecting and self-protection. Convincing a collector that he presents a danger to others and convincing a person who owns a gun for protection that she should leave that job to law enforcement officials are very daunting tasks. Most gun owners see their firearms as objects, not threats. This is not to say that firearms should not be regulated or that gun owners oppose all such restrictions.

We need to examine the potential impact of gun control laws, both positive and negative, and evaluate laws and pending legislation as objectively as we can. Most of the laws we have passed have had relatively little impact on gun-related deaths. Whether this is due to the general ineffectiveness of gun control laws or because those restrictions have not gone far enough is difficult to determine. Given that more restrictive laws are unlikely to pass, it is nearly impossible to test the latter theory. Logic would seem to indicate, though, that laws that severely restrict who can own a gun will have less impact on criminals than they will on law-abiding citizens. The criminal availability of many commodities is restricted only after we impose very serious restrictions on law-abiding citizens.

GUNS—THE COSTS AND THE BENEFITS

With approximately twenty-eight thousand annual gun-related deaths resulting from homicides, suicides, and accidental shootings, it would be foolish to say that gun violence is not an important issue. A closer look at the statistics, though, reveals that it is impossible to know how many of those deaths could be prevented through legislation. The number of deaths caused by accidental shootings is less than one thousand and is declining. Fortunately, very few of those deaths involve children. Compared to the more than forty thousand annual automobile deaths, this figure is relatively small. Firearms are used in more than half of the thirty thousand annual suicides in the United States, and about eleven thousand deaths result from gun-related homicides. There would certainly be significant method substitution for guns among those who commit suicide, and some, but probably less, weapon substitution in the homicides. Even with those "discounts," the number of deaths we can attribute to firearms remains high.

Looking more closely at the data, however, we see that gun violence is not evenly distributed across the United States, either geographically or demographically. Gun violence is a much more serious problem in urban areas and among young, minority males. City-dwelling, sixteen- to twenty-four-year-old African-American males are significantly more likely to be the victim or the perpetrator of a fatal shooting or a gun-related crime. The typical gun owner is a middle-aged white male with a mid-to upper-level income. This discrepancy is often not discussed because of the fear of being labeled a racist. It should be discussed more frequently and more seriously because it indicates an important societal problem, one that correlates with poverty, education, employment, and gangs.[2] It is also true that suicide is more common among males, and they are more likely than females to use a firearm.

Guns increase the lethality of violence in America. There is little doubt that our comparatively high murder rate is a function of a violent society that has access to deadly weapons.[3] It is axiomatic that if we removed all the guns, the murder rate would decline. However, we cannot and will not remove all of the guns. This book has tried to focus attention on the political and social realities of today. Regardless of one's opinion of the wisdom of such policies, banning firearms and confiscating those already in existence is not a part of those realities. Beyond that, the efficacy of a gun ban is very questionable.

The largest issue surrounding firearms is gun-related violence. The number of deaths related to accidental shootings is both in decline and relatively small. While we should continue efforts to improve the safety of firearms and provide adequate training to those who possess guns, our gains in this area have probably reached a point of diminishing returns. These deaths and injuries, though tragic, do not constitute an epidemic any more than accidental deaths related to other products do, with the possible exception of automobiles.

Similarly, the evidence that gun regulations would reduce the number of suicides is not convincing. Most studies show little, if any, potential impact.[4] In addition, suicide rates in the United States are lower than those of many other countries that have many fewer guns. The use of a firearm may increase the chances of death from a suicide attempt. However, a substitution effect is likely for some of those who do not have access to a gun and who genuinely wish to end their lives.

To assess the true costs of gun violence in America, we need to consider the costs of injuries and deaths related to firearms.[5] We then need to discount that number by estimating the injuries and deaths that would result from other means if guns were not available. Finally, we need to consider the likelihood that gun control strategies will reduce injuries and deaths. To measure the overall impact of firearms in the Untied States, our calculations must include the benefits of gun ownership—crimes prevented and deterred and the recreational benefit of sports shooting. The frequency with which guns are used to thwart a crime is a fiercely debated topic. It is clear that this happens much more often than most of us would expect.[6] That number can reasonably be estimated at a minimum of 1 million. There are between 13 million and 19 million citizens who hunt and perhaps another 20 million who target shoot. The fact that the overwhelming majority of gun owners are law-abiding citizens who will never use their firearms in a criminal act must also be considered. In short, the cost-benefit analysis of gun ownership is a very complex and extremely difficult calculation.

CAN WE REGULATE FIREARMS?

The debate over the meaning of the Second Amendment is not just an academic exercise. It has important political consequences. Using historical documents and analyzing the state of affairs in the twenty-first century, a strong argument can be crafted to support the notion that the Second Amendment guarantees an individual right to possess and bear firearms or that the right is a collective one that applies to the militia that provides security for the nation.[7] It may be logical to argue that the nature of any right has to evolve over time to fit the current political and social environment. However, it makes less sense to argue that the reference to "the people" in the Second Amendment does not mean individuals when that is the meaning of the term in the rest of the Bill of Rights. And while we no longer bring our guns with us when we enter military service, the thorny issue of the right to revolution has not been satisfactorily addressed.

It does seem logical, then, to conclude that the Second Amendment confers an individual right on the citizens. The nature of that right, as is true of all other rights, is subject to interpretation and is not absolute. Infringements on that right have to be balanced against the governmental or societal interest that is served. It is up to the Supreme Court to provide the guidance regarding how important that interest must be to justify an infringement. Regardless of the Court's interpretation, some infringements on the right to keep and bear arms would be permissible. Many types of gun regulations would therefore be constitutional.

Unfortunately, the Supreme Court has provided us with few precedents to elucidate the right. The major case in the field, *United States v. Miller*,[8] is vague, but the Supreme Court has not incorporated the Second Amendment to make it applicable to the states. This indicates that the Court may not view the right as fundamental to the due process of law. Still, no one knows for certain, and so the debate continues.

SHOULD WE REGULATE FIREARMS?

We now consider what Americans think about guns and gun regulations. Public opinion, while favoring many specific regulations, is not overly optimistic regarding the impact of those policies on reducing crime, accidents, and particularly suicides. In many surveys, a majority of respondents express support for a variety of gun regulations, including gun safety measures, background checks for purchasers, waiting periods, gun registration and licensing of gun owners.[9] At the same time, a large majority of respondents believe that the Second Amendment guarantees an individual right to possess a firearm. Fewer than half think that stricter gun control laws will reduce gun-related homicides or accidental shootings, and only about one-fifth think that stricter laws can reduce the number of suicides.

We are more likely to think that making it more difficult to purchase a gun will reduce crime rather than increase crime, but the margin is slim. In terms of policies most likely to decrease criminal violence, we are twice as likely to choose longer prison sentences or educating society to be less violent as we are to choose stricter gun laws. Fewer than one-fifth of respondents favor lawsuits against gun manufacturers.[10]

Public opinion on gun control may partly be a reflection one group of people (those who are not familiar with guns) being willing to place burdens on another group (those who purchase or own guns) at no cost to themselves. There is a strong relationship between both gun ownership and familiarity with firearms and opposition to gun control regulations. On the flip side, the relationship between a lack of familiarity with firearms and support for gun control is also strong. The evidence presented in chapter 4 requires that we at least consider the ramifications of a majority of citizens who do not own firearms imposing regulations on gun owners, who are the minority.

Many of our perceptions about guns and gun control, especially for those of us who are unfamiliar with firearms, are influenced by the media. There is relatively little research in this field, but it all indicates that the news media are not completely objective in their treatment of the issue.[11] First, while we hear general charges of political bias in the news from both liberals and conservatives, we hear few, if any, cries of foul from supporters of gun control. Gun rights proponents, on the other hand, are very vocal in their criticism of the news media. More important, several researchers have concluded that news accounts in the media are more likely to be biased in favor of gun control than gun rights. This is true if we look at overall coverage or references to and treatment of the interest groups involved with the issue. While the National Rifle Association receives more press than other groups, much of that attention is negative.

The elite media also over-represent children in their reporting of gun violence. School shootings are usually covered extensively. Accidental shootings, which are relatively rare, receive disproportionate media coverage, while suicides are generally ignored. Homicides are reported depending upon how many people were killed, the nature of the shootings, and, at least to some extent, who the victims were. In addition, the media tend not to use statistics in their reporting. Those data could provide some perspective to the true nature of gun violence.

Beyond that, there are parts of the issue, such as defensive gun use, which are scarcely mentioned in the news. Regardless of whether this is due to media bias or how news is defined, the fact remains. The content analysis of the *CBS Evening News* and the *New York Times* presented in chapter 7 indicates that both of these elite media outlets fail to meet the journalistic standard of objectivity in their reporting of the gun control issue. In addition, while they clearly do not violate any of the canons of journalism, editorials in the *New York Times* are overwhelmingly in favor of the gun control position.

While we can not assume a causal relationship between news coverage and attitudes, the logical connection seems obvious. Those who are familiar with firearms probably draw upon their personal experiences in forming their opinions. Those who have no direct experience must look to other sources for their information. The news would be a logical source. Even if we assume that they get their information from friends or family members, those secondary sources may have been influenced by the news media.

GUN CONTROL AND THE
POLITICAL PROCESS

As is true of many issues, the making of gun control policy is complex, and it involves many actors. This book has focused primarily on national policies, but regardless of the venue, there are many fingers in the pie. Legislators, executives, bureaucrats, interest groups, and the public are all involved in policy making to some degree.

The "garbage can model" of policy making may best describe the process as it relates to gun control. Initiatives for stronger gun laws gain momentum and are adopted when a policy window has been opened by a trigger event. That event is usually a high-profile shooting, such as a political assassination, mass murder, or school shooting, but it can also be an incident that calls attention to an increasing crime rate. When the policy window is open, solutions can be joined with problems and result in a new policy. Because of their nature, most trigger events open windows that favor the passage of stricter gun laws. It is conceivable, though less likely, that a trigger event for relaxation of gun laws would occur. The elimination of gun regulations or passage of laws that enhance gun rights are more common when crime is not a major concern and some time has passed since the most recent gun-related tragedy.

Public opinion influences gun control laws, but we know that the law does not always follow the will of the majority. Interest groups have an important impact on gun policies, and they attempt to use the gun control issue to influence elections. The strategies of the groups on opposite sides of the gun issue are different. The NRA relies heavily on the individual-right interpretation of the Second Amendment and statistics supplemented with some anecdotes, while the Brady Campaign employs a combination of statistics and emotional stories of the victims of gun violence. Both sides, of course, use scare tactics with their followers. Fear, whether it comes in the form of the threat of governmental officials conducting a house-by-house search to confiscate firearms or the threat of assault weapon-wielding mobs invading your neighborhood, is a great motivator for political involvement and spurring contributions to interest groups.

Gun rights groups, especially the NRA, enjoy a significant resource advantage with regard to direct campaign involvement. Gun rights groups spend several times as much money as gun control groups, in both direct campaign contributions and independent expenditures.[12] Money, however, does not tell the entire story. With more than 4 million members, the NRA is the behemoth of gun-related interest groups. Its members are loyal, and the NRA works diligently to communicate with its members and get them to vote. The NRA's endorsements are clear and usually reiterated numerous times during the campaign. No NRA member who is paying attention can be unaware of the group's preferred candidate.

The Brady Campaign enjoys better, though less, press coverage. It also communicates with supporters, and it frequently wins the battle in the news as well as the fight for public opinion. It generally has emotion on its side because of the tragedy associated with many of the incidents it highlights. The underlying story of Jim and Sarah Brady is also one of tragedy and inspiration. The Brady Campaign is more likely to advertise in the national news media. Still, its electoral clout is not comparable to that of the NRA.

Gun control becomes a more important issue as the number of potentially cross-pressured voters increases. In national campaigns, we see this most clearly in states like West Virginia and Tennessee. Both of these states were won by George W. Bush in the 2000 presidential election. While much of the focus in that election was on Florida, Al Gore would have won the election had he carried either of those states. Many pundits on both sides somewhat belatedly recognized the importance of gun control in that campaign.[13] Some voters in West Virginia and Tennessee who would normally agree with the Democrats on economic issues found themselves supporting Republicans because of social issues, including gun control. The NRA campaigned vigorously for Bush in West Virginia, telling coal miners that the presidential election was as much about their guns as it was about jobs. Their pleas were at least moderately successful. While the numbers of voters swayed by that appeal may not have been larger than a couple percent, they were crucial in that election.

Although it was not perceived as being as important in the 2004 presidential campaign, there was some traction to the gun control issue. Its impact was more localized to those for whom the issue is of great importance, but those voters were still critical to the reelection of George W. Bush. John Kerry tried, unsuccessfully, to shake his image as a gun control-supporting Massachusetts liberal. The NRA clearly targeted Kerry, and it made his defeat a priority. At the same time, the NRA continued its success in electing members of Congress who are more favorable toward its positions.

Candidate endorsements from the groups tend to fall along partisan lines, but electoral support is also influenced by geography and urbanization. At the national level, support for gun control is almost synonymous with the Democratic party. Individual states are a different story. Because of culture and urbanization, Massachusetts Republicans tend to be more supportive of gun control than Alabama Democrats. Within states, the lines may be drawn geographically as well. In Virginia, for example, we see a bipartisan coalition from Northern Virginia and the more urban areas aligned against a bipartisan coalition from the state's more rural areas.[14] As an example of the issue crossing party lines, U.S. Representative Rick Boucher, a generally liberal Democrat from the coal-mining area of far southwestern Virginia, was the primary cosponsor of H.R. 800, the bill that would grant lawsuit immunity to gun manufacturers and dealers.[15]

It is possible that some national Democratic candidates will begin to soften their position on gun control. Many consultants and commentators have suggested that strategic shift in the aftermath of Kerry's loss in 2004. The example of Governor Mark Warner in Virginia may also prove to be important to future Democratic candidates across the country. As part of his 2001 campaign strategy, he actively and with some success courted gun owners in rural Virginia. By largely neutralizing the NRA, Warner fared much better in southwest and rural Virginia than Democrats had in statewide elections for decades. If this position shift becomes more widespread in the party, then we will see at least a halt on future gun regulations, if not a relaxing of gun laws.

Nationally, the passage of the Protection of Lawful Commerce in Arms Act of 2005, which limited the liability of gun manufacturers and dealers, may signal this shift within the party. Opposition to the bill in the Senate was less vocal than it had been in 2004, and the strength of support was stronger, but not significantly so. The defeat of Minority Leader Tom Daschle in 2004 probably helped seal the fate of the bill. Only strongly entrenched Democrats opposed the legislation.

DOES GUN CONTROL WORK?

The competing theories of the impact of gun control legislation are relatively elementary. Gun control advocates argue that regulations will restrict the flow and supply of guns which will naturally decrease shootings. Some accidental shootings, some suicides, and many homicides could be prevented, they argue. Guns can be made safer, and we can keep guns out of the hands of some who want to kill themselves as well as some criminals who would use them to injure or kill others. They recognize that some criminals will still obtain guns, but we can prevent many of the "heat-of-passion" homicides through careful screening of gun purchasers and mandatory waiting periods to purchase firearms. At the extreme, they advocate banning certain types of firearms.

On the other side, gun rights advocates argue that criminals will find a way to obtain firearms. Restricting the supply of guns will only serve to create a black market for them. Moreover, when we make purchasing a firearm more difficult or more expensive and restrict gun ownership among law-abiding citizens, we have essentially disarmed potential victims to the benefit of the armed criminal. This could result in more violent crime against defenseless citizens. Gun rights advocates suggest that those who wish to commit suicide will simply substitute another method, and they note that accidental deaths from firearms are low and decreasing already. Of course, they also emphasize the impact of firearms restrictions on law-abiding citizens.

Gun control legislation has targeted firearms themselves, dealers, manufacturers, gun owners, and prospective purchasers. Although the data are sketchy with regard to the impact of various laws, we can make some assessments based on the policy analyses that have been conducted, as well as logical inference.

The two most common types of regulations are restrictions on the types of persons who may purchase or possess a firearm and on the guns themselves. The regulations in the first category have been in force since the Federal Firearms Act of 1938. The most recent such law passed was the Brady Bill in 1994. The purpose of such legislation is to prevent those people society feels should not have a gun from purchasing or possessing one. These laws receive near-universal support (the NRA's major objection to the Brady Bill was the waiting period, not the background check), but their effectiveness is questionable. They apply only to purchases from federally licensed dealers, so the secondary market is unregulated. With this bypass built into the legislation, the regulation is relatively easy to circumvent. While supporters may tout the number of sales that have been prevented due to Brady background checks, we can not say that those persons did not purchase a firearm elsewhere. Most crime guns are obtained through the secondary market, which is unregulated. Of course, even if we regulated the secondary market, many criminals would steal guns or buy them on the black market.

Restricting guns themselves usually takes the form of banning a certain type of weapon. With the exception of fully automatic firearms, such as machine guns, we have not enacted a comprehensive national ban on any type of firearm. The assault weapons ban, for example, prohibited only future purchases of newly manufactured firearms. Existing weapons were grandfathered in and were still legally bought and sold. Combining that with the fact that these guns never accounted for a high percentage of crime guns, it is not surprising that the ban had little, if any, impact on crime.[16] Some localities have banned other types of guns, such as Saturday night specials, or restricted gun sales to one per person per month. These laws may have restricted guns in the local marketplace, but they have had little impact overall, particularly when guns from other locales or used firearms can be substituted.

A national policy that resulted in greatly reducing the supply of firearms might yield long-term benefits. A significant impact can be realized only when the overall supply of guns is greatly reduced. Assuming that no firearms currently owned are confiscated, a policy's effects would not be felt unless and until the number of guns and the percentage of households containing a firearm were reduced. At that point, we would likely see some decline in suicides and accidental shootings. "Heat-of-passion" shootings would also probably decline, while the impact on violent crime and felony-related homicides is unclear. The latter may decline, remain constant, or increase (if criminals acted in the belief that few potential victims would be able to fight back with corresponding force because they would not be armed). The serious criminal will obtain a firearm regardless of the law, but the situational criminal may be deterred. Having said that, laws that would accomplish these goals would, by necessity, greatly restrict gun ownership among law-abiding citizens. Some of these laws may be unconstitutional. Politically, they have only an extremely small chance of being enacted.

With regard to gun safety, it seems that the technology has not kept pace with the promise. While "safe guns" and "ballistic fingerprinting" may provide future opportunities, today's technology does not allow normal firearm operation or guarantee accuracy of the tests. In addition, maintaining records of ballistics tests raises the specter of gun registration, a politically unpopular alternative.

The debate over the impact of concealed-carry laws is intense and unresolved. Both the data and logic indicate that the impact of such laws is probably minimal because only a small percentage of the public applies for and receives a permit to carry a concealed weapon. Beyond that, many who have a permit do not actually carry a firearm. Still, convicted felons have said they would be less likely to target a potential victim if they believed the victim was armed.

Owner licensing and mandatory gun registration show more promise as regulatory strategies, but they arouse both widespread and intense opposition. There is also the problem of accounting for the existing gun stock, much of which would never be registered, and those gun owners, particularly criminals, who would never be licensed. While we can not accurately predict the resistance, it is safe to assume that some owners would resist on principle while others would not comply because the gun was stolen or had been or might be used in a crime.

Studies released in the past few years by the National Academy of Sciences and the Centers for Disease Control and Prevention concluded that there is insufficient evidence of any effects of a wide variety of gun-related laws.[17] Both reports suggested that existing research was hampered by a lack of quality data on gun ownership and violent firearm-related encounters. Neither study accounted for any positive recreational impact of gun ownership, although they did consider the impact of concealed-carry laws and defensive gun use. While there are efforts underway to improve data collection regarding shootings, these studies suggest that only gun registration can provide comprehensive and reliable data on gun ownership. All sales in the secondary market would have to be regulated as well.

Enhanced sentences for criminals who use a firearm are favored by gun rights groups. Research indicates, however, that policies such as the Project Exile program in Richmond, Virginia, are often not as successful as hoped.[18] Sentence enhancements incapacitate that criminal, but the deterrent effect of such policies is doubtful.

CONCLUSION

Overall, there are serious questions regarding the utility of various gun control strategies. Most regulations would place additional burdens on law-abiding citizens while the short-term impact in terms of preventing potential criminals from obtaining guns is questionable at best. Long-term impact may or may not be more positive if more serious restrictions are enacted. In September 11 American society, enactment of a far-reaching gun control law is indeed a very remote possibility. The most likely scenario for future regulations is a continuation of the back-and-forth we have seen in the past few decades. Gun laws will become more restrictive in response to shootings that attract national attention and increases in gun violence. Laws may be relaxed during periods of relative calm and if the legislative supporters of gun control back off their position for electoral reasons. The pendulum, which seemed to be swinging in favor of stricter laws in the 1990s, is now moving in the other direction—but it can swing back if or when conditions change.

In summary, gun violence is a problem in the United States. Most gun control laws that have been passed and implemented have had minimal effect on gun-related deaths. The impact of regulations that would impose greater restrictions on gun ownership is difficult to predict. They might reduce gun-related suicides and "heat-of-passion" homicides, but they could increase more serious criminal activity. In the short term, the impact would most likely be negligible due to the large cache of firearms in circulation that could become available on the black market. None of this accounts for the potential negative consequences on law-abiding citizens who use guns for sporting purposes or for personal protection. Those benefits of gun ownership must be a part of any equation evaluating gun laws. Gun laws that impose minimal restrictions and inconvenience on law-abiding citizens will face little political resistance and may make us feel better, although their impact is doubtful. More serious restrictions will be defeated in the political process in the foreseeable future.

NOTES

1. William J. Vizzard, *Shots in the Dark: The Policy, Politics, and Symbolism of Gun Control* (Lanham, MD: Rowman and Littlefield, 2000), 27.

2. National Center for Injury Prevention and Control, Centers for Disease Control and Prevention, "Leading Causes of Death by Homicide in Various Age Groups, by Race, 2001," at www.webapp.cdc.gov/sasweb/ncipc/leadcaus.html. This is not to say that the "typical" gun owner is never involved in a gun-related death, but it is statistically much less likely.

3. Franklin E. Zimring and Gordon Hawkins, *Crime Is Not the Problem: Lethal Violence in America* (New York: Oxford University Press, 1997).

4. Gary Kleck, *Targeting Guns: Firearms and Their Control* (New York: Aldine de Gruyter, 1997), chap. 8.

5. Philip J. Cook and Jens Ludwig, *Gun Violence: The Real Costs* (New York: Oxford University Press, 2000).

6. Tom W. Smith, "A Call for a Truce in the DGU War," *Journal of Criminal Law and Criminology* 87, no. 4 (Summer 1997): 1462–69.

7. See, for example, Sanford Levinson, "The Embarrassing Second Amendment," *Yale Law Journal* 99 (1989): 637–59. The term "Standard Model" originated in Glenn H. Reynolds, "A Critical Guide to the Second Amendment," *Tennessee Law Review* 62 (1995): 461–512; Eugene Volokh, "The Commonplace Second Amendment," *New York University Law Review* 73 (1998): 793–821; and David C. Williams, "The Unitary Second Amendment," *New York University Law Review* 73 (1998): 822–30.

8. *United States v. Miller*, 307 U.S. 174 (1939).

9. Tom W. Smith, "1999 National Gun Policy Survey of the National Opinion Research Center: Research Findings" (paper presented at the annual meeting of the American Association for Public Opinion Research, Portland, OR, May 2000).

10. See chapter 4.

11. See Karen Callaghan and Frauke Schnell, "Assessing the Democratic Debate: How the News Media Frame Elite Policy Discourse," *Political Communication* 18 (2001): 183–

212; John R. Lott, Jr., *The Bias against Guns* (Washington, D.C.: Regnery, 2003); Tamryn Etten, "Gun Control and the Press: A Content Analysis of Newspaper Bias," (paper presented at the annual meeting of the American Society of Criminology, San Francisco, November 20–23, 1991); Brian Anse Patrick, *The National Rifle Association and the Media* (New York: Peter Lang, 2002); and chapter 6 of this book.

12. Open Secrets, at www.opensecrets.org.

13. Associated Press, "Democrats Play It Safe on Gun Issues," MSNBC Online, March 1, 2004, at www.msnbc.com/id/4420922.

14. See chapter 7.

15. While Boucher is relatively liberal on most other issues, he has always been conservative on gun control issues.

16. Jens Ludwig and Philip J. Cook, "Homicide and Suicide Rates Associated with the Implementation of the Brady Handgun Violence Protection Act," *Journal of the American Medical Association* 284 (2000): 585–91.

17. The National Academies, "Data on Firearms and Violence Too Weak to Settle Policy Debates; Comprehensive Research Effort Needed," December 16, 2004; and Centers for Disease Control, "First Reports Evaluating the Effectiveness of Strategies for Preventing Violence: Firearms Laws," October 3, 2003.

18. Steven Raphael and Jens Ludwig, "Prison Sentence Enhancements: The Case of Project Exile," in *Evaluating Gun Policy: Effects on Crime and Violence*, ed. Philip J. Cook and Jens Ludwig (Washington, D.C.: Brookings Institution, 2003), 251–68.

Works Cited

Abramson, Paul R., John H. Aldrich, and David W. Rohde. *Change and Continuity in the 2000 and 2002 Elections.* Washington, D.C.: CQ Press, 2003.

Adkins, Todd A. Interview with the author, Richmond, VA, January 24, 2003; February 13, 2003.

———. "Memorandum of Support RE: House Bill 1997." National Rifle Association Institute for Legislative Action, January 24, 2003.

America's 1st Freedom (January 2005): cover.

"Anti-Gun Ordinance Backfires on Falls Church." *Roanoke Times*, October 11, 2004.

Apple, R. W., Jr. "A Road Not Traveled: The New Era of G.O.P. Control." *New York Times*, January 21, 2001.

Asher, Herbert. *Polling and the Public: What Every Citizen Should Know.* 2nd ed. Washington, D.C.: CQ Press, 1992.

Associated Press. "Airport Gun Ban Stirs Up Opposition." *Roanoke Times*, February 2, 2004.

———. "Democrats Play It Safe on Gun Issues." MSNBC Online, March 1, 2004, at www.msnbc.com/id/4420922.

———. "Gun-Control Advocates Push to Keep Guns Worn in Plain Sight Out of Bars." *Roanoke Times*, January 14, 2004.

———. "Middle School Boy Shoots His Principal, Then Kills Himself." *New York Times*, April 25, 2003.

———. "Kerry Goes Hunting; Bush Meets Archbishop." *Roanoke Times*, October 22, 2004.

———. "Kerry Talks Faith, Firearms as He Tries to Lure Key Voters." *Roanoke Times*, August 2, 2004.

———. "Panel Defeats Concealed Weapons Bill." *Roanoke Times*, February 18, 2003.

Ayers, Ian, and John Donohue. "Nondiscretionary Concealed Weapons Law: A Case Study of Statistics, Standards of Proof, and Public Policy." *American Law and Economics Review* 1 (1999): 436–70.

———. "Shooting Down the More Guns, Less Crime Hypothesis." *Stanford Law Review* 55 (2003): 1193–312.

Azrael, Deborah, Catherine Barber, David Hemenway, and Matthew Miller. "Data on Violent Injury." In *Evaluating Gun Policy: Effects on Crime and Violence*, edited by

Philip J. Cook and Jens Ludwig, 412–40. Washington, D.C.: Brookings Institution, 2003.

Baker, James Jay. "NRA Issues Grades in Race for Virginia Governor, Earley Earns A-, Warner C" [letter], October 2001.

Baker, Janice. "Comment: The Next Step in Second Amendment Analysis: Incorporating the Right to Bear Arms into the Fourteenth Amendment." *Dayton Law Review* 28 (Fall 2002): 35–44.

Balz, Dan, and Jim VandeHei. "Candidates Narrow Focus to 18 States." *Washington Post*, March 15, 2004.

Bane, Michael. "Targeting the Media's Anti-Gun Bias." *American Journalism Review* 23, no. 6, (July 2001): 18.

Bardes, Barbara A. and Robert W. Oldendick. *Public Opinion: Measuring the American Mind.* Belmont, CA: Wadsworth, 2000.

Barnes, Michael D. "How Bush Neutralized the Gun Issue as Part of His Winning Strategy," November 4, 2004, at www.bradycampaign.org.

Beccaria, Cesare. "On Crimes and Punishment." In *On Crimes and Punishment and Other Essays,* edited by Richard Bellamy. New York: Cambridge University Press, 1995.

Bellantoni, Christina. "Lawmakers Seek to Close Loophole in Gun Sales." *Washington Times,* February 1, 2004, at www.washingtontimes.com/metro/20040201-105115 -6716r.htm.

Bennett, W. Lance. *News: The Politics of Illusion.* 2nd ed. New York: Longman, 1988.

Bergman, Justin. "Senate Rejects Gun Show Bill." *Free Lance-Star,* February 12, 2004, at www.fredericksburg.com/News/apmethods/apstory?urlfeed = D80LCCRO0.xml.

Black, Dan, and Daniel Nagin. "Do 'Right to Carry' Laws Deter Violent Crime?" *Journal of Legal Studies* 27, no. 1 (January 1998): 209–19.

Bordua, David J. "Adversary Polling and the Construction of Social Meaning: Implications in Gun Control Elections in Massachusetts and California." *Law and Policy Quarterly* 5, no. 3 (1983): 347–48.

Bowling, Michael, Gene Lauver, Matthew J. Hickman, and Devon B. Adams. "Background Checks for Firearms, 2002." Bureau of Justice Statistics, U.S. Department of Justice, September 2003.

Brady Campaign to Prevent Gun Violence. "After Selling Out Police, Bush Takes Delivery of the Payoff," October 13, 2004, at www.bradycampaign.org/press/release.php?re lease = 598.

―――. "The Brady Campaign to Prevent Gun Violence 2003 Report Card." www.brady campaign.org/facts/reportcards/2003/; www.nraila.org/GunLaws/Default.aspx#.

―――. "Brady Campaign United with the Million Mom March and the Brady Center to Prevent Gun Violence: A History of Working to Prevent Gun Violence," 2005, at www.bradycampaign.org/press/?page = history.

―――. "Congress Ignores Rights of Victims of Gun Violence and Grants Gun Industry Sweeping Legal Immunity President Bush Urged to Reject Bill," October 20, 2005, at www.bradycampaign.org/press/release.php?release = 697.

―――The Legal Action Project, at www.gunlawsuits.org/docket/docket.php.

―――. "Majority of the US Senate in 'Unholy Alliance' with NRA," July 30, 2005, at www.bradycampaign.org.

————. "The Morning After: Police, Victims, Democrats and Republicans Stood Up to an Extremist Agenda, Forced It Down," March 3, 2004.

————. "No Mandate for Gun Extremism," November 9, 2004, www.bradycampaign .org/press/release.php?release = 607.

————. "President Bush Supported Sensible Gun Policy on Campaign Trail—Now It's Time for Action," November 5, 2004, at www.bradycampaign.org/press/release.php? release = 606.

————. "Senate Votes down Immunity for Gun Industry," March 2, 2004.

————. "Special Protection for the Gun Industry: State Bill," 2005, at www.bradycam paign.org/facts/issues/?page = immun_stat.

————. "To Restore Sanity on Gun Issue, Brady Campaign, Million Mom March Endorse John Kerry for President," October 1, 2004, at www.bradycampaign.org/press/release .php?release = 594.

————. "Virginia Receives Grade of 'C-' on Laws Shielding Families from Gun Violence," January 12, 2005.

Brent, David A., Joshua A. Perper, Charles E. Goldstein, David J. Kolko, Marjorie J. Allan, Christopher J. Allman, and Janice P. Zelenak, "Risk Factors for Adolescent Suicide." *Archives of General Psychiatry* 45 (1988): 581–88.

Bruce, John M., and Clyde Wilcox, eds. *The Changing Politics of Gun Control.* Lanham, MD: Rowman & Littlefield, 1998.

Bureau of Alcohol, Tobacco, and Firearms. "Commerce in Firearms in the United States," February 2000.

————. "Crime Gun Trace Reports (2000)." Youth Crime Gun Interdiction Initiative, July 2002.

————. "Firearms Commerce in the United States, 2001/2002," 2003.

Bureau of Justice Statistics. "Survey of State Procedures Related to Firearm Sales, Mid-year 2002," April 2003.

"Bush vs. Kerry." *Outdoor Life*, October 2004, at www.outdoorlife.com/outdoor/news.ar ticle/0,19912,696240,00,html.

Callaghan, Karen, and Frauke Schnell. "Assessing the Democratic Debate: How the News Media Frame Elite Policy Discourse." *Political Communication* 18 (2001):183–212.

Cantril, Albert H. *The Opinion Connection.* Washington, D.C.: CQ Press, 1991.

Carney, Dan. "Brady Decision Reflects Effort to Curb Congress' Authority." *CQ Weekly Report* (June 28, 1997): 1524–25.

Carpini, Michael X. Delli, and Scott Keeter. *What Americans Know about Politics and Why It Matters.* New Haven, CT: Yale University Press, 1996.

Carter, Gregg Lee. *The Gun Control Movement.* New York: Twayne, 1997.

Catalano, Shannan M. "Criminal Victimization, 2003." Bureau of Justice Statistics, September 2004, at www.ojp.usdoj.gov/bjs/pub/pdf/cv03.pdf.

Citizens Committee for the Right to Keep and Bear Arms. "CCRKBA Hails Passage of Industry Lawsuit Protection Bill in Senate," at www.ccrkba.org/pub/rkba/press-releas es/CC_Senate_Passes_Gun_Lawsuit_Reform.

Centers for Disease Control and Prevention. "First Reports Evaluating the Effectiveness of Strategies for Preventing Violence: Firearms Laws," October 3, 2003.

Cicero, Marcus Tullius. "In Defense of Titus Annius Milo." In *Selected Political Speeches of Cicero*, edited and translated by Michael Grant, 215–78. New York: Penguin, 1969.

Coalition to Stop Gun Violence. "The Educational Fund to Stop Gun Violence," at www .csgv.org/who_we_are.

Cobb, Roger W., and Charles Elder. *Participation in American Politics: The Dynamics of Agenda Building*. Baltimore: Johns Hopkins University Press, 1983.

Cohen, Michael, James March, and John Olsen. "A Garbage Can Model of Organizational Choice." *Administrative Science Quarterly* 17 (March 1972): 1–25.

"Congress and the Gun Lobby." *New York Times*, March 3, 2004, at www.nytimes.com /2004/03/03/opinion/03WED2.html.

Cook, Timothy E. *Governing with the News: The News Media as a Political Institution*. Chicago: University of Chicago Press, 1998.

Cook, Philip J., and Jens Ludwig. "Defensive Gun Uses: New Evidence from a National Survey." *Journal of Quantitative Criminology* 14 (1998): 111–31.

———. *Guns in America: Results of a Comprehensive National Survey on Firearms Ownership and Use*. Washington, D.C.: Police Foundation, 1996.

———. *Gun Violence: The Real Costs*. New York: Oxford University Press, 2000.

———. "Pragmatic Gun Policy." In *Evaluating Gun Policy: Effects on Crime and Violence*, edited by Philip J. Cook and Jens Ludwig, 1–37. Washington, D.C.: Brookings Institution, 2003.

Cook, Philip J., Stephanie Molliconi, and Thomas B. Cole. "Regulating Gun Markets." *Journal of Criminal Law and Criminology* 86, no. 1 (Fall 1995): 59–92.

Cornell, Saul. "Commonplace or Anachronism: The Standard Model, the Second Amendment, and the Problem of History in Contemporary Constitutional Theory." *Constitutional Commentary* 16 (1999): 221–46.

———. "'Don't Know Much about History': The Current Crisis in Second Amendment Scholarship." *Northern Kentucky University Law Review* 29 (2002): 857–81.

———. *Whose Right to Bear Arms Did the Second Amendment Protect?* Boston: Bedford/St. Martin's, 2000.

Cornell, Saul, and Nathan DeDino. "Symposium: The Second Amendment and the Future of Gun Regulation: Historical, Legal, Policy and Cultural Perspectives: Panel I: Historical Perspective: A Well Regulated Right: The Early American Origins of Gun Control." *Fordham Law Review* 73 (2005): 487–528.

Cottroll, Robert J., and Raymond T. Diamond. "The Second Amendment: Toward an Afro-Americanist Reconsideration." *Georgetown Law Journal* 80 (1991): 309–61.

Cox, Chris W. Letter to NRA members from the NRA Institute for Legislative Action. August 12, 2005.

———. "Your Tools for Victory." National Rifle Association Institute for Legislative Action, at nraila.org/Issues/Articles/Read.aspx?ID = 154.

Cress, Lawrence Delbert. "An Armed Community: The Origins and Meaning of the Right to Bear Arms." *Journal of American History* 71 (June 1984): 22–42.

Dao, James. "N.R.A. Lashes Out at Kerry over Terror and Gun Issues." *New York Times*, April 18, 2004, at www.nytimes.com/2004/04/18/politics/campaign/18NRA.html.

———. "Where Kerry Is Trying to Avoid Gore's Pitfalls." *New York Times*, October 13, 2004.

Davidson, Osha Gray. *Under Fire: The NRA and the Battle for Gun Control*. Iowa City: University of Iowa Press, 1998.

Dellinger, Paul. "Group: Sign That Bans Guns Is Off Mark." *Roanoke Times*, May 23, 2004.

Democratic Presidential Candidate Debate. Moderated by George Stephanopoulos. Columbia, SC, May 2, 2003.

"Democrats and Guns." *Washington Times*, February 12, 2004, at www.washingtontimes-online.com/op-ed/20040212-081232-1419r.htm.

Dewar, Helen. "Bush Opposes Additions to Gun Bill." *Washington Post*, February 26, 2004.

Dickens, Geoffrey. "Outgunned: How the Network News Media Are Spinning the Gun Control Debate." Media Research Center, January 5, 2000, at www.mediaresearch.org /specialreports/2000/rep01052000.asp.

Donohue, John J. "A Clarification on Data Availability." *Science* (September 26, 2003).

———. "The Impact of Concealed-Carry Laws." In *Evaluating Gun Policy: Effects on Crime and Violence*, edited by Philip J. Cook and Jens Ludwig, 287–325. Washington, D.C.: Brookings Institution, 2003.

Dorf, Michael C. "Symposium on the Second Amendment: Fresh Looks: What Does the Second Amendment Mean Today?" *Chicago-Kent Law Review* 76 (2000): 291–347.

Dowd, Maureen. "Cooking His Own Goose." *New York Times*, October 24, 2004, at www.nytimes.com/2004/10/24/opinion/24dowd.html.

Dowler, Kenneth. "Media Influence on Attitudes toward Guns and Gun Control." *American Journal of Criminal Justice* 26, no. 2 (2002): 235–47.

"Down and Dirty in the Gun Debate." *New York Times*, February 27, 2004.

Drew, Dan, and David Weaver. "Voter Learning in the 1988 Presidential Election: Did the Debates and the Media Matter?" *Journalism Quarterly* 68 (1991): 27–37.

Ducat, Craig R. *Constitutional Interpretation*. 7th ed. Belmont, CA: West Constitutional Law, 2000.

Ducoff, John A. "Note: Yesterday:'Constitutional Interpretation, the Brady Act, and *Printz v. United States*." *Rutgers Law Journal* 30 (Fall 1998): 209–45.

Duggan, Mark. "Guns and Suicide." In *Evaluating Gun Policy: Effects on Crime and Violence*, edited by Philip J. Cook and Jens Ludwig, 41–73. Washington, D.C.: Brookings Institution, 2003.

———. "More Guns, More Crime." *Journal of Political Economy* 109 (October 2001): 1086–114.

Dye, Thomas R. *Understanding Public Policy*. Upper Saddle River, NJ: Prentice-Hall, 2002.

"The Election: Issues 2000: A Special Briefing; The Economy, Trade, Foreign Policy, Social Security, Health, Education, Death Penalty, Gun Control, Poverty, Race, Campaign Finance, Environment, New Technology, Values." *Economist* 356 (September 30, 2000): 59–102.

Elazar, Daniel J. *American Federalism: A View from the States*. New York: Crowell, 1966.

Entman, Robert M. "Framing: Toward Clarification of a Fractured Paradigm." *Journal of Communication* 43 (1993): 51–58.

Erikson, Robert S., and Kent L. Tedin. *American Public Opinion*. 6th ed. New York: Longman, 2001.

Etten, Tamryn. "Gun Control and the Press: A Content Analysis of Newspaper Bias." Paper presented at the annual meeting of the American Society of Criminology, San Francisco, November 20–23, 1991.

Evans, Sid, and Bob Marshall. "A Sporting Debate: George Bush vs. John Kerry: The

Field & Stream Interviews." *Field & Stream*, October 2004, at www.fieldandstream .com/fieldstream/columnists/article/0,13199,702716,00.html#.

Evans, Tom. Interview with the author, Richmond, VA, February 14, 2003.

Farnsworth, Stephen J., and S. Robert Lichter. *The Nightly News Nightmare: Network Television's Coverage of U.S. Presidential Elections, 1988–2000*. Lanham, Md: Rowman & Littlefield, 2003.

Fowler, Floyd J., Jr. *Survey Research Methods*. 3rd ed. Thousand Oaks, CA: Sage, 2002.

Friends of Morgan Griffith. "You Can Trust Republican Dave Nutter to Protect Your Freedoms" [Post-it advertisement], October 2001.

Gallia, Anthony. "'Your Weapons, You Will Not Need Them,' Comment on the Supreme Court's Sixty-Year Silence on the Right to Keep and Bear Arms." *Akron Law Review* 33 (1999): 131–62.

The Gallup Brain. "Children and Violence." August 11, 2003.

———. "Guns." October 14, 2003.

Gay, Lance. "Number of Hunters Down, but More Rich People Bag Animals." Scripps Howard News Service, January 22, 2004.

Gest, Ted. "Firearms Follies: How the News Media Cover Gun Control." *Media Studies Journal* 6, no. 1 (1992): 139–49.

Glaeser, Edward L., and Spencer Glendon. "Who Owns Guns? Criminals, Victims, and the Culture of Violence." *American Economic Review* 88, no. 2 (May 1998): 458–62.

Goldstein, Amy. "House Passes Ban on Gun Ban on Gun Industry Lawsuits." *Washington Post*, October 21, 2005.

Graber, Doris A. *Mass Media & American Politics*. 6th ed. Washington, D.C.: CQ Press, 2002.

Graff, Michael N. "Virginia Tops Nation in New Pro-Gun Laws." *Winchester Star*, July 16, 2004, at www.winchesterstar.com/TheWinchesterStar/040716/Area_VIRgin.asp.

Griffith, H. Morgan. Interview with the author, Salem, VA, April 7, 2003.

"The Gun Lobby's Bull's-Eye." *New York Times*, February 25 2004.

Gun Owners of America. "Protecting Your Rights," June 1998, at www.gunowners.org /protect.htm.

———. "Senate Passes Gun Control Amidst Protection for Gun Makers—Now the House Has to Clean Up the Senate's Mess," July 29, 2005, at www.gunowners.org/a072905 .htm.

"Guns." *Columbia Journalism Review*, February 15, 1999, 6–8.

Haberman, Clyde. "Protecting a Gun Law, or a Family." *New York Times*, February 15, 2003.

Haider-Markel, Donald P., and Mark R. Joslyn. "Gun Policy, Opinion, Tragedy, and Blame Attribution: The Conditional Influences of Issue Frames." *Journal of Politics* 63, no. 2 (May 2001): 520–43.

Halbrook, Stephen P. *That Every Man Be Armed: The Evolution of a Constitutional Right*. Oakland, CA: Independent Institute, 1994.

Hamilton, Alexander. "The Federalist No. 28." In *The Federalist,* edited by Sherman F. Mittell, 173. Washington, D.C.: National Home Library Foundation, 1938.

———. "The Federalist No. 29." In *The Federalist,* edited by Sherman F. Mittell, 176, 178–79. Washington, D.C.: National Home Library Foundation, 1938.

Hardaway, Robert, Elizabeth Gormley, and Bryan Taylor, "The Inconvenient Militia

Clause of the Second Amendment: Why the Supreme Court Declines to Resolve the Debate over the Right to Bear Arms." *St. John's Journal of Legal Commentary* 16 (Winter 2002): 41–164.

Harding, David R., Jr. "Public Opinion and Gun Control: Appearance and Transparence in Support and Opposition." In *The Changing Politics of Gun Control*, edited by John M. Bruce and Clyde Wilcox, 196–223. Lanham, MD: Rowman & Littlefield, 1998.

Harlow, Caroline Wolf. "Firearm Use by Offenders." Bureau of Justice Statistics, November 2001.

"Hate Has Found a Home in the National Rifle Association" [print advertisement]. *New York Times*, February 25, 2004.

Hemenway, David. "Survey Research and Self-Defense Gun Use: An Explanation of Extreme Overestimates." *Journal of Criminal Law and Criminology* 87, no. 4 (1997): 1430–45.

Hemenway, David, Deborah Azrael, and Matthew Miller. "National Attitudes Concerning Gun Carrying in the United States." *Injury Prevention* 7 (2001): 282–85.

Henretta, James A. "Symposium: The Second Amendment and the Future of Gun Regulation: Historical, Legal, Policy and Cultural Perspectives: Panel I: Historical Perspective: Collective Responsibilities, Private Arms, and State Regulation: Toward the Original Understanding." *Ford!:am Law Review* 73 (2005): 529–38.

Higginbotham, Don. "The Federalized Militia Debate: A Neglected Aspect of Second Amendment Scholarship." *William and Mary Quarterly* 55, no. 1 (1998): 263–68.

Holsworth, Robert, Stephen K. Medvic, Harry L. Wilson, Robert Dudley, and Scott Keeter. "The 2000 Virginia Senate Race." In *The Other Campaign: Soft Money and Issue Advocacy in the 2000 Congressional Elections*, edited by David B. Magleby, 111–28. Lanham, MD: Rowman & Littlefield, 2003.

Hsu, Spender S. "Warner, Allen Split Over Assault Weapons." *Washington Post*, March 3, 2004.

Hu, Winnie. "Council Seeks to Toughen Gun Laws." *New York Times*, August 23, 2003.

Hulse, Carl. "Senate Approves Bill Protecting Gun Businesses." *New York Times*, July 30, 2005, at www.nytimes.com/2005/07/30/politics/30cong.html

"In the Cross-hairs: The National Rifle Association's Main Strength as a Lobbying Group Has Often Been the Weakness of Its Opponents; Not Any Longer." *Economist* 356 (July 8, 2000): 27–29.

Jacobs, James B. *Can Gun Control Work?* New York: Oxford University Press, 2002.

Jarding, Steve. Interview with the author, Salem, VA, January 27, 1995.

"Joe Lieberman: Fighting Crime and Keeping Communities Safe," at www.joe2004.com.

Johns Hopkins University, Center for Gun Policy and Research. "Fact Sheet: Guns in the Home," June 2004.

Jones, Melissa Ann. "Note: Legislating Gun Control in Light of *Printz v. United States*." *U.C. Davis Law Review* 32 (Winter 1999): 455–83.

Kates, Don B. "Comparisons among Nations and over Time." In *The Gun Control Debate*, edited by Lee Nisbet, 187–94. Amherst, NY: Prometheus, 1990.

———. "Guns and Public Health: Epidemic of Violence, or Pandemic of Propaganda?" In *Armed: New Perspectives on Gun Control*, edited by Gary Kleck and Don B. Kates, 31–106. Amherst, NY: Prometheus, 2001.

———. "The Second Amendment: A Right to Personal Self-Protection." In *Armed: New*

Perspectives on Gun Control, edited by Gary Kleck and Don B. Kates, 343–56. Amherst, NY: Prometheus, 2001.

Kellerman, Arthur R., Dawna S. Fuqua-Whitley, Tomoko R. Sampson, and Walter Lindenmann. "Public Opinion about Guns in the Home." *Injury Prevention* 6 (2000): 189–94.

Kellerman, Arthur L., and Donald T. Reay. "Protection or Peril?: An Analysis of Firearm-Related Deaths in the House." *New England Journal of Medicine* 314 (1986): 1557–60.

Kellerman, Arthur, Frederick Rivara, Grant Somes, Donald Reay, Jerry Francisco, Joyce Gillentine Banton, Janice Prodzinski, Corinne Fligner, and Bela Hackman. "Suicide in the Home in Relation to Gun Ownership." *New England Journal of Medicine* 327, no. 7 (1992): 467–72.

Kennedy, Donald. "Research Fraud and Public Policy." *Science* (April 18, 2003).

Kerry for President, "Kerry Stands Up to NRA's Divisive Agenda in Letter to Blacklisted Americans," at www.johnkerry.com/pressroom/releases/pr_2003_1030.html.

Kingdon, John W. *Agendas, Alternatives, and Public Policies*. 2nd ed. New York: Longman, 2003.

Klaus, Patsy A. "Crime and the Nation's Households, 2003." Bureau of Justice Statistics, October 2004, at www.ojp.usdoj.gov/bjs/pub/pdf/cnh03.pdf.

Kleck, Gary. "Crime, Culture Conflict and the Sources of Support for Gun Control." *American Behavioral Scientist* 39, no. 4 (February 1996): 387–404.

———. "Impossible Policy Evaluations and Impossible Conclusions: A Comment on Koper and Roth." *Journal of Quantitative Criminology* 17, no. 1 (March 2001): 75–80.

———. "The Nature and Effectiveness of Owning, Carrying, and Using Guns for Self-Protection." In *Armed: New Perspectives on Gun Control*, edited by Gary Kleck and Don B. Kates, 285–342. Amherst, NY: Prometheus, 2001.

———. *Targeting Guns: Firearms and Their Control*. New York: Aldine de Gruyter, 1997.

Kleck, Gary, and Marc Gertz. "Armed Resistance to Crime: The Prevalence and Nature of Self-Defense with a Gun." *Journal of Criminal Law and Criminology* 86, no. 1 (Fall 1995): 150–87.

———. "The Illegitimacy of One-Sided Speculation: Getting the Defensive Gun-Use Estimate Down." *Journal of Criminal Law and Criminology* 87, no. 4 (1997): 1446–62.

Kleck, Gary, and Don B. Kates. *Armed: New Perspectives on Gun Control*. Amherst, NY: Prometheus, 2001.

Knight Ridder Newspapers. "Virginians Tote Guns to Celebrate New Freedoms." *Roanoke Times*, September 12, 2004.

Kopel, Dave. "Arms Alive." *National Review*, November 3, 2004, at www.nationalreview.com/script/kopel/kopel200411031134.asp.

Kopel, Dave, and Paul H. Blackman. "Gray Gun Stories." *National Review*, June 9, 2003, at www.nationalreview.com/script/kopel/kopel060903.asp.

Kopel, David B. "Assault Weapons." In *Guns: Who Should Have Them*, edited by David B. Kopel, 159–232. Amherst, NY: Prometheus, 1995.

Koper, Christopher S., and Jeffrey A. Roth. "The Impact of the 1994 Assault Weapons Ban on Gun Violence Outcomes: An Assessment of Multiple Outcome Measures and Some Lessons for Policy Evaluation." *Journal of Quantitative Criminology* 17, no. 1 (March 2001): 33–74.

Kraft, Michael E., and Scott R. Furlong. *Public Policy: Politics, Analysis and Alternatives*. 10th ed. Washington, D.C.: CQ Press, 2004.

Kraus, Michael I. *Fire & Smoke: Government, Lawsuits, and the Rule of Law*. Oakland, CA: Independent Institute, 2000.

Kristof, Nicholas D. "Time to Get Religion." *New York Times*, November 6, 2004.

Lambert, Diana. "Trying to Stop the Craziness of This Business." In *The Changing Politics of Gun Control*, edited by John M. Bruce and Clyde Wilcox, 172–195. Lanham, MD: Rowman & Littlefield, 1998.

LaPierre, Wayne. "The Case against Kerry." *America's 1st Freedom* (October 2004): 34–38.

Leddy, Edward F. *Magnum Force Lobby*. Lanham, MD: University Press of America, 1987.

Levinson, Sanford. "The Embarrassing Second Amendment." *Yale Law Journal* 99 (1989): 637–59.

Levy, Leonard W. *Origins of the Bill of Rights*. New Haven, CT: Yale University Press, 2001.

Lichtblau, Eric. "Report Questions the Reliability of an F.B.I. Ballistics Test." *New York Times*, February 11, 2004.

Lichter, S. Robert, and Richard E. Noyes. *Good Intentions Make Bad News: Why Americans Hate Campaign Journalism*. 2nd ed. Lanham, MD: Rowman & Littlefield, 1995.

Lindaman, Kara, and Donald P. Haider-Markel. "Issue Evolution, Political Parties, and the Culture Wars." *Political Research Quarterly* 55, no. 1 (March 2002): 91–110.

Lindblom, Charles E., and Edward J. Woodhouse. *The Policy-Making Process*. 3rd ed. Upper Saddle River, NJ: Prentice-Hall, 1993.

Lisk, Thomas. Interview with the author, Richmond, VA, February 14, 2003.

Lott, John R., Jr. *The Bias against Guns*. Washington, D.C.: Regnery, 2003.

———. "Media Bias against Guns." *Imprimis* 33, no. 9 (September 2004).

———. *More Guns, Less Crime*. Chicago: University of Chicago Press, 1998.

———. *More Guns, Less Crime: Understanding Crime and Gun Control Laws*. 2nd ed. Chicago: University of Chicago Press, 2000.

———. "Research Fraud, Public Policy, and Gun Control." *Science* (June 6, 2003): 1505.

Lott, John R., Jr., and David Mustard. "Crime Deterrence and Right-to-Carry Concealed Handguns." *Journal of Legal Studies* 26, no. 1 (January 1997): 1–68.

Ludwig, Jens. "Concealed-Gun-Carrying Laws and Violent Crime: Evidence from State Panel Data." *International Review of Law and Economics* 18 (1998): 239–54.

———. "Gun Self-Defense and Deterrence." 27 *Crime and Justice* (2000): 363–417.

Ludwig, Jens, and Philip J. Cook. "Homicide and Suicide Rates Associated with the Implementation of the Brady Handgun Violence Protection Act." 284 *Journal of the American Medical Association* (2000): 585–91.

Madison, James. "The Federalist No. 46." In *The Federalist*, edited by Sherman F. Mittell, 299–300. Washington, D.C.: National Home Library Foundation, 1938.

Marsh, Henry. Interview with the author, Richmond, VA, February, 13, 2003.

Marshall, Carolyn. "California Bans a Large-Caliber Gun, and the Battle Is On." *New York Times*, January 4, 2005, at www.nytimes.com/2005/01/04.national/04guns.html.

McClurg, Andrew J. "The Public Health Case for the Safe Storage of Firearms: Adolescent Suicides Add One More 'Smoking Gun.'" *Hastings Law Journal* 51 (2000): 953–1001.

McClurg, Andrew J., David B. Kopel, and Brannon P. Denning, eds. *Gun Control and Gun Rights*. New York: New York University Press, 2002.

McCombs, Maxwell E., and Donald L. Shaw. "The Agenda-Setting Function of Mass Media." *Public Opinion Quarterly* 36 (1972).

McDowall, David, and Brian Wiersema. "The Incidence of Defensive Firearm Use by U.S. Crime Victims, 1987 through 1990." *American Journal of Public Health* 84 (1994): 1982–84.

McHugh, Mike. Interview with the author, Richmond, VA, February 14, 2003.

———. "Your Immediate Action Needed" [postcard]. Virginia Gun Owners Coalition, February 2003.

McNamara, Bob. "The Issues: Hunting and Fishing." *CBS Evening News*, October 28, 2004.

McQuail, Denis. "The Influence and Effects of the Mass Media." In *Media Power in Politics*, edited by Doris A. Graber, 7–23. 4th ed. Washington, D.C.: CQ Press, 2000.

Meier, Kenneth J. *The Politics of Sin: Drugs, Alcohol, and Public Policy*. Pacific Grove, CA: Brooks/Cole, 1994.

"Middle Ground Elusive on Gun-Control Issue." *Christian Century* 122, no. 9 (May 3, 2005): 17.

Miller, Kevin. "Background-Check Gun Bill Clears Panel." *Roanoke Times*, January 22, 2004.

———. "Bill Pushing for Broader Background Checks Dies." *Roanoke Times*, February 12, 2004.

Mooney, Chris. "Double Barreled Double Standards." *Mother Jones*, October 2003, at www.motherjones.com/news/feature/2003/10/we_590_01.html.

Moore, Michael. "I'll Be Voting for Wesley Clark/Good-Bye Mr. Bush," January 14, 2004, at www.clark04.com/moore.

Morin, Richard. "Scholar Invents Fan to Answer His Critics." *Washington Post*, February 1, 2003.

Murray, Shailagh. "Senate Passes Bill Barring Gun Suits." *Washington Post*, July 30, 2005.

Mustard, David B. "Comment on Donohue, 'Impact.'" In *Evaluating Gun Policy: Effects on Crime and Violence*, edited by Philip J. Cook and Jens Ludwig, 325–30. Washington, D.C.: Brookings Institution, 2003.

Nagourney, Adam. "Baffled in Loss, Democrats Seek Road Forward." *New York Times*, November 7, 2004, at www.nytimes.com/2004/11/07/politics/campaign/07dems.html.

———. "Bush Campaign Manager Views the Electoral Divide." *New York Times*, November 19, 2004.

———. "Dean's Challenge: Turn Enthusiasm into Votes." *New York Times*, July 7, 2003.

———. "Democratic Leader Analyzes Bush Victory." *New York Times*, December 11, 2004, at www.nytimes.com/2004/12/11/politics/11dems.html.

———. "Democrats Hear from 8 Who Want to Lead Party." *New York Times*, December 12, 2004, at www.nytimes.com/2004/12/12/politics/12dems.html.

The National Academies. "Data on Firearms and Violence Too Weak to Settle Policy Debates; Comprehensive Research Effort Needed," December 16, 2004.

National Center for Injury Prevention and Control, Centers for Disease Control and Prevention. "Leading Causes of Death by Homicide in Various Age Groups, by Race, 2001," at webapp.cdc.gov/sasweb/ncipc/leadcaus.html.

National Rifle Association. "Virginia 2001 General Election Candidate Endorsement" [mail flyer], October 2001.

———. "Virginia 2001 General Election Candidate Endorsement" [postcard], November 2001.

Neal, Terry M. "Election Reflections." *Washington Post*, November 4, 2004, at www .washingtonpost.com/ac2/wp-dyn/A24733-2004Nov4.

Newton, George D., and Franklin Zimring. *Firearms and Violence in American Life: A Staff Report Submitted to the National Commission on the Causes and Prevention of Violence.* Washington, D.C.: National Commission on the Causes and Prevention of Violence, 1969.

Nibley, Anna Baker, and David B. Magleby. "Interest Groups in the 2000 Congressional Elections." In *The Other Campaign: Soft Money and Issue Advocacy in the 2000 Congressional Elections*, edited by David B. Magleby, 51–78. Lanham, MD: Rowman & Littlefield, 2003.

"No Assault Rifle for Kerry, After All." *New York Times*, September 27, 2004.

Norell, James O. E. "John Kerry's Newest Scheme to Ban Your Guns." *America's 1st Freedom* (November 2004): 42–46.

———. "Why You Can't Stay Home This Election Day." *America's 1st Freedom* (October 2004): 28–33.

Nownes, Anthony J. *Pressure and Power: Organized Interests in American Politics.* Boston: Houghton Mifflin, 2001.

NRA-ILA. "Continue to Attend Town Hall Meetings—Urge Passage of S. 397 in the U.S. House." *NRA-ILA Grassroots Alert* 12, no. 33 (August 19, 2005).

———. "Courts Reject Lawsuits Against Gun Makers," October 16, 2003, at www .nraila.org/Issues/FactSheets/Read.aspx?ID = 37.

———. "Firearms Laws for Virginia," at www.nraila.org/GunLaws/StateLaws.aspx? ST = VA.

———. "Historic Victory for NRA U.S. House of Representatives Passes the 'Protection of Lawful Commerce in Arms Act,'" October 20, 2005, at www.nraila.org/News/Read /Releases.aspx?ID = 6682.

———. "July 1 Marks Vast Improvements for Virginia Gun Laws." July 1, 2004, at www.nraila.org/News/Read/Releases.aspx?ID = 3943.

———. "Legislative Alert" [postcard], April 11, 2002.

———. "No Compromise!" June 2, 2004, at www.nraila.org/Issues/Articles/Read .aspx?ID = 139.

———. "NRA: Freedom Prevails across the Country; George Bush Re-Elected, Daschle Defeated; Overwhelming 95% Success Rate Nationwide," November 4, 2004, at www .nrapvf.org/news/read.aspx?id = 4843&t.

———. "S. 397 Passes U.S. Senate!!!" *NRA-ILA Grassroots Alert* 12, no. 30 (July 29, 2005).

———. "Statement on S. 1805," at www.nraila.org/Issues/Articles/Read.aspx?ID = 139.

———. "Taxpayer Funded Reckless Lawsuits Against the Firearms Industry," April 25, 2004.

———. "Virginia—Urge Your Senator to Oppose Gun Show Bill (SB 48) Today" [e-mail communication], January 22, 2004, at www.nraila.org/CurrentLegislation/Read .aspx?ID = 927.

NRA-PVF. "If John Kerry Thinks the Second Amendment is about Photo-Ops, He's Daffy" [print advertisement].

———. "John Kerry Wants to Ban Guns in America," at www.nrapvf.org/Kerry/default .apsx.

———."NRA Endorses George W. Bush for President," at www.nrapvf.org/News/read .apsx?ID = 4614.

O'Brien, David M. *Constitutional Law and Politics: Civil Rights and Civil Liberties.* 3rd ed. New York: Norton, 1997.

Open Society Institute. "Gun Control in the United States: A Comparative Survey of State Firearm Laws," April 2000.

Paletz, David L. *The Media in American Politics: Contents and Consequences.* 2nd ed. New York: Longman, 2002.

Patrick, Brian Anse. *The National Rifle Association and the Media.* New York: Peter Lang, 2002.

Patterson, Thomas E. "Political Roles of Journalists." In *The Politics of News, The News of Politics,* edited by Doris Graber, Denis McQuail, and Pippa Norris, 17–32. Washington, D.C.: CQ Press, 1998.

Penn, Schoen & Berland Associates. "New National Polls Show Assault Weapons Ban Wedge Factor in Election—Moves Key Swing States into 'Kerry' Column as Voters Perceive Ban as Key 'Homeland Security' Leadership Issue," October 9, 2004.

Perkins, Craig. "Weapons Use and Violent Crime." Bureau of Justice Statistics, September 2003.

Presidential Debate. Moderated by Jim Lehrer. Winston-Salem, NC, October 11, 2000.

———. Moderated by Bob Schieffer. Tempe, AZ, October 13, 2004.

Preston, Scott R. "Targeting the Gun Industry: Municipalities Aim to Hold Manufacturers Liable for Their Products and Actions." *Southern Illinois Law Journal* 24 (Spring 2000): 595–626.

Raphael, Steven, and Jens Ludwig. "Prison Sentence Enhancements: The Case of Project Exile." In *Evaluating Gun Policy: Effects on Crime and Violence,* edited by Philip J. Cook and Jens Ludwig. Washington, D.C.: Brookings Institution, 2003.

Redmond, Ian. "Legislative Reform: The Second Amendment: Bearing Arms Today." *Journal of Legislation* 28 (2002): 325–48.

Reynolds, Glenn H. "A Critical Guide to the Second Amendment." *Tennessee Law Review* 62 (1995): 461–512.

Rich, Frank. "It's the War, Stupid." *New York Times,* October 12, 2002.

Robinson, John P. and Mark R. Levy. *The Main Source: Learning from Television News.* Thousand Oaks, CA: Sage, 1986.

Rostron, Allen. *Smoking Guns: Exposing the Gun Industry's Complicity in the Illegal Gun Market.* Washington, D.C.: Brady Center to Prevent Gun Violence, Legal Action Project, 2003.

Ruhl, Jesse Matthew, Arthur L. Rizer, and Mikel J. Weir. "Gun Control: Targeting Rationality in a Loaded Debate." *Kansas Journal of Law & Public Policy* 13 (Winter 2004): 413–83.

Rushforth, Norman, Charles Hirsh, Amanda B. Ford, and Lester Adelson. "Accidental Firearms Deaths in a Metropolitan County (1958–1975)." *American Journal of Epidemiology* 100 (1975): 499–505.

Sabato, Larry J. *Feeding Frenzy: How Attack Journalism Has Transformed American Politics.* New York: Free Press, 1991.

Schapiro, Jeff E. "Extended Gun Checks Are Rejected." *Richmond Times-Dispatch*, February 12, 2004.

Schuman, Howard, and Stanley Presser. "The Attitude-Action Connection and the Issue of Gun Control." *Annals of the American Academy of Political and Social Science* 455 (May 1981): 40–47.

Scott, James. Interview with the author, Richmond, VA, January 23, 2003.

Seelye, Katharine Q. "Hammering on the 'L' Word." *New York Times*, December 6, 2002.

———. "How to Sell a Candidate to a Porsche-Driving, Leno-Loving Nascar Fan." *New York Times*, December 6, 2004.

"Sensible Gun Laws," Howard Dean for America, at www.DeanForAmerica.com.

Shah, Dhavan Vinod. "Value Judgments: News Framing and Individual Processing of Political Issues." PhD diss., University of Minnesota, 1999.

Shaiko, Ronald G., and Marc A. Wallace. "Going Hunting Where the Ducks Are: The National Rifle Association and the Grass Roots." In *The Changing Politics of Gun Control*, edited by John M. Bruce and Clyde Wilcox. Lanham, MD: Rowman & Littlefield, 1998.

Shalhope, Robert E. "The Armed Citizen in the Early Republic." *Law and Contemporary Problems* 49, no. 1 (1986): 125–41.

———. "The Ideological Origins of the Second Amendment." *Journal of American History* 69 (December 1982): 599–614.

———. "To Keep and Bear Arms in the Early Republic." *Constitutional Commentary* 16 (Summer 1999): 269.

Shaw, David. "Abortion Bias Seeps into News." *Los Angeles Times*, July 1, 1990.

Shear, Michael D. "Governor Hopefuls Hit Hard and Often." *Washington Post*, December 9, 2004.

Shuler, James. Interview with the author, Richmond, VA, February 13, 2003.

Simon, Roger. "The Doctor is In." *U.S. News & World Report*, August 8, 2003, 5.

Sluss, Michael. "Candidates Focus on Taxes, but Lobby for NRA Support." *Roanoke Times*, October 4, 2001.

———. "Guns Show Bill Gets Shot Down in Committee." *Roanoke Times*, January 16, 2003.

———. "Late-Term Abortions, Gun Restrictions Vetoed." *Roanoke Times*, April 5, 2002.

———. "NRA Stays Very Quiet on Earley, Warner." *Roanoke Times*, October 17, 2001.

———. "Warner Downplays National Attention." *Roanoke Times*, January 16, 2005.

———. "Warner Impresses Democratic leaders." *Roanoke Times*, July 29, 2004.

Sluss, Michael and Isak Howell. "Earley, Warner Have Final Say at Roanoke Debate." *Roanoke Times*, October 11, 2001.

Smith, Kenneth. "Loaded Coverage." *Reason* 32, issue 2 (June 2000): 39.

Smith, Tom W. "A Call for a Truce in the DGU War." *Journal of Criminal Law and Criminology* 87, no. 4 (1997): 1462–69.

———. "1999 National Gun Policy Survey of the National Opinion Research Center: Research Findings." Paper presented at the annual meeting of the American Association for Public Opinion Research, Portland, OR, May 2000.

———. "Public Opinion about Gun Policies (Public Perspective)." *Future of Children* 12 (Summer–Fall 2002): 155.

Snow, John B. "Targeting the Gun Vote," *Outdoor Life*, October 2005, at www.outdoorlife.com/outdoor/news/article/0,19912,688083,00.htm.

Snyder, James M., and Tim Groseclose. "Estimating Party Influence in Congressional Roll-Call Voting." *American Journal of Political Science* 44, no. 2 (April 2000): 203.

Spitzer, Robert J. *The Politics of Gun Control.* 3rd ed. Washington, D.C.: CQ Press, 2004.

Stallsmith, Pamela. "Guns Allowed in Bars?" *Richmond Times-Dispatch*, February 1, 2003, at www.richmondtimesdispatch.com/news/politics/MGBWQFZMBD.html.

———. "Hidden Gun Law Defeated." *Richmond Times-Dispatch*, February 15, 2003, at www.richmondtimesdispatch.com/news/politics/MGBETF2PSBD.html.

Stolberg, Sheryl Gay. "Congress Passes New Legal Shield for Gun Industry." *New York Times*, October 21, 2005, at www.nytimes.com/2005/10/21/politics/21guns.html.

———. "Looking Back and Ahead after Senate's Votes on Guns." *New York Times*, March 4, 2004, at www.nytimes.com/2004/03/04/politics/04GUNS.html.

———. "Senate Leaders Scuttle Gun Bill Over Changes." *New York Times*, March 3, 2004, at www.nytimes.com/2004/03/03/politics/03GUNS.html.

———. "A Swing to the Middle on Gun Control." *New York Times*, March 7 2004, at www.nytimes.com/2004/03/07/weekinreview/07stol.html.

Stolzenberg, Lisa, and Stewart J. D'Alession. "Gun Availability and Violent Crime: New Evidence from the National Incident-Based Reporting System." *Social Forces* vol. 78, no. 4. (June 2000): 1461–82.

Surette, Ray. *Media, Crime, and Criminal Justice: Images and Realities.* Pacific Grove, CA: Brooks/Cole, 1992.

Tonso, William R. "Calling the Shots." *Reason* 17 (March 1985).

———. "Shooting Blind." *Reason* 27, no. 6 (November 1995): 30–36.

Trapolin, Edward Winter. "Comments: Sued Into Submission: Judicial Creation of Standards in the Manufacture and Distribution of Lawful Products—The New Orleans Lawsuit against Gun Manufacturers." *Loyola Law Review* 46 (Winter 2000): 1275–1308.

Tribe, Laurence H. *American Constitutional Law.* Vol. 1. Westbury, NY: Foundation, 2000.

U.S. Fish and Wildlife Service. "2001 National Survey of Fishing, Hunting, and Wildlife Associated Recreation," October 2002, at www.census.gov/prod/2002pubs/FHW01.pdf.

Vandall, Frank J. "Article: O.K. Corral II: Policy Issues in Municipal Suits against Gun Manufacturers." *Villanova Law Review* 44 (1999): 547–75.

Vernick, Jon S., and Lisa M. Hepburn. "State and Federal Gun Laws." In *Evaluating Gun Policy: Effects on Crime and Violence*, edited by Philip J. Cook and Jens Ludwig, 348–58. Washington, D.C.: Brookings Institution, 2003.

Virginians Against Handgun Violence. "Lobbying Materials," February 2003.

Vizzard, William J. *Shots in the Dark: The Policy, Politics, and Symbolism of Gun Control.* Lanham, MD: Rowman & Littlefield, 2000.

Volokh, Eugene. "The Commonplace Second Amendment." *New York University Law Review* 73 (1998): 793–821.

Ware, R. Lee. "Concealed Handguns in 'Entertainment Establishments.'" Summary, H.B. 1997, Virginia General Assembly, 2003 session.

———. Interview with the author, Richmond, VA, January 23, 2003.

Weisberg, Herbert F., Jon A. Krosnick, and Bruce D. Bowen. *An Introduction to Survey Research, Polling, and Data Analysis.* 3rd ed. Thousand Oaks, CA: Sage, 1996.

"Whether the Second Amendment Secures an Individual Right." Memorandum Opinion for the Attorney General, August 24, 2004, at http://www.usdoj.gov/olc/secondamend ment2.htm.

Whitley, Tyler. "Extension of Background Checks Rejected." *Richmond Times-Dispatch,* January 16, 2003, at www.timesdispatch.com/news/politics/MGB70YY30BD.html.

Wilgoren, Jodi. "Dingell Holds Off Challenger to Win Primary in Michigan." *New York Times,* August 7, 2002, at www.nytimes.com/2002/08/07/politics/07MICH.html.

———. "G.O.P. Draws Criticism from Kerry on Assault Weapons Ban." *New York Times,* September 11, 2004. at www.nytimes.com/2004/09/11/politics/campaign/11kerry.html.

———. "In Magazine Interview, Kerry Says He Owns Assault Rifle." *New York Times,* September 26, 2004, at www.nytimes.com/2004/09/26/politics/campaign/26guns.html.

———. "Kerry Faults Bush for Failing to Press Assault Weapons Ban." *New York Times,* September 14, 2004.

Will, George. "Virginia's Democratic Contender." *Washington Post,* December 19, 2004.

Williams, David C. "The Unitary Second Amendment." *New York University Law Review* 73 (1998): 822–30.

Wills, Garry. "To Keep and Bear Arms." In *Whose Right to Bear Arms Did the Second Amendment Protect?* edited by Saul Cornell, 65–88. Boston: Bedford/St. Martin's, 2000.

Wilson, Harry L. "Public Opinion and Gun Control Utility: Not as Simple or Coherent as We Thought?" Paper presented at the Joint Meetings of the Canadian Law and Society Association and the Law and Society Association, Vancouver, BC, May 30–June 1, 2002.

Wilson, Harry L., and Mark J. Rozell. "Virginia: The Politics of Concealed Weapons." In *The Changing Politics of Gun Control,* edited by John M. Bruce and Clyde Wilcox, 125–38. Lanham, MD: Rowman & Littlefield, 1998.

Wilson, James Q., and John J. DiIulio Jr. *American Government: The Essentials.* 8th ed. Boston: Houghton-Mifflin, 2001.

Winship, Thomas. "Step Up the War against Guns." *Editor & Publisher* 127, no. 17 (April 24, 1993): 24.

Wintemute, Garen, Carrie Parham, James Beaumont, Mona Wright, and Christina Drake. "Mortality among Recent Purchasers of Handguns." *New England Journal of Medicine* 341, no. 21 (1999): 1583–89.

Wintemute, Garen J., Stephen P. Teret, Jess F. Kraus, Mona Wright, and Gretchen Bradfield. "When Children Shoot Children: 88 Unintended Deaths in California." *Journal of the American Medical Association* 257 (1987): 3107–109.

Wolpert, Robin M., and James G. Gimpel. "Self-Interest, Symbolic Politics, and Public Attitudes toward Gun Control." *Political Behavior* 20, no. 3 (1998): 241–62.

Wright, James D. "Public Opinion and Gun Control: A Comparison of Results From Two Recent National Surveys." *Annals of The American Academy of Political and Social Science* 455 (1981): 24–39.

Wright, James D., and Peter H. Rossi. *Armed and Considered Dangerous: A Survey of Felons and Their Firearms.* New York: Aldine de Gruyter, 1986.

Young, John T., David Hemenway, Robert J. Blendon, and John M. Benson. "The Polls— Trends: Guns." *Public Opinion Quarterly* 60 (1996): 634–49.

Zernike, Kate. "Kerry's Lesson: Lambeau Rhymes with Rambo." *New York Times,* September 19, 2004, at www.nytimes.com/2004/09/19/weekinreview/19zernike.html.

Zimring, Franklin E., and Gordon Hawkins. *The Citizen's Guide to Gun Control.* New York: Macmillan, 1987.

———. "Concealed Handguns: The Counterfeit Deterrent." *Responsive Community* 7 (1997): 46–60.

———. *Crime Is Not the Problem: Lethal Violence in America.* New York: Oxford University Press, 1997.

Index

About the Author

Harry L. Wilson is professor of political science and director of the Center for Community Research at Roanoke College. He has conducted numerous public opinion polls and authored or co-authored several book chapters and journal articles on gun control, the mass media, and polling.